PRAISE FOR *GLOBAL BRAND MA*

An incredibly clear-minded book. The very word brand has become increasing devalued through misuse; this book is part of a vital counter movement.
Rory Sutherland, Vice Chairman, Ogilvy, and author of *Alchemy: The Surprising power of ideas that don't make sense*

A master work. As brands define our culture and set society's agenda more and more, this book needed to be written. It comprehensively sets the ground rules and does a deep dive into how to manage the process. Lucid, covers all the bases, well organized, and accessible to the reader. Indispensable for every communications student, practitioner, and thought leader. It will be required reading in my graduate programme.
Nancy R Tag, Founding Director, Branding + Integrated Communications MPS at The City College of New York and author, *Ad Critique: How to deconstruct ads in order to build better advertising*

Students and those in the early stages of their career will certainly find Global Brand Management an effective navigator on how to build and manage brands globally. Minsky and Geva have brought together a smart combination of theory and relevant insights from leading brands and experts that will be a valuable guide in both strategy and execution.
Paul Bennett, Global Brand Director, AXA

Minsky and Geva skilfully demystify brand and branding with vivid examples in an international setting.
Salma Ghanem, Interim Provost, DePaul University, and Former Dean of its School of Communications

Whether you are a brand manager, designer or educator, Global Brand Management is a comprehensive resource for developing, building and managing an international brand. Authors Minsky and Geva write in a highly readable style that incorporates all contemporary issues facing brands in a global economy as well as recent changes in tech. As a brand designer, strategist and educator, I find this book to be an essential resource.
Robin Landa, Distinguished Professor, Michael Graves College at Kean University, author of *Graphic Design Solutions*, *Designing Brand Experiences* and *Advertising by Design*

Brand management has never been more important, yet can often be a confusing and impenetrable subject, requiring an up-to-date understanding of many topics. This book provides a much needed, clear, detailed and intelligent overview of the subject.
Darren Bridger, Consultant at NeuroStrata, author of *Decoding the Irrational Consumer* and *Neuro Design*

Whether you are a branding professional using this as a personal reference, or a professor employing it as a text, you, too, will likely come to believe, as the authors state in the opening, that 'brand managers from any country can learn from the best practices of others to improve their outcomes'. I can attest to the truth of that proposition, based on my own experience interviewing branding experts worldwide for The Branding Roundtable, and I am delighted to see the inclusion of a multitude of experienced brand practitioners here.
Chuck Kent, Contributing Editor, *Brandingmag*

Like the best travel companions, Minsky and Geva's *Global Brand Management* is conversational, engaging and has a way of making the journey richer. Together, they have written a book that appreciates the global nature of brand development today while reminding us of the importance of creating brand experiences that are personal, memorable and enriching — ones that make you feel right at home. Pick up a copy and soak up some brand-new wisdom.
Jim Misener, Principal, President, 50,000 feet

The world is changing, business is changing, and brands are changing – fast. Minsky and Geva provide key insights demonstrating the value of brands and underscores the digital transformation of marketing for the 21st century. As the 30-second ad on its own simply doesn't do the job anymore, consumer centric brand experience is now becoming the dominant focus of marketing plans and budgets. Consumers are now telling and defining what brands are. A truly insightful book and a must read for those who want to advance their careers.
Radu Florescu, CEO, Centrade-Cehil South-East Europe

This book has been written for marketing professionals and students, but it should be for everyone. As authors Minsky and Geva rightly point out, the definition of Brand keeps expanding. It's no longer about just products and services (it never was), brands can be dishwasher soap, people or nations. Today, thanks to the Internet, everything is immediately global and instantly needs a meaning and purpose, or it will not last. Deconstructing the principles about how brands are constructed, take on meaning, and persevere is the core of this book and should be the exercise of anyone who wants to make a place for themselves in the expanding universe of Branding. Whether you are a person, place or thing, this book is for you.
Patrick Hanlon, founder Thinktopia, primalbranding.co, author, entrepreneur, investor

Laurence Minsky & Ilan Geva offer the facts and reality of how brands are nowadays, how a brand is not just a brand anymore. A history of how brands evolved from iconic power to reality check where consumers actually are the new generation of brands which can make them or break them with the power of social media

Joaquin E Bonilla, Executive Creative Director, Golin Romania

Minsky and Geva have written more than a book. It's a complete do-it-yourself MBA in branding. Finally, there's an evidence-based book that covers the brand as a living, breathing being from its birth by insightful marketing to its sustenance by great communications with every relevant audience. Unlike some books by agency personnel that are love fests to the work they've done, or others that attempt to coin a clever turn of phrase for basic principles, this book is built on solid theoretical evidence and best practices, illuminated with compelling case studies. Consider it The Brand Bible.

Karen Mallia, Professor, Advertising + Brand Communications, University of South Carolina, and author of *Leadership in the Creative Industries: Principles and practice*

Branding and brand management are vital areas for businesses, business students, and, of course consumers to understand. When my students begin my brand management course, the first thing we do is explore the many – and not always similar – definitions of brand that are available. The definitions and meanings change from industry to industry and around the world. Minsky and Geva offer just the kind of comprehensive, yet heartfelt and personal, approach to brand management that today's business students need to truly understand this concept.

David Aron, Professor of Marketing, Brennan School of Business, Dominican University

Detailed case studies, practical tools and tips, clear and direct writing without the industry speak, original and insightful essays by world-class branding experts… combine to make this the most authoritative book on global brand management ever written. What makes Global Brand Management even more extraordinary though, is that it is a tremendously FUN read!

Bryan Mattimore, author, *21 Days to a Big Idea*, and Chief Idea Guy at Growth Engine Innovation Agency

Global Brand Management provides a strong conceptual base for understanding and managing brands. With engaging examples and in-depth case studies from around the world, this game-changing book clearly explains why new brand management approaches are needed, and convincingly shows how and why these approaches work. Extremely useful and insightful.

Jonathan Schroeder, William A Kern Professor of Communication, Rochester Institute of Technology, New York, co-author of *From Chinese Brand Culture to Global Brands*

If you are in need of a one-stop-shop of all concurrent brand management issues in a digital and fast changing world, don't look further. Global Brand Management tackles all the challenges marketers are facing today, summarizing the frameworks of the greatest brand thought leaders while adding the latest case studies and insights.
Joeri Van Den Bergh, Co-founder and Managing Partner, InSites Consulting, author and speaker: *How Cool Brands Stay Hot*

This book covers a vast range of topics, from basic theoretical concepts of brand strategy and planning to the practicalities of brand management. Most importantly, though, it challenges the reader to think about brands from many angles and encourages a deeper curiosity about their psychological and sociological underpinnings.
Nick Liddell, Director of Consulting, The Clearing

A really good and comprehensive read about all aspects of this gift that culture has given to commerce. A good balance of theory and real-life examples that will interest every reader.
Jacob Benbunan, Co-founder and CEO, Saffron Consultants

Global Brand Management

A guide to developing, building and managing an international brand

Laurence Minsky
and Ilan Geva

KoganPage

First published in Great Britain and the United States in 2020 by Kogan Page Limited

2nd Floor, 45 Gee Street
London
EC1V 3RS
United Kingdom

122 W 27th St, 10th Floor
New York, NY 10001
USA

4737/23 Ansari Road
Daryaganj
New Delhi 110002
India

www.koganpage.com

ISBNs

Hardback 9781789660401
Paperback 9780749483609
Ebook 9780749483616

British Library Cataloguing-in-Publication Data

A CIP record for this book is available from the British Library.

Library of Congress Cataloging-in-Publication Data

A CIP record for this book is available from the Library of Congress.

Typeset by Integra Software Services, Pondicherry
Print production managed by Jellyfish
Printed and bound in Great Britain by CPI Group (UK), Croydon CR0 4YY

To the memory of my parents, Joseph and Doris Minsky,
who shaped me and thus formed my 'brand'
L.M.

To Eileen, who's always supportive, and lets me roam around the world
while learning and experiencing all these brands
I.G.

CONTENTS

PART TWO

Practical and tactical applications 93

ABOUT THE AUTHORS

Laurence Minsky

Laurence Minsky is recognized in both professional and academic circles for his strategic and creative leadership. His broad-reaching industry expertise includes brand development, brand advertising, brand activation, content marketing, new product development, local store marketing, direct response advertising, interactive, online and mobile marketing, channel communications, and developing effective cross-channel solutions that boost marketing ROI.

He serves as an associate professor in the Communication Department of the School of Media Arts at Columbia College Chicago and as a consultant for leading agencies, corporations and non-profits across the globe.

Laurence is co-author of *The Activation Imperative: How to build brands and business by inspiring action* and *Audio Branding: Using sound to build your brand*, the executive editor of *The Get a Job Workshop: How to find your way to a creative career in advertising, branding, collateral, digital, experiential & more*, the author of *How to Succeed in Advertising When All You Have is Talent* (Second Edition) and a co-author of *Advertising and the Business of Brands.*

As an industry thought-leader, he has been published by the *Harvard Business Review*, the *European Business Review*, MarketingProfs, the Data-Driven Marketing Network, and others, and has been quoted in the *New York Times*, *Chicago Tribune*, *Chicago Sun-Times*, *San Diego Union Tribune*, *Exame* (Brazil's largest business and economics magazine), *Software Advice* and *Crain's Chicago Business*, among many others.

His agency experience includes tenure at Frankel (now Arc Worldwide) as well as engagements with more than 25 other agencies as a consultant. He has created marketing and communications solutions for many blue-chip clients, including Laila Ali, Ambius, Amazon, Bay Valley Foods, Beltone, Black & Decker Spacemaker, Bristol-Myers Squibb, Caesarstone, Connie's Pizza, Frito-Lay, George Foreman Products, Kraft Foods, LTD Commodities, Mayo Medical Laboratories (Mayo Clinic), McDonald's, Midtown Athletic Clubs, Motorola, Naples Bay Resort, The National Safety Council, PetSmart, SC Johnson, Spacelabs Healthcare, Taiwan External Trade Development Council (or TAITRA), United Airlines, United States Postal Service, Westinghouse, Vita Foods and many more.

An award-winning creative with over 125 industry accolades to date, he has served on the juries of leading industry award shows and is a long-standing member of the One Club for Art and Copy, the Authors Guild and the American Academy of Advertising.

Ilan Geva

Ilan Geva consults, teaches and execute branding projects across the globe. He currently teaches branding and consumer behaviour at the University of Chicago Graham School, and advertising, branding, consumer behaviour and creativity in advertising at DePaul University. In addition, he has taught introduction to design at the School of Hospitality Management at Kendall College; integrated marketing communications, interactive advertising and international advertising at Columbia College Chicago; brand planning & message strategy at Roosevelt University; as well as packaging design at the School of The Art Institute of Chicago. Accolades for this classroom instruction includes receiving the 2011 distinguished professional educator award from The Kellstadt Marketing Center of DePaul University and the 2006 Excellence in Teaching Award from the University of Chicago.

In addition to teaching, he currently runs Ilan Geva & Friends, a global branding consultancy in Chicago. Prior to launching his own firm, Ilan worked for some of the top global agencies, including serving as Design Head and Creative Director for Ogilvy & Mather in Johannesburg, Los Angeles and Chicago; Creative Director for Leo Burnett Chicago; Creative Supervisor at Frankel & Company (now ARC Worldwide); and as the VP, Executive Creative Director Kragie/Newell (now Integer), as well as Vice President Creative Director for Gage Marketing, Minneapolis.

Ilan develops and creates Brand platforms including the brand vision, brand strategy, brand personality, using every imaginable strategic branding solution for many of the world's largest corporations, as well as for smaller enterprises. His work has won more than 100 awards around the world including Clio, ADDY, Telly, POPAI, Caples, ECHO, Summit, Adrian and many others.

Through his work, he has helped build brands for such companies as: McDonald's, Coca-Cola, Visa, *The Chicago Tribune*, SA Breweries, Panasonic, Nestlé, American Express, Unilever, VW-Audi, Kodak, HP, Seagram, Shell, Sears, Citibank, Jahn, Israel Ministry of Tourism, Turkey Tourism, South African Tourism, British Tourist Authority, Mexico Tourism Board, State of Iowa Tourism, Lisbon Convention Bureau, United Airlines, Korean Air, Alitalia, Sheraton, Doubletree Hotels, Avis and many more.

During the last decade, Ilan has became a global expert in Medical Travel services, and assisted governments, associations and independent hospitals build their brand in that category. His articles about brand building for healthcare services were published in a number of trade magazines in Europe, Asia and the Middle East, and he was interviewed by many publications on the subject.

Finally, he is an invited speaker at global trade conferences and events and facilitates masterclasses, seminars and training sessions about branding and other marketing topics for ad agencies, trade associations and educational institutions, including being selected a faculty member of the In-Store Marketing Institute in 2007.

Plus, he judges some of the most prestigious industry award competitions in the US and abroad.

Ilan has a BFA from the Bezalel Academy of Arts and Design in Jerusalem and a Master's degree from DePaul University in Chicago. He also graduated from the Damelin College of Marketing in Johannesburg with a diploma in Marketing Management.

FOREWORD BY MARK TUNGATE

When did you first hear the word *brand*? This book inspired me to ask myself the same question, but of course I was unable to put my finger on a single moment. Branding slowly seeped into my consciousness through reading the business press and transitioning out of local newspapers into the arcane world of advertising industry trade magazines.

During that same process, I also developed an understanding of what a brand actually is. But as you'll see from the pages that follow, the word is as slippery as often-adjacent terms like *luxury* and *fashion* (two other things I write about; I really am a glutton for punishment). Indeed, perhaps it's the intellectual puzzle of defining *brand* that makes it such a compelling subject. Viewed from the exterior, branding could be perceived as a dry and clinical business. But it is nothing of the sort. Because, at the end of the day, brands are about emotion.

We all have examples of brands that seem to define the concept – again, you'll find many in this book. My go-to example is Levi's. Simply because it's one of my favourite brands. In fact – and this is what brand managers are all striving for – it's a kind of love affair.

It all began in 1985 with an ad that featured a young man taking a bath in his Levi's so that they shrank to fit. How can such a simple scene spark a lifelong relationship with a brand? Well, this was no ordinary ad. It was made by the hot London agency Bartle Bogle Hegarty. I didn't know that at the time, of course. What I did know was that it was deeply cinematic, that the hero had an aura of wry rebellion, that his apartment was insanely cool, and that the music – 'Wonderful World' by Sam Cooke – transported me to a time and a place I aspired to. Somehow all these elements combined to sear into my teenage soul and stay there. Subsequent, similar ads reinforced the emotion. I wanted those jeans. But what I really wanted was to be part of their wonderful world.

I've worn Levi's ever since, because pulling them on feels like some kind of achievement, a badge of the confident adulthood I craved at the age of 17. Daft, I know, but there's often something irrational about brand attachment. Great brands have a touch of magic about them.

The word *brand* is far more prevalent than it was when I started writing about the subject. We're often encouraged to develop our 'personal brands' – and a generation of social media influencers has proved skilled in doing so. Many brands try to hitch on to their wagon, which I personally believe is a mistake: as a friend of mine recently pointed out, the only brand an influencer is truly interested in promoting is their own.

While brands are now ubiquitous, they are also more fragile than ever. Complex from the get-go, they are exposed to threats at every turn. Multiple media platforms, myriad touchpoints, labyrinthine customer journeys, critical consumers using the megaphone of social media – as you will see, there are a thousand ways that their carefully honed strategies can be undermined by the realities of their existence.

Indeed, not all brands survive. Those that do tend to have certain traits in common. Not long ago, I was asked to give a speech about the elements that make a brand great. Having thought long and hard about it, I came up with the following list:

provenance – where your brand is from, its origin and history
values – what your brand believes in
consistency – the ability to adapt without losing your core identity
mythology – the image of your brand, created by stories
proximity – a close relationship with your customers
superb delivery of service

You may agree or disagree, especially after reading this book. But having already done so, I was reassured to note that some of the ideas above crop up here in other forms. Certainly, the influence of storytelling, the power of a mission and the importance of consistency are all addressed.

The book reminded me that great brands are also characterized by what might broadly be termed as their 'behaviour'. Strong brands are like human beings – or, at the very least, fictional characters. They have defined personalities that impact the way they act, the things they say and the manner in which they navigate the world. If they suddenly embark on a type of behaviour that's contrary to their perceived character, it can be very destabilizing for their friends and fans. This has become even more important in an era when brands are expected to have a 'purpose' beyond generating profits for their owners.

Having evoked the complexity and fragility of brands, like an establishing shot in a movie, it's time for me to step back and let the authors of this book do their work. Their achievement is to entirely update and reconfigure the tenets of brand management for a new – and constantly changing – world. Among other things, you'll read more about the definition of a brand, the challenges facing brands today and the specific problems of global brand management in the digital era. I was particularly enthralled by a section on 'nation branding', which turns out to be an even more controversial exercise than I had imagined.

Not only does the book address the myriad forms brands take, it also tackles the tricky area of brand expansion, and suggests viable approaches when working with a 'house of brands' – a collection of brands, perhaps with widely differing identities, within a single holding entity. You will also find a detailed formula for taking a brand successfully into a new overseas market. Brands are a part of a society's culture, and a failure to understand the culture you are about the engage with can lead to extreme difficulties, as some specific examples here demonstrate.

Above all, you'll learn how to become an effective and inspired brand manager.
Note the use of the word *inspired*. Building and maintaining great brands requires a large dose of creativity. Because, as I said at the beginning, they're all about emotion.

Mark Tungate is a journalist and the author of several books about branding (all published by Kogan Page), including the recent The Escape Industry: How iconic and innovative brands built the travel business.

ACKNOWLEDGEMENTS

Special thanks to Simon Anholt, Suzanne Blum Malley PhD, Jorg Borgwardt, Michael Boumendill, Heather Choi, Marcella David, Ashley Galina Dudarenok, Philippa Fiszzon, Eric Freedman, Jens Ulrik Hansen, Ames Hawkins, David Houle, Lachean Humphreys, Ki Nam Jin, Kwang-Wu Kim, Helen Kogan, Heather Langridge, Chris Malone, Mary Mattucci, Suzanne McBride, Paolo Mercado, Jeff Meyers, Ricardo Monteiro, John Morrow, Lubna Nafees, Charlotte Owen, Madison Potter, Pegeen Quinn, Rick Ray, Shaun Rein, Ruth Reisenberger, Bill Rodi, Tyler Roeger PhD, Vanessa Rueda, Danielle Sauve, Craig Sigele, Stephen Stratton, Karen Sutherland PhD, Natasha Tulett, Andy Walensa, Stanley Wearden, Cornell Wright and Jennifer Volich, and, of course, our families, the blind peer reviewers and the baristas who kept us well caffeinated.

The completion of *Global Brand Management* was partially supported by a Faculty Development Grant from Columbia College Chicago.

PREFACE

The world has changed. An obvious statement, but it has all sorts of implications for branding and brand management.

And, over the last few years, the theory and practice of brand management has been quickly changing. Any brand with a digital presence is automatically 'global' by definition. But the crossing of borders online doesn't mean that the brand understands the consumer behaviour, ethics and commerce rules in other territories.

In addition, the era of a 'matching suite of luggage' approach to branding is over. For success today, brands need to be able to flex – or have elasticity – and display a range of behaviours, so they are appropriate for the audience, location and contextual situation and the brand can be easily identifiable just by its behaviours, even without the logo attached to the element or the brand experience.

Brand managers now need to consider a wider range of opportunities and the inherent risks of each. Not being fully prepared for a global audience and conversant in the risks, particularly in light of citizen and consumer activism, can hurt the brand and its owners.

In addition, brand managers traditionally have focused on a single product in a single market, but it's rapidly changing to where they need to focus on many products across many different market situations, all under one brand umbrella.

Finally, while many Western companies focus on their financial results every quarter, the brands from many Asian countries such as South Korea and China plan for the long run. And brand managers from all countries can learn from the best practices of the others to improve their outcomes.

Meanwhile, students today – as well as many practitioners – are confused by what it means to create and maintain a brand, particularly on a global level. We've even heard marketers state that their branding activities consists of their social media posts. Others still talk about their advertising. And still others think their brand is merely their logos and, perhaps, their font and colours.

What is needed is to address the confusion is an approach that fully explores how branding and brand management is perceived and practiced differently across the globe as well as takes into account the recent developments in the theory and practice of brand management.

Welcome to *Global Brand Management: A guide to developing, building and managing an international brand*.

It is inherently teachable. We structured each chapter with a consistent format to help guide readers. Each one starts with a bulleted list of the reading outcomes for it to help set the stage and then, to help prime the reader, we follow the reading outcomes with a short introduction and an overview to the key themes of the chapter. Subheads and bullets throughout the body of the chapter help guide the reader through it. And each chapter ends with a Guest Perspective from a branding practitioner or educator, experts drawn from across the globe. We close with a list of key words from the chapter and discussion questions to help reinforce the material.

We also organized the chapters, so they build from one to the other, starting with the broader – and various – definitions of branding and the strategic roles they play and closing with a look at digital asset management platforms and other key strategies for managing global brands for today's world.

We believe that our new textbook serves as an up-to-date guide for developing, building and managing a brand that crosses borders, cultures and audience segments.

Once you read the book, we believe you'll agree.

And we believe you'll discover that *Global Brand Management* is not another dry clinical tome. But rather a book whose content conveys our passion for branding and brand management and love of learning from two educator practitioners who both admit that they stumbled along the way and want to help others avoid their mistakes. To help you understand our paths, here are our backstories.

Laurence's story

I started my career as a copywriter at an educational publisher. Not only did I learn how to create effective sales collateral, trade show booths, other integrated marketing programmes, it also gave me a grounding in what makes effective educational materials.

I knew I wanted to get into an ad agency, but was struggling with developing my portfolio, which I didn't have when I landed my job at the educational publisher. A conversation with Emily Calvo about my struggles over what I needed in a portfolio to get into an advertising gave us an idea for a book: what did the first portfolios of ad legends look like?

Emily said that someone should write such a book. I asked, Why not us?

Being an account director at that point in her career, Emily wrote a letter to a publisher with a description of the book. The publisher wrote back that they were interested in it, but that we needed a proposal. And Emily wrote back to ask, What's a proposal? They sent us an outline for one; we drafted one and landed the contract. The book: the first edition of *How to Succeed in Advertising When All You Have is Talent.*

Interviewing the ad legends who were to be featured in the book was when I started getting a firmer grounding in branding and brand management.

I implemented what I had learned, and my career grew. In sequence, I worked for a trade show company promoting business-to-business conferences across the

US and for a small ad agency with local clients, enabling me to develop a deeper understanding of what makes truly effective communications, marketing – and why brand was at the heart of that effectiveness.

My big break came when I landed a job at Frankel. I was like a kid in a candy store, because it gave me a chance to work on such brands as McDonald's, Motorola Cell Phones (back when they were a leader), Target and other leaders.

At Frankel, we looked at the entirety of the customer experience (not just the confined space of the advertising element and the brand fonts and colours). This is a lens every marketer should use but one rarely employed at companies and agencies during the day-to-day grind of producing the work. I had the chance to develop everything from in-store signage, packaging and new products to print advertising to online. Even marketing programmes designed to motivate employees to be consistent with their employer's brand through an initiative that I helped lead called The Walking Brand. In other words, we worked to shape the client's entire brand experience.

I also gained exposure to projects that were implemented in other countries.

I then moved to another agency to continue working on McDonald's, but the big career change came when I landed a tenure-track teaching position at Columbia College Chicago. Columbia has been my home ever since.

Today, I have three legs to my professional stool: consulting, teaching and writing. Each one feeds and informs the other.

In my consulting and freelancing, borders do not stop me. I have had marketing clients from Germany to New Zealand. (And, as you might have noticed, the publisher for this book is in the UK.) My consulting has also enabled me to continue working for large clients like Amazon, AON, Coca-Cola Fountain, Kraft, Mayo Medical Laboratories of Mayo Clinic and MetLife, to name just a few, to start-ups who need help thinking through all of the elements of their brand and every type in between.

I draw on my consulting experience to find examples for my teaching and to shape my research agenda, particularly of emerging trends to see if they are valid or an opportunity cost.

At Columbia, the courses I have taught have ranged from Social Media Content, Copywriter/Art Director Teams and Advertising Copywriting to Introduction to Agency, Advertising Workshop, Introduction to Advertising, Marketing Case Workshop and more. Since I am teaching at an art school, my students, in many ways, keep me on trend for music, fashion and even some apps and platforms. And my teaching requires me to think about the best ways of imparting skills, conveying information and preparing the next generation of communications professional.

Meanwhile, I've continued publishing articles and books, including the second edition of *How to Succeed in Advertising When All You Have is Talent* and *The Get a Job Workshop: How to find your way to a creative career in advertising, branding, collateral, digital, experiential and more.*

My three most recent books, prior to this one, shows my range of interests:

The Activation Imperative: How to build brand and business by inspiring action, which offers a cross-discipline marketing approach designed to impact critical behaviours and more effectively drive business results – ie, a road map to manage today's increasingly fragmented marketing landscape;

Audio Branding: Using sound to build your brand, which explores a key although often overlooked component of the brand, its distinctive sound. It serves as a practical guide on what it is, why it's important and how it can be used to enhance a brand and how to use it to enhance brand association with the consumer.

Advertising Under One Hour, a guide for marketers (to remind them of how to realize better work out of agencies), students (to help them figure out where they fit), small business owners (offering a process for creating their own ads and giving them a basis for judging them and their effectiveness) – all in a book that can be read in an hour.

If there's a theme to my writing, it's about finding clear-eyed, implementable approaches to boosting effectiveness, from finding a job in the industry to building a profitable brand.

This book is no exception. It grew out of a question from my editor, Jenny Volich, which grew into a look at how to best manage an existing global brand and equip readers with the skills to build one from scratch.

And I knew the perfect co-author to help me write such a book. I will leave the rest of the story up to him.

Ilan's story

For the longest time I've been approached by friends and colleagues who told me: 'You had such an interesting life, you must write a book.' I never got to it, because I was busy living that life, until my colleague Larry Minsky called proposing we write a book together about global brand management, and my ears perked. The subject is close to my heart.

I am fortunate to have lived and worked in four continents, served many multinational clients, and dealt with a multitude of cultures, changing technology and consumer behaviours. As an aspiring graphic designer, I found myself working in my own graphic design studio, which became successful. It was a period when print was the main media and communicating via such media was still effective. My largest account was the Israeli Ministry of Tourism, an experience that exposed me for the first time to multinational marketing. Our work was targeted to various markets in eight different languages. Needless to say, no serious attention was given to real brand building methodology in those days. It was simple, design in English and then translate it to seven other languages. Done.

Upon returning from a long travel expedition to Europe, I found a job with the then largest ad agency in Israel. The year was 1977, and the job title was Studio Manager, because the title Creative Director didn't exist in Israel back then, but that was my de facto job function.

Suddenly I was managing the creative duties for Coca-Cola, Chrysler, Levi's, as well as other national accounts in transportation, airlines, insurance, banking, construction, consumer goods and retail.

During the next four years, I moved from one agency to another, all in the Israeli market. None had any affiliation with any international agency, but some accounts were international, for example Duracell, Kodak, Sanyo, Fiat, Revlon, British Leyland, Avis and Sheraton.

'Brand management' as we define it today didn't exist. It was all about the current sales cycle of the given client.

But the combined experience of working on international accounts and travelling around the world made me ambitious. I knew, however, that the advertising industry in Israel was limited. So I started searching for other opportunities.

My break came when I met Norman Vale. Norman came to Israel to inspect the activities of the Revlon account, of which he was in charge at Grey International. As Grey International's Managing Director, Norman boosted the agency's international accounts from $150 million to $2 billion. He was a powerful and influential man. Grey was, and is, an extremely professional ad agency.

After seeing my work, he recommended me to the South African office of Grey Philips, Bunton Mundale and Blake. I also decided to send a letter of introduction to the top twenty agencies in Johannesburg and got a big surprise. Thirteen out of twenty invited me for an interview.

My visit to South Africa resulted in three job offers and I accepted the offer from Ogilvy's office in South Africa, Van Zijl and Schultze, Lund and Tredoux or as it was known VZ. I began my work there as the Creative Director of the Design group.

In one move, I finally became part of one of the biggest international agencies. Not only that, very few people knew that South Africa was a global centre of excellence in creativity, and many of its agencies are significant players on the global ad scene. I was happy to be there and be part of a wonderful group of international ad craftsmen, playing at their peak.

Everything was different. The discipline, the rules of engagement, the tradition, the way of doing business, client/agency relationship and – above all – the client's size and stature. My client list expanded to include Shell, American Express, Panasonic, South African Breweries, Nestle, Seagram, Unilever, GSK (Beecham), VW-Audi, Alitalia. Also, many other clients included the market-leading brands in tourism, consumer goods, transportation, soft drinks, alcoholic drinks and retail. Branding was a very important portion of the work, getting to know market research, brand strategy and brand implementation. That was a great experience, Ogilvy was one of the first agencies that understood the real power of branding, and not just the beauty of design.

This is where I learned that brand management is at the heart of every successful brand performance.

It is not just the advertising, or the technology used, or the coolest fonts.

It is all about the experience consumers go through before, during and after using the brand.

I spent eight years with Ogilvy in Johannesburg, Los Angeles and Chicago. I later moved to work for other international, national and regional agencies. Some got the idea about branding, others didn't.

Additional clients along my adventure included McDonald's, United Airlines, Visa, Citibank, Sears, Mexico Tourism Board, Lisbon Convention Bureau, Chicago Tribune, Hewlett Packard, Firestone, NAPA and many more.

As a result of this experience, I decided that I want to focus on building brands from the inside out. Internal branding is extremely important in brand management, and the advertising is only the tip of the iceberg.

Teaching branding became very important to me as well, and since 2000 I have been teaching the class Branding for Competitive Advantage at the University of Chicago.

I have also spent the past 13 years teaching at DePaul University in Chicago and travelled to short teaching gigs from India to Dubai. A very rewarding part of my career was giving back to the community I belong to. I have judged many advertising awards competitions. It is always great to see who's doing what and who is best at doing it.

As a global brand builder, I am now invited to speak in many international conferences about the power of brand building for destinations, trying to compete in the current global market.

Some of my experiences as well as Larry's are here for you to think about and use.

I hope this book will give you the perspective I have viewed during my career, my travels and my years of whispering in CEOs' ears what they should be doing.

PART ONE

Theoretical and strategic foundations

01

A definition of brands, branding and brand management

READING OUTCOMES

At the conclusion of this chapter, you should be able to:

- define such terminology as 'brand', 'brand development' and 'brand management';
- communicate the importance of brands, branding and brand development;
- identify and describe the various types of brands and their differences;
- describe the difference between product management and brand management.

Introduction

In our era of increasing globalization many of the traditional approaches to branding and brand management are becoming outdated and require new thinking. These days, any brand with a digital presence can be considered 'global' by default. But the crossing of borders online doesn't mean that the brand automatically understands the consumer behaviours, ethics and trade laws in the territories beyond its owner's home country. And not being fully prepared for a global audience and conversant in the risks, particularly in light of citizen activism, can hurt the brand and its owner.

Meanwhile, the era of a 'matching suite of luggage' approach to branding, where every execution looks exactly the same as the previous executions regardless of the context, is over. For success with branding today, brands need to be able to flex – or have elasticity – as well as display a range of behaviours, so that they're appropriate for the audience, location and contextual situation. Even when the brand is 'flexing', it should be easily identifiable simply by its behaviours – without the logo attached to the element or the brand experience.

In addition, while brand managers have traditionally focused on a single product in a single market, they increasingly need to focus on many products across many market situations all under one brand umbrella, given the rapidly changing global environment. Complicating the situation even further, while many Western companies focus on their financial results every quarter, brands from Asian countries, such as South Korea and China, plan for the long run.

In this chapter, we'll set the stage for an updated brand-management approach, one that accounts for how brands are perceived and practised differently across the globe, and that incorporates key recent developments in the theory and practice of brand management. In outlining this approach, we believe that brand managers from any country can learn from the best practices of others to improve their outcomes. So, if you are ready to improve the outcomes of your brand-management efforts (or future efforts), join us.

Overview

In this chapter we'll be asking what we mean by 'brand', before running through a brief history of branding and exploring the role that brands continue to play in our era of increased consumer control. We shall take a look at why brands are important for their owners, purchasers and consumers, as well as other stakeholders. Next, we'll provide a definition of brand management and touch on some of the branding and brand-management challenges and opportunities that exist, including the image-versus-action debate. We'll conclude with an extended case study on Oreo Cookies to help demonstrate one of the concepts of branding – that a brand is not a product – and to show that brands need to be managed on a global scale. We also have a 'guest perspective' from global advertising leader Jorg Borgwardt, who looks at why brand-development efforts often fail – one of the first steps towards learning how to ensure that yours will work.

Some working definitions of 'brand'

What is a brand? Some say it is the logo. A few toss in the consistent use of selected colours, fonts and/or other parts of its visual identity. Others say it's simply the name. Some include the mission and vision and/or the brand promise. And there are those who claim that it is the consumers' benefits. Some look at the physical attributes of a product, while others point to its visual manifestations. And some combine parts of all these definitions. All are partially correct, and all are wildly wrong.

While the logo, trademark, slogan, colours, fonts, advertisements, owned communications (such as the website), mission, vision, promise and more – even the product, service or other 'entity' itself – are ingredients or components of a brand, they are not the brand. So, what is a brand?

We believe that the simplest way to define it is: 'what consumers, prospects and other stakeholders think, feel and say about the product, service, person or other entity'. There are many other, more nuanced and, thus, more complicated definitions of a brand, but in the end, the intention is similar and points to the same intuitive understanding of the concept. For example, here is one definition: 'A brand is a cluster of meanings.'[1] Another definition, one that we heard in a presentation (the original source of which we can't identify) is: 'A brand is a covenant with the consumer. It is what remains from past behaviour that allows the consumer to anticipate future behaviour. The more consistent the past behaviour, the faster the brand can generate the conviction that we as consumers "understand" what it is about and anticipate what it will or will not do.'[2] Stan Richards, the founder of the US-based ad agency and design firm, the Richards Group, says that, 'a brand is a promise'. Others connect the brand with the fame and fortune of the product or service or its overall reputation. Jean-Noël Kapferer in his classic brand-management textbook defines 'brand' as 'a name with the power to influence.'[3] Meanwhile, best-selling marketing author Seth Godin defines a brand as 'the set of expectations, memories, stories and relationships that, taken together, account for a consumer's decision to choose one product or service over another'.[4] Or as Amazon CEO, Jeff Bezos, purportedly said, 'A brand is what they say about you when you're not in the room.'[5] Most of these definitions imply the same core idea – that a brand communicates meaning and offers, when positive, a form of reassurance to all, or virtually all, the brand stakeholders. Let's examine the significance of the brand for its various stakeholders – the consumers, owners and employees – in more detail.

CONSUMERS OF THE BRAND

The conveyance of meaning is particularly important for consumers and the users of the brand (not always the same) because it helps reduce any of the 'perceived risk'[6] and anxiety in making a selection. Consumers like to have confidence in the products and services that they use and, as behavioural economics shows, we naturally aim to conserve the energy in our brains by seeking decision shortcuts,[7] even becoming creatures of habit so that we don't have to think about our actions. In other words, brands create a 'cognitive bias'.[8]

Think of it this way: when we as consumers need to make a selection or decision about a product, service or other entity that we don't know much about, we seek cues for reassurance. It is for this reason that we tend to prefer brands for over-the-counter medication and cooking and baking ingredients, while consumers more educated in those areas – medical practitioners and bakers and chefs, respectively – are typically more comfortable with taking generics or using unbranded ingredients; they know what they are buying without the overlay of a brand.[9]

Brands reduce perceived risk in other ways too. Humans are tribal and seek the reassurance of other like-minded individuals – it is why we prefer to enter our neighbourhood store and be greeted on a first-name basis. But often we need a 'badge' to communicate our personality, beliefs and values so that the connection with others can happen, and often the badge is a display of a brand logo or colours.[10] In other words, the brand badge helps eliminate the perceived risk about ourselves or helps communicate that we are a risk to one group in order to appeal to another – just as strong brands that have an avid following tend to have just as fervent a group of rejecters. Think Apple versus Microsoft. People who are loyal to Apple tend to reject Disk Operating System-based computers, and people who embrace DOS tend to diss Apple users.[11]

Likewise, consumers pay attention to brands that engage with them, treat them well and provide a competent service with a human flair. In return, brands that take care of consumers are rewarded with their loyalty and that is always good for business. Which leads us to our next stakeholder.

LEADERS, MANAGERS AND OWNERS OF THE BRAND

For leaders, managers and owners of the brand, brands are important because, once established, they serve as an 'insurance policy' should something go wrong. After all, as Howard Shultz pointed out, 'If people believe they share values with a company, they will stay loyal to the brand.'[12] In addition, they can enable marketers to charge higher prices, enhancing their profit margins.

An elementary and obvious truth of business is that owners, including shareholders and other stakeholders with vested financial interests, are in it to generate profit and prosperity, and very few thrive by an ongoing series of one-off transactions. Marty Neumeier in his book *The Brand Flip* points to the sellers in Istanbul's Grand Bazaar as an example of commerce not built on the need for repeat business.[13] Other tourist spots might have the same dynamic. With these businesses, as Neumeier points out, the owners have to start over with every customer to win their trust and close the sale. And even in these one-off places, we suspect that this style of customer-churn business is going away owing to online reviews and other digitally empowered ways of researching each seller.

Even the manufacturers of durable goods, such as cars and appliances, and business-to-business big-ticket machines rely on eventual repeat purchases that a strong brand enables. In addition, consumer life cycles dictate the necessity of generating new customers indefinitely. Strong brands can help do that more affordably than weak ones. In addition, marketers can also charge more when they have a strong brand because of the trust consumers place in it. These companies thereby enhance their earning capacity and recover more quickly should an issue occur.[14]

Just as importantly, a strong brand plays a key internal role for its leaders, managers and owners because it 'aligns goals and objectives across your business units'.[15] As a result the company does need to spend as much on training and internal communications. Plus, a strong brand can reduce employee turnover and the related replacement costs, including the training of the new employees, as well as helping to attract new talent (also lowering recruitment costs). If a well-known brand is seeking new employees, you can bet that it will attract an extremely long list of applicants.

One more benefit is that a company with strong brands might not need to pay staff as much, because the employee gains a badge and emotional capital from their association with the brand. And this leads us to our next stakeholder – the employee.

EMPLOYEES SUPPORTING THE BRAND

For employees, being associated with great brands provides benefits beyond the paycheque. Firstly, just as strong brands benefit companies when it comes to recruitment, they help potential candidates decide where they might fit and might want to apply for a job. When a candidate understands the values of an organization and these values align with theirs, it can motivate them to take action and be happier with the ultimate cultural fit.

Secondly, strong brands enhance the identities of employees. It makes them more valuable to other employers, because the brand conveys a sense of the individual's worth within their industry. Strong brands promote pride within employee ranks and help make them more cohesive, facilitating teamwork. (It is one of the reasons why, as mentioned above, strong brands can pay employees less and still maintain retention rates above their category norm.)[16]

Thirdly, and perhaps most importantly, strong brands communicate guiding promises and values to which employees aspire, giving them direction in their work, and perhaps even beyond. Because strong brands are often inspirational, they can potentially guide employees into becoming better at their profession and prompt them to carry the brand values into other aspects of their life.

In other words, strong brands look inwards as well as outwards. They help their customers (and their rejecters) as well as their employees and other stakeholders.

Some types of brands

In our definition of the term 'brand', you might have noticed that we keep including 'or other entity'. That is because the concept of brand extends beyond basic products and services. A brand can be a non-commercial entity. Recognizable celebrities are brands. All politicians are essentially brands. Political parties definitely are too, plus, on a smaller scale, teachers, scholars and religious leaders. (As Patrick Hanlon points out in his book *Primal Branding*, strong brands and religions have many of the same elements.)[17] In fact, a brand could be any entity that people think and feel differently about in relation to the other entities in its category. We shall investigate in more detail some of the key speciality brands in Chapter 11, but we highlight a few of them below to show you the range of different types.

FIGURE 1.1 Types of brands

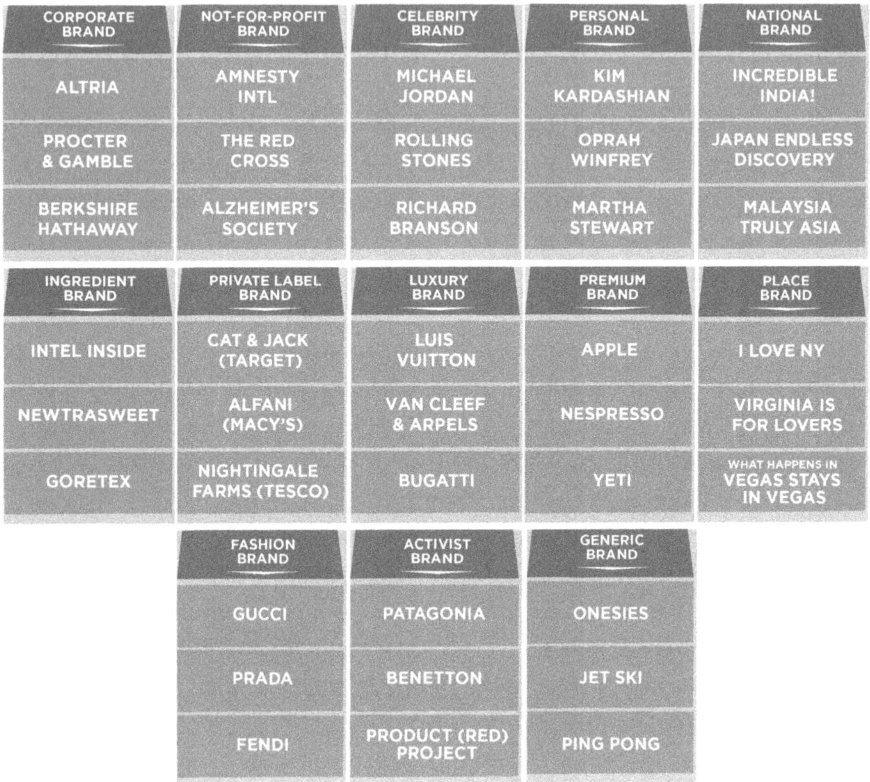

Brands span the gamut from the products themselves to the ingredients within them and can range from luxury to generic. Note that the generic examples here, as per the definition, are actually brand names that people commonly use when describing an entire product category.

PRODUCT BRAND

Adding brand properties to a product, particularly one that is at parity with its direct competitors, will help it exceed the consumer perception of its overall functional benefits and can add emotionality to the mix, inspiring greater trust and, eventually, loyalty. Consumers turn to product brands throughout their day without noticing how they have become part of their daily life. Just think of Shreddies, Heinz Beanz, Dove, Kleenex and the iPhone, to name but a few. Through familiarity with the brands as a result of repeated messaging and usage, people simply trust them and don't question their continual repurchase. Brand perception for products is becoming increasingly important as they're growing steadily more global.

SERVICE BRAND

It has been said that a service is something that people usually don't notice until it doesn't happen. Because service is invisible, brand perception becomes key in forming the underlying trust that the service will happen as anticipated or promised. And, like product brands, adding the perceived value to the service only happens if it's been branded appropriately. Traditional services – hospitality, restaurants, accounting firms, lawyers, real estate agents, home maintenance suppliers and more – were typically place-bound and relied on employees to fulfil the brand promise. However, technology is now enabling 'placeless' services (and their development is at speeds previously unknown), such as Google and Alexa, though some placeless services such as Lyft and Uber still rely on people to deliver them. Because of social media, the reaction time needed to respond when the service (or even a product) either shines or disappoints is becoming faster every day. As a result, traditional loyalty models are being challenged, something we'll explore later in the book. Another point to keep in mind is that, with the growth of such companies as Lyft, Uber, Grab, Gett, Airbnb and Zipcar, people are moving away from owning products to using them through services, making this category of brand management even more important. Finally, one more thing to think about: any start-up with a commerce-based website can be shipping internationally, making them a global brand.

CORPORATE BRAND

Or as some refer to it: 'the organization brand'. Branding guru David Aaker says: 'The corporate brand defines the firm that will deliver and stand behind the offering that the customer will buy and use.'[18] Customers may want to be reassured that the organization behind the tangible product or service that they use is solid and trustworthy. Such reassurance can come from its rich heritage; financial stability; mission, vision and values; and social responsibility. Some of the other meaningful corporate strengths could be in its global reach, innovation, adaptability to change and culture, all contributing to what people think and feel about their brands. The actions of the brand, however, must be consistent across the countries in which it operates and align with its corporate values. A break in alignment in one country can be noticed – and broadcast on social media – in the other countries in which it operates as well, hurting the brand's overall efforts.

NON-PROFIT BRAND

Non-profit or not-for-profit organizations are simply businesses with a different legal status and mission from the products and services that we have talked about above, and are, as the name implies, not focused on generating a financial profit for shareholders. However, among themselves, they are competing for donations from funders and for skilled employees (and volunteers). Many are working to shape perceptions of issues and the actions of individuals. These organizations must generate sympathy and support for their special causes. A number of the best-known non-profit brands have a long history (eg the Red Cross), while others were created following political, medical or social events. Like other businesses, non-profits can range from hyperlocal, only working in a city or even within a small neighbourhood of a city, to truly international (and somewhere in between). Those that cross borders, either in their service delivery or fundraising, experience many of the same issues faced by global product, service and corporate brands, and often need to take into account many of the same management considerations as other global brands.

CELEBRITY BRAND

Mass media and social media are creating celebrities every day, in addition to the traditional movie and television stars, sports heroes, rock and rap stars, business tycoons and others. Even cartoon characters can be considered to be celebrities. While celebrity brands are often associated with wealth, in many cases the brand creates the wealth for its owner. In order to ensure or maintain their cross-border success, the celebrities (and/or their managers and PR professionals) need to enact global brand-management strategies, just like the other entities that market across multiple borders.

PERSONAL BRAND

Brands can be built around individuals, often to advance their own personal interests. We all already have a 'brand' – the name we are given at birth. What we do with it to create value is up to us. Many build a personal brand today via social media, and others take advantage of a single event that could propel them to fame and fortune. Either way, these personal brands can be hard to build, especially since most people do not have the time and commitment to do it. A personal brand is not always positive; some personal brands have become very negative, something which can take years, if ever, to correct. Our digital footprint can remain forever without the possibility of erasing or modifying it.

PLACE BRAND

Depending on its scope, this category could be also identified as a destination or city brand. Marketing goals range from economic development to tourism (including medical tourism), often promoting a specific destination. Some of these destinations have clear tangible assets (such as the Eiffel Tower or Big Ben), while others are associated with a certain cuisine, cultural experience, musical style or history, or other key differentiators. Often, the goals require cross-border marketing efforts to achieve success, so even hyperlocal places need to implement global brand-management strategies. However, as we shall see, some argue that places can't conduct traditional branding efforts because there are too many 'moving parts' with the attributes of a place.

NATION BRAND

At the highest level of place branding, the nation in its entirety, not just a region or city within a country, becomes the brand. Many national tourism ministries and tourism boards dedicate significant budgets to building a positive image for their country, often forgetting that tourism is not the only outcome of a national brand. In today's globally interconnected economy, a nation's brand can have a tremendous impact on the country's investment, trade and place in the world. Therefore, by its very nature, a nation brand must utilize global brand-management strategies and it will experience many of the typical global-branding issues.

INGREDIENT BRAND

In this case the 'brand' is not the product or service itself, but only a part of it, a vital component that improves the perception of the parent brand. While most brands hide their supply-chain partners, they don't with well-known ingredient brands and, in fact, they add value to the parent brand. The ingredient is seen as essential to the viability of the parent brand. Often the ingredient brand substantially contributes to the parent brand's success, because prospective consumers prefer the ingredient brand over other components. In fact, ingredient brands could be the single compelling or reassuring reason for purchasing the master brand. Intel Inside is one of the best-known ingredient brands, without which certain laptop computers would not have had the credibility to generate transactions. For an ingredient brand to be an asset when the parent brand crosses a border, it too must be able to travel and offer a compelling promise. As a result, managers of ingredient brands also need to implement global brand-management strategies.

PRIVATE-LABEL BRAND

When retail organizations review the brands they sell, they sometimes realize that developing and manufacturing the same products on their own is a good practice, and they contract manufacturers to produce a unique brand, one that can be found only under their roof. Sears, for instance, developed the DieHard, Kenmore and Craftsman brands on their own. When Sears hit hard times, they sold the private-label brands, which still had significant value and equity. Grocery stores are also heavily into developing private-label products. Most private-label brands hover at the lower end of the price spectrum of products, but some have managed to penetrate the upper range, and others have been able to generate multi-country sales. Some view private-label brands as offering the same product at a lower price point and others see the added value, such as extended or lifetime warranties, that the store sometimes offers. The loyalty to these brands and the perception of them, however, are often tied to the loyalty for the parent brand, which casts a long shadow over them. Either way, the same theories and practices that apply to other brands that are available in more than one country apply to private-label brands.

FIGURE 1.2 Examples of private-label brands

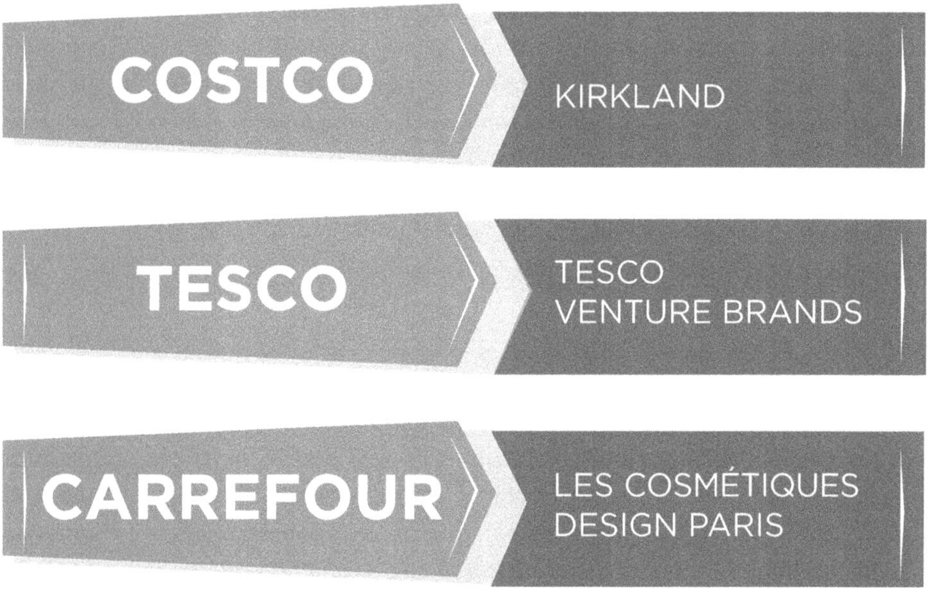

Private-label brands often rely on the brand equity of the parent brand and, conversely, extend and reinforce the experience of the parent brand.

LUXURY BRAND

The idea of 'luxury' is fluid. What is considered luxurious today could be seen as average tomorrow. And what is luxurious to one could be commonplace and expected for another. But when it comes to positioning, putting a brand in a place of luxury is a smart step. Luxury brands promise social status and demonstrate a certain exclusivity that many consumers seek. They must deliver consistent quality and, as a result, are more exposed to scrutiny than other types of brands. They generally feel more indulgent to the consumer and are stuck between the tug of needing to feel exclusive and the market reality of needing to grow sales and profits. Rarely, a brand considered luxurious in one country is not in another. Understanding what makes it seem luxurious from one country to the next – and why some brands are not seen as luxurious across the board – can be instructive, whether the marketer wants their brands to be seen as a luxurious entity or not.

PREMIUM BRAND

Jean-Noël Kapferer points out that, unlike luxury brands, premium brands are considered to be functionally better than the rest, or most of the rest, in its product or service category, and offer tangible performance benefits or are made with demonstratively better ingredients, components or materials.[19] As a result, luxury brands are generally considered more of an emotive purchase, while premium brands can have more of a rational component to the consumer's decision-making process. While not all brand experts make this distinction between luxury and premium, we mention the difference because although luxury brands might use fine ingredients and offer better functionality and premium brands might feel luxurious, these are not requirements. In other words, a premium product might not be perceived as luxurious; rather, it might be viewed as being more of a common-sense purchase or a necessity for the individual, because it is clearly better in some way. Meanwhile, a luxurious brand might not need functional or manufacturing superiority to feel indulgent.

FASHION BRAND

Clothing, as well as mobile phones and other items that can go out of fashion very quickly and therefore have fleeting value can be considered within this category. Often, these are 'badge' items that help define the individual who is sporting them. An issue with fashion brands is that they still need a long-term, differentiated brand image that enables them to remain relevant as styles change and new items are released. Some consider fashion items to be a luxury, but they are different because of the eventual steep drop in perceived value of the items and the fact that manufacturing 'superiority' is not a requirement.[20] Meanwhile, the parent brand should have brand differentiators if they are to keep producing new fashion items that sport a 'badge' quality for the wearer or user of the product.

ACTIVIST BRAND

Millennials are known for voting with their dollars and supporting the brands that give back to society – brands that put a major cause at the centre of their marketing activities, promote that activity and preach to their customers about it. In today's social-media and consumer-savvy environment, activist brands can gain traction with minimal time and effort, even across borders. As long as they seem to be authentic about their activism, they can enjoy the trust and support of many. A cause or purpose is the main ingredient of activist brands. Examples are Warby Parker, The Body Shop, Soda Stream, Benetton and the Product Red Project.

GENERIC BRAND

Also occasionally called commodities, a generic is the opposite of a brand. A generic would be, for instance, sugar without a name. In fact, many of the basic goods we consume are commodities. They were sold (and some still are) in their natural, unprocessed form. Fruits and vegetables, livestock, meats and poultry and other naturally grown products were sold in markets for thousands of years, but even many of these items are moving towards being branded. The one main place where generic brands still exist is in the pharmaceutical category, because when the patent expires others can start manufacturing it under its generic name. Overexposed brands can become generic when we start using the brand name as a verb, such as 'Xeroxing' or 'Googling'. Some marketers are claiming that they are sick of brands. The Unbranded Brand claims on its website that, 'While other companies try to create a brand image through expensive ad campaigns and celebrity endorsements, we do the opposite. Have you ever wondered why some "premium" jeans cost as much they do? What is the difference between jeans sold for $250 and others that sell for $80?'[21] Brandless.com makes essentially the same argument. Ironically, these sites are still conveying a brand image themselves, even as they attempt to claim they are not. Meanwhile, as we discussed earlier (with the case of medical practitioners and bakers), many consumers still want the reassurance and/or badge value of Levi's or Wrangler and reject the idea of unbranded fashion items – as well as other unbranded items.

As you can see from our list of brands, the types are non-exclusive – a product brand can also be a luxury brand, just as a service brand can be one too. A brand can be hyperlocal, just sold in one community, or it can be sold in nearly every country in the world. Those that are sold in more than one country, with the same name, values, promise and personality, are considered a global brand.

When considering brands, virtually every entity – even you yourself, as we saw above – can be thought of as a brand to someone, whether you or the marketer wants to be one or not. And just as your own brand status can vary between your family, friends and the world of work, the brand status of products and services can vary too. It takes brand management – a conscious branding effort – to maintain the brand values, promise and personality while enabling the status to vary. But what are branding and brand management?

A practical definition of branding and brand management

Branding is the application of a process to identify and create the core foundational elements and outcomes of an entity, such as logo, colours, font, proprietary sound, signature scent, way of talking and more, which lead consumers and other stakeholders to think, feel and say things about it in the way that the marketer would like.

If a brand is what people think, feel and say about the entity, brand management is the process of managing the brand expressions and experiences that lead prospects, customers and other stakeholders to their conclusions. In other words, if a strong brand means that people think about an entity positively, then brand management is the active process of developing 'cues' and inspiring those feelings. (Weak brands broadcast cues too – but not ones that speak well of the entity and often these are not intentional.)

Brand management, then, is all of the activities that go into optimizing the brand, from the initial branding process of identifying the essence, core promise, vision values and personality to selecting the brand name, fonts, colours, imagery, sounds, scents and textures and the intentional application of these elements at every touchpoint.[22] Therefore, the main occupation of managing a brand is managing perceptions and knowing how to continue engaging current customers, while looking to find new ones. The relationships that consumers and other stakeholders have with a brand is one of the most valuable assets that a brand can have.[23]

Strong brand managers must understand how to work well with the product managers, to evaluate product attributes and adapt product specs for changing consumer needs, habits and values. But it should be noted that *brand management is not the same as product management*, although the two are frequently confused and product managers are often given a title of 'brand manager' in corporations. The focus and responsibilities are different. Product managers are more focused on managing the supply chain, distribution and profit and loss (P&L) – the classic Four Ps still taught in most introductory marketing courses (product, place, price and promotion), with some adding a fifth P of either people or packaging or other concept.[24] A large part of these activities is internal, and only some are articulated in advertising and other forms of communications.

Product managers are also often focused on managing the relationship between 'sales' and 'marketing'. One way to think about the difference between the two groups is that sales devotes its energies to obtaining an immediate transaction (closing the sale), while marketing is concerned with longer-term growth. Therefore, their priorities are often different, with sales often desiring short-term discounts and marketing focused on increasing the perceived value and consumer demand. In sales-driven companies, marketing is typically seen as more of a support function, focused on creating effective sales-support materials, while marketing-driven companies, at the other extreme, aim to essentially eliminate the need for sales, converting sales people into simply order-takers. Of course, there are many companies that fall in between these extremes.

Because of the different traditions that companies follow in their sales and marketing activities, there is also a bit of confusion about the meaning of 'brand managers' and 'product managers'.

FIGURE 1.3 Brand manager versus product manager

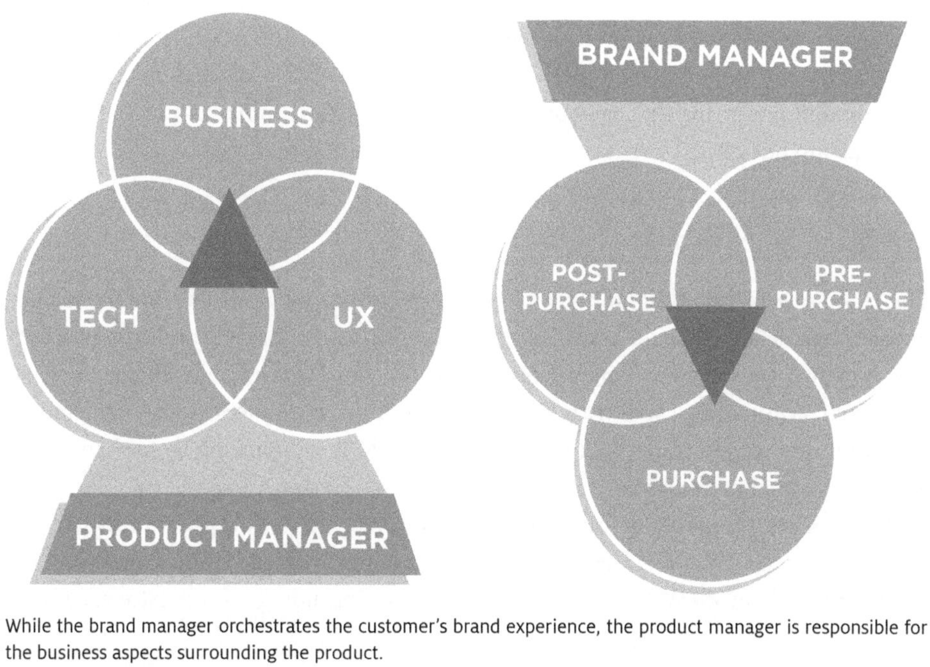

While the brand manager orchestrates the customer's brand experience, the product manager is responsible for the business aspects surrounding the product.

PRODUCT MANAGERS

Product managers are, in a sense, 'mini-CEOs' of a product or service. They are involved in all aspects of it, from the development process of the product or service and its attributes and functionality to the success and profitability of it in the marketplace. The work involved can be extremely technical and engineering-oriented, and often they must possess knowledge of materials and manufacturing methods for physical products, as well as the processes for services. Everything they do has to be closely coordinated with other departments in the organization, starting from the top management down to procurement, the manufacturing floor and logistics. As leaders of the product developers, they must also interact with potential consumers, understand how they will use the product, test its functionality and desirability, and the feasibility of introducing it into a particular market. They are also concerned with determining where the product will be sold, its price and potential profitability, as well as the other 'Ps' we mentioned above. And, they must work to keep the product or service relevant as needs and tastes change.

BRAND MANAGERS

Meanwhile, brand managers are responsible for the image of the product, service or other entity that is about to become a brand. As such, they will focus on business strategy and not functionality; they view the brand as an asset and not a functioning mechanism of some kind. Their job is to create and maintain interest in the product and its values and promote it as a brand. Brand managers have to understand the place that the brand occupies in the overall brand architecture of the organization, and make sure that it doesn't cannibalize other brands within the firm, unless that is part of the long-term strategy. Their task is to oversee the initial brand-development process, as well as the execution of the branding efforts internally and to prospects, consumers, the supply chain and other stakeholders. They need to create the emotional connections that encourage all these parties to think and feel about the brand as intended.

A brief history of branding

The technique of branding and brand management has been around for thousands of years. We believe that the term 'brand' comes from an ancient Scandinavian word meaning 'fire' or 'sword'.[25] And a later use for the word 'branding' was for marking an animal, criminal or slave with a branding iron, for example to show ownership. So, within the word's roots, there is an interesting idea of 'marking by fire' and thus leaving a permanent mark.

We see some remnants of 'branding' in the old market of Pompeii, in the form of electoral posters. That was the beginning of announcing the difference between one candidate and another. Differentiation is one of branding's cornerstones. Once special processing was added to consumer goods commodities, the opportunity for branding increased. We started to witness tea being packed for Twinings of London in 1706[26] and pharmaceutical products packed for Officina Profumo Farmaceutica di Santa Maria Novella in 1612.[27]

Culture can contribute to maintaining the reputation of businesses and brands. The Guinness Book of World Records, for instance, mentions some businesses in Japan that have been operating for centuries. One example is a hot-spring hotel called Nisiyama Onsen Keiunkan,[28] which has existed since the year 705. In addition to respect for family values and tradition, other factors have helped brands to thrive in Japan for a very long time, including political stability and a non-litigious legal system.

The Industrial Revolution in the Western world helped many organizations improve manufacturing merchandise and goods in record times, and branding started to become a recognized strategic endeavour. The different eras and concepts of marketing history, of which branding is part, are traditionally viewed as: the production, the product, the selling, the marketing and the information era.[29]

THE PRODUCTION ERA

The production era was where management focused on improving production methods and systems, while improving the distribution channel. The production concept is still useful, especially when price is a matter of survival. This is typically apparent in global markets, where price points and labour issues could be beneficial in one market versus another. Its biggest issue is that the production concept is internally focused and not concerned with quality or customer satisfaction. One thing that typifies the production era is that manufacturers were in control of the product but did not focus on controlling brand perceptions. Advertising and other marketing communications were thought of as news coming from the manufacturer and primarily consisted of announcements.

THE PRODUCT ERA

The product era was when quality, performance and incremental improvement became part of the strategy. While consumers still didn't have a voice in the product-development process, the manufacturers believed that a better product would sell. Performance was key. And the growth in product variety began to encourage consumers to compare similar items and brands. That was not well anticipated by the marketing executives, who still didn't consider consumer needs and attractive pricing as part of the mix.

THE SELLING ERA

The selling era started when manufacturers began accumulating unsold inventory owing to a weak economy and increasing competition. In addition, services were proliferating and needed a way for people to buy them. Aggressive selling, backed by

FIGURE 1.4 Consumer eras since the Industrial Revolution

long-term payments plans, incentives, discount outlets, promotions and the like were mushrooming. Consumers were coaxed into buying what was manufactured, rather than buying what they really wanted. Manufacturers and ad agencies started looking at ad messages and other forms of marketing communications as persuasion and as a surrogate for the sales person.

THE MARKETING ERA

The marketing era emerged when manufacturers, as well as service providers, started listening to consumers and answering their needs and wants, realizing that it was actually good business. When customers saw value in what they bought, they came back, leading to more sales and profitability, a departure from the concept of 'making stuff'. By responding to demands, marketers were, for the first time, creating a customer-centred business philosophy and developing marketing strategies to fit that philosophy. As a result, the concept of brand and the practice of branding and brand management became even more important. Price and functionality were no longer the only reasons for consumers to prefer a brand. The advertising creative revolution happened during the start of this era and extended to the period when the internet and its confluence of new consumer power and marketing opportunities forced a change in the marketing paradigm.

THE INFORMATION ERA

The information era began with the internet and social media becoming a dominant part of our lives. Consumers are now able to influence manufacturing, products and marketing strategies and have much more information about products and services, their functionality, their price and their alignment of brand values with actual actions. Technology has helped an entire generation of savvy consumers search, enquire, compare and make better, more informed purchasing decisions. As a result, nowadays, reputation, public opinion and opinion leaders drive many decisions even before a product is made. Business owners now have to calculate very carefully what kind of brands they are developing and must work to send the right cues or signals to get people to perceive the brand essence and values, not just separately and differently in each country, but across each one in which they operate.

Branding in an era of consumer control

The fact that we have special online channels open for public opinion and consumer reviews shows that the consumer is now in control. There are no secrets anymore, and all is out in the open. Mess up and the brand might not survive public scrutiny. Errors are typically not being forgotten, and very few mistakes are being forgiven. Many ads or other types of content are being rapidly removed because of immediate consumer backfire and negative reactions. Marketing departments are becoming more and more reactive to consumer needs and wants. Brands that have no story to tell or can't stand behind a story once told have a minimal chance of survival.

The most obvious challenge any brand faces is the amount of clutter out there. Marketers all talk about the number of brand exposures that consumers see every day. The number is in the thousands,[30] and no human brain can contain, absorb and react to such an absurd number of brand exposures. It seems that brands are chasing us into every existing space, be it in public toilets, stadiums, offices, restaurants, the street, lifts or any other frequently visited public space.

For those who treat brands as commodities or products and hope to succeed, the challenges are even greater. They are knowingly walking into a situation where their 'brand' is not filling a significant void in a consumer's life; it is just a short-term solution. Pricing is one of branding's biggest challenges, since the age of globalization has created massive price competition. And again, being the provider of the lowest price can only go so far. In other words, brands are becoming more important; meanwhile, marketers are finding it harder to achieve results merely by projecting the attributes of their brand(s) through static messaging and hoping to break through the clutter.

Building the brand by inspiring behaviour

The world of branding and brand building has changed. No longer can we just broadcast what the brand does and represents. Rather, we need brand actions too. In *The Activation Imperative*, co-written by Laurence Minsky (one of the authors of this book) and William Rosen, CEO of VSA Partners, it is argued that 'to adapt to the changing landscape, what is needed is a shift from building brands to "activating" them – from simply projecting what a brand is to optimizing what a brand *does* in order to move people closer to transaction.'[31] In other words, it's not just identifying the brand attribute that is important, but what the brand does. We believe that brand behaviours are best accomplished by inspiring action in the prospect. After all, as Adam Ferrier pointed out in his book *The Advertising Effect*, 'Action changes attitude faster than attitude changes action.'[32] When consumer behaviour becomes the marketing goal, it becomes easier to measure and opens up many more avenues of connecting with the prospect than just broadcasting messages. For example, social, mobile, events, shopper, experiential, direct, in-bound content, PR and brand journalism, sales promotions, sponsorships – even marketing disciplines that have not yet been invented – become options. And, of course, the communications using these avenues must be recognizable as coming from the brand, even if the logo, brand colours and other visual assets are absent.

In the next chapter, we'll look at the key strategic role that branding and brand management play today, particularly in our ever-changing, over-communicated, increasingly global environment, as well as examining how branding works. Join us. And learn more about the long-term profit builder that is much more than a logo. But first let's take a break and hear from Jorg Borgwardt on why brands fail and then learn about one of the leading global cookie brands, Oreos, and how its brand managers adjust product for each country in which it is available.

WHY BRANDS FAIL – A GUEST PERSPECTIVE FROM JORG BORGWARDT, GERMANY

With one of the best success records in the industry, Jorg has spent more than 40 years in international marketing communications. Multilingual and multicultural, he graduated from Cologne University with a thesis on 'International coordination of advertising agencies in Europe'. It was the first academic paper of its kind and put him in touch with leading agency networks, including Grey Advertising, which he joined.

At Grey, Jorg served in such positions as Managing Director, European, New Business Director and later Executive Vice President of Grey International, providing in-depth consultancy and advice on global communication and branding to Procter & Gamble, BAT, Block Drug, Timex, 3M, Revlon and Mars, among others. In addition to leading global strategies and teams, he dedicated himself to raising quality standards in the industry. He is a co-author of Grey's European handbook on 'Marketing and Media Planning' and also created the Grey Academy, one of the most recognized institutions for the training and advancement of practitioners in advertising.

Besides his native Germany, Jorg has worked in every continent and has lived in the US, the UK, France, Switzerland and Spain, giving him a truly global perspective. Here's what he has to say about branding, brand management and why brand development efforts often fail:

> 'Brands are the result of human effort. And it's inconceivable that brand creators strive for anything but complete success in their endeavours. Why then is it that so many fail? Misinterpretation of demand, product failure, insufficient funding, poor patience, or simply the inability to define the right brand proposition? This list could easily be extended to include additional planning errors about pricing, distribution, target reach, packaging, consumer touchpoints... but perhaps the most fundamental error is emotionless branding. Emotionless branding is the absence of powerful emotional attributes to enrich a brand promise. Emotions, however, stem from personal judgement and personal judgement is not infallible; hence mistakes can easily be made when attempting to attribute emotions to brands and the entire branding process.

'One fundamental belief has guided my professional life as a brand builder and promoter: for a brand to be successful, it has to be perceived as a "brand for me". The "Me" is the intended purchaser not the inventor or his family and friends. This "Me" is the ultimate manifestation of brand value. Just as beauty is in the eye of the beholder, a brand's value is the summation of feelings of all its users. Feelings can result from functional advantages, rational satisfaction, or emotional pleasure. This last is perhaps the most powerful but also the most difficult to define; this may be why it is not always considered for branding or under-exploited.

'Emotions are certainly difficult to measure. Procurement finds them obscure; understanding the ROI of emotions is not part of their repertoire. This is particularly true when the emotional enrichment of a brand promise is based more on intuition and less founded in facts.

'When time existed in abundance, smart managers tried to uncover the emotional "additives" that could move a brand's promise from the brain to the heart. Typically, focus groups or in-depth interviews were used, professional interpreters engaged, agencies or individuals employed to capture the right verbal and visual cues. Sometimes, market testing was funded to measure and fine-tune details before roll-out.

'Time no longer exists in abundance, markets are not protected by frontiers, planning is replaced by activism; the digital world has overrun the comfort zone of many managers. Perhaps even more problematic is the generational gap between those who have grown up with the internet and those who have an acquired knowledge of branding and brand-creation planning. Is this the end of emotional branding? I believe the contrary is true. Despite its contribution to chaos, the digital era has also permitted the arrival of new research methods that were not possible before.

'A German start-up devised a new research methodology that uncovers the unique emotional properties that a brand owns. It works for an existing brand just as well as for a new brand proposition which is not yet on the market. And what's really cool is that it can also map the emotional properties of competitive brands and hence contribute to making the brand proposition much more germane and exclusive.

'Generated data is reliable; it is based on 1,000 respondents. Each respondent attributes 50 fundamental human emotions to the tested brand. The aim is not only to uncover the single most important emotional benefit of a brand but also "next of kin" emotions which feed the fundamental feeling. What emerges is a pattern of connected emotions which the inventors call the "Emotional Territory" of a brand. These territories are found through algorithms that help sort through 10^{32} possible permutations. It is the only methodology which currently exits that provides what branding professionals need to unleash the power of emotions on their products or services.

'Thanks to supercomputers and human probing, brand promises can be defined more precisely now than ever before; a new era of emotional value-adds can emerge. More good news is that this new research tool is very affordable: costs are equivalent to three or four professional focus groups. Its results can influence everything from logo design to external and internal communication, as well as sales literature or annual reports.

'Since uncertainty can be replaced with facts and figures, brand empowerment through emotions may well see a renaissance. And, as a result, more "brands for me" may emerge – only time will tell.'

EXTENDED CASE STUDY: PRODUCT AND BRAND ARE NOT THE SAME – THE STORY OF OREO COOKIES IN CHINA AND INDIA

Founded in 1912, the Oreo brand is over 100 years old. It all started at the NABISCO (National Biscuit Company) bakery in New York City. After rounds of mergers and acquisitions it became part of the Kraft Foods family and is now owned by Mondelēz International (although still in the NABISCO division). While being an American brand for most of its existence, it is now one of the world's favourite cookie brands and, with more than $2 billion in global annual revenues (2016), it is one of Mondelēz International's 'billion-dollar brands'. But taking on the world was initially a struggle.

Oreo was first launched in China in 1996.[33] As happens with many consumer goods, the assumption was that what works in one part of the world, particularly the US, must work all over the world and, why not. The US market is not homogenous. It has many nationalities, cultures and tastes. Surely the Chinese would like the same delicious tastes that Americans love, and especially since the Chinese emulate and admire American culture.

But once they launched in China, Oreo languished and, after nine years of insignificant sales, the Kraft marketing team did what they should have done in the first place: they conducted a market research study to find out what the Chinese consumer would like in a cream-filled cookie and how to make the Oreo brand resonate with the Chinese consumer.

And to their surprise, the team learned that the Chinese consumer didn't like cookies as much as Western audiences do. Further, the research revealed that the typical Chinese consumer likes a contrast of bitter and sweet taste in food products, but that the Oreo cookie presented too much of that contrast.

And so, the first issue was the **product**. They had to modify the Oreo cookie recipe formula. The changes were in the cookie and the cream, making one more 'chocolatey', and the other less cloying. Market tests were then conducted with many different formulas to find the one that would resonate most with the average Chinese consumer – not an easy task in a market with over a billion consumers!

The second issue was **price**. Kraft came to realize that Oreo was too expensive for the value-oriented Chinese consumer. They had to change the price structure and found that a different package with fewer cookies would be the right combination of product and price.

Another part of the brand building failure was their **promotion**. While in the US, the typical twist, lick and dunk (in milk) ritual was a main theme in advertising and other marketing communications, a ritual that helped instil loyalty in its audience, it was considered foreign and strange in China, not something that would resonate with a typical Chinese consumer, especially kids.

These kinds of self-questioning and prodding processes are good for any brand. As a result of the research, Kraft re-evaluated the traditional look and feel of the Oreo product and reintroduced it in 2006. This time, there was little resemblance to the original US product. Americans would find it hard to believe that the Chinese Oreo was now made of four layers of wafers with vanilla and chocolate cream, all covered in chocolate. Further, other versions were introduced, including green tea and double-fruit. And indeed, the results were far better for Oreo in China, and the brand experienced better growth and adoption by local consumers.

Taking the lessons from China, Kraft launched Oreo cookies in India in March 2011.[34] Following the acquisition of Cadbury in 2009, Kraft had a good foothold in this market. And unlike the consumer preferences in China, the people of India generally love biscuits. In fact, it is the world's largest market for them. Also, culturally, Kraft knew that the way to the consumer's stomach in India was through maintaining highly competitive pricing, high volume and a strong distribution network, especially in rural areas.

The Oreo brand entered the market as Cadbury Oreos because Cadbury was a stronger parent brand name than Kraft in India, and exploited Cadbury's network of 1.2 million stores, something that didn't exist in China. They initially focused on generating awareness and rapid trial, sweetening the taste to better suit the Indian palate. Kraft also used locally sourced, cheaper ingredients and packed the biscuits in smaller-size packages in order to reach competitive prices. Oreo introduced the traditional chocolate cookie with vanilla cream in a pack of three to drive impulse purchases and trial; a pack of seven; and a pack of 14 for heavy usage. The cookie looked the same as its international counterpart. Unlike in China, Kraft maintained the Oreo heritage of featuring bitter chocolate cookie with sweet vanilla cream to stand out from me-too products and meet customer expectations of having the real thing.

As for the promotion in India, Kraft focused on using the togetherness concept to sell Oreos, with TV forming the main medium of communication. Social media, promotions and POP (point-of-purchase) strongly contributed to Oreo's success in India as well.[35]

The point is that with all of these introductions, the product was changed – but the brand essence stayed the same, including its unique positioning as 'milk's favourite cookie' and its 'twist, lick, dunk' brand ritual (according to a Mondelēz fact sheet, approximately 50 per cent of consumers engage in this ritual before eating, with women doing it more often than men),[36] enabling people to re-experience and experience their 'inner child'. It also maintained its unique shape in most of its markets, enabling it to serve as a strong brand signature, easily recognizable on store shelves. Also going for the brand is its name, which is easy to pronounce and has a neutral, friendly non-suggestive tone for a food product.

Today, Oreo is available in more than 100 countries; its biggest markets include the US, China, UK, Indonesia, Canada, Mexico, Spain, Argentina, India and Germany and its more recent introductions include Morocco and Russia. Unique culturally appropriate flavours include Blueberry Ice Cream and Orange Ice Cream in Indonesia, Green Tea Ice Cream and Fruit Duos (raspberry and blueberry) in China and Dulce de Leche (with banana) in Argentina. Starting in 2016, Mondelēz began running 'global' advertising campaigns for the brand, executing it in more than 50 of their markets. As the brand solidifies its dominance, we're sure the number of countries in future campaigns will expand. At least, it's something to watch as the world becomes even more interconnected.

KEY TERMS

- brand
  - global (multinational)
  - product
  - service
  - corporate
  - non-profit
  - celebrity
  - personal
  - destination (place/nation)
  - ingredient
  - private-label
  - luxury
  - premium
  - fashion
- product manager
- brand manager

DISCUSSION QUESTIONS

- Which definition of branding do you prefer and why?
- Why is brand development important to the success of a product or service?
- What is the difference between product management and brand management?
- How do brands and branding contribute to successful global marketing?
- Are your favourite brands local, regional or global?

Notes

1 Batey, M (2008) *Brand Meaning*, Psychology Press, New York

2 Brandweek (2011) 42nd ed, Adweek LP, New York, NY

3 Kapferer, J N (2012) *The New Strategic Brand Management: Advanced Insights & Strategic Thinking*, 5th edn, Kogan Page, London

4 *Kabbage* (2015) Lessons from marketing guru Seth Godin about building a brand, https://www.kabbage.com/blog/6-lessons-from-marketing-guru-seth-godin-about-building-a-brand

5 Kihlström, G (2018) *The Agile Brand*, BookBaby, Cork

6 Kapferer, J N (2012) *The New Strategic Brand Management: Advanced Insights & Strategic Thinking*, 5th edn, Kogan Page, London

7 Erskine, R (2017) Brandless, the no-brand brand, actually teaches brands the importance of branding, *Forbes*, https://www.forbes.com/sites/ryanerskine/2017/11/30/brandless-the-no-brand-brand-actually-teaches-brands-the-importance-of-branding/#3a6d620847a6 (archived at https://perma.cc/27FY-4X9W)

8 DeMers, J (2016) 8 cognitive biases that will drive the future of marketing, *Forbes*, https://www.forbes.com/sites/jaysondemers/2016/12/16/8-cognitive-biases-that-will-drive-the-future-of-marketing/#c82eb0f6be93 (archived at https://perma.cc/DK2X-WGDJ)

9 Bronnenberg, B J, Dubé, J-P, Gentzkow, M and Shapiro, J M (2015) Do pharmacists buy Bayer? Informed shoppers and the brand premium, *The Quarterly Journal of Economics*, **130** (4), pp 1669–1726, https://doi.org/10.1093/qje/qjv024 (archived at https://perma.cc/R768-MZ4K)

10 Tait, B (2015) How to manage a 'badge' brand *The Business Journals*, https://www.bizjournals.com/bizjournals/how-to/growth-strategies/2015/12/how-to-manage-a-badge-brand.html (archived at https://perma.cc/BDZ9-XT2J)

11 YouTube (2018) All 'I'm a Mac I'm a PC' ads Part 1, https://www.youtube.com/watch?v=qfv6Ah_MVJU (archived at https://perma.cc/3MQ9-WLD3)

12 Howard Schultz (1999) *Pour Your Heart Into It: How Starbucks built a company one cup at a time*, Hachette Books, as quoted in *Goodreads*, https://www.goodreads.com/quotes/387871-mass-advertising-can-help-build-brands-but-authenticity-is-what (archived at https://perma.cc/EJ74-DGC8)

13 Neumeier, M (2008) *The Brand Flip: Why customers now run companies and how to profit from it*, New Riders, San Francisco

14 Erskine, R (2017) What is a brand really worth? *Forbes*, https://www.forbes.com/sites/ryanerskine/2017/08/12/what-is-a-brand-really-worth (archived at https://perma.cc/Y9B8-YHXZ)

15 Minsky, L and Fahey, C (2017) *Audio Branding: Using sound to build your brand*, Kogan Page, London

16 Tavassoli, N, Sorescu, A and Chandy, R (2014) Employee-based brand equity: why firms with strong brands pay their executives less, 51st ed, http://faculty.london.edu/rchandy/brandequity.pdf (archived at https://perma.cc/8KEG-YH5N)

17 Hanlon, P (2006) *Primal Branding: Create zealots for your brand, your company, and your future*, Simon and Schuster, New York

18 Aaker, D (2006) *Brand Portfolio Strategy: Creating relevance, differentiation, energy, leverage, and clarity*, Simon and Schuster, New York

19 Kapferer, J and Bastien, V (2012) *The Luxury Strategy: Break the rules of marketing to build luxury brands*, 2nd edn, Kogan Page, London

20 Baicoianu, M (2015) Luxury marketing: The difference between fashion and luxury brands, *BrandUNIQ*, http://branduniq.com/2015/luxury-marketing-the-difference-between-fashion-and-luxury-brands (archived at https://perma.cc/A679-ESQR)

21 The Unbranded Brand (2018) About us, https://theunbrandedbrand.com/pages/about-us (archived at https://perma.cc/L9AC-A8KS)

22 Brakel-Schutt, N (2019) Why brand management is a key success factor for modern-day marketers, *Widen*, https://www.widen.com/blog/why-brand-management-is-a-key-success-factor-for-modern-day-marketers (archived at https://perma.cc/J7QE-K7WW)

23 Duncan, T and Moriarty, S (1998) A communication-based marketing model for managing relationships, *Journal of Marketing*, **62** (2), pp 1–13, http://www.jstor.org/stable/1252157 (archived at https://perma.cc/QKH3-7PL5)

24 Tracy, B (2018) The 7 Ps of Marketing, *Entrepreneur*, https://www.entrepreneur.com/article/70824 (archived at https://perma.cc/6FTG-8K5J)

25 Etymonline (2018) brand | Origin and meaning of brand by Online Etymology Dictionary, https://www.etymonline.com/word/brand (archived at https://perma.cc/CD8M-239U)

26 Twinings UK & Ireland (2018) History of Twinings, https://www.twinings.co.uk/about-twinings/history-of-twinings (archived at https://perma.cc/JRC2-V77X)

27 smnovella.com (2018), Officina Profumo Farmaceutica di Santa Maria Novella, https://buy.smnovella.com (archived at https://perma.cc/7FWH-M3D7)

28 Keiunkan (2018) Koshu Nishiyama Hot Spring, Keiunkan, http://www.keiunkan.co.jp/en (archived at https://perma.cc/CH99-NTHP)

29 Merritt, C (2018) What are the five eras of marketing? *AZ Central*, https://yourbusiness.azcentral.com/five-eras-marketing-3411.html (archived at https://perma.cc/W57B-VUUM)

30 Saxon, J (2018) Why your customers' attention is the scarcest resource in 2017, *AMA*, https://www.ama.org/partners/content/Pages/why-customers-attention-scarcest-resources-2017.aspx

31 Rosen, W and Minsky, L (2017) *The Activation Imperative: How to build brands and business by inspiring action*, Rowman & Littlefield, Lanham, Maryland

32 Ferrier, A and Fleming, J (2014) *The Advertising Effect: How to change behaviour*, Oxford University Press, Oxford

33 Koellmann, B (2013) How Kraft Foods won over customers in China and India, *Business Today*, http://www.businesstoday.in/magazine/lbs-case-study/how-kraft-foods-won-over-customers-in-china-and-india/story/193162.html (archived at https://perma.cc/ZT78-LMDT) Mondēlez International (2017) Oreo Fact Sheet, http://www.mondelezinternational.com/~/media/MondelezCorporate/Uploads/downloads/OREO_Fact_Sheet.pdf (archived at https://perma.cc/TF8U-WU4P)

34 *Business Today* (2011) Cadbury enters Indian biscuit market, launches 'Oreo' brand, https://www.businesstoday.in/current/corporate/cadbury-enters-indian-biscuit-market-launches-oreo-brand/story/13674.html (archived at https://perma.cc/9TN8-DEHM)

35 SIMCON Blog (2016) Oreo: Case Study Analysis, https://simconblog.wordpress.com/2016/02/25/oreo-case-study-analysis (archived at https://perma.cc/C4QF-SUR8)

36 Mondelēz International (2017) Oreo Fact Sheet, http://www.mondelezinternational.com/~/media/MondelezCorporate/Uploads/downloads/OREO_Fact_Sheet.pdf (archived at https://perma.cc/TF8U-WU4P)

02

The strategic role branding plays

READING OUTCOMES

At the conclusion of this chapter, you should be able to:

- understand how the social sciences and other disciplines contribute to branding;
- communicate the role that branding plays in business and marketing strategy;
- explain when rebranding is needed as well as describe the rebranding process;
- define brand equity and describe many common brand-valuation techniques.

Introduction

Many people do not realize that the brands to which they are most loyal have nothing to do with an app, Facebook, or Google ad and are not being used as a result of some trendy viral video or buzz marketing campaign. Rather, most of the brands we use are hidden away in our bedrooms, bathrooms and kitchens. Many follow us from our parents' homes, because they used them too. These are consumer brands that we seldom discuss, but can't live without.

Just imagine if you woke up one morning to find that your toothpaste, deodorant, shampoo and perfume had been replaced by other brands during the night. Now walk into your kitchen and imagine that the same had happened with your cereal, coffee, orange juice and favourite toaster. Then imagine if you went to your garage and found a different car parked there. Confusion, bewilderment, chaos and anger might hit you immediately – not because anything was missing, but because your brands were changed.

Many of these brands have been around longer than you. The cereal in your cabinet, the butter brand in your fridge, the shampoo and soap in your bathroom – they existed years before you. They may have acquired new packaging or a new fragrance, or contain less cholesterol, but they still carry the same brand name, with the same promises or essence, the same consistency of delivery.

Yes, we will talk about technology and the changes in the world that are putting pressure on brands and making them harder to manage. And we'll explore the new world of branding, where ceaselessly broadcasting the brand story – the ongoing and mindless repetition of the same message – is not enough. But first, let's explore what it takes to create enduring brands. And what it takes to sustain them, take care of them and build a lasting relationship with their customers. Because if we don't know these basics, all of the rest will be for naught.

Overview

What informs a brand, makes it appealing and indicates its strategic business results? Those are some of the key questions of this chapter. We shall look at some of the various social sciences and other disciplines that can help inform our understanding of brands and branding. We conclude with an extended case study on Volkswagen to help understand what happens when a brand ignores its key brand promise – instructive on how to ensure that it doesn't happen for brands that need to be managed on a global scale. And we have a 'guest perspective' from global marketing leader Ricardo Monteiro, who explores the changing world of brand building and shows why brand practices need to evolve.

Long live the brand. The brand is dead. Why the brand is important to marketers

In many ways, we have already shown the strategic importance of brands in the first chapter when we mentioned that it relieves the perceived risk of purchase. On a deeper level, for the marketer, strong brands have enabled them to charge more – think of it as a premium for the consumer on the purchase insurance. It enables them to bounce back quicker and easier should a crisis occur (providing the brand responds appropriately – think of the classic Tylenol tampering crisis of 1982, still studied in PR courses), protect against new brands from entering the field, improve internal cohesion, fuel consumer engagement and boost market capitalization, among other benefits.[1]

Not so long ago, in the 1970s and 1980s, brands and branding rose to the level of being perceived as strategic assets.[2] As marketers started understanding the power of branding, they began to realize that it is much more than a logo, symbol or slogan, but rather its entire experience.[3] In fact, brand marketers should recognize that they should be able to remove the logo and the communication and/or experience should still feel inherently like the brand.[4]

Branding and brand management are complicated subjects. Possibly because branding is not a science (science seeks to disprove the hypothesis and paradigms by continually testing them, whereas branding seeks to prove its foundation by executing tactics in the marketplace), there is no single theory or method to explain it and to help make it work. However, there are some disciplines, particularly from the social sciences, that can help us understand it.

PSYCHOLOGY

Knowing and understanding psychology is crucial for developing successful brands as well as understanding why they work. We believe that in this age, consumers control the destiny of brands, not the manufacturers. For manufacturers to be successful, they need to understand the needs and wants of consumers. And that requires a fundamental understanding of the consumer's perceptual views of the brand. To enhance the consumer experience, brands must understand consumer expectations that go into building lasting trust with them. Finally, in today's world, brands have personality and behave differently in different situations based on their values, beliefs, traits and experiences (just as we talk differently to a boss, co-worker, client, parent, spouse, child or a stranger in the street).

SOCIOLOGY

An understanding of how societies are built, structured and function – including their issues and problems – is a powerful key to understanding consumers, one which becomes even more acute for practitioners needing to cross borders – and societies – with their brands.

FIGURE 2.1 Ways to understand brands and branding

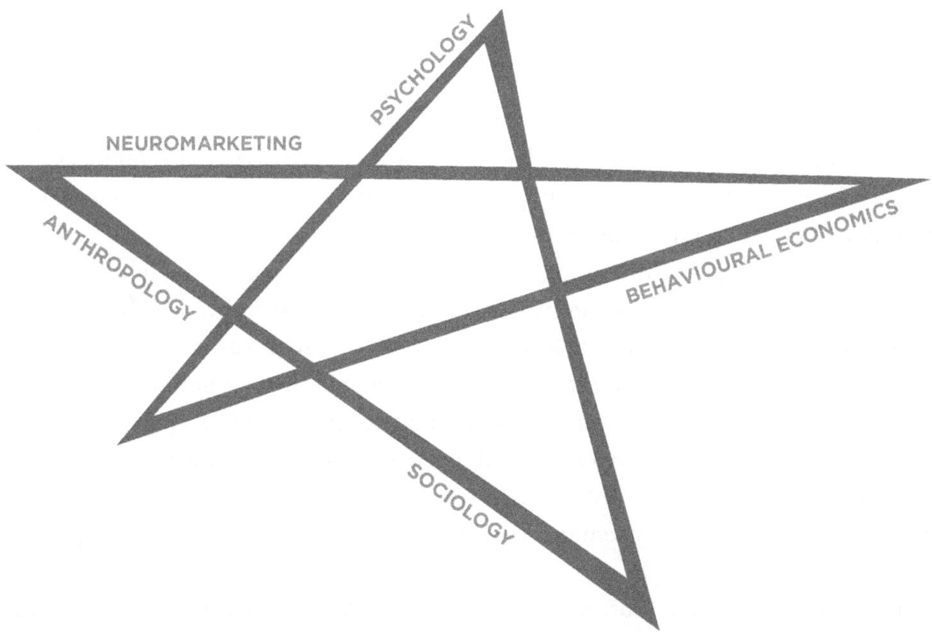

While the field of brands and brand management is not a social science, practitioners and academics draw on a wide range of social sciences to explain its power.

One example of the insights that the study of sociology can bring to branding and brand management is a paper that was published in 1980, where a new approach to consumer behaviour and branding was introduced. In the introduction to this paper the authors wrote: 'Sociology represents an area rich in its potential for contributing to research in consumer behaviour; that it has been largely neglected was pointed out by Nicosia and Mayer (1976) and by Zaltman and Wallendorf (1977).'[5]

This paper aimed to rectify the situation by introducing a subset of sociological theory called 'symbolic interactionism'. When the conceptual frameworks of symbolic interactionism – how people interact with each other – are applied to analysis of brand choices, new insight into important aspects of consumer behaviour result. More specifically, symbolic interactionism defines a concept of self that is new to consumer behaviour research, namely the 'situational self-image'.

'This concept allows a union of previous work on self-image/brand-image congruence with that on situational effects to produce a theoretical statement about brand choice for frequently purchased products which have well-developed and easily distinguishable brand images.'[6]

ANTHROPOLOGY

Like sociology, an understanding of anthropology is a necessary partner to branding. Branding by its very nature requires constant observation of human behaviour, so that product developers, manufacturers and marketing professionals can create value and turn their products and services into precious brands.

BEHAVIOURAL ECONOMICS

While tactical promotional marketing is more closely aligned with the incentives, rewards and optimizing of utility and value found in classical economics, the behavioural shortcuts that we make and that are the focus of behavioural economics – a coming together of economic theory and psychology – inform much of what makes branding such a powerful tool for marketers today.

As Darren Bridger wrote in his book *Neuro Design* (which we highly recommend), 'The old, rational model was that people seek to maximize the benefits they got from spending their money and they do this with some form of mental calculation, taking into account the potential benefits they would get from each product, its cost, volume etc – almost as though consumers had an inner accountant in their brains. While we do something like this sometimes, we usually don't have time or mental energy to perform such an exhaustive analysis of the options available. Instead, we use mental shortcuts, such as gut feeling about the options open to us.'[7]

Understanding all the shortcuts we tend to make on economic decisions (such as deciding to purchase a product or service) and what triggers our decision to make them is the core of behavioural economics. Bridger points out three main hurdles to making a purchasing decision: 1) risk; 2) uncertainty; and 3) difficulty.[8] Branding and brand management address all three. As stated in Chapter 1, strong brands reduce purchase risk and uncertainty because of its clear, understood promise. In addition, it reduces mental difficulty, because it lessens the need for the prospect to think about their purchase decision.

NEUROMARKETING

Neuromarketing, or neuroscience, is a field that uses medical technologies such as functional Magnetic Resonance Imaging (fMRI) to study the brain's activities and responses to marketing stimuli. It helps us track how brains fight to conserve energy per the observations of behavioural economics, and why we instinctively try to limit our decision-making processes. We should point out that the need of people to limit mental energy is even more acute in a world where we are exposed to approximately 4,000 to 10,000 brand messages a day.[9]

When exploring the conservation of mental energy, it is helpful to have an understanding of the neurology of learning. When we encounter a stimulus, the synapses in the brain fire, creating a pattern of associations. And the more times they fire, the stronger these pathways become, requiring less mental energy for recognition and recall of these associations. Over time, therefore, strong brands develop strong syntactical connections. As a result, individuals feel familiarity and comfort when encountering the brand and hold an intuitive understanding of the brand's meaning without needing to use much brain power. They lock out competing brands that are less familiar and thus have fewer, as well as weaker, syntactical connections.[10]

In addition, by using techniques developed for the medical profession to follow the responses of our brain to stimuli, we can learn how our brains respond to marketing messages. When certain marketing professionals claim that the logo IS the brand, we can now learn if indeed it is true. We can also measure how human brains react and respond to packaging design, videos, written and audio messages and more. Obviously, the more we know about the response rate to our marketing messages the better.

The biggest issue with this technology, which is not yet fully developed, is privacy. The study of human biological and physiological characteristics and their evolution teaches us what could be learned from the past in anticipation of the future.

Of course, there are other disciplines that contribute to our understanding of the power of branding, the practices of brand management and the need to adjust brand elements (the study of semiotics, for instance, comes to mind), but these are some of the core disciplines. And while we can only give a brief overview here, we encourage you to dig deeper into them, for they inform our approach, as you will see throughout the rest of this book.

There is one other question that we must address before proceeding to the core of managing a global brand and that is 'What is the value of branding and how do we determine it?' While we assume that you wouldn't be reading this book – and we wouldn't have written it – without assuming that branding creates value, it is always better to be armed with the evidence.

Determining the value of the brand

We address this topic, because many still even question when a brand becomes a brand. Some believe that critical mass is a qualifying measure. If so, what is the minimal size of a faithful audience that a brand needs? What is the financial threshold that a product or service must cross to become a 'brand'?

At the end of the day, since brands are intangible assets, we need some ways to measure their value. After all, many branding professionals preach the importance of building brands by emphasizing the actual monetary value to the owner. In fact, the term 'brand equity' could simply be defined as 'the value that comes from the consumers' perception of the brand (product or service), and not just from the product or service itself.'

Since we know that the consumer is now in the driver's seat when it comes to deciding the fate of brands, brand equity is also in the hands of consumers. Tracking brand equity is different in many markets. Companies such as Nielsen are using their proprietary methods to measure brand equity with market share and customer loyalty. Other similar organizations are using slightly different methodologies or technology to assess pretty much the same things: brand strength; brand image; brand behaviour; and key performance indicators.

So how do we begin to calculate the actual value? There is no 'right way' and the answer is never complete. After all, if we only measure a brand by looking at the sales, how confident are we that the sales are generated only because of the brand image? Could it not be the actual product attributes? Or the amazing customer service?

Marketers can, however, generate evidence that points to a conclusion. Several branding firms have developed methods to evaluate brands, and offer annual reports, including global brand ranking. One firm, Prophet, has developed a global index called the 'Brand Relevance Index'. This report focuses on the premise that brands are strong only as long as they are making a difference in their consumers' lives and are relevant to them. According to Prophet, the main components of brand relevance are:

- customer-obsessed – brands that we can't imagine living without;
- ruthlessly pragmatic – brands that we depend on;
- distinctively inspired – brands that inspire us;
- pervasively innovative – brands that consistently innovate.[11]

In 2017, Prophet published four different reports, one each for the UK, Germany, US and China. They surveyed 11,500 consumers on 240 different brands across 27 industries in the UK (population: 66 million) and in Germany (population: 82 million); 13,500 consumers on 275 brands across 27 industries in the USA (population: 327 million); and 13,500 consumers on 235 brands across 30 industries in China (population: 1.42 billion).

These numbers already indicate a somewhat questionable validity to the study because the percentage of consumers surveyed in China is minimal; and Chinese consumers have been exposed to 'branding' as we know it for a very limited period – of maybe 25 to 30 years at the most. But, criticism aside, Prophet wrote in their report, 'Businesses grow when their brands are welcomed into people's lives. Brands must continually find ways to engage, delight and deliver. To succeed, brands must be relevant.'[12]

Interbrand, another branding firm, looks at brands from a wider perspective. Like many other branding consultancies, Interbrand is fully behind the notion that brands are completely controlled by the consumers. As a result, the most successful brands are those that engage with consumers and understand all their unfulfilled and unmet needs. Since consumers are living in an age of constant change, a change they create by utilizing new, emerging technology, Interbrand asserts that brands need to become active, not reactive, ahead of the changes to succeed and survive. Organizations need to make the brand the centre of gravity and be prepared for an ever-shifting environment.

The annual Interbrand Best Global Brands report is indeed global, and not national or regional. In the Methodology section of its report, Interbrand mentions that the keys for evaluating brands in their index are: 1) financial forecast; 2) brand role; and 3) brand strength. All three contribute to the brand value. And to determine them, they use: 1) financial institutional data (such as from Thomson Reuters annual reports); 2) consumer goods data on brand volume and value (such as Canadean); and 3) their social media signal (such as Twitter and Infegy social media analysis). Obviously, such a ranking methodology will lead to completely different results in different parts of the world. In the meantime, Prophet's national relevance index shows a very different story when compared to the Interbrand index.

FIGURE 2.2 Comparison of top global brand rankings

Rankings differ by criteria, showing that there is no one way to judge the power of a brand. Examples shown from 2018.

And, finally, Siegel + Gale has the annual Global Brand Simplicity Index, which has been correlated to stock performance,[13] but explores completely different factors and uses its own methodology as well. In China, for instance, only Apple appears in the top five and none of the other top Interbrand global brands is even included in the top 50. Then, in the US, Apple, Google and Amazon dominate the list, but no other Interbrand-ranked brand is in the top 50. In the UK, Apple and Google are at the top and Amazon is number 10. Again no other Interbrand top 10 appears on the top 50 list. Finally, in Germany, Apple, Amazon and Google are the top three brands, and Mercedes is a distant 41. An interesting fact is that in Prophet's Brand Relevance Index many Chinese brands show up only in China, but not in Germany, the UK or the US. Chinese brands are also rare in the Interbrand BGB report: Huawei is at number 70 and Lenovo is last at number 100.

What can we learn from that? Firstly, since none of the methods relies entirely on financial results, it is extremely difficult to suggest from their studies that the best brands are also the most profitable. Secondly, brands affect our lives where we live. Tech-oriented brands invade our daily lives wherever we are. Apple, Google and Amazon are part of the global economy and provide us with the tools and technology that we depend upon. It makes sense that when judged on relevancy, we think that we can't live without them. Thirdly, as stated above, the determination of a brand's value is an ongoing debate. But, overall, strong brands have been shown to perform better than weaker ones.[14]

To help you in the short-term, however, one of the authors of this book along with Colleen Fahey have offered in *Audio Branding: Using sound to build your brand* a few informal ways to determine brand value (all the following quotes are from that book):[15]

- the company valuation (stock prices or ability to obtain loans);
- the sales close rate ('For this to be a successful metric, sales must truly adopt the new brand messaging, and the experience from one salesperson to the next must be consistent, as well as from the rest of the representatives from the company');
- the perceived price/value ('One way to do this is to ask people what they'd pay for a generic version of your product and then ask what they'd pay for one under your company's brand; calculate the difference and multiply by the size of the potential audience. .... One of the most prevalent metrics for measuring the strength of consumer brands but is also used for B2B brands.').

In addition, your 'other metrics could be unsolicited enquiries (although this also depends on the success of marketing communication programmes that reinforce the branding as well as taking into account activation programmes that can help generate leads even without strong branding); attitude towards the company; and more.'

Finally, 'you'll also need to keep in mind that branding refresh efforts tend to take between three and five years before results become truly noticeable.'

Brands should live forever, but sometimes they need to be rebranded

While we might be able determine a brand's value at a particular point in time, consumers' relationship with brands is rapidly changing, especially with new technology constantly being put in their hands. Consumers nowadays gain information and knowledge about new brands faster than they did before, and temptations that didn't affect them in the past may be effective now.

Remember Netscape, Walkman and MySpace? They were the brands to beat at one time and now they are virtually gone. There could be, as we speak, a group of Generation Z students plotting in a tech incubator to create the face of the next platform or gadget that will sweep us off our feet. Some would say that that is impossible. This is exactly what the strength of a brand is meant to prevent. It is the best possible defence against new competitors.

While we witness the invasion of a few new brands into the world's brand ranking, we can't escape the fact that the value of many old brands is unshakeable. These are the old stalwarts of the branding game: Coca-Cola, Mercedes, Toyota, IBM, GE, Philips, McDonald's and other brands that hover around their 100th birthday. If there is a lesson to learn about branding, it is one to be taken from these old warhorses. They never fall asleep; they innovate, reinvent themselves and know the rules of the branding games better than anyone. It will be very hard to beat them in the game they've played for so long.

The beauty of branding is that it allows brands to live beyond the age of being just trendy. Rather, they can gain immortality and good brand health for generations to come, but not without continual maintenance and an occasional rebranding. There are four main reasons for rebranding:

- The brand is no longer relevant. Examples could be brands like Kodak, which was the inventor of the digital camera, but hadn't realized that the digital age would come so soon. The brand was caught flatfooted when their competitors launched digital cameras and film became obsolete.
- The company is under new ownership, and the new owner has a different vision for the brand. Not all of these are successful. Motorola was a major brand, but once a new owner purchased it, no rebranding could save it and return it to what it used to be or make it a new successful brand.
- Brands that have reached a maturity stage and are stuck without being able to grow can utilize rebranding. In many of these cases the brand simply looks tired, out of style, out of touch etc. It could be that a simple redesign of the brand's packaging could be the rebranding, leading to a jump in sales and a reinstatement of the confidence of the consumers, who may have thought that the brand was lagging behind.

- 'The competition made me do it.' There are many cases where the competing brands look at each other, and noticing some changes in a competitive brand, will decide to do 'what they are doing'. Why? Because the competitive brand is experiencing success and leaving all others behind.

Just like 'branding', the term 'rebranding' is often misused. In the case of 'rebranding' one would assume that there was a brand there to begin with, but that is not necessarily the case. There could be many other reasons to 'rebrand'. It is a process of renewing, refreshing, redoing, revamping, regenerating, rebooting and some more. But the long and short of it is that it is about making your brand better than what it was before, and if it wasn't really a brand, it is an opportunity to create one.

The process of rebranding is not just an external exercise in introducing a new advertising campaign. It could be an entirely internal reorganization and the introduction of change management into a business. That process will eventually introduce a new organization to the world and with it new behaviours and relationships with consumers and the trade.

In January 2018, Philip Morris announced that it was urging the consumers of its products – cigarettes – to abandon the habit of smoking. In what seemed to be a completely suicidal business decision, the company asked people not to buy its products. The step of adopting a policy of social responsibility was a rebrand of Philip Morris. It seemed like a mad business move, but it gained a lot of favourite points for them. Although the products were not modified – cigarettes were still cigarettes – by admitting that the product was harmful, the attitude of the brand owner was completely different. Years ago, cigarettes were presented to consumers as 'something good for you', and that was the brand position for years. So far, the company has not taken cigarettes off the shelves in the UK, where the announcement was made, but claim they are aiming to remove them by the end of 2020.[16]

The solution for Philip Morris, as far as product development is concerned, has been to shift into smoke-free or tobacco-free alternatives. Significant amounts of money have been invested already in research and development of such products.

This is just one example of an old established brand that obviously sees the writing on the wall in terms of the harm presented to its clients. By taking responsibility and rebranding the entire product line, and changing public opinion about the present harmful products, this brand is really committed to the process of rebranding. It is not just another ad campaign from a new ad agency. The company even launched a website explaining everything to the world, in a fairly simple and transparent way.[17]

From this case we can see that rebranding is a tool for announcing major shifts and changes in the vision, mission and other very broad identity changes of an organization. The complete repositioning of an organization can mean changes to the promises made to consumers in a 'previous life'. It might also involve a change in what used to be the brand essence, and what made that brand different. Some brands simply have to rebrand because they have reached the end of a viable existence in that brand life cycle.

Another example of rebranding is the case of Formula 1, or as it is popularly known, F1. Formula One car racing began as the European Grand Prix championships of the 1920s and 1930s. Later, the foundation of the modern Formula One began in 1946 with the Fédération Internationale de l'Automobile's (FIA) standardization of rules. A World Championship of Drivers followed that in 1950.

British businessman Bernard Charles Ecclestone was the former chief executive of the Formula One Group, which manages Formula One and controls the commercial rights to F1. The business partly owns Delta Topco, the ultimate parent company of the Formula One Group. Mr Ecclestone controlled F1 and ran the business for a long time. He didn't run it as a brand but managed it as a cash cow without investing much in marketing. F1 sold TV rights, but neglected all the other aspects of brand development; at least, it didn't manage it as a 21st-century brand.

In late 2016, Liberty Media agreed to buy a controlling interest in the Formula One Group for US $4.4 billion (£3.3 billion). The deal was approved by regulators and completed on 23 January 2017. Chase Carey subsequently became chief executive of the Group, following a coup against Ecclestone.[18]

The brand name, Formula One, was not developed by marketing professionals. It is almost certain that in today's market environment the name would be different, but it is still a great name. The 'Formula' part of the name refers to the set of rules that racers and racing teams must comply with; the 'One' represents the fact that it is the top racing category in the FIA, comprising the fastest and most advanced cars.[19]

Each F1 race can have up to 300,000 fans attending in person, with an additional 80 million people watching live at home. The F1 owners believe the sport has 150 million global fans. While, previously, their only relationship with their fans was to sell them tickets to the race, or to let them watch the race on TV, the rebranding of F1 included developing a more dedicated relationship with the fans. They had an outdated brand model that might bring in money but didn't promise a future in an age where relationship, engagement and customer experience are the building blocks of any brand, especially in sports.

On May 17, 2017, *The Daily Telegraph* reported a story about a young boy who burst into tears when his favourite driver, Kimi Raikkonen, crashed and dropped out of the Spanish Grand Prix. He was caught crying on live TV during the race, which touched a nerve among many F1 race watchers. And it didn't go unnoticed by the rebranded F1 brand. They located him in the stands and brought him to the paddock where he could meet his hero. This sounds like a simple event, but it represented a new brand, one that cared about its customers, the audience and the fans. It would not have been possible under the previous management and represented a shift from a 'managed product' to a 'managed brand'.

Other rebranding processes might include a name change and obviously, along with this, a completely new visual and verbal manifestation of the brand, including new logo, new colours, new fonts, new design language, verbal language and brand behaviours – the way it presents itself to the world. Most of all, every successful rebranding process should introduce to the world a revised, and hopefully improved, customer experience. But any rebranding will not be an overwhelming success overnight and it comes with a steep price tag. The introduction of the new brand identity and all that comes with it has to be a well-planned campaign and managed process to guarantee success and not leave the previous customers in shock and bewilderment. Success can be declared only after the ultimate brand owners (the customers) intuitively and completely feel confidence in the new brand experience.

A more affordable route is to manage the brand, tweaking it along the way, from continually updating its visual representation in small ways to keep it up-to-date to revising its language and altering its behaviours. This is the core task of brand managers and that is what we will explore, along with the development of foundational elements of brand, in future chapters. First of all, in the next chapter, we will take a look at the differences between internal and external branding and the complete 360 degrees of branding. In the meantime, let's meet international branding expert Ricardo Monteiro, who gives his thoughts on the evolving world of branding. We also explore the results of Volkswagen's recent missteps on its brand.

BRAND BUILDING IN OUR CHANGING WORLD – A GUEST PERSPECTIVE FROM RICARDO MONTEIRO, PORTUGAL

Ricardo Monteiro has dedicated his professional life to marketing, working for Unilever, Omnicom (BBDO) and Havas. His career has led him to live in Belgium, Brazil, Spain and Uruguay, among other countries. A career man, Monteiro retired in 2017 from his position as Global President and Chairman of Havas, best known for its 'Most Interesting Man' campaigns in the US and the Evian Babies advertisements in Europe. In his 37-year long career, Ricardo worked for many of the world's leading brands and was involved in developing brand campaigns for almost every point in the globe. When he retired from Havas, the agency was already present in more than 75 countries with well over 300 operating agencies.

Today, Ricardo lives close to Estoril in Portugal with his wife of 36 years. He is a father of four and a grandfather of children of three different nationalities. He teaches at the Porto Business School and, as an Invited Professor, at the Catholic University in Lisbon. He also serves as a non-executive director in Sonae, Portugal's largest conglomerate. He is a Business Angel and a regular TV presence. He also dedicates a lot of his time to the Portuguese Diaspora as an ambassador-at-large.

Here are Ricardo's observations about how the branding world has changed, and what has remained the same, helping us prepare for and succeed in the new global brand-building environment:

'Thirty-seven years ago, I started my career in marketing as a Management Trainee with Unilever. To this day, Unilever and Procter & Gamble fight an endless battle for the wallets of people the world over, from Los Angeles to Shanghai, Oslo to Johannesburg. When I joined, it employed 330,000 people. Among the many companies on its roster you could find pearls of yesteryear like the United Africa Company or Hindustan Lever (still going strong). It had palm-oil plantations in the Ivory Coast and Indonesia and hundreds of factories across the globe. Customs duties were the rule of international trade. Multinational companies truly were multinationals; they had to cater for the local customer in every country, as cross-border trade was mostly an expensive impossibility.

'I had the privilege of joining their lengthy training programme – it took the whole of 18 months before one could become a junior manager – and went to places like Four Acres, their in-house academy in London.

'One also had to work at filling-lines in factories and learn how to mix a proper soap bar or sell to a mom-and-pop store. I did it all. I wanted to become a Marketing Director. I was lucky. Nine years later, having climbed every single step of the corporate ladder, I overshot my target and was appointed Managing Director of one of Unilever's operating companies in Lisbon, Elida Gibbs. I felt on top of the world. I was only 32 and already a senior director.

'Why the lengthy introduction? You see, the world was simpler, back then. You had ideas, you presented them to the shareholders' representatives, you got a budget, you researched them, and they would either fly or die. Good marketing would ensue. It was defined by that old acronym, the Four Ps: Product, Place, Price and Promotion. If your idea was good and your research sound, fine-tuning those four variables would guarantee you a place in the marketing Hall of Fame. Millions of bottles of shampoo or margarine tubs would fly off the shelves as you sat at home in front of your TV set, waiting for the latest advert that your Mad Men agency would have produced for you at great expense. You know the saying, "Half my marketing budget is a waste, I just don't know which half."

'And life was sweet. You read the books. You knew the rules. Your employer had both the financial clout and the organization to support your dreams. What could possibly go wrong? Nothing: marketing was the best way to convince people to part with their money, and it worked.

'My career continued to prosper, and I was already the whole of 56 when expressions like "big data", "programmatic media buying" and "automated creative" started stalking my nights.

'At that time, I had become Global President for Havas, one of the world's top marketing firms. It manages brands for Reckitt Benckiser, Louis Vuitton, Hyundai and many others in more than 75 countries. So, as I struggled to keep pace with the data onslaught, and more and more clients demanded "proof" that their adverts would work, asking for their "return on investment", I started to understand that marketing was no longer a top-down exercise where one could "push" goods through whole countries, tinker around with them and build brands so strong that "pull" was as guaranteed, as night follows day.

'So, where are we today and where are you as regards brand-building?

'Consider this: according to most agencies that rate brands for market value, the top five contenders in 2017 were Google, Apple, Facebook, Amazon and Microsoft. Not all agree on their precise place in the ranking, as Amazon has been moving fast, but at the time of writing, these are considered the five most valuable brands in the Western world.

'Now let's think a bit more. How many of those actually sell a product for a price? You can say Apple does. Microsoft too. But how much did you pay the last time you Googled something? Or went online to post that nice family picture on Facebook? You paid nothing. Vlam! Two of the world's most valuable brands do not actually sell a product or service that they charge for. So, Price has become zero. And, in the case of Facebook, the Product is you.

'Now, let's consider Place – actually making sure the product or service gets to people where they want it. At one time, Coca-Cola's mission statement made it to every marketing teaching room because it stated "Our mission is to place a Coca-Cola bottle within arm's reach of everyone on Earth." That endeavour, a physical barrier that needed overcoming, and a legal and logistical nightmare, was proof of might. Anyone trying to emulate that feat would have to spend tens of billions of dollars and many years of painstaking work, making sure every link of the chain was in place.

'As a matter of fact, as recently as 2007, Coca-Cola was still the world's most valuable brand at around US $100 billion (£78 billion). Its business has not decreased, its profitability is still impressive, but Coca-Cola doesn't even make it to the top five now. More than one hundred years of careful marketing and distribution prowess could not resist the capacity that some modern brands have of achieving immediate distribution everywhere. Take a look at that top five: all of them can be reached and actioned upon from anywhere in the world, from the top of a mountain to the middle of the ocean.

'All you need is a link. So, Placement is not physical anymore. Or, if it is, as in the case of Amazon and Apple, it has become seamless, one could argue, immaterial. Placement, distribution have become instantaneous. One of the mantras of the start-up world that every twenty-year-old will tell you is that their new company will be "global from day one"... and they can be ...

'And now for Promotion.

"Up until the year 2004, advertising agencies had a virtual monopoly on the world's advertising budgets. They fed free-on-air TV networks, countless newspaper titles, radio stations, you name it. If you wanted to advertise, you had to go through them. They did marvellous work, producing advertisements that still resonate in our memories. Think of Cindy Crawford gulping down that Pepsi bottle before three gawking teenagers ... the world would notice. Even Apple gave us the Mac "1984" Super Bowl commercial. It was only aired once and many people still consider it one of the finest, most impactful commercials ever produced.

'Can you actually remember a great commercial from the last couple of years? You probably can't – unless you're reading this the day after, well, the Super Bowl. So, if not, is it because there weren't any? No – you were just too distracted looking at your LinkedIn newsfeed, or making that WhatsApp video call to your mother back home. Ad agencies have seen their market share decline from virtually 100% a decade ago to barely 50% today. The dispersion of screens, platforms, gaming options, you name it, have taken away from traditional advertising. Google, Facebook and Amazon are simultaneously platform and content generators. You rarely watch an advertisement for them. If you live in Europe or Latin America, chances are you have never seen a single piece of advertisement for any of them. While advertising others, they advertise themselves – for free. No need for promotion, except for self, free promotion.

'Then comes consumer-generated content, or even brand content produced by companies themselves, sometimes for a few hundred dollars. Digital platforms have made it useless to look at advertising, even online, for anything else than fun. Information is everywhere. "Now available in a store near you" is a risible proposition.

'Influencers, paid or not, carry much more weight than the whole of L'Oréal. That is until they become (became?) irrelevant because people realize they're paid to do stuff for brands. Moreover, structured marketing offerings easily stumble over a bad Trip Advisor review. In a word, companies have to fight multiple promotional wars on as many fronts as there are smart phones, and have to pray for some break that might put them up there with Despacito so that the money keeps flowing.

'So, say you, what am I trying to tell you? That today's brand-building has been reduced to achieving top-of-mind awareness, no matter how fleetingly. Make no mistake, you still have to make sure your offer is relevant and that it meets some kind of demand.

"If you charge for it (bad move – make clicks remunerate you!), your price will tend to zero because sooner or later someone will come up with similar stuff for free (OK, not always if you're Louis Vuitton). Then you must make sure you can get your stuff into people's hands in the blink of an eye – that and all the rest, the endless, sleepless nights, the investment rounds, the never-ending quest for the next Netflix, Snapchat, Shazam, all modern brands known everywhere by virtually everyone.

'Immaterial offerings, at virtually no cost, that people can access seamlessly and immediately, global in their reach, that everyone will have come across because, in the ethereal existence of the digital world, an "invisible hand" has made them relevant. And – this is very important – with a monetization path and rags-to-riches trajectory that takes no longer than a few months and erupts onto everyone's mobile "from day one". These are the ingredients of a brand today.

'Unless you want to sell shampoo. But there's not much money there.

'Now, how will you do it? Let me tell you this: I know half your efforts will be wasted, I just don't know which half.'

EXTENDED CASE STUDY: VOLKSWAGEN, THE FALL OF A BRAND

One way to understand branding and how to create and maintain an effective brand on a global scale is to study one that has disappointed consumers and other stakeholders. And one of the biggest global disappointments has been Volkswagen, with its environmental scandal at odds[20] with its 'smart fun' brand promise[21] and counterculture positioning.

Go anywhere in the world and we seem to take German car brands for granted these days. Considering the not so distant past and the history of Germany during the previous century, you might have expected some German car brands to have failed. After all, Audi, under its previous name – Auto Union AG – used slave labourers from concentration camps during World War II on a massive scale.[22] BMW's owner during the 1930s and 40s, Gunther Quandt, and his son, Herbert, were friendly with Adolf Hitler and they were not afraid to use their political connections to take advantage of the Holocaust and businesses seized by the government to manufacture weapons, artillery, ammunition and U-boat batteries.[23] Mercedes Benz, during World War II, created a notable series of aircraft, tank and submarine engines. Daimler produced parts for German arms, most notably barrels for the Mauser rifle.[24] During World War II, Daimler-Benz also used slave labour and Hitler himself drove around in a luxurious Mercedes.[25]

Most notable of all German cars at the time, however, was Volkswagen. Back then, it had a very close relationship with Porsche, the Zuffenhausen-based sports car manufacturer founded in 1931 by Ferdinand Porsche, who had designed the original Volkswagen – he was hired by Adolf Hitler for the project – and was a company co-founder.[26] In April 1934, Hitler gave the order to Porsche to develop a Volkswagen.[27] The epithet 'Volks' – literally, 'people's' – had been applied to other Nazi-sponsored consumer goods.[28] Volkswagen today makes very few references to that period and considers the birth date of the VW Beetle brand to be around the Fifties.[29]

Indeed, marketing the VW to global markets was a bit of an uphill battle. It was perceived as a 'Nazi car' repackaged by a Jewish-owned ad agency, DDB, in a 'Jewish' city.[30] It was an 'ugly car' by American standards,[31] small and uncomfortable for five adult passengers.[32] The famous advertising executive George Lois said after returning from the VW factory: 'We learned that Hitler's "people's car" had a lot going for it. My copywriter Julian saw it as a dumb, honest little car, but a marketing enigma. New York was our biggest market for our new account, and that's what made it so tough.'[33]

The ad agency, DDB, took the obvious disadvantages of the product and turned them into a desirable brand,[34] establishing a car brand that stood in stark contrast to the American gas-guzzling behemoths, with their ridiculous fins, chromes and excessive weight. Brand-building is based on finding a difference, but also relevance. In this case, the VW was a great solution to the increasing parking problems in a city such as New York.

Changing consumer behaviour and consumer brand perception was key in this brand strategy. Advertising radiated confidence in a brand, broadcasting that it was superior in simplicity, quality and longevity. The brand position of VW prepared the American market for another brand introduction: the Japanese compact cars, the Honda Civic. Lois summed up the legendary campaign in this way: 'We sold the Nazi car in a Jewish town by junking all the rules of car advertising.'[35] Indeed, VW went from one success to another, and solidified its brand reputation as reliable, easy to maintain and moderate in price – features that supported the 'smart' portion of its brand promise – and, with the addition of updated models, it could even compete on design.

The company grew tremendously over the years and owns in addition to the VW brand Audi, Bentley, Bugatti, Lamborghini, Porsche, SEAT and Skoda.[36] Their brand portfolio provides them with complete coverage from luxury and mid-luxury to regular car brands.

Among the constituencies of the brand, VW clearly preferred the shareholders, and the brand strategy was to be the biggest car company in the world, pure and simple. In 2011, Martin Winterkorn, VW's chief executive, took the stage at the automaker's new plant in Chattanooga, Tennessee, and outlined a bold strategy. The company, he said, was in the midst of a plan to more than triple its sales in the United States in just a decade, setting it on a course to sweep by Toyota to become the world's largest automaker. 'By 2018, we want to take our group to the very top of the global car industry.'[37]

However, during 2015, the company was exposed in global media for installing emissions software on more than a half-million diesel cars in the US and roughly 10.5 million more worldwide that allowed them to sense the unique parameters of the emissions drive cycle set by the Environmental Protection Agency and, thus, cheat it.[38] According to the EPA and the California Air Resources Board, which were tipped off by researchers in 2014,[39] these so-called 'defeat devices' detect steering, throttle and other inputs used in the test to switch between two distinct operating modes. While this mode likely delivers higher mileage and power, it also permits heavier nitrogen-oxide emissions (NOx) – a smog-forming pollutant linked to lung cancer – up to 40 times higher than the federal limit.[40]

In short, VW diesel cars were among the top pollutants in the world,[41] although the brand presented itself as an environmentally friendly one in advertising and promotional materials. In other words, VW performed one of the major 'don'ts' in any branding strategy – never deceive your customers. At the end of the day, and especially in our generation, nothing can stay a secret for too long and VW is paying a steep price. Between 2015 and 2017 there were resignations, indictments, jail sentences and most of all a serious financial burden of around $25 billion,[42] with a significant drop in sales all across the globe, especially in the US market.[43] For 2018, the company was not offering diesel models,[44] losing a big portion of their product line.

The legal saga is not over. Future generations of consumers will be the final judge of Volkswagen. How VW rebrands and fully responds is yet to be seen. Whatever route they end up taking in rebuilding their brand, it is sure to be costly.

KEY TERMS

- anthropology
- behavioural economics
- brand failure
- neuromarketing
- psychology
- sociology

DISCUSSION QUESTIONS

- Why are the social sciences and related disciplines key to understanding branding?
- Why isn't branding dependent only on marketing and advertising?
- What role do brands and branding play in business and marketing strategy?
- Which methods of brand valuation do you prefer and why?
- When is rebranding needed and what are the steps in the rebranding process?

Notes

1 Markel, H (2014) How the Tylenol murders of 1982 changed the way we consume medication, *Public Broadcasting Service*, https://www.pbs.org/newshour/health/tylenol-murders-1982 (archived at https://perma.cc/ERV4-2U5U)

2 David, A (2014) Brands as assets: the idea that transformed marketing, *Prophet*, https://www.prophet.com/2014/07/200-brands-as-assets-the-idea-that-transformed-marketing (archived at https://perma.cc/UXX5-5D99)

3 Anderson, A (2016) Successful companies don't just have a brand identity, they create a total brand experience, *Forbes*, https://www.forbes.com/sites/amyanderson/2016/03/29/successful-companies-dont-just-have-a-brand-identity-they-create-a-total-brand-experience/#e9ab4e33cf2d (archived at https://perma.cc/BBX6-THQL)

4 Pallotta, D (2011) A logo is not a brand, *Harvard Business Review*, https://hbr.org/2011/06/a-logo-is-not-a-brand (archived at https://perma.cc/YZ5M-5NEZ)

5 Schenk, C T, and Holman, R H (1980) A sociological approach to brand choice: the concept of situational self image, *Advances in Consumer Research*, 7, eds Jerry C Olson, Ann Arbor, Association for Consumer Research, MI, pp 610–14

6 Schenk, C T, and Holman, R H (1980) A sociological approach to brand choice: the concept of situational self image, *Advances in Consumer Research*, 7, eds Jerry C Olson, Ann Arbor, Association for Consumer Research, MI, pp 610–14

7 Bridger, D (2017) *Neuro Design: Neuromarketing insights to boost engagement and profitability*, Kogan Page, London

8 Bridger, D (2015) *Decoding the Irrational Consumer: How to commission, run and generate insights from neuromarketing research*, Kogan Page, London

9 Simpson, J (2017) Finding brand success in the digital world, *Forbes*, https://www.forbes.com/sites/forbesagencycouncil/2017/08/25/finding-brand-success-in-the-digital-world/#12ffcff9626e (archived at https://perma.cc/47MX-9DLM)

10 Mundell, E (2006) Popular brands may brand the brain, *Washington Post*, http://www.washingtonpost.com/wp-dyn/content/article/2006/11/28/AR2006112800394.html?noredirect=on (archived at https://perma.cc/326Y-Z5LE)

11 Rosenzweig, F and Davis, S (2017) Three ways innovation can keep your brand relentlessly relevant, *Prophet*, https://www.prophet.com/2017/05/3-ways-innovation-drives-brand-relevance (archived at https://perma.cc/G4ZF-M5VG)

12 Brand Relevance Index (2017) https://www.prophet.com/relevantbrands-2017/united-kingdom-en.pdf (archived at https://perma.cc/M6V9-ZN6G)

13 Muldoon, M (2017) Siegel + Gale unveils seventh annual global brand simplicity index™: brands that embrace simplicity enjoy increased revenue, valuation, brand advocacy and employee engagement, *Siegel + Gale*, http://www.siegelgale.com/siegelgale-unveils-seventh-annual-global-brand-simplicity-index-brands-that-embrace-simplicity-enjoy-increased-revenue-valuation-brand-advocacy-and-employee-engagement (archived at https://perma.cc/B73V-J5UK)

14 Kumar, N (2003) Kill a brand, keep a customer, *Harvard Business Review*, https://hbr.org/2003/12/kill-a-brand-keep-a-customer (archived at https://perma.cc/8QT2-K6Y2)

15 Minsky, L and Fahey, C (2017) *Audio Branding: Using sound to build your brand*, Kogan Page, London

16 Nevett, J (2018) Major tobacco firm to stop selling cigarettes in UK as smokers will be EXTINCT by 2050s, *Daily Star*, https://www.dailystar.co.uk/news/latest-news/728750/uk-cigarettes-smoking-tobacco-phillip-morris-marlboro-chesterfield-stop-selling-shops (archived at https://perma.cc/G68V-GDY3)

17 Philip Morris International (2018) Designing a smoke-free future, https://www.pmi.com/who-we-are/designing-a-smoke-free-future (archived at https://perma.cc/K557-TX8V)

18 Robinson, J (2017) Liberty Media names Chase Carey as Formula One CEO, replacing Bernie Ecclestone, *The Wall Street Journal*, https://www.wsj.com/articles/chase-carey-replaces-formula-ones-bernie-ecclestone-as-ceo-1485210949 (archived at https://perma.cc/DH7J-DPVS)

19 Williamson, M (2018) A brief history of Formula One, *ESPN*, http://en.espn.co.uk/f1/motorsport/story/3831.html (archived at https://perma.cc/NA53-8SZ6)

20 Menzel, S and Murphy, M (2017) US monitor: VW had corrupt culture, flawed leadership, *Handelsblatt Today*, https://www.handelsblatt.com/today/dieselgate-judgement-us-monitor-vw-had-corrupt-culture-flawed-leadership/23573534.

html?ticket=ST-12992159-IkXoxg4rmZjsjOAGNEgD-ap3 (archived at https://perma.cc/98RS-JLH7). Also: Bansal, T, King, M, Sejits, G (2015, updated 2018) The Volkswagen emissions scandal: A case study in corporate misbehavior, *The Globe and Mail*, https://www.theglobeandmail.com/report-on-business/rob-commentary/the-vw-emissions-scandala-case-study-in-what-not-to-do/article26550100 (archived at https://perma.cc/XXN9-WT2E)

21 Minsky, Laurence (2007) *How to Succeed in Advertising When All You Have is Talent*, 2nd ed, Copy Workshop, Chicago

22 Audi comes clean about its Nazi past (2014) *Deutsche Welle*, https://www.dw.com/en/audi-comes-clean-about-its-nazi-past/a-17664050 (archived at https://perma.cc/G56N-H52N)

23 Massey, R (2016) German car giant BMW apologises for its wartime past, admitting its 'profound regret' for supplying Nazis with vehicles and using slave labourers, *Daily Mail*, https://www.dailymail.co.uk/news/article-3480258/German-car-giant-BMW-apologises-wartime-past-admitting-profound-regret-supplying-Nazis-vehicles-using-slave-labourers.html (archived at https://perma.cc/KD2E-V5GY)

24 Company history, Daimler-Benz in the Nazi era (1933–1945) (2019), https://www.daimler.com/company/tradition/company-history/1933-1945.html (archived at https://perma.cc/BGH4-TGK4)

25 Klara, R (2015) Hitler's car exerts grim fascination even if it just gave the Führer a lift to the airport, *The Guardian*, https://www.theguardian.com/world/2015/sep/13/hitler-car-exerts-grim-fascination (archived at https://perma.cc/BSL2-77L6)

26 German Propaganda Archive, Calvin College, http://www.bytwerk.com/gpa/vw.htm (archived at https://perma.cc/2FMK-N8N4)

27 Glancey, J (2014) The VW Beetle: How Hitler's idea became a design icon, BBC, http://www.bbc.com/culture/story/20130830-the-nazi-car-we-came-to-love (archived at https://perma.cc/NY7W-VBWW)

28 This day in history, May 28, Volkswagen is founded (2009), History.com, https://www.history.com/this-day-in-history/volkswagen-is-founded (archived at https://perma.cc/M9XX-PZGU)

29 Volkswagen Chronicle, 1950–1960, Internationalisation and mass production in the era of Germany's economic miracle, Volkswagenag.com, https://www.volkswagenag.com/en/group/history/chronicle/1950-1960.html (archived at https://perma.cc/3NV8-NTTC)

30 *Financial Times*, https://www.ft.com/content/bca651f6-6855-11e5-97d0-1456a776a4f5 (archived at https://perma.cc/CV9T-46LN)

31 John, K (2016) The Volkwagen lifestyle: Hitler, hippies, and a hint of viral marketing, *Americana, The Journal of American Popular Culture 1900 to Present*, Fall 2016, **15** (2), http://www.americanpopularculture.com/journal/articles/fall_2016/john.htm (archived at https://perma.cc/2976-EHJU)

32 This day in history, May 28, Volkswagen is founded (2009), History.com, https://www.history.com/this-day-in-history/volkswagen-is-founded (archived at https://perma.cc/M9XX-PZGU)

33 Vargas-Cooper, N (2010) An excerpt from 'Mad men unbuttoned': Selling the 'Nazi Car' to the Jews, *The Awl*, https://www.theawl.com/2010/07/an-excerpt-from-mad-men-unbuttoned-selling-the-nazi-car-to-the-jews (archived at https://perma.cc/K4NY-CWBY)

34 Stearns, T (2015) The roots of advertising: Volkswagen, *The Farm* https://www.growwithfarm.com/the-roots-of-advertising-volkswagen (archived at https://perma.cc/4RND-PPSU)

35 Vargas-Cooper, N (2010) An excerpt from 'Mad men unbuttoned': Selling the 'Nazi Car' to the Jews, *The Awl*, https://www.theawl.com/2010/07/an-excerpt-from-mad-men-unbuttoned-selling-the-nazi-car-to-the-jews (archived at https://perma.cc/K4NY-CWBY)

36 Group, Volkswagenag.com, https://www.volkswagenag.com/en/group.html (archived at https://perma.cc/G2KT-7UPS)

37 Hakim, D, Kessler, A and Ewing, J (2015) As Volkswagen pushed to be no. 1, ambitions fueled a scandal, *The New York Times*, https://www.nytimes.com/2015/09/27/business/as-vw-pushed-to-be-no-1-ambitions-fueled-a-scandal.html (archived at https://perma.cc/8WRS-6Y8S)

38 Volkswagen says 11 million cars worldwide are affected in diesel deception, *The New York Times*, https://www.nytimes.com/2015/09/23/business/international/volkswagen-diesel-car-scandal.html (archived at https://perma.cc/6U63-UZXJ)

39 Wendler, A (2015) How Volkswagen got busted for skirting EPA diesel emissions standards, *Car and Driver*, https://blog.caranddriver.com/how-volkswagen-got-busted-for-gaming-epa-diesel-emissions-standards (archived at https://perma.cc/D9ZA-3BBG)

40 Atiyeh, C (2017) Everything you need to know about the VW diesel-emissions scandal, *Car and Driver*, https://blog.caranddriver.com/everything-you-need-to-know-about-the-vw-diesel-emissions-scandal (archived at https://perma.cc/BF2E-HKWQ)

41 Mathiesen, K & Neslen, A (2015) VW scandal caused nearly 1m tonnes of extra pollution, analysis shows, *The Guardian*, https://www.theguardian.com/business/2015/sep/22/vw-scandal-caused-nearly-1m-tonnes-of-extra-pollution-analysis-shows (archived at https://perma.cc/F8MY-PSKR)

42 *Financial Times*, https://www.ft.com/content/c8c5f6f4-08a4-11e6-b6d3-746f8e9cdd33 (archived at https://perma.cc/62VB-S7FH)

43 Allen, N (2018) Sales down 18% at VW, latest auto maker dented by emissions rules, *The Wall Street Journal*, https://www.wsj.com/articles/sales-down-18-at-vw-latest-auto-maker-dented-by-emissions-rules-1539101908 (archived at https://perma.cc/6KVS-WULA)

44 The best cars, trucks, SUVs, and more for 2016: Editors' choice awards, *Car and Driver*, https://www.caranddriver.com/features/2016-editors-choice-for-best-cars-trucks-crossovers-suvs-and-hybrids (archived at https://perma.cc/CY9S-CA3S)

03

Internal branding versus external branding

READING OUTCOMES

At the conclusion of this chapter, you should be able to:

- list the primary and secondary brand constituents and describe their importance;
- recognize the key touchpoints along the 360-degree reach of brand messaging;
- understand the importance of customer-journey mapping for brand storytelling;
- describe how branding plays into the hiring, training and performance processes.

Introduction

Where do you work or go to school? Do other people recognize its name? What did you know about the place before you became affiliated with it? And what did you expect from it when you decided to become affiliated, but before you had the chance to experience it? Finally, did your experience on the job or in the school match your expectations based on the brand image? Questions such as these point to the power of a brand for those who come into contact with it.

As we mentioned in Chapter 1, brand reputation fuels employee recruitment and informs their eventual on-the-job behaviour, which in turn influences the experience of the purchasers and consumers of the brand. We call this 'the employee-customer brand experience continuum'. Each component influences the next until it forms a full circle and continues again.

The employee-customer brand experience continuum brings up a broad range of questions. For example, who is the target when creating the brand? Most think of the customers or users, but others are influenced by it too. Those of us on the outside never get a chance to see the branding efforts that go on inside and which become increasingly important as the brand boundaries grow beyond borders and employees are spread out across the globe.

There are other constituencies, such as trade partners, that are influenced by the brand image. For instance, banks do not like to do business with a brand that has a reputation for late payments. Truck drivers will not deliver the brand's products if they are not treated well by the brand's shipment department, and the supply chain can experience problems as a result.

Another question is, 'Who "owns" the brand?' Many say that it is the consumer because that is where the brand perceptions reside. Others say that the brand is 'owned' by the corporation, because they're the ones who harvest the profits from it. And some say that it is the employees, because they cultivate the brand and, with the appropriate care, keep it vibrant. But we take another approach. With the employee-customer brand experience continuum, all play a role, all benefit and, thus, all 'own' it to some degree. In this chapter, we shall look at the brand-management techniques for both the internal and external audiences.

Overview

In the first chapter, we identified the importance of a brand for purchasers, consumers, employees, managers, owners and others. But how do all of the various stakeholders interact with the brand? We start with the employee, often overlooked in the branding equation, but key in maintaining brands for service organizations. We review the entire continuum from recruitment and hiring to retirement. We then examine the role played by the other corporate stakeholders – owners, leaders and managers – and conclude with a look at the customer journey as it relates to branding. Plus, we have a guest perspective from Rick Ray, co-founder and managing partner of *brandstory,* a leading-edge European brand-strategy consultancy (which one of the authors of this book, Ilan Geva, represented in the US market). Ray talks about the need for brands to have a story. And Samsung's Manifesto, a key employee-branding tool, is the focus of an extended case study.

Welcome to the employee-customer brand experience continuum

Brands exist within companies and organizations from the moment they emerge as an idea. The impetus to create a product or a service already includes within it the 'why'. Understanding the reason why the new product or service exists, the problem that it solves, its place in the world, its essence and its promise all form the basis for the key foundational attributes of the brand. Is the new product something that didn't exist before and will it make the prospect's life easier? For instance, it is said that the concept for Uber was born one winter's night when the two founders, Travis Kalanick and Garrett Camp, were at a tech conference in Paris and were unable to get a cab.[1] On the other hand, the new product or service might be able to provide an incremental advantage over an existing brand or brands. In the US, for example, there is an increasingly popular fast-food chain called Blaze, which enables customers to 'build their own' pizza in a shorter time period than traditional pizza parlours.[2]

While new product development offers a foundation for developing the brand, it is only the beginning of a long journey that also needs to involve the employees, the other stakeholders (ie the owners, shareholders) and, of course, potential customers. Some brands, particularly not-for-profits, may also need to consider the population at large. In addition, there are brands that need to factor in distributors and others in the channel. Each group is important, but a brief inspection of any brand typically reveals that one key constituent is dominant out of the three core constituents: stakeholders, employees and customers. The preferred group, placed as the number one constituency, can define the face of the brand and reveal its character to the public.

Brands that emphasize the needs of the owners or shareholders, ie the stakeholders, often put profit above all else and do whatever it takes to generate it, even at the expense of customers and employees. While owners and shareholders literally 'own' the brand from a financial perspective and profit should be a goal, the best way to generate profit and ensure long-term health of the brand is by focusing on the other two groups – employees and consumers – and solving their problems. Starbucks, for instance, takes care of its employees and the shareholders do not seem to suffer as a result.[3] In fact, the employees create the experience and, thus, can be considered a driver of the company's growth in share value. On the other hand, Walmart aims to take care of its shareholders first, and employees do not seem to enjoy working there.[4] Consequently, Walmart's customer experience seems to suffer.[5] However, its profits and resulting ability to grow have been driven by its low costs, based on the insight that value shoppers are willing to forsake brand experience in order to obtain price savings.[6] Another example of a brand that puts its shareholders first is McDonald's. Despite being a brand built on promising its customers a 'fast, accurate, and friendly experience',[7] McDonald's ignored its customers for a period of time and started to suffer as a result. Its share price sank and customers abandoned it.[8] For a variety of reasons, employee retention has not been good either.[9]

A brand may also choose to make its employees its number one priority over the brand owners and its customers. The employees are 'walking billboards' of the brand, because they 'can serve as a key influencer during pivotal inflection points along the path-to-purchase.'[10] In other words, employees are essential to shaping the brand experience. For example, while many of us don't know the name of FedEx's or UPS's CEO and don't care, we do know the FedEx or UPS driver delivering the packages to our home or office. Likewise, customers often know the names of their local Starbucks baristas, but can't name the CEO who replaced founder Howard Schultz. While the customer-facing employees are extremely important in building the brand for consumers, the behind-the-scene, back-room operations can't escape the responsibility of representing the brand as well. After all, they facilitate the smooth functioning of the customer-facing employees. As a result, employees at every position within a company must know what their employer's brand represents.

Meanwhile, sophisticated Human Resources Departments have recognized the pivotal roles that employees and others in the channel, such as the distributors and retailers for packaged goods, play in building and maintaining the brand, and as a result, an entirely new area of brand building sprang up in the 1990s, called 'employer branding'.[11] This sub-discipline of brand management looks at the entire life cycle of an employee from being a potential recruit to a potential alumnus (ie a former or ex-employee) from a brand perspective, going beyond expressing the benefits designed to attract new recruits and retain them. One issue with merely expressing the benefits and qualities of the employer's potential work environment is that these can easily be copied, so if the employee brand were merely built around recruitment features, the results would be generic.[12]

FIGURE 3.1 The role of branding in employment

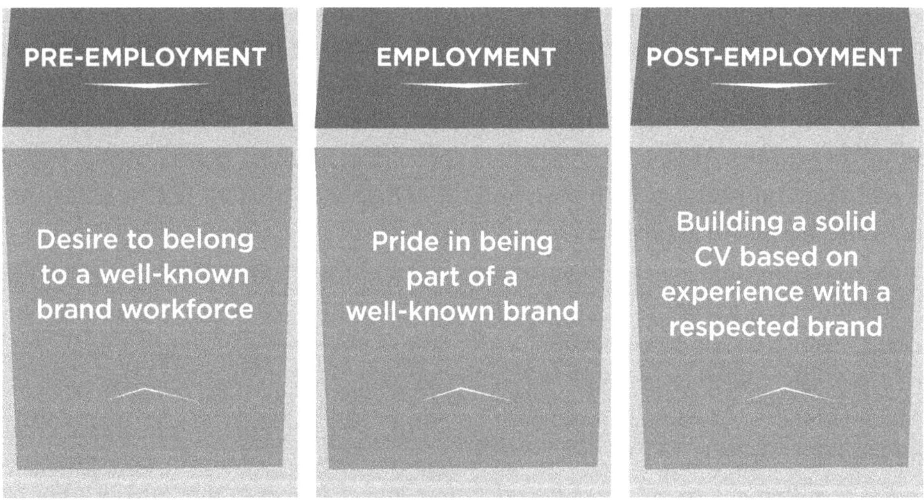

Brands with stronger equity can help attract better employees. Meanwhile the brand performance is directly connected to employee performance.

Even more important than its role in recruitment and retention, the company's brand helps employees understand the behaviours they need to express to support the brand. The brand does this through its stated essence and values (which we'll discuss in Chapter 5) as well as through 'cues' – the behaviours and signals that the brand projects. While hard and soft business skills can be taught, and the words of the brand platform (which you'll encounter in Chapter 10) can be memorized, the true depth of the brand attributes can't be verbally conveyed; just as with brand building for a consumer audience, the attributes need to be experienced to be believed. For example, merely telling potential employees that their company has a 'fun' work environment might, in actuality, make the recruit think that the place *isn't* fun. The same issues arise for other typical corporate brand values such as 'honesty', 'collaboration' and 'teamwork'. These ideas are meaningless unless modelled or experienced. In fact, if the people who work for a brand are not in alignment, prospects will perceive a different 'vibe' from different people. Branding aligns goals and objectives across a company's business units. And it helps bring the messaging together.

For brands that span the globe, particularly those providing services, the issue and hurdles of conveying experiential aspects of the brand to employees are magnified. It's easy to create a productive culture for one single office. Members of the C-Suite – the Chief Executive Officer (CEO); Chief Operating Officer; Chief Marketing Officer (CMO); and others with 'chief' in the title and their immediate reports can model the targeted behaviour. The ability to model behaviour continues to decrease as the organizational chart gets larger and the number of offices increase. One strategy for overcoming these issues is to use consumer brand-building techniques to show employees the behavioural brand's components. Media advertising can also be used for employee branding.[13] Steve Hayden, the former vice chairman of Ogilvy & Mather Worldwide, once said to one of us in an interview about a campaign that he helped to create for American Express, 'We got the client to do a brand campaign that said that they were more than a card. We took all of the components of the American Express brand and put them together in corporate messaging that reminded the employees first of all of the important global scale and quality of the company.'[14] This action was based on a key insight and produced the results they wanted: 'Knowing that employees would pay special attention to its broadcast advertising, a global media campaign helped the brand enhance morale and bring internal alignment around the key brand attributes that they needed to convey no matter where their office was located.'[15] It's important to note that media advertising can also help to explain the brand's essence, purpose, personality, behaviours and other key attributes to merchants, distributors, stockholders and others who benefit from the brand beyond the consumer.

Why internal branding is often more important than external branding

If a brand relies on the performance of its staff to execute – ie bring to life – the brand promises and convey the brand's functional and emotional values of the products and services to customers, the company will need to maintain an internal brand-building process that enables the efficient and effective management of the actions that create credibility for the brand. For these programmes, current and prospective employees at the brand become the target audience. Internal brand training then informs the employees on how to deliver the brand promises and other characteristics. In addition, the organization needs to align the daily activities, business processes, job designs, recognition programmes and rewards, including salary structure, with the brand platform to drive results. Developing the right process of internal branding within an organization contributes to:

- an atmosphere where all employees share an understanding of the brand and what it represents;
- being the catalyst for changes in the organization, while providing a common thread;
- motivating and uniting employees so that they are all going in the same direction with similar objectives (this also includes business partners such as the supply chain);
- holding the brand up to the management as a standard for appropriate behaviour.

One company that has developed an excellent formula for internal branding is The Ritz-Carlton.[16] They embody the values and philosophy by which they operate, and have developed a credo to guide employee actions. Their three-sentence statement includes the line: 'We pledge to provide the finest personal service and facilities for our guests who will always enjoy a warm, relaxed, yet refined ambience' and a motto 'We are ladies and gentlemen serving ladies and gentlemen.'[17] They also point out 'three steps of service' that identify key employee behaviours from the guest's arrival to departure, as well as '20 Basics of Service', both of which can be found on their website and which they encourage those interested in creating exemplary customer experiences to review. One of these 'basics' we especially want to point out is the company's commitment to maintaining and enforcing their promise to employees, which states:

> 'At The Ritz-Carlton, our Ladies and Gentlemen are the most important resource in our service commitment to our guests. By applying the principles of trust, honesty, respect, integrity and commitment, we nurture and maximize talent to the benefit of each individual and the company. The Ritz-Carlton fosters a work environment where diversity is valued, quality of life is enhanced, individual aspirations are fulfilled, and The Ritz-Carlton Mystique is strengthened.'[18]

Based on our experience, these steps work. One of the authors of this book consulted for a service-based brand in a different category that put its employees through The Ritz Carlton training and had management live by its principles, resulting in a better customer service than its competitors according to their proprietary research and general reputation within the category.

Meanwhile, other companies spend valuable time and money consulting with branding experts about articulating their internal values and how to manifest them, but not actually following them. Employee attrition and the pressures to make a profit at any cost are two reasons that companies often fall short. Here are the professed brand values of a well-known company:

- '**RESPECT: We treat others as we would like to be treated ourselves.** We do not tolerate abusive or disrespectful treatment. Ruthlessness, callousness and arrogance don't belong here.
- '**INTEGRITY: We work with customers and prospects openly, honestly and sincerely.** When we say we will do something, we will do it; when we say we cannot or will not do something, we won't do it.

- '**COMMUNICATION: We have an obligation to communicate.** Here, we take the time to talk with one another... and to listen. We believe that information is meant to move and that information moves people.
- '**EXCELLENCE: We are satisfied with nothing less than the very best** in everything we do. We will continue to raise the bar for everyone. The great fun here will be for all of us to discover just how good we can really be.'[19]

Reading this statement, you might say: 'I would love to work for this company.' But the statement came from ENRON, the company behind one of the best-known fraud cases in American corporate history. The systemic fraudulent methods employed by the company led to the fall of two prominent brands, ENRON and Arthur Andersen, the accounting firm that allowed their fraudulent activity to take place.[20] Obviously, none of the lofty values expressed on the company's website was implemented.

Since the image is the sum of all interactions with the brand, brands should start by identifying all of the critical touchpoints and functions that help deliver the brand experience. Current and potential consumers are exposed to many things well beyond the product or service itself, developing impressions from the salesforce and/or employees of the brand, product performance, product design, the delivery and distribution of the brand and more. To give a personal example, one of the authors of this book has had to revise his impressions of the leading natural foods grocery store chain in the US after its takeover by an online retailer owing to the manager of a cheese counter at one of its stores saying he was too busy with other tasks to help the customer, leaving the eager buyer without the object of his errand. And the impression of a computer manufacturer was shaped just as much by the rude and arrogant online-technical-support professional post-purchase, as by the beautiful, inspiring advertising pre-purchase. These kinds of imperfections in the brand's experience help to shape overall impressions and can eventually weaken the brand, eliminating years of careful grooming of the image.

Brands should develop methods to secure delivering the brand's promise and values from inside the organization. In order to achieve that, the CEO and other brand leaders should ask the following two questions:

- Which functions within the organization drive the brand delivery?
- What changes will need to be made to these functions in order to align them with the brand vision?

Having answered these questions, they should then perform the following two tasks:

- Share with employees which functions have been selected and why.
- Share with employees the changes that will need to be made to these functions.

Once the basic questions have been asked, a candid examination of the workforce can take place, identifying the key people performing the key functions and the processes that they use. Questions might include:

- What are the triggers of action for each process?
- Where does information or product come from?
- What is the outcome or result of the process?
- Where and to whom does it go?
- What works and what doesn't?

Organizations can then create the best possible scenario to present the brand in the best possible way, adding data measurement points, so that they can generate a feedback loop to ensure continual improvements. The company should also make sure that the employees are accepting of the new processes and not becoming resentful for having to change their behaviours. Finally, the organization must identify the key job holders who have the most impact on delivering brand value to the customer. This is usually a long way down the line, such as in face-to-face settings or in phone support. Identification of these jobs' functions and their descriptions may challenge traditional HR paradigms. Take the following examples:

- Disney Theme Parks discovered that their roving street sweepers are critical to brand image.[21]
- In a consulting firm, the partner is not as important in delivering the brand promise as the project manager.
- The key influencing job is the product manager in consumer products companies.
- The client implementation manager is the key job in a CRM software company.

A lot of this internal work is connected to change management and behavioural change, which ultimately will affect the brand's performance in the market. We are still humans, waiting to meet human brands that behave in a way we would like our friends and family to behave.

One more employee brand-building area that smart companies are investing in is in creating 'alumni' networks, ie people who used to work for the company, want to stay identified with it, and are likely to speak positively about it. Benefiting the former employees through referrals for new employment or clients, many firms, particularly service-based businesses, are also finding that alumni networks can be a good source of referrals to them, both for recruiting new employees and for obtaining new customers.[22] As a result, even the off-boarding of an employee can reinforce the key brand attributes.

Customer journeys and mapping the brand contacts

The third and perhaps most important group that a brand might choose to place its emphasis on is the customer. No brand is ever built on one-time purchases made by one-time purchasers, except for those selling to tourists who are unlikely to revisit the

FIGURE 3.2 A and B Customer journey map

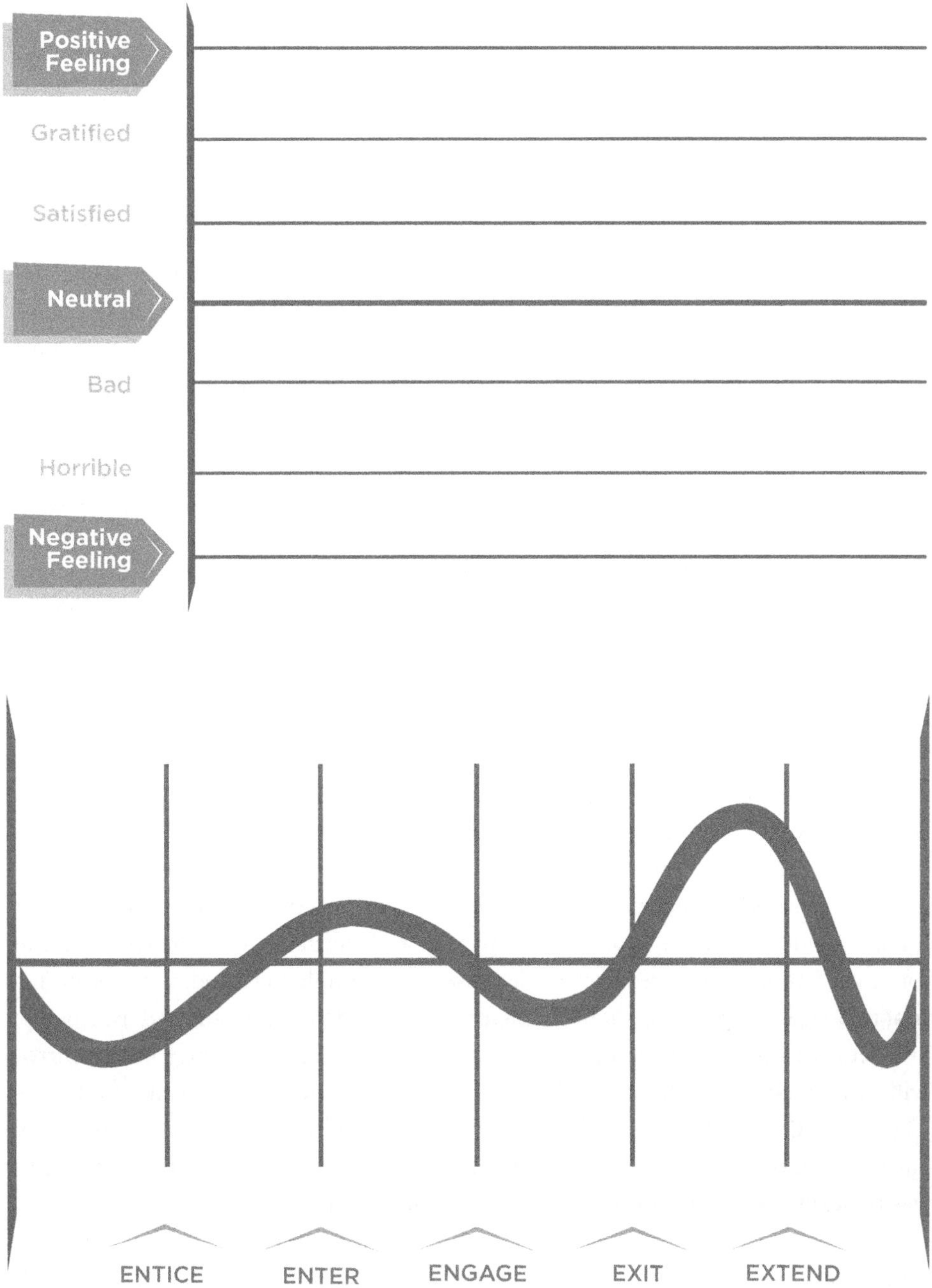

Two of many ways of creating a customer journey map. Maps vary by the nature of the business and the approach of the people constructing them.

location. Sustainability is not truly built into models that are not interested in investing in each and every customer, seeing him or her as a repeat future customer as well. It costs substantially less to retain a customer than to identify and convert new ones.[23] Brand managers must inherently know their prospects, monitor their satisfaction at every stage of their experience with the brand, and anticipate any unfulfilled needs. A very important part of managing a brand is predicting the future, and big data can help.

Just like HR professionals looking at the entire life cycle of employees, marketers need to look at the entire life cycle of customers. To start, marketers need to map the path-to-purchase or customer journey of their prospects. The length of a path-to-purchase can differ based on the customer need, situation and complexity of purchase. It can be very compressed, perhaps a matter of minutes, such as when a shopper discovers a new product on the store shelves and wants to try it or when a person is thirsty and decides to stop at a convenience store for a soft drink. It can take longer, such as when a consumer hears about a new product, reads reviews about it and then decides to seek it out in a store, or when someone makes a shopping list for the grocery. Or it can take weeks or even years of research and negotiations, which is typical when purchasing a piece of heavy equipment for a manufacturing company. An easy way to think of the customer journey is to divide it into three sections or phases: pre-purchase, purchase and post-purchase.

PRE-PURCHASE

Typically, the customer journey starts with a triggering event, a need that sets the person in motion to solve an issue, whether it is to fix a toothache, quench a thirst, take some unused holiday time, restock the fridge at home, or see an opportunity to make his or her employer more profitable and, thus, become more successful. In the pre-purchase stage, the consumer will begin to research into the product or service. For impulse items, it might be as brief as comparing products in the retail environment. But for larger items, it might require detailed research, multiple steps and, perhaps, even a trial period. A consumer might be familiar with a brand that he or she had used before and return to it without hesitation. But if a disappointing experience had occurred with a familiar brand, the consumer might spend time searching for an alternative. This is also the phase where the brand manufacturer will work to familiarize potential customers about the brand through advertising and other communications. Ad agencies typically spend most of their ad budget during this phase.

PURCHASE

The purchase period could take a few minutes online or in a store for a familiar brand or impulse item. (People also pre-schedule recurring purchases such as replacing toiletries through Amazon or other services.) If the shopper is selecting a new brand, purchasing something in a category with which they are unfamiliar, or from a new platform or process, the purchase period could be longer. Finally, for high-ticket items, complicated products or an ongoing experience, the phase can take even longer. For instance, the entire time one spends on vacation in a hotel is included in the purchase time. Likewise, the time spent in a brick-and-mortar retail environment, trying on merchandise, asking questions about the brand and options, and otherwise interacting with the store personnel, including paying, all falls within this phase. One should note that this phase is often marked with elevated stress for the consumer because he or she has to choose and commit to a product. As we have seen from our brief look at behavioural economics in Chapter 2, decision-making requires the brain to expend more energy, while humans naturally fight to conserve it.[24] Strong brands can reduce the customer's stress at this point, because the familiarity increases the brands' likeability and also decreases the defences that cause the stress.[25] Many brand marketers, however, do not pay much attention to this phase, either online or in a store environment, giving smart brands an opportunity to set themselves apart.

POST-PURCHASE

The post-purchase period is the time spent by consumers using the brand after their purchase. Crucial during this phase is the performance of the brand, because it needs to fulfill the promises it made in the marketing message. If it exceeds expectations or positively surprises the consumer in some way, they might even be willing to talk about it, providing the marketer with a valuable word-of-mouth endorsement and building awareness and credibility among the consumer's social network. Product warranties are created for this phase, as well as any follow-up messaging such as a thank-you email to the consumer from the brand. Consumer reviews are also included in this phase. These are often overlooked, but marketers should consider them, because messaging during the post-purchase period can help counteract any buyer's remorse, a typical consumer reaction that becomes more prevalent as purchase options increase. Reduce the remorse and you increase the likelihood of a positive review. In addition, building relationships with consumers during this last phase can also increase the likelihood of repurchase, starting the cycle all over again.[26]

BRAND TOUCHPOINTS

Another way to look at both the employee and consumer journey is by identifying all of the points where they come into contact with the brand from the start of the path, even before the triggering event (which could simply be dissatisfaction with prior solutions), up to the consumption of the product or service and the start of the post-purchase path. These brand touchpoints include the advertising, online and off, promotions, sponsorship associations, word of mouth among friends and associates, media reports, packaging and more – as well as, of course, the user's actual experience of it. When thinking about brand touchpoints, it is important to understand that they will vary from one brand to another, even for competing products within the same category. But even a relatively brief experience of a single brand can

FIGURE 3.3 Common brand touchpoints

It is important to remember that the actual list of brand touchpoints will vary from one brand to another, even for those in the same category.

have many touchpoints. For example, a shopper in a coffee shop might travel through a large number of 'brand touchpoints' within a very short period of time:

1 store location and appearance;
2 greeting or lack of one by the staff;
3 in-store decorations (atmospherics);
4 coffee smell;
5 any background music;
6 a long or short line of people waiting to order;
7 price perception (ie does it feel expensive, cheap or just right for the experience?);
8 coffee variety and choices;
9 staff knowledge;

10 payment methods, eg does it accept credit cards or Apple Pay?

11 does it accept coupons to purchase coffee?

12 length of wait to get the coffee;

13 the condition of the self-serving station (eg whether milk, sugar, napkins, straws etc are available);

14 ability to find a seat;

15 seating (eg is it a hard surface or comfy?);

16 taste;

17 is it a cool place to be seen at?

18 internet connection (is it working or not?);

19 washroom (clean or dirty?);

20 free sampling of new products;

21 leaving ('Goodbye' from staff or not).

Prospects, then, form an opinion about the brand through all of their contacts with it. Consequently, it is important for marketers to look at the touchpoints from every direction – known as the 360-degree reach – and to ensure that the message and behaviour of the brand at each touchpoint is sympathetic to the employee or customer mindset, consistent with the brand essence and promise, and within the bounds of its personality. This is why, in brand development, marketers need to identify a range of appropriate behaviours for the brand personality, a point we'll explore further in Chapter 5.

Segmenting prospects

Some brands, especially those in the fast-moving consumer-goods category, do not manage consumer expectations and act as if every person needs and wants their product, which is never the case. Other brands appeal to a small group of customers and are labelled 'niche brands' right from the beginning. Mastering the art of focusing on a specific target group and finding the exact compelling reasons for that group is not easy. But many Western societies enjoy a consistent supply of competing brands that are not much different from each other, so without focus and differentiation, the brand can get lost and not achieve optimal business and brand-building goals.

The marketer should start by dividing the entire market into smaller segments of like-minded individuals and then identifying the segment or segments where they can then 'win' by creating a compelling brand for this audience, one that will stand out and be appealing to what could become a very loyal audience. When identifying the initial segments, the marketers should study the different paths-to-purchase within the overall category, because they can vary by group and one path might be more appropriate. As a result, this can help inform which groups to approach, when to approach them, as well as where the marketer should place their messages and brand actions along the path. In addition, the information and subsequent selection can inform the 'shading' of the brand – ie which behaviours it needs to present. By developing a brand empathetic to its audiences, one that evolves with them, the marketers should be able to form the basis for long-term loyalty among its customers.

For brands that cross borders, the segments may or may not be the same from one country to the next. If the marketer can't identify the exact same segment in terms of customer attributes, the goal would then be to find the one closest to the ideal in each country, enabling the brand to stay within its behavioural boundaries as well as maintaining its overriding mission or purpose and essence. We shall explore these issues and strategies more fully in Part II. In the next chapter we'll look at how technology used for marketing purposes is influencing the world of global branding. Before moving on, however, we want to conclude with where we started this chapter – with the owners and the shareholders of the brand.

Some final words on the owners and shareholders

At the start of this chapter, we pointed out that some brands emphasize profit above all, focusing on the needs of the owners and shareholders. While this emphasis might benefit them in the short run, it is not in their best interest in the long-term. What is in their best interests is building a strong brand in every country that they operate in. That's because 'all things being equal, a stronger brand will win a "coin toss" between seemingly identical products or services – and, perhaps just as importantly, a strong brand can keep others with better financial positions from entering the category.'[27]

Here is another quote from Minsky and Fahey: 'If the company is ever to be sold, the owner would want to get the most for it and branding has been shown to help increase market cap – ie, it will help you get more money. In fact, according to the *Harvard Business Review*, the "branding" typically contributes between 0.5 per cent for an unmanaged B2B brand to over 20 per cent for a well-managed B2B brand to the value of the company. And the average is around 7 per cent of the company's value. In other words, on average for all B2B companies, if your brand is contributing 7 per cent to the value of your company, you're ahead of the pack; if your brand is contributing below 7 per cent to the value of the company, you're below the pack[28]. The HBR article also pointed out that "a fraction of a percentage of brand equity can mean hundreds of millions of dollars in value".'[29]

As you can see, the brand must consider and address the combined needs of all three key audience types – owners, employees and customers – and the segments in each, for the brand to produce optimal results. Maintaining a healthy balance between the three constituents enables stability and focus, which is essential for any brand that wants to ensure long-term profitability, growth and customer loyalty.

21ST-CENTURY BRAND STORYTELLING – A GUEST PERSPECTIVE FROM RICK RAY, USA

Rick recently returned to the US after spending much of the previous forty years living, working and teaching in Paris, Brussels and Milan – and spending a good deal of his professional career in airports and on fast trains. From Zagreb to Shanghai, from Calgary to Hannover, from London to San Francisco and wherever else one of his clients may have had a need, he was there. His clients included Procter & Gamble, Fiat, Nestlé, Microsoft, Budweiser and Haworth. His titles included CEO of a multinational marketing communications group in Milan, Managing Director of an Italian multinational subsidiary in Chicago and President of a leading Media Buying organization in Rome. He's currently co-founder and Managing Partner of *brandstory*, a leading-edge brand-strategy consultancy. Specializing in international and cross-cultural management, marketing and marketing communications issues, Rick also has insightful hands-on experience in the diagnosis and management of organizational culture change.

Rick considers university teaching as his 'love job'. From the European School of Economics (ESE) and the European Design Institute (IED) in Milan, to his current position at Butler University in Indianapolis, Rick has been an adjunct instructor at both undergraduate and postgraduate levels. He has worked for large multinational organizations, as well as for small family-owned businesses. It may have been unanticipated at the time, but Rick's BBA from the University of Notre Dame and MBA from Northwestern's Kellogg School of Management have combined to help take him far – both career-wise and geographically, and he wouldn't have had it any other way. So, here's what he has to say about the need for brand storytelling:

> 'First, let's all agree upfront that the success of any brand depends on an insightful understanding of the consumer, and what makes him or her tick. Agreed? But for the sake of argument here in Chapter 3, let us also agree that brand success starts with the *brand* itself. Because it is *one* and it is *unique*. And it deserves to be understood as such, in the same way, by *all* its stakeholders – both internal and external. Which also means – as you have already seen – that we must not confound these two key terms, "branding" and "brand".
>
> 'Just as "fishing" is what we do to a "fish", so "branding" is what we do to a "brand". It is consequentially logical that any branding activity in support of the brand must be coherent with the brand itself; otherwise one's activity risks being less efficient than it ought to be, or worse, even misleading or counterproductive – in effect, throwing money down a dark hole, rather than contributing to the brand's growth. In other words, before even thinking about your branding, you must truly understand your own brand. OK?
>
> 'At this point, it should come as no surprise to anyone that the folks from *brandstory*, based on our long experience in the world of brands and branding, have concluded

that the "best" way to define and successfully describe a brand is to develop its own differentiating strategic *brand story.* A brand's own, ownable *story*, an original strategic narrative that is *authentic*, *credible*, *memorable* and, above all, *motivating*.

'The success of a brand *cannot* be attributable to its "advertising" alone. Rather, brand success is the result of the unified efforts of *all* a brand's various stakeholders, both internal and external. A brand that has all of its stakeholders singing from the same hymn sheet has a genuine competitive advantage in the marketplace. Such strategic harmony can never be taken for granted.

'And the simple fact is that people are "wired" for stories. A well-told story can *motivate* internal *and* external stakeholders far more than any memo, left-brain-strategy expression or PowerPoint presentation. And there is nothing like a well-told story to provide an insightful blueprint for a coherent orchestration of the brand's multiple *touchpoints*, all of which must be woven together in an effective Integrated Marketing Communications (IMC) branding support programme.

'The validity of this storytelling approach has been amply verified by *brandstory*'s lengthy experience in Europe and with a diverse range of brands, including products and services-as-brands, Companies-as-brands, Organizations-as-brands, Institutions-as-brands and even Ideas-as-brands, in both B2C and B2B business sectors. Because *every* brand has its own differentiating strategic story to tell; it simply needs to be identified and crafted.

'Here are just a few examples of brands that have invested in the development of their own original strategic *brand stories*: a private European university brand with campuses in Milan, Florence, Rome, Madrid and London; a repositioned financial institution brand in Zagreb; a private hotel chain in Austria; a formerly obscure winery in France; an international agricultural-equipment brand headquartered in Turin; a start-up business services brand in Prague.

'Yet another such brand is the Victorian-era train station in London, St Pancras, renovated in 2007. The brand invested in the development of its own original "*Meet Me in St Pancras*" storyline, helping to position the brand as Europe's destination station as well as a meeting place – somewhere not only to "catch a train", but also a place where cultures meet, a place for adventurous diners to meet or share a glass at "the longest champagne bar in Europe"

'Or take a brand like CONAD, one of Italy's leading supermarket chains – a brand with multiple and disparate stakeholder groups, each with its own potentially conflicting business priorities. The CONAD supermarket chain is actually a national consortium, comprised of eight independent regional cooperatives, with more than 3,000 independent store owners across the nation and accounting for more than 4,000,000 individual consumer transactions each week. It has taken the brand's unifying *"In*

Celebration of Diversity" story to help ensure that these significantly diverse stakeholder groups are indeed all marching to the same beat of the brand's drummer.

'In short, while specific internal and external executional branding activity may actually differ, there is nothing like an authentic, unifying strategic *brand story* to ensure that *all* the brand's stakeholders are pulling together, in the same direction, all the time. While 20th-century marketing efforts have amply verified over time that people do prefer brands to mere products, today, in the 21st century, there is a growing body of evidence that *people prefer brands, with a story.'*

EXTENDED CASE STUDY: THE STORY OF THE MANIFESTO THAT HELPED TURN SAMSUNG INTO A GLOBAL BRAND

Not many CEOs take a 'mystery tour' and go unannounced into retail establishments that sell their brands. But in 1993, the then Samsung Chairman, Mr Lee Kun-hee, did just that. He travelled around the world determined to see for himself how Samsung products were doing at the retail level. What he found didn't make him happy. While the leading electronics brands of the time – Sony, Toshiba, Panasonic and others – were commanding the top spots on store shelves and selling in large numbers, Samsung televisions and other products were gathering dust in the least desirable spots in the store. Lee Kun-hee wanted the Samsung brand to have the same stature that GE had at the time in the US, as well as internationally. The current situation didn't promise the ability to build brand equity, or physically expand the Samsung brand and its products. He knew that something had to be done.

Lee Kun-hee didn't return to his office in Korea. Instead, he stopped in Germany and reflected on what he saw. His next move was to start writing the vision, mission and positioning statements of the Samsung brand. He then summoned his entire top management team from all corners of the world to the Falkenstein Grand Kempinski hotel in Frankfurt. Once assembled, they literally sealed themselves away from the world, and for three straight days listened to the Chairman's vision, as he read to them his writings.[30] He only broke the meeting to let his lieutenants sleep at night.

The main message that came from this vision was: 'Change everything but your wife and children.' This unusual jolt to the core of the company created the Samsung brand that we all know today. It broke all that was known within the complacent organization, calling for a complete behavioural and attitudinal change.

The speech became known inside Samsung as the 'Frankfurt Declaration of 1993'.[31] Samsung built a 'shrine' to commemorate the event, and even transferred all the furniture and decorations from the Frankfurt hotel to Samsung's HQ in Korea. The speech given to the top management is now given to each new Samsung employee in the form of a 200-page book.

In short, the company altered its vision and directed it towards a wide-range, non-product-specific human scope: 'We will devote our human resources and technology to create superior products and services, thereby contributing to a better global society.' When organizations use this language, without being specific about the products they currently manufacture, the chances are that they understand their place in the world. Better still, they know where they want to go in the future, and do not limit themselves to becoming the biggest, the richest, the most popular etc.

Samsung goes a long way to train and educate its employees, a very important step in developing an internal brand philosophy. At the end of the day, each employee, no matter what his or her role is, is a walking billboard for the company's brand. At Changjo Kwan, the Samsung Human Resources Development Centre, the company trains more than 50,000 employees each year. That is more than the number of employees that work at many global organizations and shows the level of commitment that this company has to making sure each employee understands the brand and is dedicated to it. For example, Samsung developed its own 'Three Ps' – Products, Process and People – which it teaches to its global team. Team spirit is also enhanced by having cooking classes and exposure to Korean culture. The overall culture of the Eastern world is that the community is more important than the individual – a stark contrast to the individualistic philosophy that drives Western philosophies and culture. Samsung is keen to develop that recognition among their employees, to be able to achieve supremacy via communal cooperation and collaboration.

A great opportunity was given to Samsung when Sony, the leading electronics brand and company in the world, decided to diversify into the entertainment field. Sony purchased options and stocks in Colombia Pictures and overnight became a major player in Hollywood.[32] Samsung saw its opportunity and started to implement all the learnings from the 'Frankfurt Declaration of 1993'. The declaration laid out a vision to transform Samsung from a second-tier TV manufacturer into a dominant global brand. It would require going from being a high-volume, low-quality manufacturer to a high-quality one, even if that meant sacrificing sales. It would mean looking past the borders of South Korea and taking on the world. We can gain three key insights from this move:

- A keen observer, Mr Lee Kun-hee doesn't rely on research reports, but goes to see for himself.
- Mr Lee Kun-hee is a real leader, who takes responsibility and in one gutsy move shakes the entire organization.
- A clear direction is set for the organization in terms of vision, leadership and encouragement.

Today, Samsung is the world's largest electronics brand by volume. They have surpassed Sony not only in volume, but also in brand reputation. While Sony was the undisputed leader in the market when it owned TV brands such as Trinitron, or the now obsolete Walkman, Samsung is now one of the first brand names that comes to people's minds.

This entire story is somewhat of a surprise in the current brand lore. We all know of charismatic leaders who built amazing brands: Steve Jobs at Apple, Phil Knight at NIKE and Howard Shultz at Starbucks. But Lee Kun-hee? Not many know the name, or the way he revolutionized the fate of the Samsung brand. It goes back to the Eastern philosophy of not glorifying the individual, but celebrating the community as a whole.[33]

KEY TERMS

- brand constituents
    - customers
    - employees
    - shareholders.
- brand touchpoints
- customer journey
- employee-customer brand experience continuum
- internal branding
- stakeholders

DISCUSSION QUESTIONS

- What is the importance of customer journey mapping for brand storytelling?
- What was your customer journey for your most recent retail purchase?
- Which do you feel is more important, internal or external branding, and why do you feel that way?
- What role do warranties and guarantees play in the brand experience?
- How does branding play into the hiring, training and performance processes?

Notes

1 Blystone, D (2018) The Story of Uber, *Investopedia*, https://www.investopedia.com/articles/personal-finance/111015/story-uber.asp (archived at https://perma.cc/A332-MGA5)

2 *USA Today* (2018) Is this America's best fast-food pizza?, https://www.usatoday.com/story/travel/columnist/greatamericanbites/2018/04/24/blaze-pizza-chain-growing-across-america/536335002 (archived at https://perma.cc/BBH2-3XG2)

3 Ignatius, A (2010) The HBR interview: 'We had to own the mistakes', *Harvard Business Review*, https://hbr.org/2010/07/the-hbr-interview-we-had-to-own-the-mistakes (archived at https://perma.cc/XD7A-3LBX)

4 Stewart, E (2018) Walmart is paying $20 billion to shareholders. With that money, it could boost hourly wages to over $15, *Vox*, https://www.vox.com/business-and-finance/2018/5/25/17379730/walmart-stock-buyback-worker-wages (archived at https://perma.cc/2TTX-MYES)

5 Lutz, A (2015) Wal-Mart desperately needs to fix customer service, *Business Insider*, https://www.businessinsider.com/wal-marts-wants-to-improve-customer-service-2015-2 (archived at https://perma.cc/UZZ3-LA2W)

6 Efron, L (2017) Why Wal-Mart is winning in a losing industry, *Forbes*, https://www.forbes.com/sites/louisefron/2017/05/31/why-wal-mart-is-winning-in-a-losing-industry/#6fbaeef144d5 (archived at https://perma.cc/YUT6-3SAW)

7 *The Marietta Times* (2013) McDonald's manager wins Ray Kroc Award, http://www.mariettatimes.com/news/business/2013/12/mcdonald-s-manager-wins-ray-kroc-award (archived at https://perma.cc/L32V-NSP5)

8 Peterson, H (2015) 7 mistakes that led to McDonald's downfall, *Business Insider*, https://www.businessinsider.com/heres-where-mcdonalds-went-wrong-2015-5 (archived at https://perma.cc/Z3BP-684Q)

9 Matyszczyk, C (2018) McDonald's has a massive new problem that could ruin everything the company is trying to do, *Inc.com*, https://www.inc.com/chris-matyszczyk/mcdonalds-has-a-massive-new-problem-that-could-ruin-everything-company-is-trying-to-do.html (archived at https://perma.cc/NV3M-YKHC)

10 Rosen, W and Minsky, L (2017) *The Activation Imperative: How to build brands and business by inspiring action*, Rowman & Littlefield, Lanham, Maryland, p 37

11 Hall, B (2016) Employer branding for millennials: 4 companies who got it right, *Interact*, https://www.interact-intranet.com/blog/employer-branding-millennials (archived at https://perma.cc/M7LD-46U9)

12 Schubert, A (2018) Employer branding: Another buzzword or a survival strategy? *Warc*, https://www.warc.com/content/paywall/article/atticus/employer_branding_another_buzzword_or_a_survival_strategy/99834 (archived at https://perma.cc/335G-3VV6)

13 Rosen, W and Minsky, L (2017) *The Activation Imperative: How to build brands and business by inspiring action*, Rowman & Littlefield, Lanham, Maryland, p 37

14 Minsky, L (2007) *How to Succeed in Advertising When All You Have Is Talent*, 2nd edn, Copy Workshop, Chicago, IL

15 Rosen, W and Minsky, L (2017) *The Activation Imperative: How to build brands and business by inspiring action*, Rowman & Littlefield, Lanham, Maryland, p 37

16 Michelli, J (2008) *The New Gold Standard: 5 leadership principles for creating a legendary customer experience courtesy of The Ritz-Carlton Hotel Company*, McGraw Hill Professional, New York

17 The Ritz-Carlton (2018) Gold Standards, http://www.ritzcarlton.com/en/about/gold-standards (archived at https://perma.cc/B6E5-X83T)

18 The Ritz-Carlton (2018) Gold Standards, http://www.ritzcarlton.com/en/about/gold-standards (archived at https://perma.cc/B6E5-X83T)

19 Rampersad, H and Hussain, S (2014) Authentic Governance, *Springer Science & Business Media*, p 53

20 Toffler, B L, with Reingold, J (2004) *Final Accounting: Ambition, greed, and the fall of Arthur Anderson*, Currency/Doubleday, New York

21 Devoll, J (2007) Are you 'pivotal' to your organization's success? *Harvard Business Review*, https://hbr.org/2007/07/are-you-pivotal-to-your-organi (archived at https://perma.cc/TE6W-WQ46)

22 Sertoglu, C and Berkowitch, A (2002) Cultivating ex-employees, *Harvard Business Review*, https://hbr.org/2002/06/cultivating-ex-employees (archived at https://perma.cc/S39T-DEL5)

23 Gallo, A (2014) The value of keeping the right customers, *Harvard Business Review*, https://hbr.org/2014/10/the-value-of-keeping-the-right-customers (archived at https://perma.cc/N5DE-JZFK)

24 Iyengar, S and Agrawal, K (2010) A better choosing experience, *strategy+business*, https://www.strategy-business.com/article/00046?gko=13ead (archived at https://perma.cc/9GMP-7RJV)

25 Smith, J (2015) 6 conversion principles you can learn from the mere-exposure effect, *Marketing Land*, https://marketingland.com/6-conversion-principles-can-learn-mere-exposure-effect-140430 (archived at https://perma.cc/293F-7E3T)

26 Alton, L (2017) 5 ways to avoid buyer's remorse in your customers, *HuffPost*, https://www.huffingtonpost.com/entry/5-ways-to-avoid-buyers-remorse-in-your-customers_us_58a3b46de4b0e172783aa231 (archived at https://perma.cc/WU7W-4PFL)

27 Minsky, L and Fahey, C (2017) *Audio Branding: Using sound to build your brand*, Kogan Page, London, p 28

28 Gregory, J and Sexton, D (2007) Hidden wealth in B2B brands, *Harvard Business Review*, https://hbr.org/2007/03/hidden-wealth-in-b2b-brands (archived at https://perma.cc/Z3L8-ST9M)

29 Minsky, L and Fahey, C (2017) *Audio Branding: Using sound to build your brand*, Kogan Page, London, p 29

30 Yarow, J (2013) This bizarre story about a three-day speech in a German hotel explains Samsung's culture, *Business Insider*, https://www.businessinsider.com/how-samsung-became-the-biggest-electronics-company-in-the-world-2013-3 (archived at https://perma.cc/RJ5H-T5QE)

31 Yarow, J (2013) This bizarre story about a three-day speech in a German hotel explains Samsung's culture, *Business Insider*, https://www.businessinsider.com/how-samsung-became-the-biggest-electronics-company-in-the-world-2013-3 (archived at https://perma.cc/RJ5H-T5QE)

32 Wikipedia (2018) Sony Pictures, https://en.wikipedia.org/wiki/Sony_Pictures (archived at https://perma.cc/3Y48-4BNB)

33 Yarow, J (2013) This bizarre story about a three-day speech in a German hotel explains Samsung's culture, *Business Insider*, https://www.businessinsider.com/how-samsung-became-the-biggest-electronics-company-in-the-world-2013-3 (archived at https://perma.cc/RJ5H-T5QE)

04

Programmatic and other technology in the service of brands

READING OUTCOMES

At the conclusion of this chapter, you should be able to:

- understand the opposing drives for innovative solutions and brand consistency;
- describe the ways in which marketing technology can both help and hurt brand equity;
- define programmatic as well as explain its impact on managing global brands;
- articulate the role that effective cybersecurity plays in protecting global brands.

Introduction

What is it about a product or service that grabs your attention? The answer might be more obvious than you think. Seth Godin points out in his classic book, *Purple Cow*,[1] that it's something notable or unique that people make a 'remark' about. He uses the analogy of a purple cow. If you are driving along a road and see one, you notice it and talk about it. Of course, if all cows became purple, it would become commonplace and people would not notice its colour or think it worth mentioning. Godin thinks that this uniqueness behind word-of-mouth marketing is the key to marketing success today.

Godin's observation is based on a bigger truth: marketing effectiveness, from new product development through to advertising effectiveness, is often fuelled by 'innovation'. Product innovations – which can range from new features and uses to distribution methods and processes – are what often drives category growth for marketing. For the marketing subset of advertising and other marketing communications, the slightly new and different message or new tactic is what typically breaks through the clutter and gets noticed. For this reason, marketing professionals are trained to embrace innovation in its many forms.

Taking it one step further, Peter Drucker, who is considered the father of modern management consulting, argues that, 'Because the purpose of business is to create a customer, the business enterprise has two – and only two – basic functions: marketing and innovation. Marketing and innovation produce results; all the rest are costs. Marketing is the distinguishing, unique function of the business.'[2]

But this creates a dichotomy, because one of the basic principles of branding and brand management is that these are most effective when activities, messaging and positioning are consistent, reinforcing the belief that the brand will perform as promised every time and appear in appropriate locations. In this final chapter of Section One of the book – theoretical and strategic foundations of branding – we are going to look at the concept of innovation, when to change and when to stay steady. Finally, we'll look at some of the opportunities and challenges that marketing technology, or MarTech, as it's called, creates, giving you the foundation for fully understanding Section Two, the practical and tactical applications of branding.

Overview

In the previous chapter, we explored the 360 degrees of a brand's reach and, in Chapter 1, we described why all brands are now essentially global, because of technology. In this chapter, we look at marketing technology, MarTech. While this technology creates new marketing opportunities, it also gives rise to a number of issues and areas of concern. In the following pages, we're going to explore a number of technological developments and how they can be used in growing and managing a global brand. We also hear from Jens Ulrik Hansen on how the digital shift has affected brands and branding. We end by looking at McDonald's, a global brand but with a local 'flavour' in each country that it operates in.

Branding versus the drive for innovation

Marketing effectiveness is driven by innovation. Often, the first to a new idea, insight, tactic or product feature is more successful than the followers. Because of the push towards something new, many marketers are often more willing to abandon brand DNA much sooner than is appropriate, denying the brand the chance to achieve maximum ROI and long-term brand health. The excitement of the breakthrough is one of the reasons people go into marketing. And the need to bolster one's CV and show immediate achievements, driven by the short average tenure of marketing positions (an issue we will explore more fully in Chapter 8), is another key factor in this relentless quest for change and innovation. Reinforcing this desire is the fact that being the first with on-target innovation is often the basis for achieving increased share, revenues, profits and brand loyalty.[3]

Brand-building effectiveness, on the other hand, is often driven by consistency of promise and positioning. People expect brands to perform in the same way every time. As we mentioned in Chapter 2, brands help consumers make shortcuts in their decision-making because they know what to expect. It is the comfort of familiarity that makes brands successful.[4] This is not to argue for a return to the mindless repetitive advertising of the 1950s to create the familiarity, which was based on the idea that people needed to see a message three times to understand and remember it. We now know that wear-in of a message is virtually immediate and message wear-out happens almost as fast,[5] so a greater variety of commercial messages that say the same thing in different ways, yet are consistent with the brand personality, is needed to maintain interest. Create any confusion with the positioning, personality or promise from one message to another, however, or fail to live up to the brand promise, and the marketers can hurt brand equity, loyalty and repeat purchases, opening up a window for the competition.

We bring this up, because the abundance of recent technological innovations has provided marketers with new avenues for building brand equity, but if not used wisely these advances can also hurt brand perceptions in unexpected ways. To underscore this wide range of technological advances, Ken Auletta pointed out in his recent book, *Frenemies*, that, 'Starting in the 1990s, four new technologies – first the internet, then smart phones and social media, and now AI – have transformed all business, requiring innovation.'[6]

Recognizing this dichotomy between the desire to innovate, taking full advantage of the technological advances, and the need for consistency can help marketers better manage their brands by clarifying which elements can change and where and when, and which elements should stay constant. Also, by understanding the potential issues and roadblocks, marketers can better think through and, thus, protect their brand during the innovation process. Let's start by looking at an example where one of the four technological advances has opened up brand-building opportunities for marketers.

The Huda Kattan brand start-up and social media

Social media has allowed quite a few young entrepreneurs to create brands from scratch. While we all know and have heard about the Kardashian family, especially Kim Kardashian, other young empowered females have also succeeded in building their own presence and business online. Huda Kattan is one of them. She created Huda Beauty from practically nothing, amassing a following of 26 million on Instagram[7] and 2.4 million YouTube subscriptions. With such power, no wonder she is considered one of the most advanced brands in cosmetics, owning a brand worth about US $1 billion (£795 million).[8]

Huda Kattan's story of a brand came out of her childhood dream. The secret of her success rests with her appeal to a wide audience that is tired of traditional cosmetics brands. She appears to be authentic and genuine in her communications.

It also doesn't hurt that she is good-looking and has a healthy sense of humour, making her a strong spokesperson. Combined, these brand attributes generate trust, the hardest branding currency to generate. Contributing to her success is the fact that she's not running a large corporation and she makes the decisions by herself, without relying on complicated strategies from heavy-layered marketing departments and a board of directors. Some of her family members are serving in senior positions in her organization, which is now expanding globally. It's important to point out that her small organization contributes to the authenticity, and the following she has on social media keeps motoring her forwards.

As Huda Kattan has been quoted as saying, 'I've been put in multiple boxes as blogger and as an influencer and not really perceived as a businesswoman, and that's something that I've really had to grow into.' She said in an interview with Fast Company in 2018: 'I didn't necessarily plan initially to be the CEO of the company. This transition of being a woman and a breadwinner – it took some time for my dad to get used to that. It took some time for my husband. I was like, gosh, I've worked so hard to be here, and then all of a sudden I don't know if I feel comfortable being here.'[9]

As an example of a brand that grew organically through the use of social media, Huda Beauty shows that much of building a brand today still requires 100 per cent commitment and a strong belief in an idea. With a little bit of luck, a strong idea can make a difference with a relevant audience. What's changed is that technology has given start-ups a larger, low-cost megaphone to broadcast their new idea in a unique and compelling way.

Huda Kattan is now moving her brand into bigger leagues. The tests in the larger arena will be fierce and competition can come from nowhere, because many others want the same success. One of the tasks she will have to face very soon is the decision about brand hierarchy. If the competition will be fierce, as rumour has it, she may have to consider launching sub-brands or endorsed brands in order to penetrate other market segments. This will be interesting to watch, as the influencers in this market are growing, and the social-media avenue they are using allows virtually anybody to become the next big brand. If Kim Kardashian and Huda Kattan can build brands through social media, chances are that others will too.

The new-for-the-sake-of-new versus the smart-new

Just as the rise of the internet enabled the rise of Google, Amazon, Netflix and other online powerhouse brands through new business models, Huda Kattan's story illustrates how smart innovation and the early use of social media versus 'innovating' simply for the sake of trying something new can build a brand. Of course, subsequent social-media-focused brands can't just merely copy Huda Kattan's formula. Rather, they can be inspired by her and learn from her mistakes and successes, as they create new formulas.

One lesson from examples like Kattan's is that the 'new wave of brand building' is often technologically focused, leading to new marketing tactics and business-building opportunities. For example, Google's first voice-activated coupon appeared on April 2018 for US-based discount chain Target.[10] With it, Google Express shoppers were offered US $15 off a Target order, but the shoppers who wanted to activate the offer had to say or type: 'Spring into Target' to Google Assistant via Google Home devices or the Google Assistant mobile application. This new kind of promotional activity is now considered to be part of the branding toolbox and more like it are sure to come. For some younger, more tech-proficient demographics this approach can be superior to distributing old-fashioned paper coupons, while still delivering a powerful brand-building interaction to the user. It is possible that as this book is being written, new technology is being invented that might change other shopping behaviours, followed by new brand-behavioural opportunities. We shall explore this area more fully in the following chapter, as well as corresponding business-building opportunities.

From a global perspective, media-studies pioneer Marshall McLuhan argued that a new medium actually changes culture more than the content that resides in it, and the rise of the four new technologies we identified earlier are no exception. As a result, some now argue that attempts to focus on the emotional connections for brand building are old-fashioned and are, thus, focusing solely on changing the consumer's behaviour.[11] It is a debate as old as marketing: brand building (helping prospects understand what the brand is about) versus sales building (getting prospects to try the brand, usually through incentives). We take a different approach and believe that brand building and behavioural-driven marketing can work together and concurrently, achieving the aims of both. It doesn't have to be one or the other. While it's extremely difficult to assess in advance how consumer behaviour will change after future technological introductions, we believe brand building will always involve some level of emotionality, at least in the coming generations. That is because, even with our rapid technological advances and cultural changes, our biology, physical needs and problem-solving approaches are not evolving as rapidly. An example is the rate of merchandise return of all retail brands. Not surprisingly, old-style brick-and-mortar retail outlets have fewer merchandise returns than the same brands online.[12] Many e-commerce brands that were designed to be 100 per cent online are now opening up brick-and-mortar outlets in shopping malls.

MarTech and why it matters for branding

MarTech, or marketing technology, is an industry-recognized term that refers to technology platforms that enable the automation of marketing tasks.[13] A brief audit of MarTech tools includes those for the placement of digital messages and on-the-fly digital display and mobile-marketing-message construction; email, video, content, search and social-marketing management; message testing and optimization; affiliate marketing and management; social-media monitoring; sales automation and intelligence; e-commerce; web, mobile and other marketing analytics; search engine optimization (SEO); talent (ie employees) and collaboration management and budgeting; as well as other tools that automate redundant marketing tasks and increase the marketer's ability to predict customer and prospect behaviours. Marketers use MarTech to be more efficient in their operations as well as to personalize messaging without needing extra-large teams, reducing labour demands.

MarTech's powers have increased in recent years owing to the rapid improvements in artificial intelligence, fuelled by advances in data collection, analysis and computing power. Although AI dates back to the 1950s, its growth was slow over its first 40 years. However, forecasts predict that AI will grow by 53 per cent by 2020.[14] In thinking about AI, we should note an observation from Venkat Nagaswamy, CEO and co-founder of MarianaIQ, an AI platform for one-to-one social engagement. He 'points out that one of the biggest objections to the adoption is that the AI doesn't provide new insights. And that's partially true most of the time – AI enables insights to be generated faster, automating repetitive or routine tasks at a scale that is impossible for humans'.[15] Every reader is already familiar with AI, even if they do not realize it. For example, a common AI tool that virtually everyone uses is the search engine, Google being the most popular.

One of the first major areas of AI that was invested in for marketing was programmatic media buying. Basically, programmatic involves using algorithms to draw from the data of prospects' previous online behaviour in order to target, buy and place digital advertising. While eliminating media labour costs and allowing for fast, targeted buying, programmatic, at least in its infancy, came with many unforeseen issues. For example, 'Facebook's machines inadvertently counted repeat visitors more than once when reporting total visitors,' reported Ken Auletta in his book, *Frenemies*. 'Google also reluctantly admitted measurement errors, the most egregious being programmatic buying by Facebook and YouTube that placed friendly ads on unfriendly sites, including racist, extremist and pornography sites.'[16] Needless to say, brands grow in power, positively or negatively, by their associations and these are associations many brands obviously don't want to have.

By the time you're reading this book, many of these early issues may have been addressed. We bring them up, however, because they can serve as a warning of what could go wrong with emerging marketing technology. Our goal is not to stop you from using emerging technology – after all, in marketing, innovators are often the winners – but to remind you of the need for thinking through all the potential issues and their impact on the brand, so that you can fully protect against them.

Cybersecurity as a form of brand protection

Extreme brand failures can lead to the entity going out of business or needing to merge to stay viable under a new name. This is particularly true of brands that have not yet 'banked' enough consumer goodwill. For example, take ValuJet, which was merged out of existence after being exposed for a series of safety issues, including one that resulted in a crash that killed all of the people on the flight.[17] While we don't yet have examples of a brand closing owing to a cybersecurity breach or the failure to protect its customer data, it can happen, particularly if it is still building its reputation. As a result, how marketers prepare for and respond to cybersecurity issues and protect their data is another consideration when aiming to defend a brand and build its equity.

Traditionally, when taking customers' details online, marketers aim for what is called 'low friction', ie making the transaction as easy as possible. As a result, online 'security experts have generally translated this wish into procedures that are as easy and invisible as possible for brand shoppers, while also delivering a degree of online security.'[18] However, this approach might not be as successful from a brand-building perspective. That's because customers want to know that 'your site is secure and trustworthy'.[19] Conversely, marketers can leverage 'online security measures as a way to build trust with shoppers'[20] through cues that show you're protecting your customers' privacy. While this book is not the place to explore the intricacies of cybersecurity and data protection, it is worth noting that brand managers should work with their company's Chief Information Security Officer (CISO) to develop the cybersecurity and data-protection strategies that defend the brand while facilitating business, and that might mean slightly increasing the level of 'friction' within the transaction.

Our discussion, however, also brings up a wider issue regarding the collection of data. Customers, prospects and other visitors to brand websites and related retail sites expect what is essentially a customized experience. What's more, recipients of brand messages now expect them to be relevant. Both expectations require the capture and use of data through many of the MarTech tools we just discussed. The conflict, dubbed 'the Privacy Paradox', is that people don't want to give up the data to receive the customized experience. As a result, brand managers need to be able to balance the two if they are to fulfill the wishes of their customers. One classic example of a brand going too far and showing that, through data mining, it knows more about the customer than is desirable was when the discount chain Target sent an 'addressable mailer' to a teenager who was pregnant 'before her father had discovered the same fact'.[21] In other words, how the brand treats the privacy of its customers and prospects can also influence how customers and prospects view the brand.

To explore the implications, one must first understand the cultural differences in the way people and their governments view privacy and data ownership. In the European Union, each citizen 'owns' his or her own data. Corporations can only use it with their permission. In America, on the other hand, citizens don't own their own data. Rather, the corporations who control the websites that people visit, the apps that people use, as well as the financial tools, such as credit and debit cards, that consumers rely on, own the data they're able to collect.

To underscore consumer-data ownership in the European Union, the General Data Protection Regulation (GDPR), making privacy rights more explicit, came into effect in May 2018. This spelt out that 'any company offering services to EU citizens regardless of where the citizens reside' must request 'unambiguous' permission versus 'soft opt-ins' for data capture and usage. The company must also explain how the data will be used and make it easy for citizens to remove data. To give teeth to the legislation, 'the penalty for noncompliance is up to 4 per cent of annual global turnover or 20 million euros, whichever is greater'.[22]

How brand behaviours evolve as a result of GDPR is yet to be seen. Some working in cybersecurity say privately that they believe that most brands will eventually follow the legislation worldwide, since the costs of failure – the penalties – can be crippling and the opportunities for failure are many, because EU citizens reside across the globe. (In the short-term, at the time of writing, some companies such as Facebook are approaching EU operations differently from how they approach the use of data in other countries.)[23] From a brand-building perspective, the authors believe compliance with GDPR is the right thing to do. Trust is the most important commodity a brand can earn and the need for GDPR points out the lack of it among consumers. The way a brand approaches consumer privacy rights and how it protects and utilizes customer data can impact the brand both positively and negatively. Brand managers need to approach this area wisely to ensure the long-term life of their brands.

Anyone involved in MarTech is no doubt watching with fascination the current drama of Facebook unfold: betrayal of consumers, data breaches, unfulfilled promises, disconnected and unresponsive executives, declining sales and brand equity. Facebook could be an example of a brand we all consider to be 'too big to fail' or 'too important to too many people globally', yet because it is a technology brand, it could be replaced one day by another technology we simply haven't discovered yet. The deeper the brand gets into negative publicity and stubbornly neglects to face reality, the quicker can be its demise. So far, we have witnessed brand-related controversies that have not only tarnished the company's already battered image, but have also fuelled more distrust in the social network.[24]

Before a brand can enjoy a long-term life, even on a local scale, it needs to be developed – the theme of the next section in this book. We will start with the foundational development of the brand in the next chapter and the activation or realization of it in the following chapter. We'll also explore the brand-marketing and communication ecosystem, as well as the brand life cycle in the next section. Onwards!

THE IMPACT OF THE DIGITAL SHIFT ON BRANDS AND BRANDING – A GUEST PERSPECTIVE FROM JENS ULRIK HANSEN, SWITZERLAND

Jens U Hansen is a globally recognized entrepreneur, strategic advisor, facilitator, public speaker, coach and board member. His driving principle is how to achieve the highest level of human qualities by leveraging new technologies. He inspires, facilitates and advises on leadership development and transformation for our fast-changing world. Jens works intensively in the field of leadership values and cultures, corporate strategy, new technologies, innovation, ecosystems and customer centricity – all in the light of increasing individual and collective digital maturity. Many of his client engagements are for leadership adaptation and building of strength and resilience in both running today's business and at the same time creating the digital business for tomorrow. Here's what Jens has to say about the impact of digital technologies on branding and the need to focus on the promise as a result:

> 'The digital shift, characterized in part by the continuous change and the dynamics of our digitally propelled world, seems to accelerate day by day. It is forcefully driven by the powerful undercurrent of exponentially growing complexity across technologies and data – technologies and data that can support deep profiling in part through the social behaviours of any of us as consumers, in terms of who we are, who we desire to be and have previously been. There seems to be no end to the detail that is represented in a constant flood of real-time data.
>
> 'Historically, and in contrast to these dynamics of real-time consumer data, brands have sought to represent characteristics that are relatively stable, simple and solid – a non-dynamic representation. According to AMA, the American Marketing Association, a brand is a "name, term, design, symbol or any other feature that identifies one seller's good or service as distinct from those of other sellers". Well, brands do actually change over time – read years. How to make "non-changes" changes to brands over time to demonstrate sturdiness and only make the "changes" necessary for the brand to actually remain "the same" in a changing environment has long been a separate art form.
>
> 'One of the big questions or dilemmas around brands today is how to find the best and most impactful connection between, or blend of, the dynamics of the constantly updated data around individual consumers and the historic sturdiness and relative stability around brands. Shining some light on this dilemma may reveal some important and key aspects of the impact of the digital shift on brands.
>
> 'First let's look at some of the most successful brands in our digital- and data-driven world – the American FAANG dynasty of Facebook, Apple, Amazon, Netflix and Google and let's add to these their Chinese cousins in the STAB dynasty of Sina, Tencent, Alibaba and Baidu, and also Uber, Airbnb and Tesla.

'These 12 corporations have over the past ten years gone through explosive developments. They have been developing, defining and redefining which business and even which industry each of them are operating in. They have defined and created new categories of industries, companies, products and services and they have developed and controlled new cross-industry platforms and ecosystems. All of these companies are deeply user- and consumer-centric. Driven and guided by the data they constantly collect, they exploit even the most unthinkable characteristics of their customers and their business partners. Yet all of these 12 corporations have managed to keep their company brand relatively stable. How did they do this, you may ask? Let me here focus on a couple of important elements of what these and numerous other successful companies are doing.

'Fundamental to their success is that the primary association of their company brand is with the purpose of the company, eg Google's company purpose is: "to organize the world's information and make it universally accessible and useful", expressing a strong focus on the customer experience independent of how this is delivered. The products, services, technologies and algorithms that Google at any time will use to deliver on their purpose have changed significantly over the years, but the company brand has remained stable. Similar examples may be given for the rest of the above-mentioned companies.

'In contrast to this are the brands of car companies such as BMW, known for its "ultimate driving experience", and Audi with its "Vorsprung durch Technik". These brands are, and have historically been, much more directly associated with the core products and have changed significantly over the years in line with their products changing. The digital shift is a fundamental challenge to the brand of these companies as they evolve from a product focus to serving as mobility operators with a focus on the convenience of mobility as a service.

'Even in these times of constant change, disruption and ambiguity, the purpose of the FAANG and STAB companies is unchanging – it's rock solid. How they actually achieve their purpose – or brand promise – through constantly adapting business models, services, products, people and processes is where the constant change and the dynamics play out, while keeping the brand itself stable. The digital shift is pushing the company brand, in the sea of change, to serve as an anchor, something that serves as a steady, firm point of reference in the middle of all the dynamic change that is taking place.

'As the tendency is to seek to keep the brand steady, we see the disruption and the continuous change playing out somewhere else – namely when it comes to how we play with the brand through our branding.

'Branding has never been more complex, difficult and dynamic as today. In the digital age the success of a company is directly linked to how customer-driven the company is and how successful the company is at constantly demonstrating this through its branding across the customer-driven products and services. Or in other words, how well the company is collecting and exploiting any relevant data about their customers and turning that into a trustworthy story of great customer focus, adaptation and experience.

'Data and data analytics are today the fundamental components of impactful branding – data-driven branding. This opens up a whole new discipline of branding, the AI-assisted branding. Our human-only creativity is absolutely still needed and important, but it is no longer sufficient on its own. Successful branding specialists now need to be augmented by AI and powerful data analytics in almost all aspects of their branding work. This means that to be truly successful in your branding you need constant, quality data updates about your customers and potential customers. Creative ideas and traditional branding skills are far from enough to keep on top of the game. There is a lot to unlearn, to learn and relearn about branding to master data-driven branding. This new game is just starting to become exciting and is for the most part still in its infant days.

'In brief, a couple of important aspects of the digital shift is to associate brand with the most stable characteristic of your company – your purpose – and to drive all aspects of your branding activities through all relevant and constantly updated data streams about your customers – their experiences and their behaviours – via every imaginary channel possible. This will support your brand and the branding of your company on its explorative and accelerating journey through and across countless products, services and other customer interactions over time – all on the journey towards serving the customer and creating the most sought-after customer experience.

EXTENDED CASE STUDY: MCDONALD'S MOVE INTO CHINA AND INDIA AND THE RESULTING LESSONS FOR SUCCESSFUL GLOBAL BRAND MANAGEMENT

McDonald's first launched home delivery of meals in Mumbai in 2004 and now has web-based delivery service in India. Its web-based delivery model is based on serving the customer quickly; the drive time must not exceed seven minutes because its food has to be eaten within ten minutes of preparation.

McDonald's fast-food restaurant is one of the largest restaurant chains globally. There are more than 32,000 McDonald's restaurants in 120 countries and about 80 per cent of these restaurants worldwide are owned and operated by independent franchisees. As a brand, they serve nearly 47 million customers each day.

The brand's core competency is in being able to provide convenience with fast, accurate service in clean, sanitary environments – an issue when McDonald's started, because many of their competitors then couldn't or wouldn't ensure it – when customers need and want to eat, all at competitive prices. As a result, they're perceived as providing strong value for money. As with virtually all successful brands, McDonald's offers consistency of quality in the production of food and use of all materials, globally.

They were guided by their brand mission 'to be our customers' favourite place and way to eat and drink.'[25] To achieve these goals, McDonald's focuses on putting into effect all five levers of marketing – People, Products, Place, Price and Promotion – which shapes their customers' experience.[26] Let's look at the specifics of these market introductions, starting with China.

Food, folks and fun in China

McDonald's entered the Chinese market in 1990,[27] a time when the concept and legal status of the franchise did not exist in China.[28] Its first restaurant was in the Shenzhen Special Economic Zone. More prominently, the world's largest McDonald's, with 700 seats, 29 cash registers and serving more than 40,000 customers on its first day, opened on April 23 1992 in Beijing.

In this once isolated nation, whose market only opened up to foreign commerce in around 1978,[29] McDonald's had to adapt its business model to a unique and ever-shifting commercial environment and make its products relevant to local tastes and lifestyles. At the time that McDonald's launched in China, it was already a mighty marketing-oriented organization, one that thoroughly understood the power of branding. As a company known for doing its homework, it had already identified the necessary components of a successful brand launch into a new market before deciding to tackle it. Segmentation was done according to age and life stage. McDonald's always considers children as a core customer, a group that is cultivated so that they maintain loyalty to the brand into their adult life. Children visiting the restaurants in China would often receive a balloon decorated with a McDonald's mark on it and a small gift. The traditional 'Ronald McDonald' was translated to become the 'Uncle McDonald's Club', and all children aged 3 to 12 could join. These 'brand grooming' activities were designed to win the young consumers' loyalty for McDonald's. It was a tactic that had worked in the US and in many other global locations.

Initially, McDonald's goal was to become the fast-food leader in China through American-styled beef hamburgers. Culturally, however, the Chinese preferred chicken products. McDonald's responded by launching a menu of chicken items. Suddenly, a brand known for its beef hamburger began to sell chicken hamburgers, a typical example of how brands must adapt to different markets with different consumer behaviours and preferences.

Customer behaviour is a very important element in branding strategy. The fast-food category assumes that a couple of main customer-behaviour patterns rule the market: convenience-oriented and relaxation-oriented. Convenience-oriented customers prefer McDonald's products for the convenience of purchase and eating in nearby locations, available parking and quick service. Relaxation-oriented customers like McDonald's because the chain locations are located in main shopping centres, allowing them to relax while shopping and kill time. For convenience shoppers, McDonald's activated the '59 seconds rapid service', which is the time span between making the order at the counter and the delivery of the prepared meal. The main guiding point is that the meal must be served within a minute. For the relaxation-oriented customer, McDonald's paid great attention to the interior decoration of the restaurants, making customers feel comfortable and relaxed in a place that projected a unique American culture.

The change in strategy helped McDonald's accelerate its development pace in the Chinese market. However, they did not achieve all of their initial goals. McDonald's runs one of the world's biggest franchise operations, but only 20 per cent of McDonald's restaurants in China were franchised by the end of 2014.[30] This is due to the fact that the franchise system was an unknown entity in China. The downside to franchising is losing control over certain things such as intellectual property, food sourcing and service quality. But analysts say that finding good local partners could help the brand revive in Asia quicker than McDonald's can do on its own.

Also, in another strategy adjustment, McDonald's changed its official business name in China towards the end of 2017, ditching Maidanglao, a Chinese rendering of its English name, in favour of Jingongmen, which roughly translates as 'Golden Arches'. On the face of it, the change fits with the McDonald's logo. But the switch isn't sitting well with some Chinese consumers, who have voiced their views on social media. China isn't the only global market where McDonald's uses the Golden Arches name. In the Philippines, the business is registered under the name 'Golden Arches Development Corporation'. Other Western brands have also used Chinese names in a bid to broaden their appeal with consumers in the country. For instance, Coca-Cola is known as Ke kou ke le, which translates as 'tasty and fun' and Google goes by Gu ge, or 'harvesting song'.[31]

Today, the restaurant chain has new issues to address in China. 'McDonald's is in trouble in China because it doesn't have the type of food or brand position that Chinese consumers want right now,' says Shaun Rein, founder of the China Market Research Group, pointing out growing competition from other Western brands like Starbucks, Japanese brands like Ajisen and homegrown Chinese brands like Kung Fu. 'In order to reinvigorate growth, it needs a new business model for the country,' says Rein. 'The best way to do that is to partner with folks who might know the China market a little better' and have more money to spend.[32]

Going vegetarian in India

Six years after McDonald's entered the Chinese market, the company expanded operations to India. The first McDonald's restaurant opened on October 13 1996, at Basant Lok in New Delhi. It was also the first McDonald's restaurant in the world not to serve beef- and pork-based products. The expansion was led by Amit Jatia. Since he was a vegetarian, he had never thought of trying such a place and had never even walked into a McDonald's until he was 14 when he was travelling outside India. He loved it.

Later, Amit moved to California for his studies and liked the American way of life. McDonald's approached him in 1994 and he never looked back. He is now the main franchise owner in India. It was not an easy journey, since the American brand featured a beefburger, something that is in complete contradiction to traditional Indian consumer behaviour. So, convincing his vegetarian family to invest in the business was an issue. As he told the BBC: 'From my family's point of view we thought through this carefully. What convinced us was that McDonald's was willing to localize. They promised that there would be no beef or pork on the menu.'[33]

This global brand features the Big Mac, a pure-beef product, as the company's signature product. India had to come up with its own signature product in order to launch a successful brand, despite its international standing and reputation. The new product: Chicken Maharajah Mac. Originally Amit was the local partner in the south and west of India, running the chain as a joint venture with the global McDonald's company. Later he bought out the McDonald's stake and now solely runs the chain in his territory.

During the years Amit Jatia has been involved with McDonald's, he has had to tackle many issues, primarily in the area of consumer behaviour and consumer attitudes towards the brand and its offerings. It hasn't been an easy journey. 'From a consumer point of view, I had to start with the message that a burger is a meal,' he says.

His research also showed that in 2003, of 100 meals that people ate in a month only three were eaten out. Having to convince people to enjoy a meal outside the house is a stumbling block for any fast-food operation. His solution was to invent a burger called Aloo Tikki Burger, a cutlet made of mashed potatoes, peas and flavoured with Indian spices. 'It's something you would find on Indian streets. It was essentially the McDonald's version of street food. The price and the taste together, the value we introduced, was a hit. It revolutionized the industry in India,' he says. As a result, eating out has gone up to 9 to 10 times per 100 meals and brought McDonald's in India to a level of entertaining over 320 million customers annually. The kind of customers McDonald's attracts in India is very different from other countries. There are still families with young children who frequent it. But diners also include many young people, aged between 19 and 30, with no kids. During the week, Amit says, this crowd dominates the restaurants.[34]

One of the main risks that a brand anywhere in the world faces is a potential dispute with a franchisee. This proved to be true of McDonald's in India during 2017. A long-drawn-out legal battle with one of its local joint venture (JV) partners of 22 years, Connaught Plaza Restaurants (CPRL), strained the company's business. On August 21 2017, the fast-food chain said it had issued a notice of termination on its franchise agreement with CPRL, which ran its outlets in north and east India, leaving the future of 169 of its outlets uncertain.[35] By the beginning of 2018, McDonald's had issued a warning to Indian consumers not to patronize these restaurants. The conflict concluded in 2019, when McDonald's bought out Vikram Bakshi's 50 per cent stake in their joint venture Connaught Plaza Restaurants Ltd (CPRL).[36] Although these issues are rare, multinational brands should be aware of the risks of leaving the fortune of the brand, including its reputation, in the hands of other business interests that may one day harm the master brand in general.

A new digital brand experience in Poland

During a recent trip that Ilan Geva took to participate in a conference in Lublin, Poland, he stopped at a local McDonald's on the main Warsaw–Lublin road. Suddenly, he was thrust into an experience he'd never had before at a fast-food outlet. First, the entire appearance of the establishment was more sophisticated and modern than a standard McDonald's. Whoever designed the store atmospherics made sure that it would communicate an upscale experience. It featured a slick, clean and uncluttered storefront while still sporting the brand colours and Golden Arches, a reassuring sign that indeed the place was an authentic McDonald's establishment.

Once inside, customers were greeted by a set of giant iPhone-inspired touch-screen ordering kiosks, allowing consumers to interact with the menu items and choose the combinations they wanted, offering a wide selection of different condiments and menu items that would not have been available in the past when ordering from a live person at the counter. Once an order was placed, payment was paid at the kiosk with a confirmation number, so the entire ordering process was completed without human intervention. Then the customer's number appeared on a screen when the order was ready to be picked up, making it a simple, efficient and precise process. Consumers picked up the order from a human being and went to sit in a spacious, well-lit, upscale restaurant setting – not a typical McDonald's ambiance.

This reimagined experience demonstrates that McDonald's is changing its brand positioning. Assuming that the consumer segmentation points to a younger overall target audience, it is clear why they might prefer to interact with a digital kiosk. The fact that this particular restaurant was in a petrol station on a main road suggests that the dining experience for travellers is an important ingredient of the brand and that it is paying attention to the needs of on-the-go customers who demand speedy, efficient service, without taking away from the pleasant experience that dining should be.

Some of these changes have started to take place in locations outside the US market during the last two years. We assume that these are test markets for the brand to see how to implement technology and digital store environments to enhance and in some cases replace, the human experience. No doubt these new-look restaurants will be expanded globally as McDonald's provides a needed 'face lift' to many older locations in America, Europe and elsewhere.

Other assorted brand lessons, rules and guidelines from McDonald's

Before McDonald's first engaged with the Indian and Chinese markets, they had already worked with about 40 different ad agencies in the US market. Some were in charge of the Adults' market, other in charge of the Kids' market. In addition, there were agencies specializing in reaching African American and Hispanic consumers. They also maintained contracts with sales promotion agencies, design agencies, PR agencies and others. Some of these agencies were 'national' and others were 'regional', representing the owner/operators (franchisees) of restaurants in geographic areas of the US. The main office was headquartered at Oakbrook, Illinois (they moved to downtown Chicago in 2018).

Agencies would line up every day to present their work to the relevant marketing executive in charge of their specific demographics and segmentation. Certain writing and style 'rules' were particularly important to ensure brand consistency. As a Creative Director in one of McDonald's regional ad agencies in the US, Ilan Geva had the privilege of learning from Steve Nubie, who was then a Marketing Department Creative Director at McDonald's. Ilan went through internal training to better understand the brand, its positioning and objectives. Here's a summary of Ilan's learning from Steve for TV spots:

- A BIG, SELLING IDEA;
- Brand IDENTIFICATION (key design elements and brand colours);
- A RELEVANT story to the lives of the audience;
- SENSITIVE casting (ie, present real people, not glamorous celebrity types);
- NATURAL DIALOGUE (just like ordinary people talking to each other);
- MUSIC (original, upbeat music written for the brand);
- Superior EDITING; and
- A MAGICAL MOMENT (Like Larry Bird playing against Michael Jordan for a Big Mac).

During this period, McDonald's also paid attention to the appearance of the food in their TV advertising. After all, appetizing food was at the core of their brand. Among the directions to keep the brand cohesive globally, McDonald's insisted that their food:

- be dynamic, not static (it should move and have a life of its own);
- look pretty (but not too much; we're not talking Michelin-starred restaurant here);
- be slightly imperfect (look real and convey that the food is homemade, not mass-produced);
- seem fresh (not taken from a deep freezer) and prepared for a specific customer;
- evoke the senses.

These 'rules' reflected a tremendous flair for understanding human nature, consumer behaviour and habits. In judging the ideas for proposed TV spots presented by the agencies, McDonald's developed a list of key triggers for making a choice.

During the 1990s, when McDonald's was expanding globally, TV advertising was still at its prime and was the main workhorse in promoting the brand all over the world. They insisted that all of their TV commercials had to feel 'real, relevant and respectful of the consumer (reflected in casting)'. They also needed to 'remain likeable (must not annoy over time)' as well as 'provide insight into human nature to evoke a "that's just like me!" response'.

The fact that McDonald's invested so much time in training the staff of many ad agencies shows that they really cared about their brand. Say what you want about them, they were amazing marketers (still are) and they knew exactly what to do and how much to invest in order to become the brand they are. The competition could only watch and try to catch up.

It is interesting to note, that during the years since these rules were drawn up by McDonald's, many other fast-food brands took notice and started following the same rules. Today, there is almost no difference between food shots of one fast-food company or another and rarely is there a difference in brand personality, giving a brand manager an opportunity to find something new and reset the category.

KEY TERMS

- AMA, the American Marketing Association
- Chief Information Security Officer (CISO)
- FAANG (Facebook, Apple, Amazon, Netflix and Google)
- General Data Protection Regulation (GDPR)
- STAB (Sina, Tencent, Alibaba and Baidu)
- product innovation

DISCUSSION QUESTIONS

- What are the opposing drives for innovation and brand consistency and why do they exist?
- In which ways do marketing technology help brand equity?
- In which ways do marketing technology hurt brand equity?
- What is programmatic and what is its impact on managing global brands?
- What role does effective cybersecurity play in protecting global brands?

Notes

1 Godin, S (2016) *Purple Cow*, Joosr Ltd, Hove

2 Trout, J (2006) Peter Drucker on marketing, *Forbes*, https://www.forbes.com/2006/06/30/jack-trout-on-marketing-cx_jt_0703drucker.html#5f165945555c (archived at https://perma.cc/X3LP-YF69)

3 Reichheld, F (2018) Loyalty-based management, *Harvard Business Review*, https://hbr.org/1993/03/loyalty-based-management (archived at https://perma.cc/R42C-MP4W)

4 Fabrikbrands.com (2018) Passion for the past: Nostalgia marketing and the retro revolution, http://fabrikbrands.com/nostalgia-marketing (archived at https://perma.cc/SDJ9-V9CJ)

5 Rosen, W and Minsky, L (2017) *The Activation Imperative*, 1st ed, Rowman & Littlefield, Lanham Maryland

6 Auletta, K (2018) *Frenemies: The epic disruption of the ad business (and everything else)*, Penguin, London

7 Jedrzejczak, A (2018) How a makeup mogul built a $1 billion business on Instagram, *Bloomberg*, https://www.bloomberg.com/news/articles/2018-08-22/how-huda-kattan-built-a-1-billion-beauty-business-on-instagram (archived at https://perma.cc/YT7B-5EHE)

8 Jedrzejczak, A (2018) How a makeup mogul built a $1 billion business on Instagram, *Bloomberg.com*, https://www.bloomberg.com/news/articles/2018-08-22/how-huda-kattan-built-a-1-billion-beauty-business-on-instagram (archived at https://perma.cc/YT7B-5EHE)

9 Ifeanyi, K C, (2018) How Huda Kattan built a multi-million-dollar beauty brand from a blog, *Fast Company*, https://www.fastcompany.com/90180015/how-huda-kattan-built-a-multi-million-dollar-beauty-brand-from-a-blog (archived at https://perma.cc/5X88-R9LK)

10 Lacy, L (2018) Google and Target issue the first voice-activated coupon for Google Assistant, *Adweek*, https://www.adweek.com/digital/google-and-target-issue-the-first-voice-activated-coupon-for-google-assistant (archived at https://perma.cc/868T-LY7F)

11 Coupland, D (2018) Why McLuhan's chilling vision still matters today, *The Guardian*, https://www.theguardian.com/commentisfree/2011/jul/20/marshall-mcluhan-chilling-vision (archived at https://perma.cc/6D6S-4UZF)

12 Dennis, S (2018) The ticking time bomb of e-commerce returns, *Forbes*, https://www.forbes.com/sites/stevendennis/2018/02/14/the-ticking-time-bomb-of-e-commerce-returns/#7b300dd04c7f (archived at https://perma.cc/L8JP-QWCG)

13 Levine, B, Phelan, R, Marvin, G, McGee, M, Infographics, Burka, K, Wright, T (2018) What is MarTech or Marketing Technology? *MarTech Today*, https://martechtoday.com/library/what-is-martech (archived at https://perma.cc/CC2A-SHDC)

14 Levine, B, Phelan, R, Marvin, G, McGee, M, Infographics, Burka, K, Wright, T (2018) What is MarTech or Marketing Technology? *MarTech Today*, https://martechtoday.com/library/what-is-martech (archived at https://perma.cc/CC2A-SHDC)

15 Minsky, L (2018) The intelligent way to prepare your sales team for AI adoption, *Salesforlife.com*, https://www.salesforlife.com/blog/the-intelligent-way-to-prepare-your-sales-team-for-ai-adoption (archived at https://perma.cc/7CMG-L7QS)

16 Auletta, K (2018) *Frenemies: The epic disruption of the ad business (and everything else)*, Penguin, London

17 Langewiesche, W (2018) The lessons of ValuJet 592, *The Atlantic*, https://www.theatlantic.com/magazine/archive/1998/03/the-lessons-of-valujet-592/306534 (archived at https://perma.cc/XB42-HVP4)

18 Minsky, L (2018) Good cybersecurity can be good marketing, *Harvard Business Review*, https://hbr.org/2016/09/good-cybersecurity-can-be-good-marketing (archived at https://perma.cc/R5WX-ZB22)

19 Minsky, L (2018) Good cybersecurity can be good marketing, *Harvard Business Review*, https://hbr.org/2016/09/good-cybersecurity-can-be-good-marketing (archived at https://perma.cc/R5WX-ZB22)

20 Minsky, L (2018) Good cybersecurity can be good marketing, Harvard Business Review, https://hbr.org/2016/09/good-cybersecurity-can-be-good-marketing (archived at https://perma.cc/R5WX-ZB22)

21 Rosen, W and Minsky, L (2017) *The Activation Imperative*, 1st ed, Rowman & Littlefield, Lanham, Maryland

22 Minsky, L and Quesenberry, KA (2018) Hunter or hunted? How digital media and GDPR increases importance of inbound B2B sales, *The European Business Review*, https://www.europeanbusinessreview.com/hunter-or-hunted-how-digital-media-and-gdpr-increases-importance-of-inbound-b2b-sales (archived at https://perma.cc/6JCC-T8V4)

23 Khanna, T, Palepu, K, and Sinha, J (2018) Strategies that fit emerging markets, *Harvard Business Review*, https://hbr.org/2005/06/strategies-that-fit-emerging-markets (archived at https://perma.cc/E3NQ-DHAG)

24 Wong, Q (2018) Fixing Facebook? Zuckerberg falls short of his New Year's goal, *c|net.com*, https://www.cnet.com/news/fixing-facebook-zuckerberg-falls-short-of-his-new-years-goal (archived at https://perma.cc/3XPJ-SZTN)

25 Meyer, P (2018; updated 2019), McDonald's mission statement and vision statement (an analysis), Panmore Institute, http://panmore.com/mcdonalds-vision-statement-mission-statement-analysis (archived at https://perma.cc/78HS-Z9EZ)

26 Jurevicius, O (2013) Mission statement of McDonald's, *Strategic Management Insight*, https://www.strategicmanagementinsight.com/mission-statements/mcdonalds-mission-statement.html (archived at https://perma.cc/YCM5-STHX)

27 Dondon, R, Timeline (2017) In the 1990s, McDonald's fought the Chinese Communist Party… and won, https://timeline.com/china-mcdonalds-food-history-95cd7e2d1fb9 (archived at https://perma.cc/5H68-SCXT)

28 *Financial Times* (2018) McDonald's and its challenges worldwide: a market-by-market look, https://www.ft.com/content/f8ac22fc-a7c1-11e4-8e78-00144feab7de (archived at https://perma.cc/YDP8-679J)

29 Yaleglobal.yale.edu (2018) China joins the Global economy – Part One, *YaleGlobal*, https://yaleglobal.yale.edu/content/china-joins-global-economy-part-one (archived at https://perma.cc/T5WT-JN5Q)

30 Burkitt, L, (2015) McDonald's aims to sell Taiwan stores, expand China franchise business, *The Wall Street Journal*, https://www.wsj.com/articles/mcdonalds-aims-to-sell-taiwan-stores-expand-china-franchise-business-1435219854 (archived at https://perma.cc/Y34U-3HWN)

31 Wang, D (2018) McDonald's puzzles Chinese customers with name change, *CNNMoney*, https://money.cnn.com/2017/10/26/news/companies/mcdonalds-china-name-change/index.html (archived at https://perma.cc/C2KQ-UA8G)

32 Horwitz, J, *Quartz* (2016) McDonald's plans to revive its brand in China by getting out of the restaurant business, https://qz.com/713411/mcdonalds-plans-to-revive-its-brand-in-china-by-getting-out-of-the-restaurant-business (archived at https://perma.cc/K7M3-MNH2)

33 Kannan, S (2014) How McDonald's conquered India, *BBC News*, http://www.bbc.com/news/business-30115555 (archived at https://perma.cc/GL4P-VU4Y)

34 Kannan, S (2014) How McDonald's conquered India, *BBC News*, http://www.bbc.com/news/business-30115555 (archived at https://perma.cc/GL4P-VU4Y)

35 Tandon, S (2017) Want to know why McDonald's may shut down in half of India? Ask its first Indian business partner, *Quartz India*, https://qz.com/1058465/want-to-know-why-mcdonalds-may-shut-down-in-half-of-india-ask-its-first-indian-business-partner (archived at https://perma.cc/X24L-DSJ2)

36 Tandon, S (2019) McDonald's buys out Vikram Bakshi; temporarily shuts over 160 outlets, *LiveMint*, https://www.livemint.com/companies/news/mcdonald-s-buys-out-vikram-bakshi-ends-six-year-long-dispute-1557429965862.html (archived at https://perma.cc/YH4N-3QVL)

PART TWO

Practical and tactical applications

05

Brand foundational development

READING OUTCOMES

At the conclusion of this chapter, you should be able to:

- describe the typical brand life cycle of launch, adoption, maturity and decline or rebranding;
- understand the elements of and the process for developing a comprehensive brand foundation;
- define and explain the key concepts of 'brand essence', 'brand promise', 'brand positioning' and more
- recognize brand pyramids, onions and keys, message maps and other brand management tools;
- communicate the importance of brand research for ensuring consumer resonance and validation.

Introduction

'Branding' can seem like a very simple process now that technology makes it so quick and easy to create logos, select fonts, refine photos, develop content and other visible elements of a brand foundation. As a result, those outside professional marketing and branding circles may assume that the brand-development process requires little time and cost and that the branding elements can be ready to implement immediately – and they want it immediately. In addition, many people who start businesses try to do it themselves without professional help or do it cheaply by choosing the lowest-priced offer. Once a product or service is ready, business owners and many CEOs and CMOs are eager to get going and recoup their development costs. Many entrepreneurs with more of an engineering or tech background might not even understand the need for a brand-development process.

The problem? Customers will assign a personality, values, positioning, associations and more to your product or services based on the visual and verbal cues you give them in your product design, brand experience, packaging, advertising and more. So, you will have a brand no matter what; it just might not be an advantageous one and it could even be one that suppresses sales and profits.[1]

What's missing from this 'hurry up' approach is all of the thinking and decisions that should inform the development of the logo, colour choices, the image style (and whether it should even be a photograph or illustration), tone of voice and, most of all, the brand actions. The goal of a brand-development process is to bring alignment to all of the elements and give the brand room to accommodate and be relevant to various audiences and situations, but still consistent enough to be seen as coherent and believable.

The good news is that developing a brand foundation – its DNA – is not as hard as it looks. There's a simple process for thinking it through and there are tools to help you organize the elements. But it does take time, discipline and attention to detail. In addition, there are just a few foundational elements that need to be determined. So, if you only have a product or service – or are in the process of creating one – but have not given much thought to your brand, read on and learn how to avoid the peril of launching a new product without properly thinking through the brand foundation.

Overview

What is brand development, brand positioning and brand essence, mission or purpose? And what is value proposition and a comprehensive brand foundation? Who among the various audiences come first and why is it necessary for the marketer to pay attention to them? Why do we need to go through all these time-consuming phases when we launch a brand or try to revitalize a dormant one? We'll answer these questions in this chapter, starting with the common life cycle of a brand. We'll then go into the various ways of organizing the brand's foundational elements as well as defining these elements. We will also look at the types of research that marketers can conduct to provide feedback on all of the decisions made during the brand-foundational-development process. To conclude, Ashley Galina Dubarenok, an expert on marketing in China, provides her perspective on how international brands can succeed there, and we present a case study on Coca-Cola in Israel.

Welcome to the never-ending brand-development process

Product development always starts with ideation, the process of generating new ideas. It can take place among new, inexperienced entrepreneurs or within existing organizations. Depending on the nature of the product or service, a significant amount of money could be spent on Research and Development (R&D). All this effort and investment, however, can be wasted if budgeting doesn't include the next crucial phase, brand development. In fact, brand development requires the same level of attention as R&D.

Often, however, products and services are developed without determining the desired brand image and might even be initially successful for purely functional reasons, eg offering clear competitive advantages such as being noticeably easier to use or operate or cheaper to obtain. When this happens, the brand still develops an image, but it just might not be an image that positions the brand for the long term, protects profit margins, ensures against potential business missteps, or offers other benefits marketers enjoy through maintaining strong brands. A good way to understand the perils is to look at the typical life cycle of products or services, which go through four stages: introduction, growth, maturity and eventual decline – unless the brand is continually tweaked, pruned and imperceptibly updated on a regular basis. Even then, some brands wither away because of shifts in culture, consumer perceptions and needs.

The very first phase is the actual development of a brand. It should be concurrent with the product or service developmental process, starting with the idea. It might be for something completely fresh or some improvement in an existing product or service. Once the new product idea seems to be a good one, ideally validated through research or testing, brand-foundational development should begin. The first step is a thorough examination of the marketplace to understand where the new brand will fit and be placed. Some key questions to ask are:

- What consumer value will it deliver?
- Who will find it appealing?
- Will it be a brand that people 'need' or one they just 'want'?
- How will it be different from and similar to already existing brands?
- How will it be priced?

Your decisions will impact the entire life of the brand and all of them are strategic in nature. This kind of analysis will have to be conducted in every country where the organization expects to market the brand.

After the market has been examined, opportunities are identified and the intended audience is fully understood, it's time to craft a distinct positioning for the brand, making sure it has a chance to stand out in a market of parities. In other words, a brand must stand for something. So, what is positioning? It's a term with multiple meanings and definitions, which can vary depending on who you ask within marketing. A good place to start for a solid one is with Ries and Trout's classic definition of it from the 1970s: the product's 'position is in the prospect's mind.'[2] This definition is slightly dated because it assumes that a brand's position actually resides in a specific place within the brain, like a slot within a computer, when memory, as we now know, is actually a construction of associations assembled by synapses firing throughout the brain.[3] According to Ries and Trout, product positioning in packaged goods was the product 'form', packaging and more – in other words, as John P Maggard pointed out, the differentiating factors for the product.[4]

Even as far back as the 1960s, advertising icons inherently understood positioning and started to deliver communication to customers, expressing the positioning for their products and brands. Bill Bernbach, the founder of DDB, used to say: 'If you stand for something, you will always find some people for you and some against you. If you stand for nothing, you will find nobody against you, and nobody for you.'[5]

Since every definition of positioning seems to boil down to how the product or service differentiates itself from the competition, we take the classic approach that there are four main positions: leader, anti, niche and starting a new subcategory.[6] Being able to claim the leadership position is best, but every leader needs a clear rival. Think Coke and Pepsi; Microsoft and Apple; McDonald's and Burger King. Brands that own a position between the leader and the rival often get overlooked but can 'own' a niche and develop a loyal following among a select group of consumers. If your brand can't be the leadership or rival or have a niche that attracts a select few, create a difference in your product or services – it might not even be a functional or financial benefit – and start a subcategory you can own. This is the key point of the best-selling book *Blue Ocean Strategy*.[7] The authors say: while everyone within a category is fighting amongst themselves, creating a bloody red ocean, make a change so you can own something new. One key example they give is Cirque du Soleil. This highly successful brand eliminated two of the three 'rings' out of traditional circus, creating a one-ring circus within a nicer environment; they were able to own the new category and charge a higher price for the tickets as well.

It's also important to note that the product form and brand positioning are not the same and, in fact, a company can offer two different brands (or more), each brand with its own unique positioning, but with the same product form. Nestlé, for example, markets Nestlé Extrême, a premium ice cream in a waffle cone, in some countries and Nestlé Drumstick, which has the same form – ice cream served in a waffle cone – but is positioned for the masses, in others.

Whichever position your brand takes, your positioning claim should be in relation to the other products or services within your category. While the economy on a macro-economic level – GDP growth – is ever expanding[8] on a micro-level, marketing is a zero-sum phenomenon.[9] To get people to buy one thing, they must give up something else. People aren't going to eat two full dinners in a single night just because two restaurant brands advertised or developed attractive promotional offers. Except for the top 2 per cent or so, people aren't going to need to furnish more than one home. So, marketing's ultimate goal is to get people to select their brand over the other options and branding's goal is to make that selection choice easier, even automatic.

The power of positioning is simple: it can make similar-functioning products feel different. The tools of delivering the message aren't important, whether it's social media or old-fashioned newspaper ad – but the product or brand position – its promise – must be clearly different from its competitors in a meaningful way. One of the most famous positionings of a brand was David Ogilvy's decision to call Dove soap a 'beauty bar' for women with dry skin. Obviously, the soap could be used for a multitude of purposes, but the clear positioning, differentiating Dove from other soap brands, was extremely refreshing and successful. It not only related to the functional benefits, but also to the aspirational and emotional benefits of the target audience.

A good way to develop a positioning statement is to start by identifying the audience segment, then describing the product or services and its key difference or promise. You should then identify the competing brands and their main promises.[10] Finally, you should identify why your difference is important to your key prospects.[11] If the difference doesn't offer a significant benefit to your prospects that they find appealing, you should start over with the statement and you could even change your product to include one.

Overall, the brand's positioning should be consistent from country to country. However, the direct and indirect competitors may change to account for regional and local brands, so some adjustments to the positioning might be needed to take this into account. In addition, when the brand represents a cultural or behavioural aspect of its country of origin, it can also take the positioning of providing a more authentic taste or experience and be seen as more of a premium brand in the exported markets.[12]

During the product-development stage, other very important considerations are the manufacturing location, production processes, material and component choices (key cues for quality level), assembly requirements, distribution methods, shipping methods and costs to the various channels, pricing (also cues for quality and exclusivity) and trade participation, as well as other key choices in the classic four Ps of marketing (product, placement, price and promotion).

Selecting a brand name or would Apple have been Apple with a different name

When Steve Jobs and Steve Wozniak started Apple, they didn't actually have a name, a strategy or even a vision for the brand. Walter Isaacson in his biography of Steve Jobs, wrote that Jobs, a 'fruitarian' – someone who primarily or only eats fruits, nuts and seeds – had just come back from an apple farm and thought the name sounded 'fun, spirited and not intimidating'.[13] Some also claim that he also admired and was inspired by Apple Records Company, which was owned by the Beatles.[14]

Conversely, when Phil Knight founded Blue Ribbon Sports, he didn't plan on changing its name to Nike.[15] But on May 30 1971, the company adapted the new name and the 'swoosh' as its official logo.[16] Carolyn Davidson, a student at Portland

State University, created the logo for $35, while attempting to convey movement and speed in its design. The name Nike (Greek goddess of victory) and the swoosh logo were not liked by Phil Knight and his partners, but they had delivery deadlines for a new shoe line, and they just had to go forwards.[17] They never looked back.

What could be learned from these stories? It's not the name or the logo or personal preferences of the company's leaders that create a successful brand. Rather, it's the exceptional satisfactory delivery of its products and services to consumers that truly counts. Nothing matches the customer experience and the consistency of delivering that experience for as long as possible. Changes to a brand should always be aimed 'upwards', and should not involve making compromises, shortcuts or savings on the assumption that customers won't notice inferior delivery or product performance.

Launching a new brand

Depending on the product or service, the introduction of a new brand will have a very different character and performance. If the product or service is completely innovative, a new invention or in a new category, the level of acceptance among customers can be quite low. Only innovators and people seeking new experiences will adopt it and they tend to constitute no more than 2.5 per cent of any given population.[18]

When it comes to launching a new brand, many brand managers consider the introduction phase the most critical in creating awareness and interest in the new product. This is also the time to make sure that all the introductory messages convey the brand purpose, character and positioning (explored more fully below) in order to create a clear difference from the competition. Chances are that this is the time during which the majority of the advertising budget will be spent. It makes sense, because the introduction phase will determine the future of the brand for the long run. A brand introduction can take a fairly short time, owing to new technology and social-media influence. Likewise, if there is no quick momentum, the brand can disappear within a few months.[19] Brand managers might want to start with launching in just one country, or even a region within a country, before expanding globally to ensure focused efforts.

A good place to start with launching a brand is the AIDA model (Attention, Interest, Desire, Action), although some consider it to be out-of-date,[20] because it emphasizes one-way communication rather than two-way communications enabled by mobile, social and other technology and it does not account for the often illogical approach to decision-making that people use, ie adopting mental shortcuts and rules to conserve mental energy.[21] In the AIDA model, which was first developed for direct-selling presentations, the time allotted to each phase is getting shorter as one goes through each one.[22] It can be helpful, however, because it reminds marketers that some level of disruption or surprise is often needed to get consumers to notice and expend the extra energy to logically and rationally try something new. Specifically, the steps of AIDA are:

- **Attention**
    - Convey something provocative or surprising that makes prospects stop and think, so they become aware of the new brand, product, service or category.
- **Interest**
    - Increase consumer interest by exposing the brand benefits, advantages and lifestyle promise of the new brand.
- **Desire**
    - Develop a favourable consumer disposition towards the new product or service, including a 'need' or 'want' of the brand.
- **Action**
    - Encourage engagement, trial and the purchase of the new product or service, which can lead to loyalty.[23]

In many ways, AIDA is the 'anti-brand', because brands facilitate decision-making short-cuts. As Nobel Prize-winning economist Daniel Kahneman described in *Thinking, Fast and Slow*, people have two systems metaphorically speaking – fast thinking and slow thinking.[24] Fast thinking is intuitive, requiring very little energy. Meanwhile, slow thinking is deliberative and rational. Our brain's default goal is to conserve energy, driving us to rely on habits, until something interrupts it. This kind of decision-making without thinking is the realm of branding. AIDA, on the other hand, requires that the prospect's brain expends energy – attention is the instigator of the brain powering up. Therefore, the AIDA model is good for selling situations requiring deliberate, rational thought, which can be effective in driving some changes in behaviour, but not all. Often, it's more effective to get people to just act on something, however irrationally and then define the experience through brand messaging. As we mentioned earlier, action drives a change in beliefs faster and more assuredly than beliefs drive behaviour change.[25]

Another way to think about it is that while many decisions are anchored in rational thinking and are sequential in nature, many are not. People often develop emotional connections to their favourite brands and many unconsciously consider their brand choices as a reflection of their self-concept. There are also deeper psychological brand connections that go back to childhood experiences and habits. Emotional branding is irrational, and to be effective the marketer must peel away the consumer's defence mechanisms.

Growing a brand after the launch

Once early adopters get word of a new product, service or trend, they begin experimenting with it. That small number of first customers can open the floodgates. Following that early period, and if the brand is satisfying certain portions of the

FIGURE 5.1 The arc of the brand life cycle

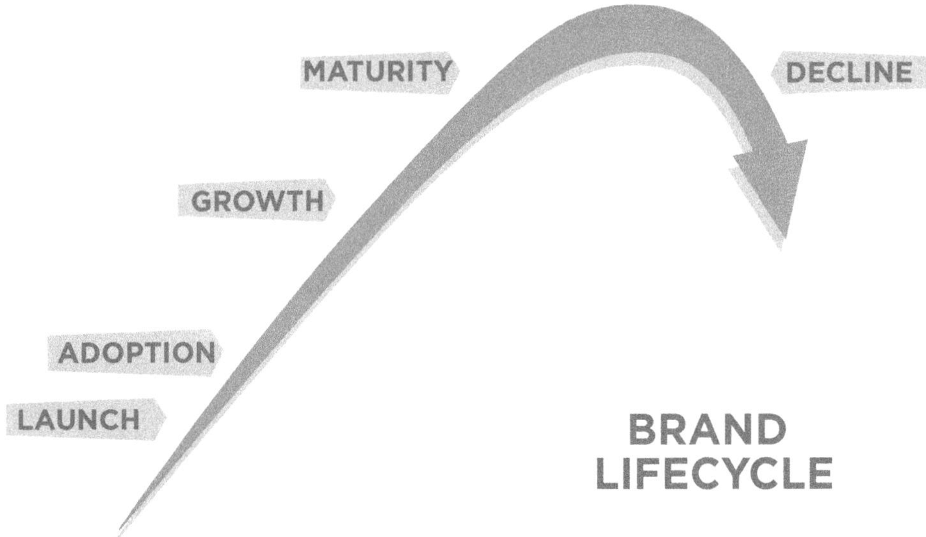

Brands, like all living things, are born and die – some brands just 'live' longer than others, because they're better nurtured.

market, it enters the growth stage and sales start increasing in significant numbers. Favourable word-of-mouth and consumer reviews are very important here.

Growth is a very crucial stage, where the entire supply chain and distribution channels are put into test. Brand managers may want to increase distribution during the growth stage to further enhance sales and make sure that supply meets demand. The growth stage is also a great period for enhancing product attributes, following the responses of the early adopters. Great sensitivity to consumer needs at this point can go a long way to securing the long-term health of the brand.

During the growth stage, brands should pay close attention to fulfilling the brand promise, being aware of and responding to any consumer feedback and satisfying the trade and supply channels. As a result, the marketer will create a complete brand ecosystem that will support it for many years to come. In addition, keen attention should also be paid to quick imitators and 'me too' products and services based on the brand success that can mushroom during the growth period. Obviously, marketing indicators such as price, place, promotion and product are now in play and the focus begins to shift from product development to brand management.

It is reasonable to assume that while the new brand is becoming known and shows signs of early success, competitors can pop up. As they enter the market during the growth stage, the 'defending brand' can expect improvements and new features coming into the market in order to steal customers. All of the activity expands the market size, the number of distributors and points of sale, but it can also take market share from the brand. To combat competitors, the brand must increase its promotional activity and along with it, the marketing budget. While creating awareness and preference is not over yet, the new brand should now be investing in defence as well as offence. While making these investments, marketers should:

- Never compromise the quality of the product, service or brand, or sacrifice the integrity of the brand foundational elements to drive sales in response to competitors.
- Avoid adding new features, sub-brands and brand extensions in response to competitive actions; rather, marketers should hold them back until brand habits and image have been fully established.
- Shift advertising and marketing activities from awareness-building and trial-driving to brand loyalty and repeat purchases.
- Expand into countries that have similar markets, opportunities and culture, as well as easy ability to build the infrastructure, before venturing into other markets.

Reaching the brand's maturity stage

Most of the brands that we use today are already in the maturity stage. It might even be hard to believe, as mentioned earlier, but many of the brands that we use every day are older than us. During the maturity stage, brands often develop sub-brands and brand extensions in order to remain relevant to their current customers and add value to the product, as well as to respond to changing tastes and niche competitors.[26] Brands, and especially brand managers, should become obsessive with market share and consumer mind share throughout the maturity stage of their brand's life. Collecting data is easier today, but it is crucial to understand how to use it for building and protecting brands.

The potential long life of a brand can lead to changes forced by outside influences such as the economy, consumer behaviour, technological advancements and overall trends. Brands might also need to act to respond to the competition catching up with them, which doesn't take much time these days, because the ability to imitate or copy the successful aspects of another brand is easy. (The one thing that can't be copied is the distinctive brand foundational elements.)

Since we aim to build brands that last once they reach the maturity stage, it is assumed that they could live for a long time. Certainly, longer than at all the previous stages. As a matter of fact, most brand managers will manage brands in the maturity stage. Many brand managers spend most of their careers maintaining their brands, fending off competitors and keeping an eye on inventories, distribution and profit margins. The real 'branding' assignments here are typically associated with external aspects, such as advertising, but will be less urgent, which could lead to complacency.

During the brand's maturity stage, the brand manager should continually evaluate its condition by conducting an annual brand audit, including a thorough inspection of the product itself, the consumers, the competition and the market environment. The product and service details to be inspected should include the functional and emotional benefits; the product attributes; brand ingredients (including ingredient brands); the product and packaging design, accumulated history and heritage; and successes and failures of marketing activities. Brand managers should understand the balance between the heavy users, light users, current and past users, their attitude towards the brand, their lifestyles and, in the case of brands that cross borders, changing needs and trends throughout the globe. Competitive details that should be examined include a confirmation of the direct competitors versus the indirect ones; their strengths and weaknesses; their brand promises and delivery, as well as their market share and influence. The market environment details should include a review of the social, economic, political, cultural and technological aspects affecting the brand in each country it operates. Any changes and how they could affect the brand should be noted and acted upon. The most important thing for brand managers during the maturity stage, however, is not to feel comfortable, because comfort can lead to the next stage: brand decline.

The eventual, but not inevitable, decline of a brand

At any given moment, a brand can start to experience a decline in sales, but sales are not the only reason for brand decline. Neglecting certain business aspects can drag an organization into cutting corners, and that can influence the quality of the brand and hurt its basic promise to the consumer. Usually, when brands are introduced, the novelty, media exposure and good PR can lead to curiosity and a corresponding increase in sales. Once brands get into the routine of being accepted by specific segments of consumers, however, those people might find a 'new and improved' version of the product or service and abandon the original one. Some brands decline because shareholders demand increased profits that result in trimming budgets for marketing, research, brand audits, distribution and much else. Each cut can contribute to eventual decline.

The decline can be faster, or it can be a slow and agonizing death spiral that will eventually lead to the termination of the brand. The US car brand Oldsmobile was an example of a slow brand death, and despite large spending in advertising, the brand managers at General Motors and the ad agency at the time failed to observe that Oldsmobile was no longer relevant to the American buyer. The famous last brand positioning statement, 'It is not your father's Oldsmobile' failed to see the consumer reaction which was 'Yeah, my father's Oldsmobile was better.'[27] Dead brands in the restaurant industry include once booming chains such as Chi-Chi's, Lun's, Steak & Ale and Burger Chef. As of writing, we witness the rapid decline of Sears, which was essentially the Amazon of the 20th century.

A brand may also decline at different rates within different countries, depending on the competition. In fact, brands that disappear globally might have regional pockets or even a country or two where the brand lingers. For example, one of the leading bookstore chains in the world, Borders, which had 19,500 employees in 2010, went out of business in most countries in 2011,[28] but not all. We recently spotted a Borders store still in operation in a hospital shopping mall in Malaysia and there might well be other pockets in the world where a store or two exists, but as a global brand, it has gone. Blockbuster, once the leading video-rental chain in the US, filed for bankruptcy and started closing stores in 2010, but a small handful of final locations – mostly in the wifi-poor state of Alaska – didn't close until 2018. As of writing, there is only one remaining Blockbuster store, which is in Bend, Oregon.[29]

Some brands can be saved once they start to decline. Brand managers should conduct thorough market research to identify the reasons for the decline, which could also reveal that a simple solution might help. A new packaging design, for instance, saved a toothpaste brand and increased the sales by 30 per cent.[30] In most cases, however, the efforts put into saving a brand should be holistic and not just result in a new ad campaign.

Brands could also decline because the actual product category, not the brand, becomes obsolete through technological advances or shifts in consumer tastes. Examples include the Sony Walkman as well as VHS and beta tapes. Sales may plunge to zero or they may drop to a low level where they continue for many years. As mentioned in the previous section, a brand audit could be useful for brand managers at this stage as well.

Breck Shampoo is a classic example of a declining brand. In 1930, Dr John H Breck, Sr founded the brand. His brand insight was that 'every woman is different'. Breck advertisements regularly appeared in magazines such as *Ladies' Home Journal*, *Woman's Home Companion*, *Seventeen*, *Vogue*, *Glamor* and *Harper's Bazaar*. They were most often on the magazine's back cover. The models chosen to represent the brand were known as 'Breck Girls'. During these years, Breck Girls were identified through the company's sponsorship of America's Junior Miss contests and, among them, were the names of prominent models and actresses such as Kim Basinger, Patti Boyd, Christie Brinkley, Farrah Fawcett, Cybill Shepard, Jaclyn Smith, Brooke Shields and Cheryl Tiegs. The brand shot to a commanding position in the US shampoo market and the Breck Girls ads are now in the advertising history records in the Smithsonian National Museum of American History.

In 1990, Breck was sold to the Dial Corporation; in 2001, Dial licensed Breck to The Himmel Group and in 2006 it was licensed to Dollar Tree. Dial continues to market Breck shampoo in the institutional market, but not as a fast-moving packaged good. Breck lost its leading position to many other competing shampoo brands and ended up in the bottom shelves of supermarkets and pharmacies and certain Dollar Stores, [31] a sign of its reduced status.

When faced with a situation such as this, companies must decide whether to maintain, harvest or drop the brand. If they decide to maintain it, they can reposition it and allocate an additional marketing budget, so they can aggressively promote it. They may decide to harvest the brand, by reducing costs such as R&D, advertising, capital costs and human resources, with the goal of 'milking' the profits from any of the sales they realize. While some companies aim to 'milk' the profits from their declining brands, it can also be a costly proposition. In addition to suffering monetary declines, there is also the stigma of maintaining an unsuccessful brand, which can prompt investors to sell their shares in the enterprise, resulting in serious financial peril. Finally, the organization might decide to drop the brand or sell it, relegating the name and logo to clickbait listicles on social media of failed brands from one's youth that might be remembered.

An overview of brand foundational elements

The brand foundational elements – its DNA – should be consistent across the globe but should be broad enough to allow it to 'flex' from one country to the next. Every executional decision needs to align and support the DNA. If the brand's foundational elements do not work in a specific country, but the product or services can still be sold there, a different product name with a separate set of foundational elements should be considered.

The first foundational element of the brand's DNA is the positioning, although specific competitors may vary. In addition, as noted earlier, the positioning can be elevated, increasing its claim of offering a 'premium' in the exported country in certain situations, such as when it represents a cultural experience related to the country of origin or when the original country is known for providing 'better-quality' products than the other market or markets. Product examples include Swiss watches, Swiss or Belgian chocolate, Italian dried pasta, French wine and German engineered machines such as cars.

The next key foundational element is the brand essence (some call it brand promise), which is the 'soul' of the brand. Unlike an explicit functional promise, which would deliver tangible rewards, the brand essence delivers behavioural cues as well as emotional rewards. It has no smell, physical presence, taste, colour, texture or sound. It's the key idea. The brand essence appeals to our feelings and connects with us on many subliminal levels. The brand essence is what we want shoppers and users to believe about the brand. While products can be easily copied, it's hard to copy a brand essence. Each brand essence in a category should be clearly unique and ownable. As a result, it becomes the ultimate differentiator.

There are many ways to think about the brand essence – it can range from one word such as 'safety' for Volvo to two or three words or a complete sentence. We've even seen long brand-essence statements. All can work. We recommend, however, that the core brand-essence statement be reduced to just two words. Some examples: 'servant leader' for Walmart; 'affordable style' for Target; 'stay alive' for Orangina; and 'ridiculous masculinity' for Old Spice. Many brands have an essence that consumers take for granted because it is consistently delivered without compromise. From years of exposure to the brands, people automatically think of Disney as 'family magic', Apple as 'easy technology' and BMW as 'ultimate driving'.

By cutting the statement down to two words, marketers set the boundaries for the brand's behaviour, enabling situational flexibility while ensuring a consistent space for the brand to operate in. Often oxymoronic – people don't often associate 'affordability' and 'style' or 'easy' and 'new technology' per the examples above – the brand essence can serve as the 'screen' for making business decisions and guide the development of its activation programmes and communications. Products and marketing programmes must either emphasize one of the words or both. For instance, consider Nike. The long-time creative leader on the Nike account at Wieden + Kennedy is Susan Hoffman – she defines the brand essence as 'performance sport'. The messaging can celebrate 'the athlete within you'[32] (performance), the sport itself (usually by recognizing the athletes and their attitudes) or a combination of the two. But it also serves as a guide for other decisions. For instance:

> 'When they started doing sunglasses, I wondered how that fitted the brand. But if you think about it, you need good equipment – shoes, glasses, hat or gloves – whether you are a runner or a skier. On the other hand, Nike lost their focus when they had a jewellery line. That was years ago, and it was a total mistake. Some guy had designed all this jewellery, and Nike got all excited. But if you define the brand as 'performance sport', whether it's in their communication or in their product, it's clear what works and what doesn't: jewellery doesn't, sunglasses do.'[33]

Other brand foundational elements that need to be determined are the mission (typically needed for services) or purpose (typically required for packaged and durable goods) and the vision. 'Think of mission as your internal motivation beyond money, just as a missionary is set on some goal – to wipe out disease; empower humanity in some new way; create happiness or some other emotion – and the vision as where you want to go or what you want to be as a brand.'[34] As with the brand essence, some brands use different models for mission and vision, essentially reversing our recommendation by having the mission be the end state and the vision be some internal motivational phrase. We find that our version is easier to use, because of the relationship between mission and missionary as well as between vision and seeing the future. Ultimately, which version you select doesn't matter, as long as it provides direction and is motivating to all of the internal stakeholders.

Some believe that packaged goods and durables can't have a mission, because they are inanimate objects. However, the people creating the products can have a mission such as putting a computer on every desk by making it affordable for people living in impoverished countries.[35] As far back as 1960, leaders of great organizations understood the power of having a purpose for starting a business and leading a mission-driven organization. For instance, in a speech that David Packard, a founder of Hewlett Packard, gave to his employees, he said: 'I want to discuss why a company exists in the first place. In other words, why are we here? I think many people assume, wrongly, that a company exists simply to make money.'[36] Packard understood that every company and every brand should have a reason for being and a purpose for starting its life beyond merely making money. Indeed, he believed that a new brand should solve a problem and improve life. A brand's *raison d'être* should enable it to exist for many years to come, long after the founders and originators have passed on and left the brand for other like-minded people to carry the torch. Without it, the brand could turn into another mere commodity. If the purpose statement is the 'why' of the brand, the vision is the ultimate outcome.

The phrases of a brand's mission statement should be short, clear, motivating, directional and unique to the category and brand. If you need to explain the phrase, create a sub-point. For instance, state, 'Our mission is to: [drop in the short phrase]. The brand will achieve our mission by [drop in the explanation].'[37] We recommend the same structure for constructing a vision statement. However, we also think that this recent vision statement, called Vision 2020, works: 'No one should be killed or seriously injured in a new Volvo car,'[38] reaffirming a focus on enhancing automotive safety that dates back to the founding of the company in 1927.[39]

The brand foundation should also define the product's or service's personality or brand character, tonality, manner and range of expression, 'so the team can get a sense of how the brand should behave.'[40] It isn't enough to focus only on product attributes, it is imperative to think of brand personality and character, one of the few attributes that can't be copied by the competitors. Use words like 'funny', 'sarcastic', 'irreverent', 'brave', 'caring', 'upbeat', 'energetic', 'approachable' – the same words that you would use to describe the personality of an individual. We recommend selecting from three to five words for the personality statement. You should ensure that these descriptions are appropriate to the category (you wouldn't really talk of a funny perfume, for example) as well as unique within it.

When developing the personality statement, special attention should be given to the touchpoint wheel before, during and after purchase to help determine the specific brand behaviours at these points. Like a person adjusting how he or she talks depending on the situation and audience(s), brands can do the same. The emphasis can also change depending on the culture of a particular market. For instance, with a brand that is both 'caring' and 'slightly irreverent', the brand's emphasis can be on 'caring' with slight undertones of 'irreverence' in one market and 'slightly irreverent' with just a hint at its 'caring' approach in another market. With three to five words in the personality statements, one or two can even be completely underplayed or overplayed in a selected country to better appeal to its local culture. What brands shouldn't do, however, is invent new personalities for different countries, so the overall personality becomes incoherent. Rather, it should be one character, just slightly adjusted for the needs of a particular country.

Finally, the brand's values should always be clear to consumers. There are many values appreciated by most people. As they appreciate them in humans, so they look for them in brands. Values are society's constructs about what is worth pursuing and, more importantly, how those pursuits should be conducted.[41] If humans value honesty, a dishonest brand will never resonate with them. A fundamental list of 'values' might be very different in various parts of the globe. Western values often focus on individualism and materialism, while in Eastern cultures, collectivism, harmony, tradition, hierarchy, particularism and consensus tend to be highly valued.[42] Like the personality statement, the brand values should be globally consistent in every market, although the difference may create completely different brands, and those may offer different qualities, functions and emotional connections to the consumer.

Finally, a newer method of product and brand development is utilizing crowd sourcing from many different outside resources to generate the options and identify what consumers find appealing.

Pyramids, onions, keys, ladders and maps – tools for displaying the brand foundations

FIGURE 5.2 Organizing brand foundational elements

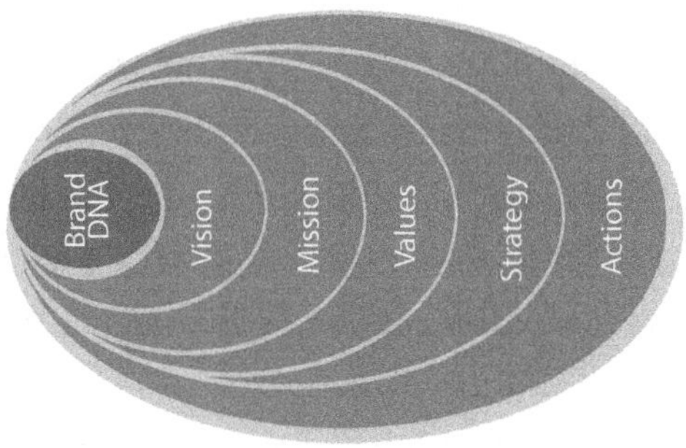

In addition to the 'onion' shown here, other common ways of organizing the brand's foundational elements include pyramids, quadrants and brand keys.

Brand pyramids, onions and keys are models for pulling together the brand foundational elements into one- or two-sheet documents showing the relationship between each component. Each model looks the way it sounds. With brand pyramids, the basic information such the audience and competitive environment is on the bottom; features and benefits are next; the product or service differentiator is the following 'floor up'; then comes the personality statement followed by brand values; next comes mission or purpose; vision is the second from the top; and brand essence is at the pinnacle. The brand onion follows the same order as the brand pyramid, but with concentric circles going from the competitive environment and audience on the outer two circles to the brand essence in the centre. Placement of the other elements follows the same hierarchy of the brand pyramid.

A brand key is a hybrid of the brand pyramid and onion. The contextual information of the market environment – competition, audience and insight – forms a base on which sits an 'onion' showing the brand-specific attributes, benefits, values, personality, discriminator and proof points (or reasons to believe). In the centre of the onion is the brand essence. While we recommend the brand key model because we believe that it provides a better visual representation of how the elements work together, the most important factor is just having one and fully training every employee to refer to it, so they accurately and consistently represent the brand to external constituents.

Another tool for ensuring brand consistency is the message map. Like pyramids, onions and keys, the message map pulls together pertinent information about the brand to help tell the brand story, but it also provides key overall messaging and identifies customer needs and concerns and how to succinctly answer them, including the 'proof' that the individual can provide. Message maps are key tools for aligning sales and marketing messages across all offices and countries.

Finally, a brand ladder is like a pyramid and can be visualized like one, but is more of an 'internal' marketing tool that contains just four stages:

1 **attributes**, including all the physical features of the product;
2 **functional benefits** – the actual physical 'utility' of the brand or its category usefulness;
3 **emotional benefits** – the emotional rewards that the brand provides: self-expression, a feeling safety or security, self-confidence and more;
4 **social benefits** – the brand's contribution to increasing the status of the consumer within society.

Identifying these benefits – most brands have the first three and some also offer the fourth option of a social benefit – enable the marketer to think about which type of benefit needs to be emphasized in the advertising and other marketing-communication vehicles. In most cases, the brand manager will select the benefit to be emphasized based on the following criteria: 1) what the prospect will find most appealing, 2) what the competition is claiming and 3) whether the brand can stand out by making the claim.

Validating the brand foundation

Once the foundational elements have been identified, they should be validated. When marketing professionals are asked such inevitable questions as 'Are you sure the campaign will bring results?' or 'Do you think this new product will catch fire in the marketplace?' they can never guarantee the answer, but they can give qualified reassurance if they have done their research. Here are some key points about the brand that should be examined thoroughly in order to validate its value:

- **Product or service uniqueness:** Product-development teams often get bogged down in the process and they simply forget to look at the uniqueness. Lacking a clear, meaningful differentiator can render any brand irrelevant, unless the goal is to provide it at a cheaper price point. The one thing that a brand manager should never forget is creating absolute perceived value for the consumer.
- **Bulletproof product or service:** Protecting a product and brand is getting increasingly tougher. Virtually every product or service today can be imitated, copied and even surpassed in terms of construction and benefits. Obviously, patent registration and other legal protections are important, but even they can't completely provide protection. The only true differentiator in the long run is the uniqueness and appeal of the brand foundation. Do you have one that prospects will embrace?
- **For how long?** Many brands have a shelf life of just six months[43] before the competition can copy it and, in some categories, the shelf life is even shorter. Do you have the resources to successfully launch the brand and build repeat business within your time window?
- **Can you remain profitable?** What does your price point say about your brand? Can you offer the product for less or more than the competition? Can your price be matched by a 'me-too' product? If so, how can you protect against it? Since we're talking about price competition, how long can you sustain low prices before suffering financial ruin?
- **Can you build loyalty?** The biggest indicator of brand validation is creating a loyal following and generating repeat purchases. All of the points above can contribute to either positive or negative brand loyalty, depending on your situation, the competition and more.

Research methods to validate your brand

Here are some research techniques that you might want to employ to validate your brand:

- **Qualitative research:** Get your potential consumers to indicate actual perceived quality and price of your brand. Is it perceived to be more than a generic? Your competition? If you can answer yes to both questions, then your brand has value. Also, take time to test the product's functionality and usability to discover what could go wrong. Research can uncover unmet consumer needs as well as indicate consumer benefits. While it is always recommended to conduct product research during the development stage, it's never too late.
- **Focus groups:** Avoid gross mistakes and uncover the language that consumers would use to describe your product or service through small focus groups featuring an intimate discussion with up to six participants. Smaller groups often yield

better results than larger more 'democratic' forums. Make sure you have several different sessions to avoid participant bias from a single group. Also, keep in mind that the findings can only be directional owing to the small sample size. Finally, while focusing on the product attributes and functionality is important, paying too much attention to them could be a trap – technical perfection should be a given. It is better to focus on customer service, warranties, innovation, overall product design, potential pricing and other key areas that can contribute to the perceptions of value.

- **In-depth one-on-one interviews:** These discussions are often a great way to share complicated concepts with consumers, developments that require concentration and attention to detail such as new packaging concepts and user-experience innovations.
- **Problem research:** We all know a problem when we see one. The issue here is finding a problem without knowing it even exists. That is a tough one, but it does help marketers identify and find the unmet consumer needs during the product-development stage. In some cases, the participants for this type of research could be experts and, in other cases, daily users and other consumers.
- **Archetype research:** Psychologist Carl Jung believed that people divide others into 12 different 'archetypes': the Innocent, Orphan, Caregiver, Warrior, Seeker, Lover, Creator, Destroyer, Ruler, Sage, Magician and Jester. These archetypes enable marketers to construct brand personalities, tell brand stories and define behaviours that people intuitively understand.[44] Validating one or blending two can help ensure adoptions of brands that best fit into the consumer's life and worldview.
- **Loyal customer insights:** Some of the most valuable insights can come straight from consumers who are already brand loyalists. They already appreciate the attributes, functionality, emotional connections and much else. More importantly, they already have a commitment to the brand's success. Once the brand is established, their insights could offer some of the most important feedback for developing enhancements that can ensure the brand's future.

HOW INTERNATIONAL BRANDS CAN SUCCEED IN CHINA – A GUEST PERSPECTIVE FROM ASHLEY GALINA DUDARENOK, CHINA

Ashley Galina Dudarenok is a China marketing expert, entrepreneur, professional speaker and vlogger. She is the founder of several China-focused businesses, including social-media agency alarice.com.hk and resources platform ChoZan.co. She runs the world's largest vlog about China market, consumers and social media on YouTube, @AshleyTalksChina. Her latest bestseller *Unlocking the World's Largest E-Market: A Guide to*

Selling on Chinese Social Media is available on Amazon. Here's what Ashley has to say about what is takes for international brands to succeed in China:

'With a population of over 1.3 billion, China is a market that many international brands can't wait to enter. As an important pillar in the global economy, China is developing at a rapid speed. It has a growing number of middle-class consumers and there's rising demand for more diverse products. However, along with all the opportunities come challenges. China is a large market and its numerous domestic brands have a definite advantage when competing with international brands. They understand local consumers, know sales channels, have lower production costs and already have most of the market share. International brands need to adapt to China's unique language, culture, customs and consumer behaviours. They can't just copy what has worked successfully in other countries. This requires an in-depth understanding of the country and its consumers.

'Coca-Cola has always been a strong performer in regional branding. In 2011, it debuted its packaging customization initiative in Australia, which later became part of the 'Share a Coke' global campaign. A lot of English names were printed on the packages so that consumers could search and try to find their own name or the names of friends and family. The campaign was a huge success and led to a healthy sales increase. Later, it spread to other countries and areas.

'However, Coca-Cola didn't copy all the details of their successful campaign in each region. The brand made an important change when they brought it to China. Instead of Chinese names, which are too diverse and would have resulted in a much lower chance for consumers to find their own names, the packages featured internet catchphrases to describe different groups of people like 'baifumei / 白富美', an attractive lady from a decent family, 'wenyiqingnian / 文艺青年', a hipster or 'yueguangzu / 月光族', someone who always lives from paycheck to paycheck.

'These terms were fun, descriptive and popular, especially among Chinese youngsters. Getting a bottle or can of Coca-Cola was like showing their personality. Not surprisingly, these special editions soon became a hit. Later, they continued the campaign with well-known lyrics and movie lines in Chinese, which were also well received. Coca-Cola succeeded because it knew the culture, grasped popular trends and understood the mindset of Chinese consumers, so the campaign echoed with consumers.

'Another good example comes from New Balance. In early 2017, the Boston-based shoemaker kicked off a campaign called 'Letter to My Future Self', which featured videos of several high-profile athletes who had written a letter to themselves in the future, talking about their goals and what would drive them to do their best. New Balance launched the campaign later in China. But instead of Chinese athletes, the brand featured Papi Jiang, one of the most popular key opinion leaders (KOL) in China who is famous for her short funny videos. In her video, Papi talked about how she had managed to carve out her own niche, build a business and gain fame during her 12 years in Beijing.

'As Papi had a large follower base on the internet who could relate to her life and experiences, her video struck a chord with many viewers and her endorsement for New Balance created huge buzz on social media. Her followers are mostly young people who fit New Balance's target market. In fact, less costly KOLs, who more effectively speak to specific audiences, are approached more and more by brands for online promotion campaigns. This is now a major way for brands to build their presence and attract new audiences. Familiar with all these marketing trends in China, New Balance found a great spokesperson who successfully maximized their influence on the internet and boosted sales.

'However, there are also international brands that overlook the impact of local culture and consumer behaviours or aren't sensitive enough to changes in the market. Usually they end up losing money or even having to retreat from the market. Marks & Spencer, which specializes in clothing and luxury food products, opened its first Chinese flagship store in Shanghai in 2008. The London-based retailer later began to expand, and by mid-2013 there were 14 Marks & Spencer stores in China. However, in November 2016, Marks & Spencer announced its plan to close all their brick-and-mortar stores in China because of continued losses.

'So, what went wrong? For one thing, they lacked an in-depth understanding of the market. For example, the British retailer used UK or European clothing sizes instead of the S-M-L size standards that Chinese consumers were familiar with and this left shoppers confused. What's more, many Chinese consumers complained that the clothes in stock were too large for them or that the styles were too old-fashioned. They also failed to keep up with changes in the market. As online sales and digital payments began to grow, many fashion brands caught on and developed their online sales channels. However, Marks & Spencer was slow to respond and was eclipsed by quickly evolving fast-fashion brands. All these contributed to its failure in the China market.

'An international brand's performance in China depends on how well it understands the market and its consumers. Before entering a new market, brands need to understand themselves and their products, cultivate an in-depth understanding of the local market, develop insights into their target consumers and stay sensitive to changes in the market that might influence their brand.'

EXTENDED CASE STUDY: THE GLOBAL BRANDING OF COCA-COLA

Back in 1977, the Israeli franchisee of the Coca-Cola manufacturing, bottling and distribution operations had been running for ten years and had succeeded in establishing awareness as well as the following of many eager customers, who looked at this iconic American brand as superior to the local light beverages. Coca-Cola hired Israel's largest ad agency to help promote the brand. There was no affiliation between the global ad agency, McCann Erickson, based in New York, and the Israeli agency. However, being a multinational brand, Coca-Cola insisted on adhering to very strict rules.

While the Coca-Cola logo was first created in 1887, there were many variations and changes to it over the years, especially to accommodate the growth and the global expansion of the brand. In 1969, for instance, they introduced the 'white wave' and the Arden Square logo was unveiled.[45] In a red box, the Coca-Cola script is underlined with a white 'wave' or 'Dynamic Ribbon Device'. The beauty of this logo allowed the Coca-Cola logo to be written in as many languages as possible, while still embracing the name in a familiar all-inclusive simple shape and colour that is immediately recognizable all over the world. This logo is still used today.

It is worth noticing that among all the different languages in which the Coca-Cola name appears, the Hebrew version is the closest to the original in design style, despite the fact that Hebrew lettering and Roman lettering are worlds apart. The designers who developed the logo's Hebrew version stayed true to the spirit of the brand. Even if one doesn't read Hebrew, there is absolutely no doubt about the brand when looking at the Coca-Cola logo in Israel.

The Israeli agency was given a series of three ring binders with clear instructions, as well as ready-to-use 'slicks' for creating ads and any other local market promotional materials. There were logo sheets plus ready-to-use photography and illustration materials. The Israeli agency was told to use them without any deviation and there was a limit on the kind of photos they could take – just product shots that showed the Hebrew script on the bottle, since they were not available outside of the country.

Looking back at the early ads for Coca-Cola in Israel – Ilan helped create them – it is clear that less attention was paid to values and lifestyles. The young people appearing in the photography provided by an American ad agency to an Israeli ad agency didn't reflect the local market. While they showed fresh-faced young people, they definitely looked more like 'Americans' than Israelis. Today, it's important to note, Coca-Cola ensures that its imagery reflects local markets. This brings us to a concluding question that any global brand manager should be asking themselves: do I want my target audience to aspire to become something they're not by using my product, such as emulating American youth in the Coca-Cola example above; or do I want my brand to appear as part of the local culture and show that it understands the local needs and wants, enabling the local population to identify with it?

KEY TERMS

- brand development
- brand essence
- brand positioning
- brand purpose
- ideation
- mission
- value proposition

DISCUSSION QUESTIONS

- What is a typical brand life cycle and what happens at each of its stages?
- What is the process for developing a comprehensive brand foundation?
- What are the key elements within a comprehensive brand foundation?
- Which format of organizing brand elements do you prefer; why do you prefer it?
- Why is brand research necessary for ensuring consumer resonance and validation?

Notes

1 Getman, P (2017) Why you should launch a brand, not a product, *Entrepreneur*, https://www.entrepreneur.com/article/295306 (archived at https://perma.cc/5RRR-9EB6)
2 Maggard, J (1976) Positioning revisited, *Journal of Marketing*, 40 (1), p 63
3 Mayford M, Siegelbaum SA, Kandel ER 'Synapses and memory storage', *Cold Spring Harbor Perspectives in Biology*, 4 (6), https://doi.org/10.1101/cshperspect.a005751 (archived at https://perma.cc/7APC-QT8K), https://www.ncbi.nlm.nih.gov/pmc/articles/PMC3367555 (archived at https://perma.cc/92CW-TMMH)
4 Maggard, J (1976) Positioning Revisited, *Journal of Marketing*, 40 (1), p 63
5 Boches, E (2014) Bill Bernbach and the beginning – thoughts and lessons for my students, *Medium*, https://medium.com/what-do-you-want-to-know/bill-bernbach-and-the-beginning-7e49c2242390 (archived at https://perma.cc/945A-A6MV)
6 Bendinger, B (2009) *Advertising & the business of brands*, The Copy Workshop, Chicago
7 Kim, W and Mauborgne, R (2015) *Blue Ocean Strategy*, Harvard Business Review Press, Brighton, US
8 Product2Market micro marketing vs marco marketing – understanding the differences (2019), https://product2market.walkme.com/micro-marketing-vs-macro-marketing-understanding-differences (archived at https://perma.cc/SZ8R-8CQ4)
9 Poduct2Market micro marketing vs macro marketing – understanding the differences. (2019), https://product2market.walkme.com/micro-marketing-vs-macro-marketing-understanding-differences (archived at https://perma.cc/SZ8R-8CQ4)
10 Stayman, D (2015) How to write market positioning statements, *#CORNELL360*, http://blog.ecornell.com/how-to-write-market-positioning-statements (archived at https://perma.cc/6RJA-DH2Z)
11 Neumeier, M (2006) *The brand gap*, New Riders, Indianapolis
12 Kapferer, JN (2012) *The New Strategic Brand Management: Advanced Insights & Strategic Thinking*, 5th Ed, Kogan Page, London
13 Rivkin, S (2018) How did Apple Computer get its brand name? *Branding Strategy Insider*, https://www.brandingstrategyinsider.com/2011/11/how-did-apple-computer-get-its-brand-name.html#.W8gDlhNKgcg (archived at https://perma.cc/RLD7-8UZ7)
14 Telegraph.co.uk (2018) Steve Jobs: ten things you didn't know about the Apple founder, https://www.telegraph.co.uk/technology/apple/8574277/Steve-Jobs-ten-things-you-didnt-know-about-the-Apple-founder.html (archived at https://perma.cc/7LNW-7C92)

15 Levinson, P (2018) How Nike almost ended up with a very different name, *Business Insider*, https://www.businessinsider.com/how-nike-got-its-name-2016-1 (archived at https://perma.cc/EZ2W-E859)

16 Creative Market (2016)The $35 Nike logo and the woman who designed it, *Creative Market*, https://creativemarket.com/blog/the-35-nike-logo-and-the-woman-who-designed-it (archived at https://perma.cc/U3NE-XJCM)

17 *The Vintage News* (2018) The ancient Greek goddess Nike, representing victory and speed, inspired the Nike company logo, https://www.thevintagenews.com/2017/10/11/the-ancient-greek-goddess-nike-representing-victory-and-speed-inspired-the-nike-company-logo (archived at https://perma.cc/5PU6-NU4Q)

18 Tanny, S M, and Derzko, N A (1988) Innovators and imitators in innovation diffusion modelling, *Journal of Forecasting*, 7 (6), https://onlinelibrary.wiley.com/doi/abs/10.1002/for.3980070403 (archived at https://perma.cc/F5NX-BTCW)

19 Gatignon, H, Weitz, B, and Bansal, P (November 1, 1990) Brand Introduction Strategies and Competitive Environments, *Journal of Marketing Research*, https://journals.sagepub.com/doi/abs/10.1177/002224379002700402 (archived at https://perma.cc/YZE8-PMJN)

20 Rosen, W and Minsky, L (2017) *The Activation Imperative: How to Build Brands and Business by Inspiring Action*, Rowman & Littlefield, Lanham, Maryland

21 Rowley, J, (2002) Information marketing in a digital world, *Library Hi Tech*, 20 (3), pp 352–58, https://doi.org/10.1108/07378830210444540 (archived at https://perma.cc/K8RR-597X), https://www.emeraldinsight.com/doi/abs/10.1108/07378830210444540 (archived at https://perma.cc/X9SC-J2TQ)

22 Corporate Finance Institute (2018) AIDA Model – understand the steps in the AIDA model hierarchy, https://corporatefinanceinstitute.com/resources/knowledge/other/aida-model-marketing (archived at https://perma.cc/UW5S-5VHW)

23 Lyong, H C (1998) The theory of reasoned action applied to brand loyalty, *Journal of Product and Brand Management*, 7 (1), pp 51–61 (11), https://www.ingentaconnect.com/content/mcb/096/1998/00000007/00000001/art00004 (archived at https://perma.cc/E58X-6HVN)

24 Holt, J (2018) Thinking, Fast and Slow – By Daniel Kahneman – Book Review, Nytimes.com, https://www.nytimes.com/2011/11/27/books/review/thinking-fast-and-slow-by-daniel-kahneman-book-review.html (archived at https://perma.cc/FLV9-8PAS)

25 Rosen, W and Minsky, L (2017) *The Activation Imperative: How to Build Brands and Business by Inspiring Action*, Rowman & Littlefield, Lanham, Maryland

26 Hardie, B G S, Lodish L M, Kilmer, J V, Beatty, D R, Farris, P, Biel, A L, Wicke, L S, Balson, J B and Aaker, D (1999) *Harvard Business Review*, The logic of product-line extensions, https://hbr.org/1994/11/the-logic-of-product-line-extensions (archived at https://perma.cc/B2CQ-5NRG)

27 Postaer, S (2008) The story of 'not your father's Oldsmobile'. Or how some really bad advertising changed the culture forever! *Gods of Advertising*, https://godsofadvertising.wordpress.com/2008/10/14/this-is-not-your-fathers-oldsmobile-how-a-portfolio-tarnishing-piece-of-creative-changed-our-culture-forever (archived at https://perma.cc/8W3C-UB92)

28 Merced, J (2018) Borders' Bankruptcy Shakes the Publishing Industry, Nytimes.com, https://www.nytimes.com/2011/02/17/business/media/17borders.html (archived at https://perma.cc/HJQ5-M4SC)

29 Shannon, J (2018) Soon there will be only one Blockbuster video store left in the US, *USA Today*, https://www.usatoday.com/story/news/nation-now/2018/07/12/soon-there-only-one-blockbuster-video-store-left-u-s/781653002 (archived at https://perma.cc/B52S-XZFT)

30 Lin, D (2017) Money in packaging: how it drives up sales, *Packaging of the World*, https://www.packagingoftheworld.com/2017/07/money-in-packaging-how-it-drives-up.html (archived at https://perma.cc/YK5E-SHMS)

31 Frayer-Luna, G R (2017) Who sells Breck shampoo? *bizfluent*, https://bizfluent.com/facts-5828012-sells-breck-shampoo-.html (archived at https://perma.cc/WV2V-WMZV)

32 Coffee, P (2018) Wieden + Kennedy establishes new global leadership team, *Adweek.com*, https://www.adweek.com/agencies/wieden-kennedy-establishes-new-global-leadership-team-with-4-promotions (archived at https://perma.cc/8LZU-HU4J)

33 Minsky, L (2007) *How to Succeed in Advertising When All You Have is Talent*, 2nd Ed, The Copy Workshop, Chicago

34 Minsky, L and Fahey, C (2017) *Audio Branding*, Kogan Page, London

35 People Helping People (PHP) (2019) http://syvphp.org (archived at https://perma.cc/7MN2-8F2S), https://www.syvphp.org/about/mission (archived at https://perma.cc/4GZM-PVSG)

36 Gizmodo.com (2018) https://gizmodo.com/5634378/the-hp-way-how-bill-hewlett-and-i-built-our-company (archived at https://perma.cc/M5LS-3WHH)

37 Kolowich, L (2019) 17 truly inspiring company vision and mission statement examples, *Hubspot*, https://blog.hubspot.com/marketing/inspiring-company-mission-statements (archived at https://perma.cc/93WP-P4P9)

38 Volvocars.com (2018) Vision 2020, Volvo Cars, https://www.volvocars.com/en-ca/about/our-stories/vision-2020 (archived at https://perma.cc/5RKR-AD8Z)

39 OSV (2018) Volvo history: how the Swedish manufacturer became the leader in safety innovation, https://www.osv.ltd.uk/volvo-history-timeline (archived at https://perma.cc/AY7Q-HEHM)

40 Volvocars.com (2018) Vision 2020, Volvo Cars, https://www.volvocars.com/en-ca/about/our-stories/vision-2020 (archived at https://perma.cc/5RKR-AD8Z)

41 Anderson, J, and Narus, J A (2018) Business marketing: understand what customers value, *Harvard Business Review*, https://hbr.org/1998/11/business-marketing-understand-what-customers-value (archived at https://perma.cc/7VPM-3HR2)

42 Page, R C and Berkow, D N, Concepts of the self: Western and Eastern perspectives, *Journal of Multicultural Counseling and Development*, https://onlinelibrary.wiley.com/doi/abs/10.1002/j.2161-1912.1991.tb00625.x (archived at https://perma.cc/63HY-XBHH)

43 Hurwitz, J (2016) Your brilliant Kickstarter idea could be on sale in China before you've even finished funding it, *Quartz*, https://qz.com/771727/chinas-factories-in-shenzhen-can-copy-products-at-breakneck-speed-and-its-time-for-the-rest-of-the-world-to-get-over-it (archived at https://perma.cc/5BSM-VX97)

44 Insights-qualitativos.com (2018) Using the power of archetypes as a qualitative research tool, http://www.insights-qualitativos.com/2008/05/using-power-of-archetypes-as.html#ixzz5C5zJUQMg (archived at https://perma.cc/6U88-L9MX)

45 Coca-cola.co.uk (2018) The history of the Coca-Cola logo, Our History, Coca-Cola GB, https://www.coca-cola.co.uk/stories/the-logo-story (archived at https://perma.cc/W62Q-SQHW)

06

Creating the brand foundational elements

READING OUTCOMES

At the conclusion of this chapter, you should be able to:

- describe basic visual branding practices and their contributions to overall brand building;
- appreciate the importance of naming and how the brand foundational elements can inform it;
- understand the basics of audio branding and when and where sound should be employed;
- articulate the basic considerations when branding through olfactory, taste and other senses.

Introduction

Back in 2005, Martin Lindstrom published a book called: *Brand Sense*, in which he described the way that brands connect with consumers by 'activating' our five senses. To reinforce his argument, he used a quotation from Benjamin Franklin – often considered the 'father' of American advertising – at the book's opening: 'Tell me and I'll forget. Show me and I might remember. Involve me and I'll understand.'[1]

We believe that Franklin's quote is a brilliant way to describe brand actualization, because we all touch, taste, smell, see and hear our favourite brands, even service brands. The sound of crunching cereal – or lack of it – communicates flavour and whether we're eating something healthy or fun. The smell of a new car conveys luxury, that of a hotel room a feeling of comfort. The feel and texture of the cover of this book, we hope, convey quality and the promise of valuable information inside. The shape of a bottle of water conveys its purity and health-giving properties. The visual cleanliness of a restaurant and the comfort of its chairs tell us about the quality of the meal we are about to enjoy.

In other words, each one of our senses contributes to our expectations about the product or service performance, which then influences our experience of it. Think of it this way: if we believe that something will perform better, through our confirmation bias we interpret that it often does perform better.[2] We may also turn away from brands because they do not appeal to our senses or have contributed to a negative experience.

More importantly, although often overlooked beside the sense of sight through visual design elements, the sensory attributes of smell, sound, taste and texture can either make or break a brand. In the following pages, we're going to take a look at the considerations regarding the sensory attributes of brands. Let us get started, because with sensory branding, success can be so close you can almost taste it.

Overview

Once you have the brand foundation or DNA, the actual brand needs to be brought to life, and this is what this chapter is all about. The first area we investigate is visual branding – the creation of the brand's visual manifestations such as symbols, emblems and colours. We then discuss creating the brand name based on the brand foundation, a step that should be completed before beginning the logo design. We'll also briefly explore the complete world of branding through our senses – sound, smell, touch and taste – and home in on an innovative brand, Illy, which is expert at activating all of its customers' senses. We conclude the chapter with a contribution from brand strategist Chris Malone, who takes an unusual angle on logos, as well as an extended case study on the classic American brand, Harley Davidson. Join us to see how to bring your brand to life.

Set your sights on visual branding

As we've already discussed in earlier chapters, the concept of a brand is intangible. Brand marketers should never forget that besides the physical product features and functional utilitarian benefits, a brand is an idea. Bringing it to life and making it 'actual' to consumers – actualizing it – is the most important thing we should know and appreciate. There is no strict formula for brand actualization, but there are quite a few reasonable and rational ways of bringing a brand to life and make it a consistent part of a consumer's life.

During the product-development phase or while planning to launch, the first things that most marketers focus on are the logo, brand colours, fonts, imagery, as well as other visual branding elements. Typically, the first touchpoint of a brand that consumers experience is visual. Other sensory brand experiences follow.

Many branding experts, including advertising legend Rich Silverstein, co-chairman and co-creative director at Goodby, Silverstein & Partners, San Francisco, claim that the logo is at the core of the brand,[3] making it the most important visual branding element. But other elements should be considered in tandem with the logo development. First, the brand name is core and should be selected (and approved by the company's legal department for usage in all of its markets) before logo work even begins. Colour is also an easy identifier of a brand; some brands even get known by their colour. For instance, IBM used to be known by many consumers as 'Big Blue', because of its logo colour. The Golden Arches of McDonald's are an obvious signifier of the brand. UPS built a branding campaign around its distinctive brown colour.[4] Other famous brands use a distinct colour to identify themselves, and no one can take away the robin-egg blue colour that distinguishes Tiffany's.

Ideally, a brand should have its own distinct font, at least in its category. When possible, the font could be customized like the unique one for Renault and McSans for McDonald's and, for more visionary brands, they can also include exclusive icons and pictographs. In some cases, brands develop a distinct shape that is related to the brand and serves as an ownable brand icon, such as the Coca-Cola bottle. Legend has it that the instructions to the designers who created the bottle were to make it 'so distinct that you would recognize it by feel in the dark or lying broken on the ground.'[5] Those instructions are a good way to think about package design overall – make your package distinctive even when its form has been changed.

Other visual branding elements might include:

- signage, both exterior and interior and directional and informative for all company locations;
- employee communication tools, including stationery, envelopes, forms, invoices and emails;
- vehicles, including commercial vans, trucks and trains, and even aeroplanes, when possible;
- uniforms – male and female, including name tags with options for seasonal and cultural occasions
- interior design, including HQ, branches, stores, trade-show stands and franchised operations;
- packaging, including shopping bags, bulk packaging, wrapping paper and shipping boxes;
- online presence, including every single element of websites, social media, blogs and audio.

The goal is: if it can be branded, it should be branded.

When developing the visual identity, the designer should create a brand-identity manual to show the brand manager as well as other art directors and designers the dos and don'ts of utilizing the elements. Most comprehensive identity manuals include:

- a welcome that explains how to use the manual;
- an overview of the brand foundational components – mission, vision, values, personality, essence – either displayed in a pyramid, onion, or key format (described in Chapter 5);
- how to implement all of the design equities, including the logo, colour palette, illustration or photography style, the approved fonts and other executional considerations that can ensure a consistent tone of voice;
- possibly direction on the tone of voice, key-word choices, house style (usually focusing on capitalization and punctuation) and other verbal guidelines, so the brand 'speaks' consistently as well.

It's all in the name – some key considerations

When talking to a friend, you may mention the brand Mac and be referring to the famous Apple sub-brand of personal computers. But your listener may mistake it for another MAC brand, the cosmetics company. Granted, the chances of that are slim, but it is still a risk. Others may simply use the Google brand name as a verb, and some have already doing it for years with the Xerox brand, even though the Xerox Company is no longer in the copying machine business.[6]

While working for a naming company may be a great deal of fun and provide the thrill of creative exploration, there are many professional considerations and many roadblocks to the final 'ownable' brand name, one that is unique in all of its primary markets, separating it from the competition. A good name should firstly create a positive impression, be easy to remember – or, even better, be unforgettable – and align with and, ideally, convey the brand essence, brand positioning and other elements of the brand foundation. Just as importantly, the company needs to be able to get the domain name across all of its key markets. Your goal should be to purchase all of the obvious extensions –such as .au, .cn., .com, .in and .uk – so that your competition and cybersquatters can't reserve them or create confusion. Finally, the name has to be legally protectable through a trademark.

Brand names tend to fall into one of five categories:

1 **Product.** These types of names convey the product category or key output such as International Paper, US Steel, envelopes.com, or Foodstuffs, a local small food market near the home of one of the authors. Most professional association names

fall into this category as well. Because these types of names can feel expected, they are less memorable and can come across as generic, but they can work if the marketer is first to the category. Another key issue with these types of names: They can limit expansion opportunities into related product categories.

2 **Functional Benefit.** While names of this type help promote the primary outcome of the product usage or communicate what the brand does, they suffer much of the same issues as product-type names. Some examples include: Healthy Choice Frozen Entrees, Sea Harvest (a South African seafood company), Post-it, Tractor Supply Co., Band Aid. A common subset is the pun or cute variation such as Ben & Jerry names for their ice-cream flavours: Cherry Garcia, Chubby Hubby, Coffee, Coffee BuzzBuzzBuzz. We caution against these 'cute names', because they can make the business seem immature, small and/or unsophisticated, though, in some cases, it can reinforce a feeling of 'fun'.

3 **Person.** Usually the founder, partners, or other person instrumental to the business. Most law firms and old-school ad agencies use this naming approach. On the plus side, this approach often allows for it to be unique in the category and, occasionally, memorable, but it can also feel disconnected and meaningless, especially if the individual is not a celebrity, requiring greater marketing efforts to create positive associations for the brand.

4 **Symbolic.** Here, the name implies a deeper meaning, as well as emotionality, and because it's not logically connected with its functional category, it could provide an opportunity to expand beyond it. Examples are Virgin (a brand which we'll explore in Chapter 12) and Spirit (although this airline rarely lifts ours whenever we use it). Brand marketers should also make sure that the brand name enables it to be separated out from its competitors. We've noticed that certain words are commonly selected in particular categories. For instance, numerous newer ad agencies include the word 'octane' in their name, because they want to imply that they produce better 'fuel' for the brands of prospective clients. When this happens and a word becomes common in a category, we recommend staying away from it, because the brand loses its point of differentiation.

5 **Invented.** Created names are generally easier to trademark and obtain as the web URL, but like brands named after individuals, they will require greater marketing efforts to create positive associations for the brand. Finally, we recommend that the name must be easy to pronounce and spell in all of its markets. Marketers should note that a subset of 'Invented' is using a Product, Functional or Symbolic product name as the base and then deleting, adding or altering phonemes – unique units of sound – to create a name that implies its root. For instance, one of the authors of this book contributed to the development of the name 'Carent' for a medical laboratory network, a combination of two symbolic ideas: care and parent. Both parts of the word help contribute to the implied meaning of the name.

Naming a brand often has a significant influence on its success or failure. When it comes to over-the-counter (OTC) drugs, naming becomes both serious and, to our ears, a bit weird. Consider the names Adcetris, Anakinra, Cisplatin, Domperidone, Farxiga, Hetlioz, Incivek, Moxifloxacin, Otezla, Pancuronium, Viibryd, Yervoy, Xgeva, Xylometazoline, Zykadia and Zytiga. Pronouncing them or remembering them is nearly impossible. The reason for these strange names, however, is that the United States Food and Drug Administration (FDA) requires that OTC drug brand names be totally different from each other. The frequent use of X, Q and Z in OTC drugs ensures that they do not sound like existing English words and that there will be no mistake in confusing one drug with another. One thing is sure: it's getting harder to find new, simple names not only for OTC drugs, but for other products and brands as well.

We live in an age where millions of people are entrepreneurs, starting new businesses and building new brands. One website that helps in the process is namechekr.com, because it can help determine the domain and social username availability across most networks, including Facebook, Instagram, YouTube, Twitter, Tumblr, reddit, meetup and StumbleUpon. It is one of many tools that can assist newly minted brands to start the process without getting into any legal issues. Of course, none of these tools can replace the legal review to ensure complete trademark protection. And there are companies that do nothing but specialize in the creation of brand names and are experienced in developing them for products and services that span a wide variety of cultures and countries. Just like hiring an experienced design firm for the logo, hiring a naming company for important brand launches might help as well.

Whichever approach you use, there is one more key consideration when selecting a global brand name: it must not imply a negative in any country where it is being marketed. While it might not 'decrease' sales, since results are an outcome of both the marketer's actions and its competitor actions, it certainly won't help in the brand manager's efforts to build positive associations for it.

Audio: the next biggest sense for branding

After vision, 'the most used sense in branding',[7] the next area to determine is the sound of your brand. Virtually everyone can recall the sound of an Apple Macintosh booting up or the roar of a Harley Davidson, even if there is no computer or motorcycle around. It's enough to mention the brand name and the sound comes to mind. Conversely, if you hear a motorcycle starting up you might well be able to distinguish whether it's a Harley or a Honda. We are surrounded by branded audio sounds almost all day, but many marketers fail to pay attention to creating one. Almost all cars today produce their own recognizable sounds as we open the door, before we snap our safety belt on and as we start driving. Smartphones, computers and tablets broadcast unique branded audio sounds too. Meanwhile, an increasing number of people, especially millennials and Generation Z, have been relying on social media and platforms like YouTube for the bulk of their entertainment and content consumption for some time.[8] And the brick-and-mortar world is becoming more audio-enabled as well. To bring a seamless consistency to all of these experiences – a must if Generation Z and millennials are among your prospects – you need to develop a branding strategy for audio, just as you would for the visual world.

Once overlooked, audio or sonic branding is becoming more important to marketers. As Laurence wrote with Colleen Fahey in the book *Audio Branding: Using sound to build your brand*, 'The strategic use of sound can play a pivotal role in positively differentiating a product or service, enhance recall, creating preference, building trust and perhaps most importantly, increasing sales and marketing return on investment (ROI).'[9] Sounds should be considered for the actual product such as the snap of a lid or click of a car door closing, as well as a complete audio language for all of the communication touchpoints. Included would be an audio identity, just like a visual logo, plus a complete audio-identity system. Overlook the sound of your brand, and your product, service or company can come across as disjointed and confusing. Audio branding can help companies in the following ways:

- in regulated industries, communicate emotions without making verbal claims;
- increase the effectiveness of rebranding campaigns (or any campaign), because your messaging will work on an additional level;
- bring greater consistency across all touchpoints, even apps, on-hold messages, corporate meetings, smartphones (think ringtones), enabling all of them to reinforce your brand;
- suggest other types of sensory experiences such as taste, texture or scent;
- lower licensing fees and the management of them across across platforms, mediums and channels when producing branded content;
- create a better branded experience in retail environments, experiential programmes and other places where you may encounter prospects and customers.

And these are just a few of the reasons more and more companies are investing in developing their audio brand. However, it is extremely important to remember that registering a sound as a commercial protected trademark could be a long process. Harley Davidson submitted applications to register several components of its products, including the sound, in 1994, only to withdraw them in 2000. The company said it had dropped applications for federal trademark protection for various design elements on its motorcycles, including its teardrop-shaped gas tanks, the curve of its front and rear fenders and the overall shape of its motorcycles. The simple reason was financial; the process is long and expensive.[10]

More importantly, we are now entering the era of screenless web. More and more consumers are using voice-based devises – currently branded as voice-activated assistants – to search the web and even shop on it. To encourage adoption of voice-based shopping, the first voice-activated coupon was recently tested by Google: a US $15 discount voucher for Target which could be claimed using voice-only Google Assistant.[11] Within two years, it is predicted that over 50 per cent of all web searches will be screenless and within four years, shopping online by voice-only is expected to reach $40 billion.[12] For additional insights on how to identify and create your brand sound, check out *Audio Branding: Using sound to build your brand.*[13]

Why branded scents can make sense

Sight and sound are not the only ways you can build your brand. Another opportunity is scent branding. The olfactory bulb is a structure located in the forebrain of vertebrates that receive neural input about odours detected by cells in the nasal cavity. The smell-receptor cells extend directly into the highly organized olfactory bulb, where information about odours is processed,[14] making it a highly efficient system. As Neil Gains wrote in his book *Brand EsSence*, it's 'the only sense with a straight line to our emotions'.[15] Smells are directly linked to our emotions and memories, therefore triggering strong emotional responses,[16] important since long-term memories are extremely influential in forming positive or negative opinions among consumers.[17] Smell is closely linked to memory because it is a strong defence mechanism, warning us of rotting food that might make us sick. In his book, Martin Lindstrom wrote that '75 per cent of the emotions we generate on a daily basis are affected by smell. Next to sight, it is the most important sense we have.'[18]

No one is really sure how far back the habit of using the smell sense in marketing goes. One story dated it at 1921, when Coco Chanel was preparing to introduce her first commercial fragrance: Chanel No. 5.[19] She had contracted the most renowned perfumer in Europe to create her No. 5 scent, designed the bottle herself and sent samples to all the pivotal society movers and shakers in Paris. She also sensed that an extra push was needed to help sell the fragrance at her boutique at 31 rue Cambon. Legend has it that she ordered her salesladies to spray the perfume all over the boutique from the entrance to the dressing rooms.

Today, we take such activity for granted, especially in the retail environment. As a matter of fact, many brick-and-mortar establishments have used scent to attract consumers and make their time memorable. Hotels, casinos and airlines have all used scents for years. Diffusers and air machines are located in discreet locations throughout many retail locations. They produce scents that sometimes have nothing to do with the actual products sold but are creating the right ambiance that will influence the consumers' mood and willingness to purchase. Behind-the-scenes diffusers have also largely freed Abercrombie & Fitch employees from spraying the air with the clothier's muscular array of colognes. In an interview with *Adweek Magazine*, Andrew Kindfuller, CEO of ScentAir, the largest manufacturer of scent diffusers in the US said: 'Brands realize now that this is a part of doing business. We're implementing these systems in many different environments – not just hotels and retail, but funeral homes, retirement villages, and medical and dental and law offices.'[20] Other examples include a scent of fresh laundry in Thomas Pink stores[21] and a floral-infused rainforest scent for the Equarius Hotel at Resorts World Sentosa.[22] However, 'the true power of olfactory branding (also known as scent branding) is in its unique ability to form immediate, powerful and differentiated emotional connections with customers, particularly within a category of functionally similar offerings'[23] when the brand has a unique signature scent.

Branding through the sense of touch

For physical products and branded environments, there's also the sense of touch. We respond to texture, weight, temperature, quality (a spectrum from softness to ruggedness), movement and more. All of these contribute to brand associations for physical products. Our sense of touch is often considered to be second to our eyesight[24] in that we see things first and then tend to examine the item by touching. Just watch any shopper in a store.

All of us know exactly how we feel about our smartphones, our keyboards or the steering wheels of our cars, to take just a few examples. We develop an emotional connection to those tools exclusively through the sense of touch.[25] Video gamers appreciate a joystick and judge its sensitivity to be a contributing factor when choosing one brand over another. When clothes shopping, we pay attention to the texture and softness of the cloth, leather or other material. These experiences are all brand experiences.

Many brands utilize our sense of touch in the packaging design, not just during the product design. Apple, for instance, has demonstrated great sensitivity to the experience of unwrapping Apple products and slowly taking them out of their packaging. Many cosmetic brands activate the sense of touch by employing a multitude of materials. Some say that the cost of packaging is reaching 40 per cent of the total cost for some luxury cosmetics brands.[26] All for a good reason.

Even a product's taste is part of its branding element

The final sense that a few marketers can activate is the sense of taste. As mentioned in the book *Audio Branding*, 'Unless it's a food product, physical taste typically isn't a consideration for any marketer's branding effort.'[27] In addition, 'physical taste is a result of chemical reactions being initiated at receptors in the mouth, and are limited to sweet, sour, salt and bitter, though others add the taste of "umami" (savoury) as well' and 'the actual understanding of a taste is the combination of the chemical reactions as well as the scent, the tactile inputs (such as the temperature and texture), memory, context (which is why people can enjoy the "warning" taste of sour in candy), expectations and more... In other words, the perception of taste is really a multisensory experience.'

The illy coffee brand

Let's look at a brand that has captured most of the areas of sensory branding, illy Coffee, an Italian coffee-roasting company that specializes in the production of espresso. Francesco Illy founded the company in 1933, and it was later led and expanded by his son, Ernesto Illy. The company is based in Trieste, Italy, and operates single-brand stores, *espressamente illy*, all over the world.

Any coffee brand possesses great advantages that many other brands lack, because it has a very strong hold on our senses. For many people the smell of freshly brewed coffee is the sign of a great new day. The entire process of coffee brewing is an emotional one for many, and they pride themselves on the particular way they make coffee, or want it served to them. It is personal.

Coffee first appeared around the 1400s, which generally corresponds to the beginning of the use of metal pots.[28] Coffee leaves, seeds and cherries were boiled together in water, leading to the discovery of coffee as we know it today. It took a long time for people to figure out how to make a cup of it.[29] Coffee became a commodity, traded, bartered and changing hands just like sugar, salt, oil and wheat. It was first described by European travellers in 1573, and imported to Italy by way of the Ottoman Empire.[30] North Africans and Egyptians included coffee in their trade. Venetian merchants also contributed to the widespread popularity of coffee in Europe, introducing the drinking of it to its wealthy residents. In 1720, the famous coffee house Florian was opened there, still in business today.[31]

By the late 1800s, coffee had become a worldwide commodity, attracting the attention of investors and traders. In 1864, John and Charles Arbuckle purchased the newly invented self-emptying coffee-bean roaster and began selling pre-roasted coffee in paper bags by the pound. They named their coffee 'Ariosa', and found great success selling it to the cowboys of the American West. Just like the history of many other brands, differentiation of it in the 'general store' of early settler towns was needed. Individually branded, pre-weighted bags were used. It wasn't long before James Folger followed suit and began selling coffee to the gold miners of California. This blazed the trail for several other coffee producers, including Maxwell House and Hills Brothers.[32]

Meanwhile, in Europe, Trieste was part of the Austro-Hungarian Empire, and, as one of the most important Mediterranean ports, it had a strong coffee culture, with historic cafés steeped in a Central European atmosphere and teeming with lots of rituals and myths.[33]

Illy, a relatively new coffee brand, was established in Trieste in 1933, taking the initiative to be more than just a coffee roaster and distributor. Throughout the history of the brand, the company took steps to differentiate itself. Its innovative packaging of the coffee was an important step in preserving its aroma and taste under any condition and for as long as possible. In 1934, merely a year into the brand's life, illy Caffè patented its revolutionary pressurization system, which it still used today. The properly ripened coffee could thus travel worldwide whilst keeping its aroma and freshness. For consumers who buy illy packages in supermarkets all over the world, this is a very important point, because they are confident of its freshness.

Not even a year later, in 1935, Illy invented Illetta, the first high-pressure espresso machine with a patented system of separating water heating and pressure, forever associating its brand with espresso coffee. This was not merely a technical achievement; illy immediately positioned itself as an innovative purveyor offering the best roasted and brewed coffees.

It didn't take long for illy caffè to become the ambassador of espresso culture, exporting to its first foreign base in Switzerland and becoming an international brand. But illy understood that it needed to keep innovating. Ernesto Illy, the founder's son, set up their first research laboratory in 1957, making coffee a science at Brand illy.

While the 1960s saw growth and expansion, the brand created other 'first to market' products, such as the first single-serve coffee pods that make the perfect espresso at any time and in any location, enhancing their reputation. Illy quietly entered the US market in 1980, bringing the real espresso experience with it. Another 'revolution' in the brand's history was that they started using digital sorting machines in 1982, which analysed the colour and shape of the coffee beans to ensure that each one was perfect.

Enhancing their brand personality, illy introduced the illy Art Collection in 1992. Elevating coffee and coffee-making into an art form was not a popular concept at the time. But then Francesco Illy had the idea for their iconic espresso cup, an interpretation of the country's old art of decorative porcelain. The illy Art Collection has been added to over the years by established and upcoming artists, and has become one of the world's largest collection of art objects.[34] Among the artists who have contributed to the illy Art Collection are Robert Rauschenberg, Francis Ford Coppola, David Byrne, Jeff Koons, Julian Scnabel, Yoko Ono and Anish Kapoor. On a promotional piece distributed through illy's stores, they say: 'For the last 25 years we have been entrusting our coffee cups to the hands of some of the greatest talents in contemporary art. They have interpreted the white canvas of the cup, so you can enjoy not just coffee, but an experience that involves the mind and the senses.' We believe that the art collection enables illy to stand out and build connections despite the increasing proliferation of coffee brands around the globe.

Building on the association, after an encounter with the great photographer Sebastião Salgado in 2002, illy decided to pay homage to the men and women growing coffee through a photography project that lasted 14 years and extended to 10 countries, culminating in the 'Scent of a Dream' exhibition.[35]

Today, illy continues to invest in advancing its espresso-machine technology and design, bringing it to the home for personal consumption in 1995, setting up Francis Francis! and launching the X1. A year later, illy's logo was redesigned to allow for more artistic interpretations.[36]

The consumer experience in the illy store involves all of the senses. Obviously, the first impression is from the sense of sight: the whole environment is decorated with the illy logo, colours and the famous illy espresso cups. Following up is a strong smell of great coffee, something that immediately evokes the 'need for coffee' feeling, and as the customer waits to order, the sound of the espresso machines assures them that a great-quality coffee is brewing. The store environment radiates high-quality Italian design, apparent in every detail: the furniture, lighting and even the merchandise display. It is a total experience, one that envelopes the five human senses, and once we get that cup of coffee, the taste, of course, becomes one of the most important aspects of the experience.

Illy is a great example of not just a company that makes coffee, but one that pays close attention to all aspects of its brand, celebrating coffee and 'all things Italian'.[37] They not only pay close attention to the quality of their products, they also focus on the details of their product and packaging design and ensure fair-trade measures and responsibility, establishing coffee-industry awards for coffee-growers around the world and celebrating coffee in global events.[38]

It's worth noting that Starbucks used a similar brand-strategy model, underscoring the importance of paying attention to all of the senses when developing one's products and branding elements. In fact, when Starbucks first launched breakfast sandwiches, they weren't going to keep them, because their aroma was overpowering the smell of coffee and threatened the company's image for having a passion for coffee, one of its key brand attributes. They were able to limit the smell, however, giving them a profitable line extension.[39]

THE SURPRISING TRUTH ABOUT FACES, LOGOS AND LOYALTY – A GUEST PERSPECTIVE FROM CHRIS MALONE, USA

Award-winning author, speaker, thought-leader and strategic adviser, Chris Malone is a former C-level executive with multiple Fortune 500 companies and the co-author of *The Human Brand: How we relate to people, products and companies*. His category experience includes the consumer packaged-goods, food service, hospitality and consulting industries and his specialities include growth acceleration, strategic planning, innovation strategies, consumer and B2B marketing, e-commerce, sales management, P&L management, product development, customer loyalty, client retention and public speaking. Here's what he has to say about the relationship between human faces and brand logos.

'As online shopping and trade proliferate, it seems clear that we are encountering live, human faces less and less frequently in commerce. Instead, we are greeted by the logos of faceless, digital monoliths like Amazon, Netflix and Google. At first glance, this seems to be a natural consequence of the increasingly wired world around us. But what if something essential to commercial success has been unwittingly lost in the steady migration of human to digital interactions? New research suggests that that may be exactly what's happening as our culture moves further into the digital age.

'Humans are remarkably adept at studying, interpreting and recalling the faces and facial expressions of other humans. For our ancestors who lived thousands of years ago, the ability to recognize people, to correctly judge their intentions and collaborate productively was crucial to their survival. Through natural selection and evolution, faces became the focal point for all human interactions. It allowed our ancestors to rapidly distinguish friends from foes and build trusting relationships with others.

'Over the past several decades, social psychologists have deduced that as humans struggled for survival they had to develop an ability to make two kinds of immediate judgements: what do other people intend towards me? How capable are they of carrying out those intentions? Researchers call these two critical categories of human perception 'warmth' and 'competence'. These perceptions of others, largely detected through facial expressions, have been shown to guide over 80 per cent of human behaviour towards others.

'More recently, my colleagues Dr Susan Fiske and Dr Nicolas Kervyn and I showed that customers also perceive, purchase and become loyal to brands on the basis of their warmth and competence.[40] This led to a wide variety of follow-up studies investigating how perceptions of brands are similar to perceptions of humans.

'One such study investigated how perceptions of human faces are similar to those of brand logos. Researchers at the University of Lüneburg in Germany recently published the findings of a study designed to evaluate how humans perceive and form opinions of both faces and brand logos. Their conclusion was that humans use the same psychological framework to process and judge brand logos as they do to evaluate the faces of the people around them. Both are judged on the basis of their warmth and competence.

'To reach this finding, Dr Rainer Hoeger and colleague Anne Lange had German test subjects evaluate 18 face variations and 16 well-known brand logos using established predictors of human loyalty and commitment, such as warmth, trustworthiness, competence and dominance.

'The participants' ratings of both faces and brand logos yielded a strikingly similar pattern of warmth and competence perceptions. The researchers concluded that we assess brand logos using the same skill and trustworthiness criteria that guide all other loyalty and commitment towards others. Humans evaluate dynamic faces and static logos using the same warmth and competence criteria.

'There's a crucial difference between face and logo interactions, though. Human facial expressions change during the course of an interaction to telegraph crucial information about emotions and intentions. Brand logos, on the other hand, are static and unchanging. They lack the nuance and variation of a human face.

'As a result, their ability to elicit trust and loyalty is impaired relative to that of an expressive human face. Perhaps this helps explain the steady decline in loyalty towards companies and brands over the past decade. This troubling finding was well documented recently by researchers at Northwestern University in the *Journal of Brand Management*.[41]

'Despite the scale, efficiency and ever-present availability of electronic commerce, it seems that something significant and crucial has been lost in the transition from human to digital interactions. While e-commerce, social networks and mobile devices continue to grow and change at a breakneck pace, the human psychology of trust and loyalty has remained unchanged despite thousands of years of evolution. That's not likely to change anytime soon.

'We remain heavily dependent on the dynamic facial expressions, the tone of voice and body language that have shaped human interactions for eons. The challenge is to find a balance between human and digital commerce that delivers the best of both worlds.

The key insight

'A growing body of evidence indicates that people were the first brands and faces the first logos. Therefore, all the branded trade and commerce that humans have engaged in over the past several thousand years has simply been an adaptation of the way we were wired by evolution to perceive, interact and form relationships with one another. This makes clear that digital technology is best used to support and enable human interactions, rather than replace them entirely.

Ideas to consider

- Don't overuse your logo
  - One of the most common and misguided practices in business is the overuse and reliance on company and brand logos. Potential customers certainly need to know you exist to buy from you, but a logo alone does very little to encourage purchase or loyalty. Logos should be used only to identify the communicator, they are not the communication itself.
- Come out from behind the screen
  - Our first instinct as humans is to assess the intentions and abilities of the people and organizations we encounter, both in person and in cyberspace. Make it easier for your online visitors to figure out who you are and what you care about by bringing the people in your organization to the forefront of your digital presence.
- Preserve human interactions
  - Automating most interactions with customers through digital technology may sound like a great way to reduce costs, but the resulting loss of trust and loyalty will far outweigh the savings. Instead, use technology to automate mundane, low-value tasks and free up time for your staff to have more personalized, meaningful and memorable interactions with customers.'

EXTENDED CASE STUDY: THE BIG BRAND DILEMMAS OF HARLEY DAVIDSON

As any serious motorbike rider knows, there are Harley riders and then there are the rest: Kawasaki, Honda, BMW, Suzuki, Motor Guzzi, Ducati etc. The reason is simple. For over 100 years, Harley cultivated a strong brand with tough, macho, manly associations. It was not just for men who wanted a means of transport, but for those craving the freedom of the road.

A Harley says 'I'm a rebel,' notwithstanding the fact that most Harley owners are middle-aged, suburban residents, at least in America.[42] What's more, the brand legends are designed to make the owners feel as though they belong to a unique tribe.

Twenty years ago, women were not thought of as an audience for Harley.[43] Harley reinforced imagery associated with male activities, while the 'girlfriend' was relegated to the back seat – if the model had a back seat, as it was also a brand designed to serve single riders.[44] With changing times and cultural mores, however, this approach was in danger of rendering the brand irrelevant.

To avoid such a fate, Harley Davidson adopted a new brand strategy. They would market to women as well. To do this they changed their brand architecture. Placing Harley as the master brand and endorser, they developed a whole new brand architecture that competed with other well-known motorcycle brands such as BMW, Ducati and Suzuki, and launched a sub-brand that catered to a more diverse audience. In this new structure, one sub-brand under its name could become what the master brand could not: their product as a daily mode of transport.

Beyond its brand image in its home country, Harley is seen as the ultimate American brand, on a par with Coca-Cola and McDonald's.[45] During its many years of success in the USA, it has also acquired many enthusiastic fans across the globe, inspiring the organization to open manufacturing facilities in other parts of the world.

Today, the current US Administration's policies of trade wars is making Harley look at its strategy again. Facing stiff competition beyond America, they had to make a decision about their country of origin, an important consideration in branding. In the public's eye, some brands convey an aura of authenticity because they're manufactured in their home country. Swiss-made watches are considered to be of higher quality than other watches. The same goes for German-manufactured cars. Coca-Cola and McDonald's are seen as American.

What if, however, the products were actually manufactured in another location? What if your Coca-Cola was made in Pakistan? It turns out that, often, it isn't the place of manufacture, it's the brand's place of birth and heritage that contributes to the brand image. By the same token, Harley will continue to be viewed as an American brand, even though it's moving some of its manufacturing outside the United States. There might yet even be undiscovered benefits of manufacturing the brand in other countries. For example, it might lead to developing new sub-brands that relate better to a local population, creating new markets and generating new loyal consumers. It is a tall task for a brand that has always been identified as having a strong American male persona, but it could be accomplished with the right brand-management steps and market conditions. Only time will tell.

KEY TERMS

- audio branding
- brand names
- scent branding
- sonic branding
- visual branding

DISCUSSION QUESTIONS

- What are the basic visual branding practices and their contributions to overall brand building?
- How should the brand foundational elements inform the creation of a brand name?
- When and where should sound or audio be employed for brand-building purposes?
- What are the basic considerations when branding through olfactory, taste and other senses?
- Will brands have to deliver on all five senses through technology in the future? Why or why not?

Notes

1 Minsky, L (2018) *Advertising Under One Hour*, Under One Hour LLC

2 Shotton, R (2018) *The Choice Factory. How 25 behavioural biases influence the products we decide to buy*, Harriman House LTD, Petersfield

3 Minsky, L (2008) *How to Succeed in Advertising When All You Have is Talent*, 2nd edn, The Copy Workshop, Chicago

4 Dawson, T (2018) The importance of color in brand strategy, *Branding Strategy Insider*, https://www.brandingstrategyinsider.com/2013/07/the-importance-of-color-in-brand-strategy.html (archived at https://perma.cc/X5BD-HZVY)

5 Ryan, T (2015) The story of the Coca-Cola bottle, Coca-Cola Journey, https://www.coca-colacompany.com/stories/the-story-of-the-coca-cola-bottle (archived at https://perma.cc/T2BE-YM6R)

6 Holusha, J (1994) Xerox's new strategy will not copy the past, Nytimes.com, https://www.nytimes.com/1994/12/18/business/xerox-s-new-strategy-will-not-copy-the-past.html (archived at https://perma.cc/6DJF-BY58)

7 Gains, N (2014) *Brand esSence*, Kogan Page, London

8 Premack, R, (2018) We asked 100 teens how they watch television – and the results should horrify cable companies, *Business Insider*, https://www.businessinsider.com/youtube-netflix-teen-generation-z-moving-away-from-cable-2018-6 (archived at https://perma.cc/NKD6-4YU7)

9 Minsky, L and Fahey, C (2017) *Audio Branding: Using sound to build your brand*, Kogan Page, London

10 O'Dell, J, (2000) Harley-Davidson quits trying to hog sound, *Los Angeles Times*, http://articles.latimes.com/2000/jun/21/business/fi-43145 (archived at https://perma.cc/CLH3-3RZX)

11 Lacy, L (2018) Google and Target issue the first voice-activated coupon for Google Assistant, Adweek.com, https://www.adweek.com/digital/google-and-target-issue-the-first-voice-activated-coupon-for-google-assistant (archived at https://perma.cc/868T-LY7F)

12 Council, F (2018) How voice technology is changing the way we work, *Forbes*, https://www.forbes.com/sites/forbesagencycouncil/2018/07/27/how-voice-technology-is-changing-the-way-we-work/#780591564a4d (archived at https://perma.cc/GFN5-A7JJ)

13 Minsky, L and Fahey, C (2017) *Audio Branding: Using sound to build your brand*, Kogan Page, London

14 Chapman, R and Bernays, E (2018) Olfactory bulb anatomy, *Encyclopedia Britannica*, https://www.britannica.com/science/olfactory-bulb (archived at https://perma.cc/B46E-H87E)

15 Gains, N (2014) *Brand esSense*, Kogan Page, London

16 Gains, N (2014) *Brand esSense*, Kogan Page, London

17 Murrt, P N (2012) How memories of experience influence behavior, *Psychology Today*, https://www.psychologytoday.com/us/blog/inside-the-consumer-mind/201210/how-memories-experience-influence-behavior (archived at https://perma.cc/RVC7-XBMT)

18 Lindstrom, M and Kotler, P (2009) *Brand Sense*, Kogan Page, London

19 BBC News (2011) Chanel No 5: The story behind the classic perfume, https://www.bbc.com/news/world-13565155 (archived at https://perma.cc/8CJ4-PQPM)

20 Klara, R (2012) Something in the air, Adweek.com, http://www.adweek.com/brand-marketing/something-air-138683 (archived at https://perma.cc/YVZ2-SPFV)

21 Gains, N (2014) *Brand esSence*, Kogan Page, London

22 Faure-Field, S (2012) This is what sensory branding can do for your business, *Singapore Business*, http://sbr.com.sg/media-marketing/commentary/what-sensory-branding-can-do-your-business (archived at https://perma.cc/Q54Y-Q4QN)

23 Minsky, L, Fahey, C and Fabrigas, C (2018) Inside the invisible but influential world of scent branding, *Harvard Business Review*, https://hbr.org/2018/04/inside-the-invisible-but-influential-world-of-scent-branding (archived at https://perma.cc/UH8T-N9TT)

24 Gains, N (2014) *Brand esSense*, Kogan Page, London

25 Chillot, R, (2013; last reviewed: 2016) The power of touch, *Psychology Today*, https://www.psychologytoday.com/us/articles/201303/the-power-touch (archived at https://perma.cc/92WT-MWB8)

26 Gauthier, P (2017) 5 advances and packaging trends in the beauty universe, *Packaging Digest*, https://www.packagingdigest.com/cosmetics/5-advances-and-packaging-trends-in-the-beauty-universe-2017-05-15 (archived at https://perma.cc/A9YU-M2BY)

27 Minsky, L and Fahey, C (2017) *Audio branding: Using sound to build your brand*, Kogan Page, London

28 Earthstoriez.com (2018) COFFEE history: a timeline, https://www.earthstoriez.com/coffee-timeline (archived at https://perma.cc/4AYQ-7LYR)

29 Castle, T (2000) *The Great Coffee Book*, Ten Speed, Berkeley

30 Gourmetcoffeelovers.com (2018) The history of coffee, http://www.gourmetcoffeelovers.com/the-history-of-coffee (archived at https://perma.cc/BZ42-TVX9)

31 Coffeefacts.org (2018) History of coffee in Europe, http://coffeefacts.org/history-of-coffee/coffee-in-europe-a-brief-history (archived at https://perma.cc/EN7K-NDQ2)

32 Avey, T (2018) History of coffee, PBS Food, http://www.pbs.org/food/the-history-kitchen/history-coffee (archived at https://perma.cc/TG6N-K5GL)

33 Morelli, R (2018) The city of coffee, Discover Trieste, https://www.discover-trieste.it/code/15907/The-city-of-coffee (archived at https://perma.cc/S8E3-NCP8)

34 illy (2018) illy: a heritage of taste, tradition and coffee culture, https://www.illy.com/en-us/company/company/illycaffe-history (archived at https://perma.cc/NH2Q-MFN7)

35 illy (2018) illy: a heritage of taste, tradition and coffee culture, https://www.illy.com/en-us/company/company/illycaffe-history (archived at https://perma.cc/NH2Q-MFN7)

36 illy (2018) illy: a heritage of taste, tradition and coffee culture, https://www.illy.com/en-us/company/company/illycaffe-history (archived at https://perma.cc/NH2Q-MFN7)

37 illy (2018) illy: a heritage of taste, tradition and coffee culture, https://www.illy.com/en-us/company/company/illycaffe-history (archived at https://perma.cc/NH2Q-MFN7)

38 SpA, E (2018) Andrea Illy, Expo Milano 2015, http://www.expo2015.org/archive/en/andrea-illy.html (archived at https://perma.cc/W586-KGF4)

39 LaMotta, L (2008) Starbucks: Ooh, that smell, Forbes.com, https://www.forbes.com/2008/01/31/starbucks-sandwiches-mcdonalds-markets-equity-cx_lal_0131markets24.html#179dbe44b324 (archived at https://perma.cc/ZMH2-C544)

40 Kervyn, N, Fiske, S and Malone, C (2012) Brands as intentional agents framework, *Journal of Consumer Psychology*, https://doi.org/10.1016/j.jcps.2011.09.006 (archived at https://perma.cc/R2JA-5R22)

41 Fidelum.com (2018), https://fidelum.com/wp-content/uploads/2014/09/BRAND-PREFERENCE-BEING-CHALLENGED-Journal-of-Brand-Management-August-2014.pdf (archived at https://perma.cc/VD3A-69Y5)

42 Ell, K (2018) Harley tries to regain its coolness factor, CNBC, https://www.cnbc.com/2018/02/03/harley-davidson-tries-to-regain-its-coolness-factor.html (archived at https://perma.cc/CDU7-8FUH)

43 Krauss, C (2018) Harley woos female bikers, Nytimes.com, https://www.nytimes.com/2007/07/25/business/25biker.html (archived at https://perma.cc/TR5Q-SZ5X)

44 Plueddeman, C, Story of One (as featured in H.O.G.® Magazine Issue 037) Harley-Davidson.com, https://www.harley-davidson.com/us/en/owners/hog/HOG-article/story-of-one.html (archived at https://perma.cc/3WPN-CWK6)

45 Rifkin, G, How Harley Davidson revs its brand, *strategy+business*, https://www.strategy-business.com/article/12878?gko=dcfc8 (archived at https://perma.cc/46X9-MF9Z)

07

Branding and the marketing communication ecosystem

> READING OUTCOMES
>
> At the conclusion of this chapter, you should be able to:
>
> - understand the historic brand-building role of media advertising as well as clues to its future roles;
> - identify the strengths and weaknesses of the marketing communication ecosystem;
> - describe the importance of post-sales customer massaging and support in building the brand.

Introduction

We live in a world where we are bombarded with news, information and, of course, paid marketing communication. Some say the average person is exposed to 5000 brand messages every day.[1] These brand 'exposures' could be anything from seeing a passing bus carrying outdoor ads to using a branded napkin in a fast-food restaurant, or simply taking a glance at a smartphone, but they all have one goal – to get you, the consumer, to be aware of and use the product.

It is even becoming difficult to distinguish between what is a plain marketing message and what is someone simply posing in their branded sneakers for a selfie. Marketers are trying to hide their brand messages behind the camouflage of branded content, and publishers, even highly respected ones like *The New York Times*, are all too happy to facilitate the delivery of these messages. Cynicism regarding marketing messages is at an all-time high.[2] People just don't trust what they're seeing. Perhaps some now consider all marketing messages 'fake news'.

The brand, however, should live beyond the product or service itself, which means marketers need to know how to fully employ the marketing communication ecosystem to build their brands. Although it is fraught with dangers through inauthentic messaging and other marketing missteps, used well, it can powerfully fuel the growth of your brand.

In this chapter, we shall discuss many of the marketing-communication components that create this jungle of messaging, all designed to engage consumers, get them to buy and try or repurchase the sponsor's brand. We shall examine the influence that they have on consumers and the methods of utilizing each one of them within the big orchestra of marketing communications, understanding the strengths and weaknesses of each one. To round up, we shall explore post-sales support, which can also advance the brand.

Overview

A successful brand obviously requires people to use the product or service, so getting prospects to try and reorder is the primary goal of marketers. For the promotion of brands, brand managers have only a limited ecosystem: advertising, direct-response marketing, direct sales, public relations, social media and digital and mobile marketing. In this chapter, we'll look at the role that the marketing communication ecosystem plays in the creation and maintenance of successful global brands. We'll start with advertising and cover all the elements of the marketing communication spectrum. You will learn the meaning of terms such as 'direct mail', 'direct selling' and 'direct response' and we'll try to cover the latest ways in which marketing is using the fast-moving world of digital, mobile and social media. Bill Rodi gives us a 'guest perspective' on shopper marketing, and our case study looks into a rebranding effort for Tropicana that didn't work and created a backlash – obviously a reaction that brand managers need to avoid.

Blah blah blah: some words on advertising and other marketing communication channels

The list of marketing activities below includes many that may seem familiar. The way they're used in an ever-changing marketing environment, however, poses challenges and their effectiveness is open to question. That is because while channels and platforms are proliferating, our understanding of how to best use these channels is also changing thanks to a greater awareness of behavioural economics – how people make decisions – and a better ability to track consumers, among other related reasons which we'll explore.

The first and still far oldest and biggest discipline to consider is advertising. One of the earliest known examples of advertising is a printing plate from China under the Song Dynasty (960 –1297 AD) promoting a sewing-needle shop.[3] In China, between the 11th and 7th centuries BC, ads were often conveyed through words and music.[4] As for the Western world, advertising on papyrus was used across ancient Greece and Rome.[5] Some examples of political ads from the Roman Empire include these from Pompeii, discovered during the excavations of the ruined city: 'The late drinkers ask you to elect Marcus Cerrinius Vatia eadile. Florus and Fructus wrote this' and 'If integrity in life is thought to be of any use, this man, Lucretius Fronto is worthy of great honour.'[6] Finally, 'Tourists in Pompeii can spot a well-preserved not-safe-for-work ad from 79 AD promoting the world's oldest profession.'[7]

The use of advertising continued during the Middle Ages. The first ad in Great Britain, however, was published in 1477, an ad to promote a book named *The Pyes of Salisbury*. Also, according to the same source, advertising started to become a serious business and it wasn't long before people started to offer themselves as specialists in advertising, with the earliest known advertising agency dating back to 1786.[8]

Advertising took off as a force during the industrial revolution because of the confluence of three developments: mass education (people could read the advertising), mass production through the industrial revolution (meaning there was an abundance of items that needed to be sold) and mass media (providing a place to run the advertising).[9] Other developments during this time included the concept of creating a campaign of related messaging, an innovation created by showman P T Barnum.[10]

During the growth period, advertising was primarily associated with media buying and placement. The first agents acted as representatives of publishers and, in the next iteration, as resellers of media space – they bought blocks of it from the publications, breaking it down into smaller segments to resell to the advertiser. Creative development was then added as a service to help sell the advertising space. Market research and other planning tools were the next to be added, again for the same purposes of facilitating the sale of ad space. The first full service ad agency was N W Ayer and Son, founded in 1869 by 20-year-old Francis W Ayer, who took his father's name as the agency name, because he feared clients wouldn't trust someone so young. They were the first firm to offer account services, market research, creative services such as copywriting, art direction and design and media planning and buying.[11]

Until the start of the 1900s, advertising was seen as – and constructed as – delivering 'news' (and still is used that way by retail brands with a sale). The switch came in 1905 when the persuasive power of advertising was recognized by Chicago-based agency Lord & Thomas (known as FCB today); John E Kennedy, a copywriter seeking a writing job at the agency, pitched the idea that 'advertising is salesmanship in print'.[12]

The role of advertising in creating a brand could be defined as 'external branding', as the term 'advertising' is a very wide and generic description of all activities connected to informing consumers about the available brands, products and services. Advertising can help build brand awareness, enable prospects and consumers to formulate their opinion about the brand, and drive trial and repurchase among other things. Advertising is also the external voice that carries the message of and conveys the difference between brands. Finally, of the various disciplines, it is the one that most easily enables and ensures consistency of global messaging.

Advertising is an industry built on innovation, with the goal of 'getting the right message in the right place at the right time'. From the early days of messages on papyrus – the start of 'outdoor advertising' – and 'roving barkers' (people walking through villages 'barking out' promotional messages) to print, radio and then television advertising to in-store marketing, to digital and mobile advertising, the available and effective platforms are ever-evolving and expanding, ever increasing media options for global brand managers. It is also very expensive, although the cost per exposure can be lower, because it's a form of mass communication. Some even argue that a reason it is effective is because people see it as being expensive, with the underlying message that if a brand can afford to advertise, it must be successful and, if it's successful, the brand must be effective at delivering on its promise.

The big question for a global brand manager is should the ad campaign itself be global, with the same message and even creative execution in every country, or should each country develop its own campaign? The answer isn't easy and depends on the brand's situation. Our rule-of-thumb is to ensure consistency of promise, personality or attitude and brand element usages (such as logos, colours and imagery style), while making sure that the specific images, stories and messaging emphasis are appropriate for and align with the intended audiences.

Some direct comments

At the heart of any marketing and advertising activity for a brand is the call to purchase it, try it, or at least become aware of its existence. The mass communication discipline that directly reaches out to the consumer and requests that prospects return the favour by purchasing the item, or at least requesting more information, is direct response. The term itself doesn't necessarily point to printed messages; it includes any marketing activity that requires or generates a response from the target audience, including those messages that are digitally delivered. Some even argue that digital, including mobile, is the ultimate direct-response medium, because everything can be tracked, tested and optimized, all with the goal of inspiring consumer behaviour.

FIGURE 7.1 The history of direct marketing

The tools and the platforms of direct marketing have changed and evolved, but the principles have remained the same. Content has always been king.

Defining direct response today can be tricky, simply because of constant changes in technology allowing consumers to engage in many different ways and respond accordingly. For example, a consumer who responds to favourable recommendations from complete strangers on a consumer review board could fall under the rubric of 'direct response', even if the review was not intended to 'sell'. After all, any click-to-buy on an e-commerce website falls under direct response. One way to define the direct-response relationship is as that between a marketer or brand and a consumer, where the marketer or brand advertises a product or service and the consumer then immediately responds. While direct-response mechanisms constantly change and develop, they can include sales-promotion coupons, emails, toll-free phone numbers, online banner ads, search engine pay-per-click links, personal sales calls and surprise offers at point-of-sale.

One term that has become notorious in the direct-response family of offerings is 'junk mail, or direct mail. Ever since technology has made it possible to personalize printed materials, the amount of direct mail has increased. Offers include everything from insurance plans to credit cards, club memberships, fund-raising appeals and more. Suppliers of direct mail claim that it 'hits home' and technically they are right. Direct-mail envelopes and packages do appear in our mailboxes and on our doorsteps. The question remains, do they generate the desired response? Since they are trackable, the answer for individual mailings can be determined and often they are very profitable. As a member of the US Postal Services pointed out to one of the authors, virtually 100 per cent of direct mail gets reviewed, because the recipient has to determine if it's important or not. A catchy message or offer on the envelope can be enough to get the recipient to consider the rest. But not only should direct-response materials be customized to each specific country in which a global brand operates, they should be (and often can be) customized to the needs, desires and stated interests of each intended recipient.

While working at Ogilvy & Mather Direct, Ilan learned that a hand-addressed, 'non-commercial'-looking envelope will always be opened and the content reviewed. With all the data that marketers have on consumers today, however, care should be taken that the brand doesn't come across as too 'familiar' with the recipient, as people often find that creepy. Just as with media advertising, the brand promise, personality or attitude, and brand elements (such as logos, colours and imagery style) should be consistent globally, while the specific images, stories and messaging emphasis should be appropriate for and align with the intended audiences.

Retail atmospherics

In marketing models developed by Professor Philip Kotler and others in the 1960s, among the Four Ps of product, place, price and promotion, 'place' gained attention as another point of differentiation between one brand and another. In earlier days, retail atmospherics – the delivery of the sensory branding opportunities we described in the previous chapter– were not given the attention they deserved, because buying and shopping were looked upon as functional activities that needed to be efficient and merely offer choice.

Over the past years, the retail business has witnessed amazing developments in attention to detail, including lighting, scenting, sound and tactile displays; in short, our five senses are getting close attention in many stores. However, brick-and-mortar stores are on the decline. Not only do we all live in a world of extremely saturated branded environments, we have a very wide selection of channels through which we can buy. Consumers need not leave their house to purchase an item or access a service. It's all online, and voice-activated devices can now deliver to our many needs and wants. Physical retailing, however, is not doomed. There are still plenty of opportunities to convey brand experiences and engage key prospects through 'place'. Recently, some e-commerce brands, such as Warby Parker, founded on the idea of operating completely online, have started opening brick-and-mortar stores as well. Apparently, consumers demand the presence of certain brands near their homes and work. They want a physical brand experience.

Many in the retail business have warmed to the idea of branding but do it primarily in the areas of advertising and website presence. Others, however, still lag behind when it comes to their retail atmospherics. Visit any shopping mall or other concentration of retail establishments, and you can't help noticing the 'sameness' of many brands. The branding concept of retail atmospherics also holds for professional service industries, including law firms, medical offices and advertising agencies. One ad agency has even developed a unique scent that it employs across all of its offices.[13]

To connect the brand to the atmospherics of a retail location, one needs to consider the physical ambiance of the space. It has to create a pleasurable sensory experience for the consumer. Just as a recruiter forms an opinion of an applicant in the first few seconds of a job interview, consumers form opinions of stores during the first steps into them. The wrong smell, sound or display can send them away, but the right elements can attract them deep into the environment. A good brand strategy can help in determining what kind of environmental attributes could be connected to a given brand. In the case of a supermarket with lots of organic produce, one could consider using lots of organic natural materials in the store interior. For a luxury brand, such as expensive, high-end jewellery, the store ambiance should project this exclusive quality through the materials on the walls and the lighting used to highlight the products. Meanwhile, big-box retailers imply frugality by operating on simple concrete floors, with simple, crude shelving systems and bright fluorescent lights.

When an emphasis is put on store image, it translates to a brand personality that is human-like. The brand experience is not limited to the store fixtures alone. When building the overall brand personality of a retail environment, the following criteria should be considered:

- Genuineness of staff
  - It goes without saying that the staff have to be honest, sincere, reliable and true to the brand values they represent. Training is essential, as they are your 'walking brand' and can communicate the most about the brand's care of their customers.
- Enthusiasm
  - How welcoming the staff are, how lively the atmosphere in the store is and how dynamic the space feels all contribute to the feeling of enthusiasm, communicating that the brand wants to help the customer.
- Sophistication
  - For some prospects, a less sophisticated store environment can feel more welcoming, while other customers might feel more at home in an elegant, upscale environment. In the case of a high-profile brand, the brand is ultimately judged by the store's appearance: is it elegant or merely glitzy, is its style understated or over-the-top, does it feel fresh and modern or old-school?
- Success level
  - The retail environment should convey that the brand is successful. Staff should make sure that the shelves are stocked, as empty shelves could be seen as a sign of neglect and an indicator that 'we are about to close shop soon'. Huge mark-down sales can also be a sign of desperation that the brand isn't performing well. Negative retail atmospherics could include having too strong a scent or playing music that is too loud. Some brands, such as Abercrombie and Fitch, on the other hand, have used just such atmospherics to drive parents and other older adults from their stores.[14]

Finally, store design can also consistently convey the brand promise, personality and attitude across all the brand's locations worldwide, with perhaps some localization in the offerings and imagery to better appeal to the shoppers.

Packaging priorities

Packaging became an important part of the marketing process when commodities, such as coffee, salt, sugar, oil, soap, tea and beans, started requiring some form of protection in stores, enabling the producer to take full credit for the product as well. Take Philadelphia Cream Cheese for example. Now a global brand, it was born 120 years ago and sold with foil packaging to protect the product from spoiling. 'We still use foil for our brick Philadelphia Cream Cheese,' said Lynne Galia, a Kraft spokeswoman. 'Foil provides a strong light and oxygen barrier for our product, limiting oxidation, which helps maintain the great taste and quality of our Philadelphia Cream Cheese. ... While we don't have details on the origin of the brick shape, it certainly makes sense to package this dairy product in foil.'[15]

Beyond the protective aspects, however, packaging is extremely important for brand identity and is especially important for brands sold in environments controlled by others. In fact, shoppers often look for the package shape and colours to find the item they want and are confused if the design gets radically changed. A package design is like a face in a crowd. For brands, it is extremely important to be able to show your unique, familiar and friendly face to millions of loyal customers, or to introduce your face to millions of potential customers in the most positive way. One indicator of an inexperienced brand manager new to a brand is a move to completely redesign the packaging. Packaging, however, can get out-of-date and sometimes need a redesign. Redesigns should be carried out with caution, so that the brand doesn't confuse or lose customers. A strategy that we've used in our consulting practices for updating packaged goods is to create a long-term plan and evolve the label, box or bag in stages. The goal should be to keep the product familiar for loyalists as well as fresh for attracting new consumers and should be consistently executed worldwide. The only localization should be the language on the packaging and perhaps the usage imagery if it's needed to better appeal to the shoppers in the market. Brand managers who oversee packaging, including the shopping bags, for stores that control their own brand have slightly more leeway, but the new design should be branded sufficiently so that the new packaging can be recognized from a distance. By being recognizable from a distance, it can then serve as a billboard advertising the store, and since the packaging or bag is being carried by a shopper, it also provides 'social proof' that people are frequenting the brand, which can drive additional prospects to them.

The ultimate importance of the packaging, and the role it plays, depends on where the product is being sold. If it's for a product sold in a store controlled by the brand, such as shopping bags for clothiers, the packaging becomes an extension of the brand experience – think Tiffany's turquoise box and bag – and it should merely convey the brand personality and essence. For brands sold in stores controlled by others such as grocery items sold in Tesco, Sainsbury's and so on – the packaging has to also convey the entire sales story. The decision to pick up the product, explore its label and drop it into the shopping trolley is considered to be the 'moment of truth'.[16] If the brand manager can't get prospects to review the label, all of the prior branding efforts have been in vain.

Shopper marketing in brand building

The discipline of shopper marketing involves studying the behaviours of shoppers and recognizing that the shopper might not be the same person as the consumer. The resulting findings then form the basis for optimizing the shopping experience and developing in-store, pre-store and online marketing programmes, so shoppers spend more (for retail brands) and select your brand (for packaged goods). To create an effective shopper-marketing programme for packaged goods, it's important for the brand manager of the packaged item to understand the priorities and brand of the retail establishment or establishments where the programme will 'live.' In this way they can ensure that the retail establishment will adopt the programme as well as execute it properly. In other words, both brands need to benefit from the programme, and the 'behaviours' or actions of the programme need to align with the brand personalities of both entities (or more, if the programme is being carried out by multiple retailers). For additional considerations on the application of shopper marketing regarding global brands, take a look at Bill Rodi's 'Guest Perspective' at the end of this chapter.

Social, mobile, digital and more

One of the most difficult areas of branding is dealing with social media. Social media continues to evolve quickly. A look at the history of social media shows that advertising and promoting brands was an afterthought. The prime reason for using social media was social. In 1979, Usenet allowed people to post news into newsgroups. Bulletin board systems, after a login, gave participants an interaction option. Compuserve introduced the first chat option for participants, and Prodigy ventured into online portraits and online news. By 1988, 'advanced technology' enabled file sharing and ICQ technology took us into multi-user messaging, games and an introduction to abbreviations such as LOL.

Six Degrees was already attempting to give us the kind of connectivity we experience today with the creation of profiles and adding friends. Dynamic content was first introduced by LiveJournal in blogs and forums. From this stage, around 2001, we stepped into the 'golden era' of social media, with the introduction of Wikipedia and a short time afterwards the introduction of Friendster. Hi5 was a great jump forwards, combining the ability to include photo sharing, user groups, social gaming and status update all in one programme, which paved the way for Myspace and subsequently The Facebook, which was open only to Harvard University students at the time.

Google tried to get into the game with Orkut, and the next big hit was Flickr with its photo-sharing platform. YouTube was a game changer since it allowed video sharing and video-streaming platforms of the like never seen before. More niches were added in the form of Reddit, an entertainment and social-networking platform. Facebook in its current form joined the party in 2006 and became the leader until the summer of 2018, when it started to experience a consumer revolt because of privacy concerns. In addition, Twitter, Tumblr, WhatsApp, Snapchat, Tinder, Pheed and others are adding to the noise and quite frankly to the confusion among both consumers and advertisers.[17]

There is an ongoing debate about the efficiency of social media and its return on investment (ROI) for advertisers. There are no clear answers, because there are no reliable tools for measurement. Research from the American Direct Marketing Association (DMA) shows that only 48 per cent of marketers agree that social media gives them any return on investment.[18] Nevertheless, it is clear these days that marketers are using social media in vast numbers. Close to 80 per cent of all marketers, both B2C and B2B, are engaged in some form of social-media activity of one kind or another.[19] While 32 per cent of marketers aim to achieve brand awareness through organic social media (39 per cent B2C, 26 per cent B2B), only 20 per cent of them aim to achieve brand awareness via paid social media (26 per cent B2C, 19 per cent B2B). Rather, their main goal for paid social media is to generate leads.[20]

At the end of 2017, Marc Pritchard, P&G Marketing Chief, in his acceptance speech while being awarded the Master of Marketing award by *Marketing Week* magazine in London, talked about the digital immersion, especially the social-media component of it, in everyday marketing strategies, mentioning that he was disappointed by the lack of ROI data. Moreover, he also expressed concerns about brand safety, a topic we covered in Chapter 4. Pritchard said that P&G had to rethink where its ads appear. While people in the industry were shocked by *The Times* investigation, which revealed that Google ads were appearing next to unsavoury content from people including terrorists and white supremacists, he half-joked that he is also questioning how many cat videos Google needs its ads appearing alongside.[21,22]

While marketing ROI is clearly an issue, social media can't be ignored, because too many people are using it. The first place to start is with social-media monitoring, because it can uncover trends, as well as unmet needs, that can lead to brand extensions, dissatisfaction with product performance and other issues and opportunities central to maintaining brand health. If an issue appears, we recommend a quick response, which should be localized to fully reflect the culture, concerns and conversational language of the specific market, but in the personality or attitude of the global brand. The social-media specialist who responds should be aware that their messages could quickly become global, shared among the social-media user's network. Therefore, centralized internal online resources should be developed to ensure consistency of messaging across markets – a domain of the global brand manager. For additional considerations when using social media in global branding, take a look at Dr Karen Sutherland's 'Guest Perspective' in Chapter 11.

Another discipline that falls under the digital rubric is mobile, which is inherently local. When users access mobile, they are generally concerned with immediate goals, the here and now. It might be to find a nearby store location, an online store to compare prices, or technical and user reviews to help decide between various options. The content, therefore, of any marketing material should be highly localized. To ensure its accuracy, we recommend that it be maintained by staff or an agency within the market, but with global oversight to ensure consistency of branding.

Of course, owned online properties such as websites, fall under digital too. While local sites can be developed, all of them are inherently global, because they can be easily discovered and accessed across the world. It follows that the sites should all convey the brand promise and personality, as well as display the branding elements – logo, colours, font, imagery style and sound – of the global brand. The sites, however, can, include localized information such as store locations.

Though it's an offline initiative, we should also mention experiential marketing. Highly engaging with the right concept and experience, it is generally also very expensive to execute. We reference experiential here because the way to spread its reach is to inspire participants to share the experience on their social media. The event planners should be able to explain how the event is facilitating sharing and why participants would even want to share it in the first place. Experiential is, of course, highly local and should be executed by people working in the market, but the stunt should display the brand personality and dramatize the brand promise. It goes without saying that the design should convey the branding elements as well.

The importance of public relations for brand building

The practice of public relations (PR) is also a prominent factor in the marketing mix. According to the Public Relations Society of America (PRSA), the formal practice of what is now commonly referred to as PR dates back to the early 20th century.[23] The roles and functions of PR have changed because of the advances in technology, allowing the use of it in ways well beyond influencing printed messages. The earliest definitions of PR, for instance, emphasized the activities of 'press agents' and publicity, while more current definitions incorporate the concepts of 'engagement' and 'relationship building'.[24] These terms are more suitable to the strategy of brand building and the public perception of the brand and what the brand represents. More specifically, the PRSA adopted the following definition in 1982: 'Public relations helps an organization and its publics adapt mutually to each other.'

According to 'Marketing in China', a Shanghai-based marketing consultancy, the role of PR in China is a bit different. On their website, they claim that: 'In China you have to adapt your Geolocal Marketing to this particular market, you need also to adapt your public relations. The public relation subject is one of the touchiest subjects in China. Lots of companies fail because they don't understand the role of the government in media and how powerful it is. This role must be taken in account when you engage a strategy in China. Nearly all forms of media have some sort of relationship with government organizations.'[25]

Just like anything else in the world of communications, advertising and publicity, the evolution of technology has had a tremendous effect on the definitions, roles and functions of PR. Obviously, the impact that PR has on brands had evolved as well. Brand marketers using PR must adopt messages to the local cultures that communicate a meaningful difference between their brand and competing brands and project a positive brand image, while being ready to defend the brand should it encounter any crisis or consumer protests, product recalls, or negative publicity from other sources, including social media.

Because brand marketing is about influencing public perceptions by engaging and building a relationship with key stakeholders across a myriad of platforms, PR professionals can and should play a key role in all aspects of this process and be the voice of the brand both in announcing future plans and reacting to events that affect the brand. Considering some of the key PR activities, it is easy to understand why they are crucial to the success of the brand; they include branded journalism, content creation, corporate communications, crisis communications, events, executive communications, internal communications, marketing communications, media relations, multimedia, reputation management, social media (monitoring and placing) and speechwriting.[26]

Moreover, because PR professionals need to be accessible to local media, they should be retained in all of the markets where the brand is available. A brand manager should ensure that these professionals are fully versed in the mission, vision, values, purpose, personality and key messages of the brand, as well as in the application of the brand behaviours, so that they know how to properly respond. They will, however, also need leeway to respond to local issues in the most efficient, effective and, most of all, ethical way possible. No matter what, brand managers should always include the PR professionals in charge of their brand in all communications, briefings and updates.

Direct selling for global brands

Direct selling is often defined as a retail channel but without a fixed real-estate location. It is a person-to-person contact that generates sales and is used by top global brands and smaller, entrepreneurial companies to market products and services to consumers, including consulting, cookware, cosmetics, energy, financial services, healthcare, housewares, insurance, jewellery, nutritional supplements and real estate. It can be an economical way to engage with potential consumers and can offer an avenue for entrepreneurs to build their business with low start-up and overhead costs. Many consider the beginning of direct selling to be when Earl Tupper introduced branded products named 'Tupperware' in 1946. When he started, he actually sold them through traditional retail channels, stores, but they weren't successful because consumers didn't understand their uniqueness and differentiation from other containers, which needed to be demonstrated.

Luckily for him, he met someone experienced in direct selling, who began organizing Tupperware home parties. Two years later, this person, Brownie Wise, became the Tupperware's sales director and also became the face of the brand, promoting it via interviews on TV, radio and print media. Brownie Wise became a model for many who followed her direct-selling techniques, among them Mary Kay and Martha Stewart.

Direct selling is also a main component of B2B marketing. Overall, the value of a single sale in the B2B environment is much higher than an average B2C sale, creating a different dynamic between the buyer and seller. The B2B salesperson, however, often presents their products and services in the context of the prospect's offices. As a result, the only clear brand representations during these sessions are the elements on the slide show, the entirety of the leave-behind collateral and the tone, attitude, delivery and personality of the salesperson.

While all customer-facing staff, especially those in sales and service, functions as their employer's walking brand, a concept we discussed in Chapter 3, direct salespeople become even more important to the delivery of the brand experience because the retail atmospherics are absent. Therefore, the brands that use direct selling must employ salespeople that are a truly authentic representation of the brand. Imagine the direct-selling team of a brand such as Boeing, selling a new aeroplane model to a team of executives from an airline, or imagine a situation where an innovator tries to sell a new invention to a brand such as Nike. The need for a direct seller to understand the brand that they represent is acute. It is not enough just to know facts, figures and product attributes. It is important to know the brand being represented at the sales event and to be a good model and ambassador for that brand. It is the global brand manager's job to ensure that there are materials and a programme that fully trains the direct sellers in the mission, vision, values, promise and, most of all, personality, of the brand. Another key way to bring alignment of a brand's salespeople, a strategy which we mentioned earlier, is through the use of advertising, particularly for far-reaching global brands, as the messaging not only reaches prospects, it reaches employees as well. Brand managers can enjoy the benefits of appointing personal selling staff who know the local population, live among the prospects and intimately understand their needs and wants. This approach may sound old-fashioned, but it has many advantages.

Post-sales customer support

As you might recall, the 360-degree wheel of brand touchpoints that we illustrated in Chapter 3 started with the pre-purchase points, moved into the actual purchase experience, and ended with the post-purchase customer experiences with the brand. Most brands invest heavily in the first phase, pre-purchase, through spending on advertising, packaging, sales promotions and other disciplines that drive prospects down the path-to-purchase. Next, the actual purchase phase gains attention and budgets for engaging prospects. Store atmospherics and a general understanding of sense activation became relevant and influential in the consumers' choice and preferences. In-store promotions and other shopper-marketing techniques became major contributors to brand success.

With the advances in technology, particularly social media where customers can report on their experience with the brand, the last phase, post-purchase or post-sales, is becoming just as important, if not more important in brand building. After all, it's easier to re-sell to an existing customer than to get a new one to try the product or service. Before social media, the consumers' opinions and the reports on their actual brand experiences were not public. At best, they were relegated to a small circle of friends and family through direct word-of-mouth. Those days, as we all know, are long gone. As we've already mentioned, in today's digital-driven reality, customers have more power and control than ever. If customers have a great brand experience, something unexpected, they'll share it with friends, family and connections, which in turn can lead to new customers, all at zero cost to the marketer. The practice of inspiring people to broadcast their brand experiences is known as word-of-mouth marketing. If the customers don't have a positive brand experience, however, research shows that they are even more likely to broadcast it on social media. In fact, research shows that 13 per cent of unhappy customers will share their complaint with 15 or more people.[27]

Maintaining a consumer-complaints channel in every market that the brand serves is actually a great resource for uncovering unknown problems and new product opportunities. Any customer complaint points to a problem. It could be a functional issue with the product, an employee's behaviour, processes or some other issue. By paying direct attention to these problems from customers, a brand can explore and improve production, design, service, price, location, store environment and other attributes. As we mentioned earlier, brands employ experts who watch the Twitter feed and other social platforms all day and respond to consumers' comments, complaints and observations. Often this responsibility falls to the brand's PR professionals or it could be handled under a separate contract with an agency specializing in social media. For brands spread across multiple countries, it is often wise to have someone or some firm responsible for customer complaints in each market. If the responsibility is centralized, the brand manager should ensure that those responsible for uncovering and responding to customer complaints are conversant in the market's conversational language, including slang, and are fully empowered to immediately resolve the complaint. Provide a good experience by quickly and efficiently handling the customer's post-purchase issues and he or she could become even more loyal to the brand and could even become a brand advocate.[28] Create a bad experience and you might never recover the customer for future purchases. The most basic strategies for responding to post-sale issues are to be on the alert, monitor, document, learn and respond. Some best practices for responding include:

1. Educate the sales team, marketing staff and other key stakeholders on the value of post-purchase (post-sales) brand strategies.
2. Learn to listen to the exact nature of the complaint and evaluate it.
3. Be prepared to admit mistakes, both in person, as well as in public (depending on the scope of the issue).
4. Investigate all the possible ways to find a solution to the current complaint and in the future.
5. Never leave a customer without an appropriate answer and a solution.
6. Develop the next steps with your team to exceed customer expectations in the future.

Of course, brand marketers should also be aware of buyer's remorse, particularly for higher-cost items and for those brands that offer an extensive range of options. Research shows that the fewer choices a customer has to make, the better because they question less of it.[29] So even if a customer didn't complain, the post-sale period could be a chance to reinforce the value of the brand and its purposes. Some key ways to accomplish this goal is through snail mail, email and other forms of outreach. The response, of course, needs to be culturally appropriate to the market, another area where global brand managers need to focus.

SHOPPER MARKETING – A GUEST PERSPECTIVE FROM BILL RODI, USA

Bill Rodi currently leads Mosaic's US Shopper Marketing business, with an emphasis on growth strategy, business development and operations. He brings to the role more than 20 years of brand and creative-strategy experience garnered across leadership positions at Kraft Foods, Landor Associates, MSI, Schawk/Anthem, GfK Consumer Brand Consulting and his own firm, Rodi Platcow Malin Advertising. His work for clients, including P&G, Unilever, ConAgra, Kellogg's, Yum! Brands, RJ Reynolds, Monster Beverage, Volvo, Sony BMG and Diageo, has garnered him awards, including two EFFIE Awards for marketing excellence. Here's what Bill has to say about shopper marketing:

'What is shopper marketing? It probably depends whom you ask, and perhaps even at what point in its history you do so. In classic Four Ps vernacular, one might think of Shopper Marketing simply as 'promotion' – or a means to convey a pricing offer or incentive to purchase a given product at a specific time and place. And while this definition wouldn't be completely incorrect, classifying what's become a much more nuanced, integrated brand-marketing discipline today in such lifted and tactical terms would be unfairly limiting.

'Today's best-in-class shopper marketing does so much more: building the brand and its equity, delivering on a brand's promise, complementing other marketing activities and, most importantly in this new age of near-limitless choice and information to inform it, understanding deep human insights to engage in a thoughtful, one-on-one conversation with the consumer.

'All that being said, it should be known that shopper marketing, at its core, was born to focus on personal connections to better understand consumers and inform their purchase decisions. While learning the concept of Shopper Marketing, it's not only important to understand how it has the potential to evolve brands, but also how it affects the daily lives of consumers and retailers alike.

'For the consumer, shopper marketing can be most commonly defined by the total sum of their digital and physical interactions before purchase – with or without the brand in the forefront – that ultimately inform their purchase decision. For retailers, Shopper Marketing has the power to dramatically shift the shopper's daily in-store experience towards tailored programmes, driving a personalized brand experience that's uniquely their own. And lastly for brands, shopper marketing can be seen as not only generating increased sales year on year, but also as the science of intercepting the shopper during their daily routine to propel brand equities and interest.

'When determining where shopper marketing lives in the broader marketing mix, industry leaders have commonly divided communication into two distinct sectors: ATL (above the line) and BTL (below the line). In a space we call the ATL, messaging and brand building at a macro scale allows for mass communication. The sector where shopper marketing lives, BTL, is hyper-focused on sales via one-on-one consumer conversations leading to the point of purchase. It should be noted that, as the journey of shopper marketing is explained, it will be evident that the practices of BTL have evolved with it.

'So, to fully understand its complete (and ever-evolving) journey, let's consider its past, present and future, tracing its arc from its origins as a brand-driven promotional tactic, to its efforts to drive the loyalty of retailers, to a collaborative consumer-centric effort shared by both parties in an ongoing effort to capitalize on shopping behavior – securing added display placement in-store and ultimately driving incremental sales.

'Indeed, relative to many marketing disciplines, shopper marketing remains a relatively new specialization – and there is an ongoing interplay between remaining consumer-packaged-goods (CPG) marketers and their major accounts that followed in the retail boom of the 1980s and 1990s. As for all the growth and investment surrounding it in recent years, it remains an elusive moving target of sorts. Depending on whether you're the stakeholder employing it or the organization in which it operates, shopper marketing can be defined as a tool to spark measurable sales of select products, or a strategic enterprise designed to grow brands and brand/product portfolios.

The past – 'recognizing the store as a medium'

'In the golden age of marketing, CPGs followed a much less complex playbook predicated on 'pushing' messaging out to consumers through broad, mass media and then intercepting and 'funnelling' them into store aisles with price and other incentives to purchase their brand or product.

'In a popular example, Procter & Gamble's Tide detergent made its first debut in stores across America with a universal TV and radio commercial. Its target audience, stated simply, was anyone. After the commercial's airing, consumers steadily became more familiar with Tide, keeping the commercial and print piece top of mind. Their simplified purchase journey then ended at their local grocer when they were incentivized to purchase Tide off the shelf. All this to say that in the past, in light of original marketing strategies such as Tide, brands regarded shoppers as a homogeneous audience to be merely spoken to in different ways, across different 'touchpoints', based on where they were along a 'path to purchase'. All the while, managing brands represented little more than logos, colours and packaging to decorate that path in a consistent, recognizable way.

'And it worked, for a while. Dollars then began to pour into routine weekly circulars and FSIs (free-standing inserts in Sunday newspapers), timed to advertising media buys and trade support (price discounting), driving a steady stream of extra measurable sales to a given retailer or chain, thus solidifying a manufacturer's position on-shelf at a given account and currying favour with it.

'This 'Account-Specific' marketing, programmes targeted to a particular retailer change, and its attendant innovation and investment, would eventually be co-opted, however, by the stores who seized upon their new customer intimacy and data-driven insights and set out to own the consumer – and thus gain the upper hand with manufacturers – themselves. This multimedia complexity drove a prolonged battle to gain shoppers' attention, with stakeholders simultaneously campaigning to place their interests at the forefront. In plain terms, there were too many cooks in the kitchen. Unfortunately, this propelled complexity led to both brand and programme fails, ushering in the next era of 'Retail Marketing'. This era, in short, also welcomed the concept of stores as *de facto* media and customer-loyalty vehicles, leveraging new CRM (customer relationship management) technologies and the oceans of new, highly-targetable information on store shoppers it yielded.

'All of which presaged the concept of 'Shopper Marketing', as we've known it for some 20-odd years – in which retailers and manufacturers joined hands in a resounding truce of collaboration and information-sharing that placed the shopper at the centre of both parties' efforts. Together, their *shared* goals drove growth by improving shopping experiences overall: tailoring offerings, suggesting pairings and delivering solutions to consumers that went well beyond the early days of coupons, circulars and limited promotions to truly engage and have a dialogue with *shoppers* as distinct from *consumers*. Shopper marketing helped to build brands over time and engaged with shoppers at every stage of their purchasing process, rather than just driving short-term sales through offers and tactics at the retail 'point-of-sale'.

The present – 'always-on/on-demand'

'So, what's changed as regards shopper marketing today? Two things really: technology, and the importance of strong brands to help consumers navigate the increasingly complex world it's created. Contrasted with that bygone era of FSIs and coupons described above, today's new generation of shoppers raised on technology have come to view the world and their path through it in entirely different ways from before. And this has upended much of marketing's established beliefs about how to 'manage' them. Before this era the retailer and/or brand had control of funnelling the shopper to a purchase, but now with technology such as Amazon, Google *et al*, it is the shopper who is in total control.

'There are many options for engaging with the shopper. Media have fragmented exponentially, and product variety has exploded through online shopping and e-commerce applications – while access to both has become almost constant through ubiquitous mobile devices. This puts the shopper even further at the centre of this complex new commercial ecosystem and marketers areincreasingly at odds about how best to navigate it, as well as serve an 'always-on/on-demand' population with access to endless information and choice.

'More to the point, for a shopper marketer in today's highly fragmented and hyper-accelerated world, the notion of any predictable 'path to purchase' has quickly become more of a conceptual model than an accepted axiom: a quaint memory of what was once held as a central truth just years before, replaced by a new emphasis on personalized marketing, and the need for brands and retailers alike to extend their view well beyond mere physical environments to meet shoppers with the right message and right offer, in just the right place, at any hour of the day.

'Push' tactics like coupons and sales promotions have been replaced by 'pull' strategies, wherein brands seek to position themselves as a like-minded or favourable friend that one enjoys a relationship with. For, ironically, all this new media and technological complexity has only wound up reasserting the vital importance of two things that people understand: trust and favour.

The future – 'curated, tailored commercial experiences'

'Looking ahead, it's safe to say a few of the above-mentioned cultural, commercial and technological forces will continue to play themselves out and shape the next era of shopper marketing. No doubt it will result in a much more singular view of 'commerce' that delineates less between 'in-store' and 'online' and leverages technology to create more seamless, intuitive experiences.

'Retailers today are already rethinking ways to keep up with 'always-on' shopper behaviour. And, in the future, this will continue to evolve into a dual-role approach that marries complementary digital and physical activities in ways that highlight the different roles of each, to create shopper experiences that differentiate them from other stores. To do so they will first strive to create unique in-store experiences, assortments and offers that cannot be replicated digitally, giving the shopper a reason to visit a store versus buying online. As for all the talk of brick-and-mortar stores becoming extinct, the reality is that they'll continue to play a vital role in the shopper mix – but a more specific one: there will be smaller, more curated and creative stores designed to build loyalty with targeted audiences versus ones that sell mass volumes of product like the big-box formats in decline today.

'Retailers will then complement this with enhanced online availability of products, making it convenient and easy to shop online, while providing dynamic unique pricing and proprietary content to again differentiate themselves from competitors. Supporting this will be increasingly personalized and tailored offers and messaging, driven by vast streams of data and technical platforms to help interpret and manage it.

'On the other technological front, digital shopping will become easier with the expansion of voice-activated technology and virtual reality, resulting in a world where, through interactive VR, you can perhaps one day visit the grocery store and pick your preferred products right off the shelf from your couch.

'Meanwhile, delivery options will continue to become more efficient with drone delivery and on-demand delivery services. Retailers will also find efficient ways to automate inventory control for improved back-of-store efficiency, for example, evolving robotic automation to complement, or even replace, human labour services from warehouses to increase efficiencies.

'All said and done, it can be seen that technology, through trial and error, has enabled a highly personalized path-to-purchase, closing the loop and establishing the arc of shopper marketing. And the core of its existence resides in one quintessential objective affecting purchase behavior: having a one-on-one conversation with the consumer.

Key takeaways

'Within most large consumer-goods enterprises today shopper marketing stands alone as a distinct, specialized function, often aligned with either sales (ie as a velocity, category and basket-building effort) or marketing (ie as an extension of a brand's positioning and presentation, integrated with other activities). But in both cases it is classified as a 'below-the-line' (BTL) operation: activity that remunerates the agency by paying a fee per project, not a commission from a given media budget spending.

'Shopper marketing, at its core, focuses on shaping purchase decisions through personalized, one-on-one conversations (within or without retailer-centric programmes) throughout their path-to-purchase. The savvy brand manager understands that shopper marketing is only supplementary to the ensemble of all marketing and branding activity. Shopper marketing in itself will not be the only brand-building strategy.'

EXTENDED CASE STUDY: THE TROPICANA PACKAGING REDESIGN DISASTER

Back in 2009, Tropicana decided to 'rebrand' by redesigning its package, introducing it with an awareness campaign employing advertising, PR and other disciplines. Their rebranding attempt is considered a failure; some even consider it one of the biggest rebrand blunders of all times.[30] Understanding what happened and how they recovered should be an important lesson to every brand manager.

Prior to the rebranding effort, Tropicana was already a mature multinational brand, launched in 1947. The brand was purchased by Pepsi in 1998. Tropicana's website tells the story of a single person, not a corporation, and the battles that he went through to establish his business: 'The Tropicana story begins with Anthony T Rossi, who arrived in the US with just $25 in his pocket. He founded Tropicana in 1947 with the mission of making the goodness of the finest fruit accessible to everyone. He developed flash pasteurization and pioneered orange juice transport in 1970 via train from Florida to New York. As Tropicana continues to grow, we have Anthony Rossi to thank for creating the spirit of innovation and fresh thinking that continues at Tropicana today.'[31]

Notice the solid mission and vision in the brand story and that the promise of delivering a pure orange juice 'from the fruit into your glass' was there from the beginning, despite the fact that mass production forces certain artificial processes to be involved. For years, the loyal customers of Tropicana saw comfort in the extremely clear image of an orange, with a straw in it, delivering juice directly from the fruit into their glass.

But then on January 8 2009, Tropicana unveiled a new packaging design for its best-selling brand, Tropicana Pure Premium, a brand that had enjoyed sales revenues reaching more than US $700 million (£560 million) a year.[32] We can't uncover the strategic rationale behind the rebrand. One guess is that it was driven by the overall rebrand that Pepsi went through at the same time, and by the same designer.[33] The new design, however, was considered cleaner, removing the orange and the straw.[34]

In an article by Peter Merholz in the *Harvard Business Review*,[35] he mentioned that seen in isolation the newly designed carton would probably pass muster, but when stocked on the shelf in the supermarket environment, it didn't resonate or compete with other brands,[36] a reminder that all brands work in the context of other brands in their own and similar categories.

Pepsi invested US $35 million (£28 million) to create Tropicana's package redesign and accompanying advertising materials[37] and then had to spend much more to remove it from the supermarket shelves,[38] apologizing to customers,[39] and losing market share to the competition.[40] There are some useful lessons to be learned from Tropicana's mistake. Understanding brand origins and brand legacy is a powerful tool for guiding future brand development programmes;[41] [42] extensive packaging changes all at once, as we pointed out earlier, can confuse existing customers;[43] and, most of all, it is important to keep the imagery and content that form the customers' emotional ties with the brand. It is these ties that enable long-term loyalty towards the brand. Therefore, with package redesigns, as stated earlier, the brand manager should always proceed cautiously.

KEY TERMS

- art direction
- atmospherics
- copywriting
- direct response
- direct mail
- shopper marketing

DISCUSSION QUESTIONS

- What is the historic brand-building role of media advertising?
- What are retail atmospherics and why are they important to brand building?
- How do you see advertising being used for brand building in the future?
- What are the strengths and weaknesses of direct response for brand building?
- Why is packaging design one of the most important brand-building influencers?
- Why is post-sales customer massaging important in supporting and building the brand?

Notes

1 StopAdBlog (2019) How many ads do you actually see daily?, https://stopad.io/blog/ads-seen-daily (archived at https://perma.cc/26WD-K93D)

2 Creighton, K (2019) Branding in an age of cynicism, *Simpson Scarborough*, https://www.simpsonscarborough.com/branding-in-an-age-of-cynicism (archived at https://perma.cc/5DNW-6HD8)

3 Commercial Advertisement, https://depts.washington.edu/chinaciv/graph/tcommain.htm (archived at https://perma.cc/FR8R-M639)

4 Eckhardt, G and Bengtsson, A (2008) Pulling the white rabbit out of the hat: Consuming brands in Imperial China, *Advances in Consumer Research* [European Conference Proceedings] 8; Eckhardt, G and Bengtsson, A (2010) A brief history of branding in China, *Journal of Macromarketing*, 30 (3)

5 Minsky, L (2018) *Advertising Under One Hour*, Under One Hour LLC

6 Cartwright, M (2019) Pompeii: Graffiti, signs & electoral notices, *Ancient History Encyclopedia*, https://www.ancient.eu/article/467/pompeii-graffiti-signs--electoral-notices (archived at https://perma.cc/6KJ8-44RL)

7 Campaign US (2015) History of advertising: No. 142: The Pompeii penis, https://www.campaignlive.com/article/history-advertising-no-142-pompeii-penis/1357977 (archived at https://perma.cc/58S6-43KJ)

8 A brief history of advertising (2007) OpenLearn, http://www.open.edu/openlearn/money-management/management/business-studies/brief-history-advertising (archived at https://perma.cc/N76P-VGU9)

9 Minsky, L (2018) *Advertising Under One Hour*, Under One Hour LLC

10 Applegate, E (2012) *The Rise of Advertising in the United States: A history of innovation to 1960*, Scarecrow Press, Lanham, Maryland

11 Applegate, E (2012) *The Rise of Advertising in the United States: A history of innovation to 1960*, Scarecrow Press, Lanham, Maryland

12 Lord & Thomas: advertising & marketing profile, adbrands.net, https://www.adbrands.net/files/us/lord-and-thomas-us.htm (archived at https://perma.cc/GSF5-QWDC)

13 Minsky, L, Fahey, C, and Fabrigas (2018) Inside the invisible but influential world of scent branding, *Harvard Business Review*, https://hbr.org/2018/04/inside-the-invisible-but-influential-world-of-scent-branding (archived at https://perma.cc/UH8T-N9TT)

14 Lutz, A (2014) Abercrombie is killing the nightclub vibe in its stores, BusinessInsider.com, https://www.businessinsider.com/abercrombie-changing-store-design-2014-5 (archived at https://perma.cc/92R2-HHR2)

15 Kasperkevic, J, Cream cheese has a history wrapped in tin foil, *Marketplace*, https://www.marketplace.org/2017/04/26/your-money/ive-always-wondered/cream-cheese-has-history-wrapped-tin-foil (archived at https://perma.cc/5PBM-HZCL)

16 Moments of Truth, *Mercuri International*, https://mercuri.co.uk/moment-of-truth (archived at https://perma.cc/S7SL-46PJ)

17 Colaiacovo, K. (2017) An interesting timeline of the evolution of social media, *Pepper It Marketing*, https://www.pepperitmarketing.com/facebook/evolution-social-media (archived at https://perma.cc/4XZQ-KFJ6)

18 DMA Insight: Social data Integration report 2016, DMA.Org.UK, https://dma.org.uk/uploads/ckeditor/Social_Data_Integration_2016.pdf (archived at https://perma.cc/TFZ9-DMW7)

19 Chaffey, D (2018) Using social media marketing in B2B markets? *Smart Insights*, https://www.smartinsights.com/b2b-digital-marketing/b2b-social-media-marketing/b2bsocialmediamarketing (archived at https://perma.cc/5NU7-VYN2)

20 Allen, R (2018) Does social media marketing actually generate ROI? *Smart Insights*, https://www.smartinsights.com/social-media-marketing/social-media-analytics/social-media-marketing-actually-generate-roi (archived at https://perma.cc/JY7R-TC43)

21 Vizard, S (2018) 'Marketer of the Year' Marc Pritchard on his quest for transparency, *Marketing Week*, https://www.marketingweek.com/2017/10/04/marc-pritchard-quest-transparency (archived at https://perma.cc/NWE2-JKD4)

22 Google faces questions over videos on YouTube (2017) Smart Insights, https://www.thetimes.co.uk/article/google-faces-questions-over-videos-on-youtube-3km257v8d (archived at https://perma.cc/VT85-4GLK)

23 About Public Relations, PRSSA, Public Relations Society of America, https://www.prsa.org/all-about-pr (archived at https://perma.cc/5NXU-JB3E)

24 Dühring, L (2017) The history of public relations thought, https://link.springer.com/chapter/10.1007%2F978-3-658-18034-8_5 (archived at https://perma.cc/G9JG-PPVE)

25 Marketing to China (2018) How PR (Public Relations) in China differs from advertising, https://www.marketingtochina.com/role-of-public-relation-china (archived at https://perma.cc/F2JL-A3JE)

26 About Public Relations, PRSSA, Public Relations Society of America, https://www.prsa.org/all-about-pr (archived at https://perma.cc/5NXU-JB3E)

27 McDonald, S (2019) Why customer complaints are good for your business, *Super Office*, https://www.superoffice.com/blog/customer-complaints-good-for-business (archived at https://perma.cc/44M2-VEYT)

28 Sheehan, A (2017) Post-purchase communications: expert tactics to stay in touch with customers, *Shopify*, https://www.shopify.com/retail/examples-of-great-post-purchase-communications-you-should-steal (archived at https://perma.cc/DF3Y-6XWF)

29 Spenner, P and Freeman, K (2012) To keep your customers, keep it simple, *Harvard Business Review*, https://hbr.org/2012/05/to-keep-your-customers-keep-it-simple (archived at https://perma.cc/L4ZJ-L53H)
30 Merholz, P (2009) Tropicana's marketing folly, *Harvard Business Review*, https://hbr.org/2009/02/tropicanas-marketing-folly.html (archived at https://perma.cc/6KQR-L2B5)
31 The Tropicana Tradition (2019) Tropicana.com, https://www.tropicana.com/our-story (archived at https://perma.cc/8CGF-XNLL)
32 Marion (2019) What to learn from Tropicana's packaging redesign failure? *The Branding Journal*, https://www.thebrandingjournal.com/2015/05/what-to-learn-from-tropicanas-packaging-redesign-failure (archived at https://perma.cc/2VDL-4968)
33 Marion (2019) What to learn from Tropicana's packaging redesign failure? *The Branding Journal*, https://www.thebrandingjournal.com/2015/05/what-to-learn-from-tropicanas-packaging-redesign-failure (archived at https://perma.cc/2VDL-4968)
34 Vinh, K (2009) Orange you sorry about Tropicana? Subtraction.com, https://www.subtraction.com/2009/02/24/orange-you-sorry-about-tropicana (archived at https://perma.cc/AUB7-Y4TQ)
35 Merholz, P, (2009) Tropicana's marketing folly, *Harvard Business Review*, https://hbr.org/2009/02/tropicanas-marketing-folly.html (archived at https://perma.cc/6KQR-L2B5)
36 Marion (2019) What to learn from Tropicana's packaging redesign failure? (2019) *The Branding Journal*, https://www.thebrandingjournal.com/2015/05/what-to-learn-from-tropicanas-packaging-redesign-failure (archived at https://perma.cc/2VDL-4968)
37 Marion (2019) What to learn from Tropicana's packaging redesign failure? (2019) *The Branding Journal*, https://www.thebrandingjournal.com/2015/05/what-to-learn-from-tropicanas-packaging-redesign-failure (archived at https://perma.cc/2VDL-4968)
38 Marion (2019) What to learn from Tropicana's packaging redesign failure? (2019) *The Branding Journal*, https://www.thebrandingjournal.com/2015/05/what-to-learn-from-tropicanas-packaging-redesign-failure (archived at https://perma.cc/2VDL-4968)
39 Marion (2019) What to learn from Tropicana's packaging redesign failure? (2019) *The Branding Journal*, https://www.thebrandingjournal.com/2015/05/what-to-learn-from-tropicanas-packaging-redesign-failure (archived at https://perma.cc/2VDL-4968)
40 Marion (2019) What to learn from Tropicana's packaging redesign failure? (2019) *The Branding Journal*, https://www.thebrandingjournal.com/2015/05/what-to-learn-from-tropicanas-packaging-redesign-failure (archived at https://perma.cc/2VDL-4968)
41 Cbs News (August 8 2018) https://www.cbsnews.com/news/arnells-explanation-of-failed-tropicana-design-resembles-his-nonsensical-pepsi-document (archived at https://perma.cc/UL4K-6E6E)
42 Marion (2019) What to learn from Tropicana's packaging redesign failure? (2019) *The Branding Journal*, https://www.thebrandingjournal.com/2015/05/what-to-learn-from-tropicanas-packaging-redesign-failure (archived at https://perma.cc/2VDL-4968)
43 Marion (2019) What to learn from Tropicana's packaging redesign failure? (2019) *The Branding Journal*, https://www.thebrandingjournal.com/2015/05/what-to-learn-from-tropicanas-packaging-redesign-failure (archived at https://perma.cc/2VDL-4968)

08

Brand management

> READING OUTCOMES
>
> At the conclusion of this chapter, you should be able to:
>
> - detail the tactical applications for optimizing the key phases in a typical brand's life cycle;
> - explain when and how to rebrand, and why it is better to slowly evolve the brand;
> - understand the 'when' and 'why' of co-branding, as well as some of its key best practices;
> - understand the common job titles and various requirements in a marketing department.

Introduction

When does a brand become a brand? Was GE (General Electric), a company that manufactures jet engines, a brand when Thomas Edison invented the light bulb? When did the power of its brand go into decline and will it be able to turn itself around? Think of all of the once powerful brands that are now shells of themselves, including Sears, Netscape, RCA and Circuit City, and those no longer in business such as online site Vine or television manufacturer Quasar.

Brands have a very distinctive life, defined by periods, just like humans. They're born out of the imagination of business entrepreneurs and innovators or new product-development groups within corporations; they either fail within a matter of months[1] or grow up and reach brand 'adulthood'; then they slow down and eventually vanish or get reborn. Others chug along year after year.

As we discussed in Chapter 5, marketers have named the life-cycle periods of brands: 1) launch; 2) adoption; 3) maturity; and 4) decline or rebranding. There are many different activities associated with these different eras in the lifetime of any brands and, while we covered some in Chapter 5, we will dig deeper and discuss more of them here. Rebranding, another key topic we'll cover in this chapter, also becomes a greater issue for global brands because the repositioning has to be executed across all of its markets for the brand to feel truly consistent. Looking deeper into the brand life cycle is important because it repeats itself in every country in which it is available. In other words, in every market, a brand experiences many evolutions until it becomes an entrenched brand concept in the consumers' minds.

As the brand grows stronger in a market, opportunities also arise for it to join forces with another brand. Called co-branding, these opportunities can help advance the brand, often with cost-savings and greater reach. The considerations and issues for this strategy as it relates to a global brand, however, are different.

Finally, a brand can't grow without the professionals who carefully tend and shepherd it through its birth and growth stages and, once established, help maintain it. Since the theme of this chapter is brand management, we'll look at the titles, roles and responsibilities of these individuals as well. Let's get started.

Overview

In Chapter 5, we outlined a brand's life cycle – from birth to death for some of them and 'rebirth' for others. In this chapter, we shall examine these stages more closely as we explore the steps for growing a brand into a global one. We shall also look at co-branding, a strategy that a brand manager can use to help expand a brand's presence. Finally, we'll look at the titles and roles of various marketing professionals who help grow the brand, whether local or global, and we shall conclude with a 'guest perspective' from Michaël Boumendil, founder and president of Sixième Son, the world's largest audio-branding firm; he discusses audio branding across borders. We also feature an extended case study on Rotary International's rebranding effort.

Taking a brand global and the people who do it

While we have explored the all-important product- or service-development stage, most 'brand launches' officially start with the introduction of the brand to consumers and the strategic and creative work leading up to it, which will be different depending on whether it is a completely new-to-market entity or if it is part of an extension of a brand already in the market. For a completely new entity, of course, market research should first be conducted to identify category dynamics and the situation. For brand extensions, basic research should already exist.

As we said earlier, the new brand should come into the world with a clear definition of its place, be it a niche or one that should generate wide appeal, and with a solid understanding of the product promise. There must also be a complete vision of how it will fit into the environment. The new brand could either be part of an existing group of products, part of a house of brands (a concept we'll explore in the next chapter), a consortium of related entities or a completely stand-alone entity.

It's important to remember that launching a brand never takes place in a vacuum. Brands that do everything 'right' can still fail because the competition outmanoeuvres them. And though it's less likely, brands that do everything 'wrong' can still succeed – at least in the short-term – perhaps because the direct competition makes even worse mistakes, only to be replaced when (and only if) a 'smarter' marketer enters the field to create a stronger brand. It's all fluid.

There are steps, however, that brand managers can take to increase their odds of success. First, brand managers should work to ensure consistency along the consumer brand touchpoints as well as optimize the brand experience along it. To achieve this goal, the brand launch plan should detail each and every possible contact point with the consumer: the retail environment, online, call centre, advertising messaging points and, most importantly of all, product usage. Often the product itself is not as important as the consumer experience prior to the purchase, during the purchase and immediately after the purchase. The brand experience actually matters more if it is a service because people in these transaction situations tend to pay more attention to their interaction with the brand representatives.[2] For tangible products, consumers tend to pay more attention to its design and functional attributes, but the overall brand experience along all of the touchpoints still matters.[3] A simple and practical strategy for brand managers is to be a customer of the brand you manage. Buy it, use it and be aware of the experiences that real customers go through while using it. Having first-hand experience is sometimes superior to market research!

Brands are living creatures and the initial growth stage is one of the most crucial steps in its life cycle. The research company Kantar Millward Brown claims that size alone doesn't constitute brand growth. Brands can be large in size but may stop growing owing to lack of differentiation and relevance to the target audience.[4] In fact, we've seen huge brands like Nokia climb to the top spot in their category only to lose it,[5] with – as we noted earlier – some brands disappearing completely. Nokia paid attention to growth only when it was done according to the parameters known to them, without an eye towards technological innovations. When smartphones appeared, they ignored them as a passing fad,[6] resulting in their loss of global market dominance.[7] The fact is that no matter its financial size or success, the work of growing a brand never stops. It is like the act of breathing or the pumping of blood. Stop and the consequences are deadly. To extend the analogy, advertising and other marketing activities are like feeding a body. Junk foods like discounting may quickly fuel the creature, but a well-balanced, nutritious diet is better for ensuring a longer life. Seybold, Marshak and Lewis in their book, *The Customer Revolution*, underscored the importance of the relentless pursuit of growth, writing that: 'The real leaders in today's economy run their businesses based on things like customer retention, customer satisfaction, growth in the number of customers, growth of customers' spending, and the predictors of customer defection.'[8]

It's important to remember that branding-growth activities should not be solely measured by monetary gain. Tom Peters, the American business management guru, said: 'In an increasingly crowded marketplace, fools will compete on price. Winners will find a way to create lasting value in the customer's mind.'[9] How do you create lasting value? For a multinational brand, consider the following:

- **Product need**
  - Just because the brand was successful in one market it doesn't mean that it will be successful in another. Manufacturers traditionally export successful products they developed for their own country, concluding that, based on local demand, there might be demand elsewhere. But this might not be the case or the selected market might not be the best one for expansion. One strategy is to identify the markets that are close in make-up to the original one. This works often, but not always. For some brands, a better strategy would be to find a market where the brand's country of origin is viewed as a benefit. There are other strategies as well. Whichever way, research is needed.
- **Brand structure**
  - It's simple to structure with one product, but as the number of extensions grow, the brand manager will need to develop an architecture that accommodates diverse offerings, such as sub-brands being marketed to multiple segments that enables the best results for the overall brand. (The topic of brand architecture is covered in more depth in the next chapter.)
- **Market conditions**
  - While brands tend to first be available in a single country, usually one with a successful economic environment, a brand launch for market expansions can take place in many countries at once. A thorough understanding of each market is necessary. As we've previously mentioned, brands that are available in more than one country should maintain a global perspective and launch brands accordingly. Companies like Nestlé have understood it for a long time and have developed global brands for countries unlike theirs, such as Nescafé for underdeveloped countries, with great success.
- **Infrastructure scope**
  - One final consideration is: can you consistently get the product to the intended consumers? Do you need to find an in-country partner or do you need to hire staff for that country? Can you support it from your headquarters? What are the tax laws in the country and what do you need to do to maintain compliance? Where will you produce the product? Do you need to manufacture or assemble it in the expanded market, perhaps to keep down costs, or can you produce it as part of your current operations? It is perishable? If so, how can you keep it fresh? The goal is to keep the brand stocked and make it part of the consumer's life in every market in which it is available.

Maintaining a brand

Brands can live and be profitable for a very long time, even hundreds of years. According to the *Guinness book of Records*, the hot-spring hotel Nishiyama Onsen Keiunkan in Yamanashi, Japan, has been in operation since 705.[10] The secret of this brand's success is rooted in the private family ownership, lasting over 52 generations, and consistent commitment to, as they claim, courteous hospitality. Not all brands, however, are as lucky. The average life of a brand today stands at about 50 years.[11] Checking Interbrand's list of Top-Ranking Global Brands at the time of writing, we find that the top five include four tech brands (Apple, Google, Microsoft, Amazon), with just one 'traditional, old-school' brand among them: Coca-Cola, a 126-years-old brand.

To achieve longevity, skilful maintenance of the brand starts with senior management (not the marketing department professionals), who must develop and uphold the internal systems to control how the brand is handled inside the firm. Brand management begins with providing complete clarity to all employees about the brand's values, vision, mission and behaviours. After all, the company's senior management are the real brand ambassadors and champions for the brand. They have to instill a complete commitment to continuing the task of brand management throughout the organization's rank-and-file. Many employees who do not work in a customer-facing function do not understand that they are also responsible for maintaining their brand's vitality. Brand-oriented organizations need to establish the right governance systems and be able to monitor and collect data about brand performance. In addition, consistent training and education programmes must be provided to reinforce and sharpen the skills of all employees, starting with the C-suite executives. Of course, new employees have to become deeply versed in the brand as well. Employee turnover in organizations is a constant source of inconsistency in delivering the brand experience.[12] The more a company can do to prevent this inconsistency, the better.

An important part of maintaining a brand is keeping its integrity. Brands must stay true to their positioning in the marketplace and the relationships they develop with their customers. BMW, 'The Ultimate Driving Machine,' will not sound credible if it manufactures cars that do not perform, or they do not offer superior customer service. BMW owners have become accustomed to a level of integrity from the brand. Ongoing disappointments or a failure to address and correct them can result in a break in the brand promise. While some say the BMW car lags behind in design innovation,[13] it is not the reason loyal customers flock to it. Rather, they select BMW for its superior ability to handle the road.[14] Walmart's integrity is connected to the part of its brand that promises merchandise for low prices.[15] While some accuse Walmart of hurting communities because of their practices,[16] the integrity of the brand – the low-price promise – remains intact.

Of course, maintaining a brand can involve changes, but they should be gradual, not too extreme and executed over a period of time. Within the industry, it's said that the sign of an inexperienced brand manager new to a position is that he or she immediately wants to change the packaging. But when consumers are confronted with a new logo, new typography, new slogan etc, they can become confused. As we stated in the previous chapter, the colours, shapes and imagery of packaged goods help consumers home in on the brand they're looking for when out shopping. Loyal consumers can even become confused with extensive brand changes for services. For both products and services, extensive brand changes can provide the opportunity for competitors to take a share, something we saw with the Tropicana example in the previous chapter, so while it might look good for the CV of the brand manager in the short term, it might not be the best for the brand in the long run. Senior brand management needs to be aware of these tendencies and clamp down on them, particularly for global brands where the expense of new packaging is compounded. When gradually updating the packaging, brand managers should ensure that existing consumers become aware of the changes. Brand managers can also make these brand updates country-by-country, a strategy that can also be used when launching new product forms.

The lesson for marketers and brand strategists for successful brand maintenance is that they should maintain a great respect for aligning each brand touchpoint, especially packaging, and hold a deeper commitment to methodically evolving brand assets. This will ensure consumers accept the change in a positive manner.

Evolving and extending a brand

Branding is traditionally considered the responsibility of the marketing department within the organization; they create the name, symbol, logo, product or service, promise, expectations, ad campaigns, positioning and, ultimately, monitor the profits. The reality in the marketplace these days, however, is that customers are expecting an 'experience' from their favourite brands and this has become the most important element in developing and maintaining brand loyalty.[17] As a result, organizations need to expand responsibility for the brand to every employee. Some large corporations even understood it long ago and designed the brand experiences at the launch of a new brand. Such examples include Google,[18] Starbucks[19] and Apple Computers.[20] Even Oreo, as you might recall from Chapter 1, offers a unique brand experience built right into it – the twisting apart of the biscuits and dunking of them in milk, a ritual that captured loyal consumers.

After consumers are attracted to a single-product brand, support it and become loyal to it, the brand owners often see an opportunity to evolve and extend the brand. One example is Dove. On its website, Unilever, the corporation that owns Dove, says 'Dove started its life in 1957 in the US, with the revolutionary new beauty cleansing Bar. With its patented blend of mild cleansers and ¼ moisturizing cream, Dove's iconic Beauty Bar rinses cleaner than soap, leaving skin clean, soft and smooth. It is the #1 Dermatologist Recommended brand in the US, Canada and France and strongly endorsed by Dermatologists across the world.'[21] For many years, from 1957 until 2000, Dove was an all-purpose moisturizing soap bar. But the way it was made, and the clever differentiating position of the product, suggested it wasn't soap at all. Instead, it was a beauty bar with 'moisturizing cream' in it. Because Dove beauty bar didn't dry the skin like other soaps, it set itself apart from the others. Its performance was obvious.

Since 2000, Dove has expanded its product line to include hair-care products, exfoliating body polish, body lotions, antiperspirants and deodorants. They launched sub-brand 'collections' like Go Fresh, Clinical Protection and DermaSeries. They also grew with endorsed sub-brands to reach new audiences, creating Baby Dove wipes, soap formulas and other products for infants, as well as a full range of male-oriented products in five countries with the sub-brand Men+Care.[22]

Just as we explained above that consumers are now expecting brand experiences, Dove has embraced a purpose beyond moisturizing skin: 'to make beauty a source of confidence'.[23] The brand, which is now available in over 80 countries, aims to be 'an agent of change to educate and inspire girls on a wider definition of beauty and to make them feel more confident about themselves'.[24] To activate their newfound mission, they launched its 'Campaign for Real Beauty' in 2004, sponsoring a photography exhibition called 'Beyond Compare: Women Photographers on Real Beauty'.[25] They followed up in 2006 with a video that went viral showing a model being groomed and the resulting image being retouched to produce an unrealistic vision of beauty.[26] Also in 2006, they started a 'Dove Self-Esteem Fund'.[27] These types of campaigns for Dove continue today and throughout all the countries where the brand is available.[28] To extend the social mission to men, they also claim 'commitment' to paternity leave.[29]

Refreshing and rebranding

When they reach the maturity and decline phases, successful old brands may work to improve brand experiences at key customer touchpoints. It's why brands as old as Officina Profumo Farmaceutica Di Santa Maria Novella, an Italian brand founded in 1612, keep doing interesting things.[30] They have never 'rebranded' themselves in the traditionally accepted sense of changing their language, tone and manner. Their brand is so successful and mature that any change in these elements could alienate existing customers and their implied promise of 'authenticity'. Instead, the brand must walk the fine line between continually fine-tuning the brand and maintaining their brand foundation and image by adapting new technology, having a technologically up-to-date online store and equipping existing stores with the latest technology.

In other words, while they have continually adapted to changing customer needs, their logo, packaging and products have not changed for generations. In fact, any change could have implications for their bottom line and their unique positioning as being one of the oldest pharmacies – if not *the* oldest – in the world.

On the other hand, much younger brands, such as Yahoo, need tweaks and rebranding after just a few years of brand maturity. Yahoo lost its relevancy in the eyes of many, lost its unique position in the market and quickly became a stale tech giant.[31] Upgrading the logo didn't help. AOL also couldn't use a logo makeover as a rescue strategy either.[32] Hiring a recognized ad agency to come up with new creative ideas didn't do much either. Simply put, a logo redesign alone will never suffice as a method of rebranding.

Many organizations and corporations use the term 'rebranding' when sales are sagging. They change their agency, launch a new ad campaign, or fire their Chief Marketing Officer. In most of these cases, refreshing the brand is a reactive move, not a well-thought-out strategic move initiated by an identification of an opportunity, an insight into the direction of their market, and/or inspiration into where the brand should be positioned in the future. At other times, the brand refresh is driven by a merger or an acquisition – 'the product mix has changed, or the brand execution was not well maintained' and the brand elements need to be modernized. Any brand refresh, however, should be approached 'cautiously and hesitantly'.[33]

When considering a companywide rebrand, the marketing executives should review their current brand portfolio, decide which ones deserve to be refreshed, which should get less support, and/or which should get sold, an activity called 'brand rationalization', which we will explore in the following chapter. The macro environment could significantly influence rebranding decisions. The demographics of the consumers who use the brand, for instance, could have changed. As a result, two separate brands owned by the same company could end up competing for the same audience. If the audience is getting older, one step that brands take is to reposition the brand for a younger audience, which may require a deep examination of not only the brand elements and experience but also the product itself and its key attributes. Other brands, particularly those in non-luxury categories, might require a rebranding effort if the economy takes a down turn and they become victims of price wars.

When technology advances, the brand itself might have to change to incorporate relevant new distribution and payment opportunities, which could also require a rebranding effort. In some cases, the political landscape shifts and with it, certain brands can suffer, or become more relevant, and call for a brand reposition and a rebranding effort. And finally, cultural shifts could heavily impact fashion and food brands.

When exploring a brand refresh, here are the key considerations:

1. Review your key branding challenges. What is the situation and objective?
2. Map all the brand touchpoints along the customer journey – pre-purchase, during purchase and post-purchase. Have they changed? Are there more now or fewer?

What are the most important ones? What are the most likely customers' paths-to-purchase? What are the key inflection points within it?

3 Assess the opportunities to build your brand. How can you add value at the key points and speed up prospects along their journey?
4 Calculate the costs for the rebrand – everything from the development of the brand assets to the roll-out costs. Falling short on funds can doom the launch – obvious, but often overlooked. Make sure you have enough for success.
5 Create the timeline for the brand refresh – from the initial research and strategic work to the creation of the communication elements. Make sure it's realistic. Often, brand refreshes are rushed because they're carried out to reverse lagging sales or address other issues; if an insufficient amount of time is allotted, the proper research and foundational initiatives can't be accomplished.
6 Review staffing. What additional skills and resources will you need to be successful? Do you have them in-house? Do you need to hire experts?
7 Plan ahead. What is the roll-out plan? Should the new branding be premiered market by market or should it be global to create a bigger splash and trigger cross-market conversations?
8 Avoid situations where only a portion of a market sees the rebranding, while other market segments are still experiencing the 'old brand'.

When a firm refreshes its brand, brand managers need to keep in mind that 'marketing is fluid. Other issues and new competitive actions can come into play.'[34] In addition, 'because competitors are reacting in real time, the end result might be that the company doesn't slide as much. Can we tell you how much a company will make as a result of rebranding? No, but we can assure you that in many instances, the cost of not acting could be greater.'

SEVEN REASONS FOR REBRANDING

In *Audio Branding: Using Sound to Build Your Brand* Minsky and Fahey identified seven additional reasons a company might want to rebrand:

1 if the current perception of the brand differs from how the organization wants it to be seen and it's not because of issues with product or services (which should be acknowledged and fixed, accompanied by communications showing how the changes have corrected the issues);
2 'if you have never formally defined its DNA';[35]

3. if the brand is not growing as fast as competitors I(it means the pie is growing, but not your share);
4. if your brand imagery or messaging is dated, disorganized and/or inconsistent;
5. if the company's people are not in alignment (eg you might have a solid brand foundation, but it's just not being executed very well);
6. if the brand is not attracting world-class talent;
7. if the brand for B2B companies is not contributing at least 7% of the company's value, the average according to the *Harvard Business Review*.[36]

The when, why and how of co-branding

Co-branding is simply a marketing strategy that features more than one brand name in combination when offering a product or providing a service. It is surprisingly very common, so common that many take the participating brands for granted as being part of the same brand. McDonald's has had a co-branding partnership with Coca-Cola for many years. Patrons of McDonald's restaurants order Coca-Cola products as if they were part of the restaurant's brand. Many credit cards now have special co-branded editions of their cards with airline, store, hotel, bank, investment firm, insurance and hospital brands. In fact, almost every airline has a co-branded partnership with either Visa, Amex or Mastercard. Note that other terms, such as 'brand partnership', are sometimes used in place of co-branding to describe the same kind of activity.

In the early 2000s, two leading brands in separate categories, Nike and Apple, uncovered a connection point and then collaborated in creating a co-branded product, Nike+iPod, which allowed fitness buffs to listen to their favourite music while exercising. Nike+iPod produced sneakers and clothing that tracked fitness activities while connecting people to their music. It might sound simple today, only because we take it for granted.

Nike CEO Mark Parker and Apple CEO Steve Jobs unveiled Nike+iPod at an event in New York attended by seven-time Tour de France champion Lance Armstrong and marathon-world-record-holder Paula Radcliffe. Parker of Nike said, 'Nike+iPod is a partnership between two iconic, global brands with a shared passion for creating meaningful consumer-product experiences through design and innovation. ... We see many more such Nike+ innovations in the future.' Specially designed Nike apparel, including jackets, tops and shorts, and armbands for the iPod Nano were developed, bringing together the Nike+iPod experience with waterproof pockets that accommodated the iPod and were designed to make it easy to operate while staying tuned to your music during an active workout.[37]

While we can't do justice to the various strategies and tactics of co-branding in this book – it could probably fill a book just on its own – we outline below the three main types co-branding:

1. **An endorser brand**, where one brand recommends the other. The endorser tends to be top in the communication hierarchy. Think back to the Dove case study above for an example. They market Dove Go Fresh, Dove Clinical Protection and Dove DermaSeries, among others. Generally, sub-brands are owned by the same company as the endorser brand, but it doesn't have to be the case. With this model, the endorser brand provides credibility to the one being endorsed.
2. **Equal brands**, such as the Nike and Apple partnership example listed above, where the strength of the two are the same or close and they use the partnership to create a new category or line of products. In these cases, both brands should have equal weighting, as it's the unique combination that gives the marketing effort its power.
3. **Supporting brand**, were strong brand is featured as the 'ingredient' of the other to give the main product a 'proof point' for its quality, functionality or unique experience. Examples include the Intel Inside logos on computers to indicate its quality; various restaurant chains offering Sriracha hot sauce or Heinz ketchup as a key ingredient to imply a taste experience; and a Gore-Tex tag hanging from various jacket and shoe brands to show that they are indeed waterproof. Even the Coca-Cola in McDonald's example cited above could fall into this category. In these instances, unlike endorser brands, the ingredient is secondary to the primary brand in the messaging hierarchy.

For global brands, a co-branding strategy can be implemented universally, regionally or locally, depending on the needs of the brand and the strengths of the partner brand in the various markets. In addition, co-branding partnerships can be long-term such as the Intel processor chips in various computer brands and the availability of Coca-Cola products in McDonald's, or they can be short-term and promotional like a Sriracha-infused sandwich, available for a limited time in some fast-food or fast-casual restaurant chain.

Does the job title 'Brand Manager' mean what it says?

According to the global recruitment company Spencer Stuart, Chief Marketing Officers (CMOs) stay in their job for an average of 44 months, an improvement from earlier times (around 2004) when they served for an average of only 23.6 months.[38] However, neither is enough time to fully influence, modify and build meaningful growth for a brand. The job tenure might be long enough to plan a new ad campaign, but truly building brands takes much longer.

As previously discussed, one way to influence the growth of a brand is to change the brand packaging right away; it's good for one's CV – and for creating confusion among customers. Another way is to adopt new technology just because it is there. CMOs however, should be strategic in what they adopt. To be able to make informed choices, they need to develop a broad spectrum of new technological skills. During the American Marketing Association's Brand Smart conference that was held in Chicago in April 2018, we learned some interesting facts regarding new technological skills. The keynote speaker, Jens Ulrich Hansen from Switzerland, in his talk about the growth and maturity of brands in the digital age, described some fundamental mega shifts that CMOs must master when aiming to achieve brand growth and future success, including: Anticipation, Augmentation, Automation, the Cloud, Cognification, Datafication, Disintermediation, Mobilization, Personalization, Platformization, Robotization and Virtualization. Not all job requirements, however, are digital. The brand manager still has to have simple human qualities for success: compassion, conscientiousness, creativity, empathy, emotions, ethics, imagination, intuition and values.[39] Professionals just starting out should take note of these technological and human skills. Mastering them can help speed up one's career trajectory.

Tenure for professionals at the start of their careers can be very short, because many either move up quickly or leave the profession. With the constant change, however, there are many opportunities to start a brand-management career.

Some common job titles are Brand Manager, Brand Specialist and Brand Ambassador. It might be tempting to apply for these jobs, even if they are at the bottom of the corporate ladder. However, a closer examination reveals that many of the positions that have the word 'brand' in their titles have very little to do with brand development or management. Some of the descriptions on job boards are also confusing, since they emphasize different sets of skills, expectations, qualifications and job functions. What's more, there is often confusion between 'marketing' and 'sales'. Many include skill sets interchangeably for these distinctly different career paths.

The brand manager position is a much lower one than other positions within a marketing department. Because it is considered to be a junior position, most brand managers are relegated to performing tasks that are not strategic, but rather executional in nature. These positions require the professional to be a quick learner and detail-oriented, so they can perform without fault. If they don't come up to the marketing department standards, they'll be asked to leave, because the brand can't stop. Those in the early stages of their careers, and even those in the middle stages, should attach themselves to a mentor. Beginners shouldn't expect more experienced employees to volunteer to be mentors. Rather, in this fast-paced environment, the beginner needs to recruit the mentor, which requires dedication, ambition and confidence.

A brand manager's job description

The job of the brand manager is to create an appropriate enduring impression among its prospects and users that improves both sales and market share. This one sentence illustrates the difference between a brand manager and a product manager. While brand managers should be involved with the creation of consumer impressions, product managers are responsible for sales. It is the difference between a brand and a product. Factors beyond the brand contribute to the sales, such as costs, distribution, sales force, channel marketing programmes and competitor actions. Often, because of this difference in outlook and workload, it makes sense for a company to split the responsibilities along these lines: someone who is responsible for building the brand and someone who is responsible for building the sales. Of course, the two would need to collaborate closely. In addition, when there are multiple sub-brands, a company can employ one brand manager working alongside multiple brand managers.

Success as a brand manager, according to another definition of the role, can be 'achieved by making sure their organization's advertising and marketing activities send out the right image. Key aspects of the job include creating brand guidelines and making sure that employees follow them.'[40]

Here are some examples of real-life recruitment adverts for brand managers. Note the level of experience, skills and disciplines required. The first advert is for a 'brand manager', but the actual job is not about branding or brand management. Rather, it is focused on sales:

> 'We are seeking an energetic, detail-oriented Brand Manager to fill a full-time position in our headquarters. You'll oversee development and manufacturing of new and emerging products. You will develop and maintain product roadmaps, provide financial and technical justification for product selection and conduct market research on market trends within the industry. Position requires creative thinking and excellent verbal and written communication skills.
>
> Responsibilities include:
>
> - Manage entire product life cycle
> - Oversee cost and pricing changes
> - Create, prioritize and maintain customer and market requirements
> - Lead market research initiatives into customer perceptions and behaviours
> - Analyze competitive materials against ours
> - Formulate marketing strategies to achieve visibility and optimal performance
> - Collaborate with engineering, marketing, manufacturing and operations to ensure that products meet customer needs and take advantage of market opportunities
> - Coordinate and develop product marketing, sales, engineering and financial plans

- Research and develop new product requirements and coordinate manufacturing
- Estimate potential profits and develop technical justification of new products
- Provide technical expertise and product training to other departments
- Prepare product development objectives
- Schedule all phases of product development and market launch
- Identify complementary third-party partnering opportunities
- Manage manufacturer alliances
- Participate in key product sales situations

Qualifications:

- Bachelor's degree or above; or 1–3 years related experience and/or training; or equivalent combination of education and experience
- Proficient with Microsoft Office (Word, Excel, PowerPoint and Outlook), email and Internet Explorer browser software
- Ability to plan, organize and control an assigned product line from conceptual stages through product life cycle
- Exhibit strong leadership abilities, good communication and social skills, strong analytical skills and ability to multitask

Here is a job advert for a 'brand specialist', though in fact the job description shows that they are seeking a car salesman:

> 'The largest-volume dealer in the region is currently looking for Brand Specialists to add to our team. Why is it important that we are the largest-volume dealer… because our large volume creates numerous opportunities for you, and the more opportunities you have, the more money you can make. There is no limit to how much money you can earn here; in fact, top performers have earned over $200k a year. If you are hard-working, dedicated and professional, you will be well rewarded. No prior sales experience necessary and we'll provide the n training. We're certain that you'll enjoy being a part of a record-setting brand and also a part of a dealership that is extremely well respected and has been family-operated for more than 40 years.
>
> We take care of our team:
>
> - 401k
> - Health, Dental and Vision Insurance
> - Unlimited earning potential
> - Up to 5 weeks paid vacation
> - Bonus programmes and incentives

What you'll do:

- Provide an unrivalled level of service to high-end customers
- Follow up with leads distributed to you by our ABC department
- Greet walk-in customers and help them proceed into the sales process
- Assist the customer in finding the vehicle that is perfect for their needs
- Work closely with the management team to ensure every customer has an exceptional experience
- Follow the processes put in place by our management team

What you'll need:

- Driven personality and strong work ethic
- Personable and friendly demeanour
- Stellar listening and communication skills
- The ability to work well with computers, iPads and in-vehicle technology
- Ability to successfully respond to customer objections
- Self-motivation
- Capable of processing management feedback and making changes
- Professional appearance

Finally, job seekers might also come across the title of 'branding consultant', which often turns out to be a junior account executive or sales position. A typical job posting for this title reads:

'Blah Blah International, a nationally renowned (blank) solutions company seeks new branding consultant to drive our presence. This person is responsible for prospecting and closing profitable sales. Candidate will receive ongoing best-in-industry training/education. The branding consultant serves as the client's primary contact during the sales process while simultaneously working with internal support functions (special order, creative services, account services, sales management, merchandising and more). We're looking for self-starters who are interested in building a career with an industry leader.

Core job responsibilities:

- Identify and cultivate new business opportunities through research, networking, social media, email and cold calling.
- Develop and deliver sales action plans with key strategies, objectives and targets to increase revenue and aggressively acquire new accounts.
- Create target prospect lists based on industry, company size, number of employees and other metrics.

- Manage marketing resources to develop prospect proposals and presentations, including needs assessments, customer expectation management and follow-up needed to close or expand existing business.

Skills

- Sales experience with prospecting and cold calling.
- Self-motivated and goal driven with a balanced focus on sales and customer satisfaction.
- Understands the start-to-finish campaign development process.
- Strong presentation and project management skills, comfortable performing to tight deadlines.
- Conduct effective market research, creating effective ways to obtain new clients and expand existing client business by staying current with industry trends and market activities.
- Must be detailed, organize and reliable with a positive and professional attitude.
- Proficiency with Microsoft Word, Excel and PowerPoint necessary.
- College Degree preferred.
- Sales experience not required, however is a plus.

As you can see, when it comes to finding a brand management position, titles don't mean responsibilities. Rather, seek indicators that correspond to the responsibilities outlined in this book. It might keep you from being sidetracked on your way to becoming a brand manager.

BRANDING ACROSS BORDERS – A GUEST PERSPECTIVE FROM MICHAËL BOUMENDIL, FRANCE

Michaël Boumendil is Founder, President and Chief Creative Officer of Sixième Son. A musician, composer, producer and branding expert, Michaël founded Sixième Son in 1995 and, with it, invented the concept of branded audio identities and musical design for companies. At the age of 23, he foresaw a new horizon in the application of music to brand communications. Today, Sixième Son has become global leader in audio branding with clients spanning the globe. The agency's unique expertise is widely recognized in the world of branding and communication. And Michaël, who speaks French, English, Spanish and Italian, spends a lot of his time travelling and nurturing his ever-growing company. Here's what he has to say about audio/sound/sonic branding:

'A heart that beats, the wind that blows, a bird that sings, a baby crying, an iPhone ringing, Michael Jackson performing Billie Jean: we are in a world where sound is universal. We generally have an audio vocabulary that spans countries and cultures. There are a wide range of songs that we all know. Our parents, grandparents and their parents all knew them too. For decades now music has become universal. Whether you like it or not, communicating a 'brand' in a globalized world points to the use of music.

'Research shows that audio sounds and music are among the most effective content available when it comes to crossing borders and cultures[41] and now brands have the opportunity to have their own vocabulary with a strong, consistent audio-branding approach. Audio branding is an amazingly helpful and powerful tool for conveying a clear and unified message across languages and countries. If the marketer does things properly, audio branding can give the product or service a strong competitive edge. Brands that have created their own music, their unique audio DNA, have the ability to express their identity with sometimes even more impact than their visual identity. As a result, I believe that few branding tools contribute as much to a company's brand success as having and properly executing a consistent audio identity.

'Music needs no translation. Does it mean that managing an audio identity around the world is easy? No. Does it mean that it is easier than most of the other aspects of branding? Yes, most definitely, as long as you create the right environment for your organization to use it and keep in mind the customer experience and that expectations are key in a proper audio branding approach.

'So how do you create these good conditions? Here are five tips for implementing a successful cross-border audio-branding approach:

1 **Educate the people within your company about the power of audio branding**. Not all countries have the same experience of audio branding. In fact, it is just in its infancy in North America while it is well-established in Europe and Asia. Also, not all of your peers have the same understanding of what it takes to manage audio-branding content. Finally, not everyone knows how impactful and effective it is when you use proper audio-branding guidelines. That is why it is important to share the right content, do the research and give some key examples that show how big the added-value of a strong audio-branding approach is.

2 **Clearly define the 'flexibility' of the rules to remain coherent**. Managing audio branding across borders often leads to the need for creating adaptations for specific local needs. It is key that all adaptations keep a strong link to the audio DNA. To see to it that creativity does not lead to confusion, the rules and guidelines for adapting audio content must be clear. It is crucial, for instance, that you precisely define the elements that shouldn't change whenever a new version is developed.

3 **Always keep in mind local customer-experience expectations**. There is no doubt that the understanding of music has now become global. What is not global, however, are the audio-experience expectations. Developing a corporate ringtone, for instance, should be done at the local level. For an event also, you sometimes need something very specific, just like music for radio messages. Allowing local expectations to lead to new development is a perfect way to keep your whole system alive and pertinent to your audience.

4 **Regularly feed your peers examples of the good use of music**. If a new need appears in one country, there might be an interest in it in other countries. Develop a gallery or an audio newsletter to share contents and give ideas or inspiration, a great way to encourage people to use your audio-branding system to enrich prospect and customer experiences.

5 **Audit your audio applications and system at least every three years** Like every system, ageing can be good and bad. If you have the right audio-branding system, the older it gets, the more effective it becomes. Awareness and attribution become bigger with time. When ageing, your system can enrich itself with all the new adaptations and contents that you and your peers develop. But it is good to audit your system to see that rules have been followed, to analyze how new people within your company understand the system, one that was built before they joined. An audit is a good way to regularly analyze how you are managing across borders and determine if it's a good reason to update your tools and assets.

'Try these steps with your global brand and experience the benefits of having a brand that extends beyond the visual. It just might be the soundest brand investment you've ever made.'

EXTENDED CASE STUDY: ROTARY INTERNATIONAL'S GLOBAL REBRANDING

Twelve Years ago, Ilan became a member of the Rotary Club of Chicago. When joining, he had no idea what Rotary was. He was simply 'recruited' by a longtime member, and didn't know what to expect at all. He only knew that they had a lunch meeting every Tuesday. The brand image of the club was that of a place where old people met. Ilan's business partners agreed that Rotary could be a great place for networking, so off he trudged to his first Chicago Rotary Club luncheon. His first impression was positive, but it had nothing to do with the brand. Rather, it was the members and their openness, warmth and actions.

Rotary International is not a product or service. It's a goodwill organization where members engage service to the public. Unlike with many other brands, when you ask the average person, 'What is the Rotary Club?' the chances are you will not get two answers the same. Goodwill organizations, such as the Red Cross, The Cancer Society and the Alzheimer Association, are defined by one clear purpose. Rotary is a different kind of brand.

Rotary's main brand presence in many cities is a road sign welcoming drivers into town. The Rotary logo is accompanied by other civic organizations such as Lions, American Legion, Kiwanis International, Optimist International, Masons and Zontas International. Unless the Rotary logo is displayed on its own, the brand is completely diluted by the presence of all the others. Brands like Rotary depend heavily on word of mouth and members recruiting others. They get some other exposure in public-ribbon-cutting ceremonies at Rotary-supported public works, initiatives and community projects.

The first Rotary Club in the world was organized in Chicago, Illinois, USA, on 23 February 1905. Paul P Harris, a young lawyer, gathered together a group of men, each of whom was already engaged in a different form of service to the public. They didn't have a business plan, but there was an agreed mission among the members. The name Rotary came simply from the group's early practice of rotating meetings among member offices, not from a branding firm or highly paid marketing team. Today, Rotary is a truly international brand, present on all continents and with more than 1.2 million members in 35,000 clubs across 530 districts.[42]

Because of its global expansiveness, until the recent past, many people, including its members, misunderstood and misinterpreted Rotary's goals and objectives. Many could not even define Rotary's reason for being. In 2013, the Rotary Club embarked on discovering facts and perceptions in order to change the situation.[43]

A branding firm was hired to conduct research and find out how the brand could gain recognition and understanding of its personality and the 'why' of the brand essence. Working with Siegel+Gale, Rotary conducted two additional worldwide studies.[44] The first one assessed a donor's motivation to give money or time by comparing the non-profit organization to 12 international peers and two local charities in each of four global regions to see how people perceived Rotary, as well as the respondent's 'brand preferences' among these organizations. This survey found that, while some non-profits were positioned clearly in people's minds, Rotary wasn't. The second study revealed that neither their members nor staff could consistently answer the question, 'What is Rotary?'[45]

These studies demonstrated that the Rotary brand was misunderstood. On the positive side, the study showed that members joined and stayed because they made great connections and felt positive about the actions and activities that they performed. Important to notice was the fact that members felt good about giving back to their communities. That was the discovery of the brand essence, the core benefit, promise and purpose of the Rotary brand.

Simplifying the definitions of Rotary's activities was primary in the process of 'cleaning' the message, important since Rotary doesn't focus on one defined activity, like cancer, famine, Alzheimer's or clean water. To define their activities, Rotary organized them into three core areas aligned with this brand essence:

1 'join leaders' for their club meetings;
2 'exchange ideas' for their work in finding solutions to community problems;
3 'take action' for their efforts to create positive change in their local communities and in the world.

As a result, Rotary was able to imply the benefits of getting involved with the organization, and explain how to do it, through one simple structure. Now, the brand message was clear; it sent a message that people with worthy intentions could contribute locally to the global community.

The next step was how to deliver the message in a clear way, so they updated the logo and redesigned the website. Rotary's exercise demonstrates that when considering a brand refresh, the first thing to do is to exactly understand the issues. Finding the brand essence – the core of the brand – is not easy and requires a deep understanding of its constituents. Jumping into a quick fix of simply redesigning a logo is not going to solve the underlying problems or clear up confusion. By taking the time to simplify and clarify its essence, Rotary became much easier for people to understand and continues today to function, thrive and march on.

KEY TERMS

- brand manager
- brand structure
- co-branding
- market conditions
- product manager
- rebranding

DISCUSSION QUESTIONS

- When should a marketer consider rebranding and how should they go about it?
- Why it is better to evolve a brand than to wait until a complete rebranding is needed?
- When should a brand engage in co-branding and what are some of its key best practices?
- What are the common positions in a marketing department and their job requirements?
- Why should job descriptions convey the essence of the brand to future employees?

Notes

1 Suttlr, R (2019) Brands & product life cycle, *Chron*, https://smallbusiness.chron.com/brands-product-life-cycle-785.html (archived at https://perma.cc/XS2Y-NKB9)

2 Schwager, A and Meyer, C (2007) Understanding customer experience, *Harvard Business Review*, https://hbr.org/2007/02/understanding-customer-experience (archived at https://perma.cc/D5N6-844C)

3 Schwager, A and Meyer, C (2007) Understanding customer experience, *Harvard Business Review*, https://hbr.org/2007/02/understanding-customer-experience (archived at https://perma.cc/D5N6-844C)

4 Hollis, N (2018) How brands really grow, Millward Brown, http://www.millwardbrown.com/Insights/Point-of-View/How_brands_really_grow (archived at https://perma.cc/SDV2-GXCX)

5 Hollis, N (2018) How brands really grow, Millward Brown, http://www.millwardbrown.com/Insights/Point-of-View/How_brands_really_grow (archived at https://perma.cc/SDV2-GXCX)

6 Hollis, N (2018) How brands really grow, Millward Brown, http://www.millwardbrown.com/Insights/Point-of-View/How_brands_really_grow (archived at https://perma.cc/SDV2-GXCX)

7 Hollis, N (2018) How brands really grow, Millward Brown, http://www.millwardbrown.com/Insights/Point-of-View/How_brands_really_grow (archived at https://perma.cc/SDV2-GXCX)

8 Seybold, P, Lewis, J and Marshak, R (2001) *The Customer Revolution*, Random House Business Books, London

9 Seybold, P, Lewis, J and Marshak, R (2001) *The Customer Revolution*, Random House Business Books, London

10 Baer, D (2014) How 16 of the oldest companies on earth have been making money for centuries, *Business Insider*, http://www.businessinsider.com/oldest-companies-on-earth-2014-8#705–nisiyama-onsen-keiunkan-in-yamanashi-japan-1 (archived at https://perma.cc/VRZ6-RH45)

11 Keiunkan.co.jp (2018) Koshu Nishiyama Hot Spring, Keiunkan, https://www.keiunkan.co.jp/en (archived at https://perma.cc/HQ8Q-GW35)

12 Harris, R and Short, T (eds) (2014) Workforce development, https://doi.org/10.1007%2F978-981-4560-58-0_2 (archived at https://perma.cc/P3Q9-W8WW)

13 Behrmann, E and Rauwald, C (2016) BMW's new electric car set for 2021, lags behind Audi, Mercedes, *IndustryWeek* (*Bloomberg*), https://www.industryweek.com/emerging-technologies/bmw-s-new-electric-car-set-2021-lags-behind-audi-mercedes (archived at https://perma.cc/S52M-FHEF)

14 Simona (2007) Topspeed.com, https://www.topspeed.com/cars/bmw/2008-bmw-x6-ar49149.html (archived at https://perma.cc/KB3L-Q4NX)

15 Stern, M (2018) Walmart's low-price strategy breaks down online, *Forbes*, https://www.forbes.com/sites/retailwire/2018/02/22/walmart-com-wants-to-sell-higher-not-a-typo-priced-products (archived at https://perma.cc/B6XV-N4U4)

16 Stern, M (2018) Walmart's low-price strategy breaks down online, *Forbes*, https://www.forbes.com/sites/retailwire/2018/02/22/walmart-com-wants-to-sell-higher-not-a-typo-priced-products (archived at https://perma.cc/B6XV-N4U4)

17 Goldstein, N J (2017) What you need to know about luxury consumer trends for 2018, *Forbes*, https://www.forbes.com/sites/njgoldston/2017/12/29/what-you-need-to-know-about-luxury-consumer-trends-for-2018 (archived at https://perma.cc/5YYH-5L2C)

18 Google.com (2018) Google, About, https://www.google.com/about (archived at https://perma.cc/UL3Y-B79P)

19 Starbucks Coffee Company (2018) About Us, https://www.starbucks.com/about-us (archived at https://perma.cc/DU23-QWQQ)

20 Apple (2018) Site Map, https://www.apple.com/sitemap (archived at https://perma.cc/5LY9-L8QC)

21 Anon (2018) Dove, Unilever global company website, https://www.unilever.com/brands/personal-care/dove.html (archived at https://perma.cc/8DYP-KR9S)

22 Live strong (2018) Dermatologist recommended soaps, https://www.livestrong.com/article/77820-dermatologist-recommended-soaps (archived at https://perma.cc/N57L-DDRN)

23 Anon (2018) Dove, Unilever global company website, https://www.unilever.com/brands/personal-care/dove.html (archived at https://perma.cc/8DYP-KR9S)

24 Global Cosmetic News (2015) Dove – company profile, https://globalcosmeticsnews.com/dove-company-profile (archived at https://perma.cc/QTT4-43NJ)

25 Murrills, A (2018) Beyond compare: women photographers on beauty, *Straight*, https://www.straight.com/article/beyond-compare-women-photographers-on-beauty (archived at https://perma.cc/7NQY-ZE3F)

26 YouTube (2018) Dove evolution, https://www.youtube.com/watch?v=iYhCn0jf46U (archived at https://perma.cc/L2DJ-MYAY)

27 Dove US (2018) Dove self-esteem project, https://www.dove.com/us/en/dove-self-esteem-project.html?gclid=Cj0KCQiAi57gBRDqARIsABhDSMo3JEX0aYJL1M4fXbOdiyyCWyjZ7QkEUrCJk1p1ruu_oUgLj3slpXkaAr4ZEALw_wcB&gclsrc=aw.ds (archived at https://perma.cc/GF9J-XGG6)

28 Dove US (2018) Dove self-esteem project, https://www.dove.com/us/en/dove-self-esteem-project.html?gclid=Cj0KCQiAi57gBRDqARIsABhDSMo3JEX0aYJL1M4fXbOdiyyCWyjZ7QkEUrCJk1p1ruu_oUgLj3slpXkaAr4ZEALw_wcB&gclsrc=aw.ds (archived at https://perma.cc/GF9J-XGG6)

29 Dove US (2018) Paternity leave – Dove Men+Care, https://www.dove.com/us/en/men-care/paternity-leave.html (archived at https://perma.cc/WC87-GJ6E)

30 Buy.smnovella.com (2018) Home page, https://buy.smnovella.com (archived at https://perma.cc/7FWH-M3D7)

31 Kosoff, M (2018) How Yahoo lost its way, *The Hive*, https://www.vanityfair.com/news/2016/07/how-yahoo-lost-its-way (archived at https://perma.cc/3H3X-8JGX)

32 Velarde, O (2018) How do you know when it's time to rebrand? Visual Learning Center by Visme, https://blog.visme.co/rebranding-strategy (archived at https://perma.cc/Y8LG-DS5M)

33 Minsky, L and Fahey, C (2017) *Audio Branding: Using sound to build your brand*, Kogan Page, London

34 Theseus.fi (2018) https://www.theseus.fi/bitstream/handle/10024/66822/ositioning%20and%20Networking%20in%20the%20Globalization%20Process%20of%20a%20Small-Sized%20Brand%20-%20Case%20SabrinaTach.pdf?sequence=1 (archived at https://perma.cc/8Z5E-F998

35 Minsky, L and Fahey, C (2017) *Audio Branding: Using sound to build your brand*, Kogan Page, London

36 Minsky, L and Fahey, C (2017) *Audio Branding: Using sound to build your brand*, Kogan Page, London

37 Apple Newsroom (2006) Nike and Apple team up to launch Nike+iPod, https://www.apple.com/newsroom/2006/05/23Nike-and-Apple-Team-Up-to-Launch-Nike-iPod (archived at https://perma.cc/9YLT-LBL8)

38 Spencerstuart.com (2018) Chief Marketing Officer average tenure increases to 44 months, https://www.spencerstuart.com/research-and-insight/cmo-tenure-2017 (archived at https://perma.cc/A28E-AYUD)

39 Jens Ulrich Hansen, Founder and CEO, www.futureassociates.com (archived at https://perma.cc/YM6B-WH42), Brand Smart Conference, Chicago, April 26 2018

40 Butler, N (2018) How to create a powerful brand identity (a step-by-step guide), Column Five, https://www.columnfivemedia.com/how-to-create-a-brand-identity (archived at https://perma.cc/9CUL-XA6C)

41 Minsky, L and Fahey, C (2017) *Audio Branding: Using sound to build your brand*, Kogan Page, London

42 Rotary Club of Eureka (2018) 101 Things About Rotary, https://rotary1.org/101-things-about-rotary (archived at https://perma.cc/G89R-QYR2)

43 Minsky, L, and Fahey, C (2014) Rotary strengthened their brand by simplifying it, *Harvard Business Review*, https://hbr.org/2014/09/rotary-strengthened-their-brand-by-simplifying-it (archived at https://perma.cc/BA6S-GJ64)

44 Minsky, L, and Fahey, C (2014) Rotary strengthened their brand by simplifying it, *Harvard Business Review*, https://hbr.org/2014/09/rotary-strengthened-their-brand-by-simplifying-it (archived at https://perma.cc/BA6S-GJ64)

45 Minsky, L, and Fahey, C (2014) Rotary strengthened their brand by simplifying it, *Harvard Business Review*, https://hbr.org/2014/09/rotary-strengthened-their-brand-by-simplifying-it (archived at https://perma.cc/BA6S-GJ64)

PART THREE

Branding issues and opportunities

09

Branding in a global economy

READING OUTCOMES

At the conclusion of this chapter, you should be able to:

- communicate the fundamental management decisions at the brand life-cycle inflection points;
- describe key considerations that help determine whether a brand should expand into a new market;
- understand the dos and don'ts when localizing multinational brands through customization;
- describe the basic conditions for success in vast and competitive marketing environments.

Introduction

Wherever in the world you reside, never forget that the business of branding is 24/7. There are no 'breaks'. Branding is the equivalent of breathing: it's a condition needed to sustain life, so you can only stop for a minute. If a brand does start to suffer from a decline in sales or some other ailment, a number of common remedies can be administered. One of the least effective is advertising, the equivalent of using a Band-Aid (yes, it's a brand name) to treat a serious medical condition. In many situations, the act of rebranding can help resuscitate an ailing brand. But by far the best method of maintaining a brand in good health is continual grooming and tweaking of the branding elements and a re-visiting of the brand touchpoints so that it's always up-to-date.

As part of this ongoing maintenance, management should treat even the most basic marketing activities as a global endeavour. As we said earlier, every brand that has a website is global, intentionally or not. Brands should consider the fact that their website might be viewed by millions of people around the world and should cater to the needs and wants of as many of them as possible. Failure to do this could be fatal, because truly disruptive competition can spring up from virtually anywhere, while embracing global branding could be an advantage even for the tiniest start-up. Let us not forget that some of the examples of global brands that we have mentioned in this book started as a young person's dream in some university dorm or their parent's garage.

Being a global brand throws up many issues and considerations that the manager needs to address. Understanding linguistic and cultural differences is just the beginning. Suffice to say that many brands aiming to attract customers from across borders should have an inherent knowledge and appreciation of what it takes to appeal to each audience in the countries in which it operates. Young entrepreneurial spirits should be ready for the onslaught of rules they will encounter when launching a global brand and will need to be ready to take common-sense actions.

The global economy has opened the doors to many brands and put them centre stage in markets they didn't know before. If not currently, one day, you may be in a position to determine the fate of a brand that will go global or already is. You should get a fairly good idea from this chapter of the basic conditions for success in this vast and competitive environment. Technology might be the backbone of the global economy – facilitating more economical distribution channels, financial transactions and, some say, relative world peace – but technological savvy alone is not enough to achieve success. What is? Read on to find out.

Overview

What are the steps to consider when your local brand is so successful that management begins calling for its introduction and launch in foreign and sometimes unknown markets? We'll answer this question using as our basis the brand life-cycle model introduced in Chapter 5. Next, we'll examine the political, economic, social and technological issues that a brand manager should take into consideration before entering a market. We look at a concrete example of how a marketer in medical tourism attracted international patients to his practice. To tie up the chapter we have a 'guest perspective' on the localization of global brands from Paolo Mercado, the Senior Vice President for Marketing, Communication and Innovation at Nestlé Philippines, followed by extended case study on how Phillips became a global health and wellness brand.

Key management considerations and strategies

A brand's impact on prospects depends on the information, feelings and thoughts that it transmits, and this should drive every strategic decision about brands and branding.[1] Branding is the business of humans behind the brand influencing and impacting other humans. Technology is merely a mode of transferring data, information and some emotions, providing reassurance that the brand indeed meets the functional requirements, while empathizing and sympathizing with its customers. As advertising legend David Trott said in his talk 'Predatory Thinking for Copywriters', given at the Professional Copywriter's Network Copywriting Conference 2013, the ultimate medium or platform is the human brain; every other medium or platform is just designed to affect it.[2]

It boils down to evolution. We humans have not changed much in our physical appearance and sensory capacities for many years. The principle of the five basic human senses can be traced back to Aristotle's *De Anima* ('On the Soul')[3] – we still have the same five senses, two ears, two eyes, one nose, a pair of hands and one mouth – but the world around us has drastically changed.

We now have an enormous amount of information broadcast to us everywhere we look and at our fingertips; for many of us it is overwhelming and impossible to digest. As a result, we're relying more and more on mental shortcuts and heuristics to make our decisions.[4] This means that brand marketers need to remember that when they suggest that their brand is better, cheaper, sweeter, lighter, larger than or amazingly different from the competition in some other way, the entire effort may go unnoticed. So how should brand managers get their product or service noticed, tried and adopted as a constant part of the consumer's life? Let's answer that question by using the typical life cycle of a brand that we first outlined in Chapter 5.

LAUNCH

Usually, start-ups do not begin their life with 'brand managers' on board. They start with a bunch of entrepreneurs who have an idea for a product/service/brand. Once the brand becomes a viable entity, however, its owners tend to form an organization. To these new business owners at the beginning of their market adventure we say: success and failure come in all sizes. Whether you're a corporate giant or a small mission-driven start-up, you compete in the same cluttered, information-bloated, confusing marketplace as everyone else. You need to get your brand noticed, differentiate it from others and make it grow. Do you dream about growing stronger or bigger? Do you imagine that you can achieve more, expand your mission or accomplish it more effectively? If so, seek help to determine if your dream is really possible and to work out how to turn it into reality.

Even at the beginning, when your organization is small and budgets are limited, strategy, brand development and marketing communications shouldn't be seen as a luxury, but an investment. To make your brand work harder than your competitors, you might need to invest and/or find a business partner or an outside reliable source who can help by providing experience, resources and extra creativity. By seeing things differently, thinking strategically, not focusing on making immediate profits and planning everything step by step, new businesses can perform better than their competitors. It all boils down to building a great brand, not just developing new technology or a shiny new feature.

Whether you have just finished your MBA studies with a brilliant business plan or already secured your angel investor funds, your newborn brand is still just a baby. Will it live to grow into the next Facebook or Starbuck's, or will it die early like Google+ or Vine? And if you are already functioning as a wobbling young infant brand, there is still a long road ahead, where the wolves are waiting at the next curve in the road. Are you ready? Building a great brand via the steps we outlined earlier helps erect a strong defence, enabling a longer commercially viable life.

ADOPTION

The point here is to avoid 'waiting on the runway'. Imagine that you already have a brand that has registered some success and is profitable, but it is not increasing activity, revenue, awareness or its number of customers. In other words, the brand simply isn't taking off. Some businesses are stuck on the runway for years. While typical, this is not a healthy situation and, in many cases, it can lead to early decline in the brand life cycle. As with the Launch phase, if you don't have the resources or experts at this stage, get them. By building the brand equity, not just sales, at the Growth stage, brands can:

- command premium pricing;[5]
- secure protection against price wars, or be able to weather a crisis;[6]
- successfully expand with new products in their portfolio;[7]
- gain leverage with channel partners;[8]
- attract co-branders (look at all of the brands that are incorporating Sriracha);[9]
- attract licensers;[10]
- become a new employee-recruiting magnet;[11]
- drive up employee pride;[12]
- find customers who won't consider competitors, will refuse substitutions[13] and request and recommend that brand.[14]

MATURITY

If you are a mature business, honestly review your company and brand(s): in the classic brand-management system, your brand manager is often a relatively inexperienced person who rarely stays in any job for more than two years.[15] In fact, 60 per cent of MBA graduates do not have previous applicable marketing experience,[16] and the job they often get first is that of product manager. From a strategic perspective, the brand manager should have a higher-ranking position in the organization, possess the wisdom that comes from experience and have a longer-term employment horizon; in the brand leadership model,[17] the brand 'manage' is the top marketing professional in the organization and, ideally, is the CEO. The brand (or brands for multi-brand companies) – and particularly the brand equities – must at least reside with the CEO and be promoted by him or her.

Think of it this way: managing the brand image – the communication elements that drive short-term results – is tactical and, while the messaging development needs to be informed by the current brand equity, it can be comfortably left to the advertising and promotion specialists. Brand equity, in contrast, is strategic. How consumers feel about the overall brand and whether these feelings contribute to or detract from what consumers are willing to pay for it[18] is an asset that can be the basis for long-term profitability and give the company the ability to introduce new products and extensions under the same name and logo. As a result, brand equity needs to be monitored closely by top management. The goal of brand leadership is to build brand equity – the price that consumers are willing to pay for a brand against a generic and competitors – rather than simply managing brand images. After all, other key factors contribute to the brand equity, including the brand story, brand essence, functionality, features, packaging and distribution.

DECLINE

If your brand ever experiences a decline in brand equity or sales, don't panic – even if things don't look good. There are solutions, and they don't start with going to the bank for another loan or filing for bankruptcy. It might just be that your brand is a bit under the weather.

Rather than panic and immediately go into discounting mode, brand managers must calmly examine the situation. Some multinational brands were saved by simply evolving the packaging and others by reminding long-term customers of their love for the brand.

To save the brand, you must find the critical point of disconnect with the audience. A simple brand audit or comprehensive check-up could reveal symptoms that might not deal a lethal blow to the business if addressed properly. These situations have occurred many times, all over the world. Many businesses don't understand the difference between a product and a brand, and that alone could be an issue. While the product is selling, the brand is the ultimate memory in consumers' minds. Remember that when you try to save an underperforming brand.

How to build an international brand for a single medical tourism provider

In order to help us better understand the Launch and Growth stages of a global business, let's look at a brand within the medical tourism industry, in which people travel to other countries to receive medical care. Medical tourism gained presence on the world's economic radar thanks to a 2008 Deloitte report, entitled *Medical Tourism, Consumers in Search of Value*,[19] which provided a clear picture of the potential opportunities afforded by this industry. The reaction to this report was far-reaching, with many hoping to make quick money from the industry, while assisting the development of healthcare in poorer nations. The report cited a potential US $100-billion (£80 billion) market, with an average annual growth rate of 25 per cent. Many people have based their business decisions on these figures, which have not yet been obtained.

At the time of writing, more than 100 nations are involved in or aim to become medical tourism destinations. In addition, individual cities within these country destinations are also trying to bill themselves as the place to go to for medical procedures and wellbeing treatments. They are essentially competing for the same global patient, offering similar medical solutions and services and claiming to charge lower prices than the competition. One common way of comparing global healthcare prices is taking the costs of medical treatments in the US as the benchmark, a flawed approach, since most medical travellers live far away from the US and never consider going there for treatment anyway. With all of this global competition, the simple market factors of supply and demand already show a clear tilt towards supply, while demand is barely measurable.

Marketing, including clear brand positioning, is therefore an essential element to get right if a country, city and/or facility is to stand out in a crowded global marketplace. When other products on the global open market are examined, we find that consumer products with similar multinational distribution and an equivalent price point (cars, for example) are professionally marketed. But medical services are known for being marketed in a slightly different way because medical procedures are rarely planned or budgeted for in advance. Medical-tourism marketing overall is currently deficient in government support, budget allocation, as well as legal and ethical implementation. Where governments support medical tourism in their country with professional and cohesive marketing efforts, their hospitals are more often found on lists of the 'best hospitals in the world'.[20]

One country that has done a notable job of supporting their medical tourism industry is Korea. They have created a single body, the Korean Health Industry Development Institute (KHIDI), which supports the activities of their industry and helps market the facilities. By studying Korea's medical tourism industry and how they are marketing themselves to those who are willing to travel for medical care, we can learn how countries build their international reputation and brand alongside their established tourism brand. This example can also help us understand the brand launch and growth phase. To start, let's look at a business plan to establish a recognized brand within medical tourism. This plan was created and the following content was written by Professor Ki Nam Jin of Yonsey University and is being used with his permission.

BRANDING ONE KOREAN MEDICAL TOURISM PROVIDER FOR GLOBAL CONSUMPTION

Background

Located in the south of South Korea, Busan is one of the main tourist destinations in the country. Busan is South Korea's second-largest city with a population of 3.6 million. The city is famous for its beaches, natural hot springs and beauty clinics. Dr O & Ananti Private Clinic is located at Ananti Cove which is a large town consisting of a hotel, hot spring, private beach, walking trails, shops and private residences. Ananti Cove is positioned as a luxury oceanfront resort. Its aim is to provide customers with an unprecedented range of ways to relax and a distinct culture and lifestyle.

The clinic

Dr O & Ananti Clinic works within the anti-ageing niche, providing services to refresh customers' minds and bodies with the promise of enhanced longevity. It offers four programmes: Immune System; Obesity; Stress Management; and Beauty. The private clinic developed these services in line with Ananti Cove's goal of providing luxurious experiences. In addition to the actual medical clinic, facilities include a restaurant, bookstore and fitness centre, all coordinated to deliver a coherent brand experience.

Problems of clinic branding

The clinic initially failed to differentiate itself clearly and appropriately from the competition. It did not create a clear brand identity of how it wanted to present itself to its prospects and patients and how to be perceived by them. Even though the clinic uses advanced technologies for diagnosis and treatment, it described itself as a sanctuary place for the soul on the clinic's website – eg, 'DR O & Ananti Private Clinic aspires to be a sanctuary for the soul through relaxation and healing to ensure time and space for those seeking further direction in life.'[21] Anyone familiar with the clinic will immediately see that its overall description does not reflect its core service and technological strength in the anti-ageing market. In other words, the clinic's description of brand identity and actual services were not aligned.

Brand building

IDENTIFICATION OF CLINICAL SERVICES

To develop the clinic brand, my client and I first needed to identify the clinical services and their characteristics. We created a diagram showing the flow of clinical services and highlighting the unique technologies that were different from the competition's. We started with the health check-up (a holistic health examination), which included advanced testing. We then organized the main and unique treatments into three groups and named them ABC (A = air detox; B = blood detox; C = cell treatment), as portrayed in Figure 9.1. Other ancillary services were combined with ABC to create the individual programmes, including the immune-system program, as portrayed in Figure 9.2.

FIGURE 9.1 ABC Treatment as core service

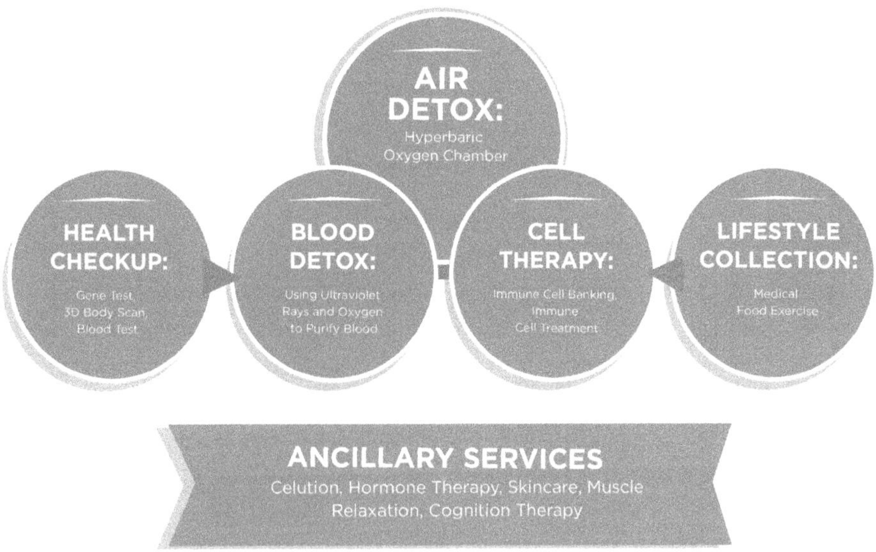

Health checkup and treatment services.

IDENTIFICATION OF CUSTOMER-SERVICE CHARACTERISTICS

Next, we explored their customer-service delivery, the key aspects of which are characterized as the 5 Cs:

- customization;
- crew (eg, doctor, nurses, therapist etc) cooperation;
- coordination with other service providers (eg, restaurants, fitness centre etc) inside the resort;

- communications;
- commitment to continuity. These 5 Cs are practical guidelines for designing most customer experiences.

FIGURE 9.2 Programmes and treatment services

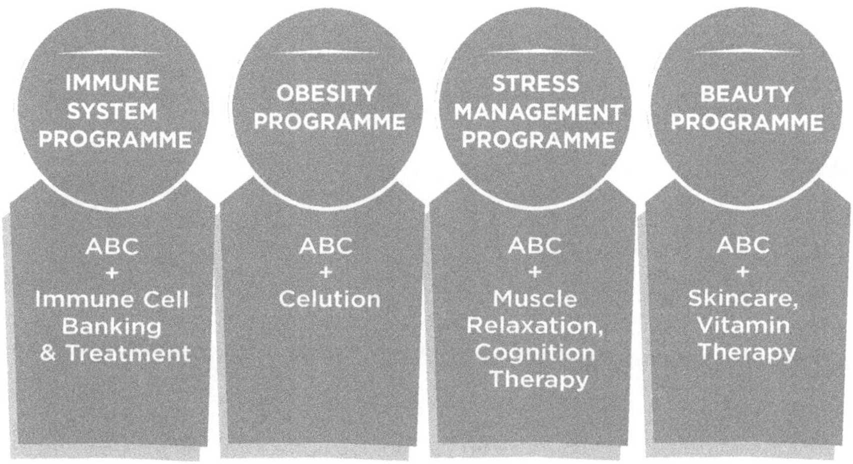

© Ki Nam Jin. Used with permission.

IDENTIFICATION OF SERVICE PHILOSOPHY

To help assess the customer services, we also identified the key service philosophy inherent in the programmes, listing it as the shift:

- from disease-focused to patient-centred care;
- from simple disease detection to prevention and health improvement;
- from person-centred care to family-centred care with a focus on the family background (such as genetic inheritance);
- from traditional medical care to hybrid care, aligning the body, mind and soul.

IDENTIFICATION OF SERVICE GOAL

The goal of a health check-up is not the simple detection of disease but rather detection of deterioration of holistic functioning. The goals of treatments are the enhancement of vitality and the increase of longevity. The health check-up and treatments are all aligned to achieve long-term goal of vital longevity.

IDENTIFICATION OF PATIENT NEEDS

The patients of anti-ageing clinics have the following service needs: 1) advanced treatment using state-of-the-art technology; 2) holistic care; 3) personalized care; 4) elegant service. The patients want these services for healthy ageing. Healthy ageing entails vitality and longevity.

Brand creation

All services aligned towards enhancing vitality and increasing longevity correspond to patient needs. Hence, 'companion for vital longevity' was proposed as the brand identity of the clinic. We considered the clinic as a 'companion' with commitment to the customer. This reflects the service philosophy.

FIGURE 9.3 Brand identity: companion for vital longevity

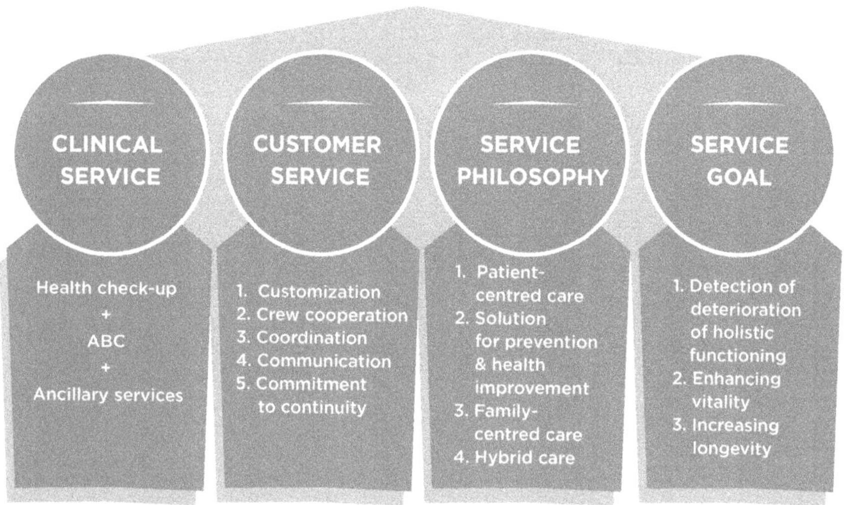

As you can see, the clinic was initially stuck 'waiting on the runway' after their launch, because they had not done the proper upfront branding work to differentiate themselves and tell their complete story in an easy to remember, approachable and believable way. As we have mentioned, all was not lost, because they brought in an outside expert, Professor Ki Nam Jin, who authored the case study and set them on the right track. Examples of underperforming brands can be found in each stage of the brand life cycle and they are usually underperforming as a result of a missing strategic initiative and, often, the necessary resources to implement such an initiative.

Conditions for success in new local markets

Planning on penetrating any market requires deep investigation. Never assume that if a brand is already popular in one market that it will immediately be popular in other markets. The global marketer will need a deep understanding of the new market, including its culture, values and practices. The reasons for being cautious are many. The opportunity cost of a failed market entry can take efforts away from programmes in successful countries, stalling the brand in an area in which it was already successful. A cultural misstep can spread across the borders and affect overall brand perceptions. Gucci recently removed an US $890 (£700) sweater from the shelves after an uproar because it resembled blackface. In their apology, they wrote, 'We consider diversity to be a fundamental value to be fully upheld, respected, and at the forefront of every decision we make.'[22] But if diversity were really at the forefront of every decision, the sweater wouldn't have made it to the market in the first place, because they would have had people in place who understood the implications of their design earlier in the product development stage.

Likewise, in their move to grow their brand in the Chinese market, Dolce & Gabbana launched an ill-fated campaign themed #DGLovesChina. As part of it, they produced a video of a model using chopsticks to eat a range of Italian foods – pizza, spaghetti and a *cannoli* (pastry) – accompanied by a voiceover from a man who asks during the *cannoli* serving, 'Is it too big for you?' Not only did they have to incur the costs of cancelling a huge fashion show featuring 300 models,[23] a small step for justice in light of their actions, they were (rightly) branded as being racist in a key market, an image that will be even more costly for them over the coming years.

Both examples show the implications of not fully knowing their audience, semiotics (the meaning of imagery) and cultural currents of their markets. One way to study a new market to see if conditions are right is by conducting a PEST Analysis, a tool created by Francis Aguilar,[24] who was a professor at Harvard University. PEST, as he set out in his book, *Scanning the Business Environment*,[25] stands for 'Political, Economic, Societal-Cultural and Technological' (it was originally ETPS); some also add environmental and legal (PESTEL) as well as other categories such as demographics.

Often compared with the ever-ubiquitous (and often useless) SWOT Analysis created by Albert Humphrey of Stamford University,[26] these two tools have different usages and provide different types of insights. According to MindTools.com, a great resource, the PEST Analysis looks at 'big picture' factors that might influence a decision, a market or a potential new business. SWOT Analysis explores these factors at a business, product-line or product level.[27] Often a brand will craft both a SWOT and a PEST. If so, create the PEST first and use it to inform the SWOT.

We mentioned above that SWOTs are often useless and it's for a very simple reason: most don't dig deep enough. They are crafted in brainstorm sessions, rather than being deeply research-based. Often, the weaknesses are just the reworded opposites of the strengths and the same for opportunities and threats. When Humphrey created the SWOT in the 1960s and 1970s, he was trying to identify 'why corporate planning failed'[28] and in conducting his research, he drew from a large database.[29] We mention it as a cautionary tale, because, if misused, both the SWOT and the PEST analysis can be, at the very least, useless and, at worst, harmful, leading you astray. The more you know and the more data you have, the better your results will be.

Based on the PEST, here are some considerations to help you decide if you should enter a market:

- Demographics
  - A very close study of the population make-up is essential for any brand to succeed. You should look at the size, age, gender, occupation and education level of the population to help you understand the market potential. Of course, geographics should also be considered – just as it doesn't make sense to sell snow shovels to to warm-weather countries, so too it doesn't make sense to promote swimming suits in Chicago during the winter.
- Economics
  - The economy has a direct effect on the buying power of potential consumers. But the economic conditions can change rapidly and any projections far into the future may not be accurate. The price of anything that contributes to the cost of the brand, from raw materials to transport, can fluctuate. A stable, growing economy would be, obviously, the best conditions for launching into a new product, giving your brand a chance to claim a stake in a new market. At the very least, you need a large enough potential audience with enough means to make your market entry profitable, based on exchange rates and other costs (such as shipping and labour rates in the market).
- Legal system
  - Understanding the stability of the new market's legal system in order to ensure protection for your brand and familiarity with the local laws to make sure you don't inadvertently break any of them are also key before deciding on any move.
- Natural resources
  - The actual location and the natural resources in that location can, and will, affect the brand performance in any market that you want to penetrate. Natural resources such as water, forestry and minerals can affect the manufacturing of a brand in a given location and, thus, product costs. A lack of a natural resources might mean that you have to rely on bringing in the necessary raw materials (or the ready-made product) from the country where the brand originated.
- Politics
  - The political environment is important to understand, because it affects the economy. At the time of writing, certain trade wars are impacting the global balance between east and west and the brands manufactured in both. Many brands, such as Harley-Davidson, are building manufacturing facilities in markets that they want to dominate, because import tariffs from a trade war

are standing in the way of success. A small number of people in powerful political positions can, and are, changing the face of trade and the fate of many brands. Local politics are also important to understand, because it can affect decisions on whether to adopt the new brand. Finally, overlapping with the legal issues, politics plays a role in the enforcement of laws. It doesn't pay for a brand to consider entering markets where their assets can be seized in a political move.

- Social-cultural issues
  - Will the social norms in the potential new market make adoption of the product likely? That is the predominant question in this category. Also, in countries with a sizeable market, will the brand and its elements need to be adjusted? In certain locations, especially in countries with large immigrant communities, it is critical that brands consider social behaviours. Recent immigration waves into Europe have created new communities of consumers, whose behaviour patterns are completely different from those of the local population. These groups will eat, wear and consume different brands, until a full assimilation takes place. Other reasons for different consumer patterns include religious restrictions, especially again when it comes to food and fashion brands. Brand imagery won't necessarily translate either. For instance, a brand once ran a campaign in the US with an ad showing a girl on the rug reading to her dog. The brand wanted to run the campaign in a selected array of Middle Eastern countries, but many people in those countries consider dogs to be dirty, not a pet to cuddle while reading, so the imagery had to be reshot showing a girl reading to her cat.
- Technology
  - It seems that tech is everywhere and increasingly controlling our lives, and it has an impact on brands as well. Does the potential new market have the technological capabilities to adopt your product? After all, on a basic level, if the product is an app, there need to be enough smartphone- or tablet-users with enough towers for it to work. It's increasingly likely that there will be a degree of technological infrastructure, but it might not be enough to support your brand. Many newer brands are completely e-commerce-dependent, but not every market has the internet connectivity, which obviously could interfere with the buying process and with it the consumer's brand experience. Even internally, with back-end operations, the technological infrastructure can influence the consumer's brand experience, affecting the supply chain's 'just-in-time' delivery of product – ie consumers getting what they want, when they want it.

Local customization of multinational brands

Throughout the book, we've pointed out some of the areas that need to remain the same for the product to be seen as a 'brand' and some areas that can and perhaps should be localized. For instance, the brand foundational elements should remain consistent in every country, but some of the brand's atrributes, such as tonality and personality, can be adjusted to correspond to the cultural norms of each individual market and the prospects' needs and interests within it.

As a result, brands that penetrate other global markets face major decisions as they expand. They should begin with the most fundamental considerations such as the brand name. Generations of marketing professionals were told that the Chevy Nova model didn't sell well in Spanish-speaking markets, because the word in Spanish means NO GO.[30] Apparently, further studies proved that this particular story wasn't the case.[31] But the meaning is clear and lessons that could be learned from this false legend are clear. Do your homework when you try to establish a global brand, and make sure the brand name is not offensive in any way possible to the local market. Taking chances isn't worth it.

GLOBAL BRANDS IN A LOCAL WORLD: THE CHALLENGE OF BRAND BUILDING ACROSS MULTIPLE COUNTRIES – A GUEST PERSPECTIVE FROM PAOLO MERCADO, PHILIPPINES

Paolo Mercado is currently the Senior Vice President for Marketing, Communication & Innovation at Nestlé Philippines. Responsible for overseeing the company's advertising, media, digital marketing, promotions, marketing intelligence, innovation, corporate communication, consumer services and marketing competency development, he is a seasoned international marketing and advertising executive with over 12 years of working outside the Philippines for Nestlé and his previous company, Publicis. He has been based in China, Switzerland and France, and has run projects in Europe, the US, Middle East and Asia Pacific. He is the first Filipino to graduate from the Berlin School of Creative Leadership Executive MBA programme. He is also the founding president of the Creative Economy Council of the Philippines, a think tank that is advocating for the recognition of creative industries as the country's next economic growth driver. Here's what Paolo has to say about building brands across countries:

> 'I was born, raised, educated and learned the ropes of my advertising and marketing craft in the Philippines. An emerging economy of more than 100 million people, the Philippines is one of the top consumer markets not only for my company, Nestlé, but for many other multinational fast-moving-consumer-goods (FMCG) companies such as P&G, Unilever, Colgate-Palmolive and Mondelēz.

'As a former Spanish then later on American colony, the Philippines has long been an eager consumer market for Western FMCG brands and products, which were a far superior offer to locally available products at the time they first entered the market. Nestlé, for example, first entered the Philippines with the Milkmaid condensed milk product more than 107 years ago when it was first imported into the country. Milkmaid in fact was also the very first ever Western food product ever registered for commercial sale into China via Hong Kong. Fresh cow's milk was an inaccessible luxury in the Far East in the early 1900s. Thus the 'breakthrough' technology of condensed milk allowed milk from Switzerland to have the long shelf life needed to make the long, slow journey across the oceans and still be fit for consumption when it reached the Philippines.

'This was the pioneering era of global packaged food. This was the story of Nestlé's business from the early 1900s all the way perhaps to the 1980s. Nestlé's food manufacturing technologies brought previously inaccessible food to new emerging markets such as the Philippines. Condensed milk (then later on evaporated milk, powdered milk and UHT milk), instant coffee, chocolate milk powder, bouillons and powdered iced tea were all new to the market. These product innovations were of a much higher quality than local alternatives and they allowed Nestlé to build new categories and highly profitable businesses for years. Competition usually came from other multinational companies as no local company at this time had the capital and know-how to match the food expertise of the multinationals.

'Though the brands were global, much of the brand building at this time was very local. Advertising was seen primarily as product education, and the concept of global brand building wasn't really a thing yet. Thus, marketing was more about on-the-ground distribution, and advertising shifted consumers from traditional options into the new and modern solutions from the multinationals. As each local market had a different situation, advertising and brand building was developed from the ground up in order to convert consumers into adopting essentially new consumption habits.

'Things began to shift in the 1980s to the late 1990s. The advent of global media through cable, satellite and, later on, the internet, encouraged marketers to start doing global brand-building campaigns. For American brands such as Nike and Coke, this just meant pushing their US ads to all markets, as this was part of the broader agenda of democratizing the world through Hollywood and consumerism.

'For non-American multinationals like Nestlé, the approach taken was more of 'best practice sharing'. Thus, a Nescafé campaign that worked well in Brazil or Japan would be adopted/localized in the Philippines. The spirit behind these efforts from Nestlé was more about learning from success rather than the 'One World, One Consumer' approach of American mega brands.

'During the late 90s to the present day, things started to shift yet again. Global media and the digital media revolution had taken root. It was at this time that I shifted from being an advertising strategist in the Philippines to becoming a part of the Global Advertising Team for Nestle, and then later on joining Nestlé as a global communications manager. During this period, global brands now worked with global aligned agencies, both of whom paid more attention to global financial markets and global advertising awards than they did local consumers. Thus, the current era of global brand building with 'Global Big Ideas' began. From Nike's 'Just Do It' to Dove's 'Real Beauty' and OMO's 'Dirt Is Good', global marketers all drank the Cool-Aid of Universal Human Truths that would change the world and pick-up a Cannes Lion or two along the way.

'At Nestlé, we also got into the game with 'Have A Break, Have A KitKat' (an idea born in the UK in the1960s but globalized in the 90s) and Nespresso's 'What Else?' campaign with George Clooney. Other brands like Nescafé and Maggi, though, struggle to this day to find the elusive Global Big Idea that changes the world. Alignment of advertising execution was no longer just a matter of sharing of best practice, rather it was about having global advertising that built global brands. The situation was further compounded by Procurement (with a capital P), seeing how globally or regionally produced campaigns would save a lot of money versus each local market producing their own local campaigns.

'While this made sense from the global HQs of marketers and ad agencies (and I have worked in both), local competitors who stayed close to local consumers saw things differently. When Jollibee, the Filipino fast-food giant, launched fried chicken, sweet spaghetti and rice meals, it took a couple of years before McDonald's could convince their head office to do the same. P&G and Unilever, bitter rivals in home care, were so busy watching each other, that they didn't notice a local low-cost brand gain market share through traditional channels and radio advertising. For our part, Nescafé initially ignored an Indonesian brand that first entered the market as a coffee-flavored hard candy sold in small stores. Then with lighting speed, this competitor introduced their own powdered coffee and quickly gained market share with those who grew to like their coffee candies! Similarly to McDonald's, the need to align all product and communication strategies with our Head Office slowed down our response time enough for the competitor to gain significant ground in the marketplace.

'A recent multi-market study done by McCann Erickson called 'The Truth About Brands' gives concrete data behind the rise of local and regional brands. In 2015, 67 per cent of consumers trusted global brands more than they did local brands. In 2018, the situation had reversed, with 56 per cent of those surveyed trusting local brands more than global brands. McCann posits that while the internet age was thought to help create a single global community, it has in fact highlighted the importance of local diversity and uniqueness in an otherwise generic world. The internet has allowed local brands relatively cheap access to consumers through digital advertising and e-commerce.

'Furthermore, local brands have caught up with the big FMCG's manufacturing capabilities. While some multinational technical experts scoff at the inconsistent quality of local products, for many consumers an overly standardized product isn't special; it's actually boring. The imperfections of local brands are sometimes seen as a sign of authenticity, while the technical perfection of big-brand products are seen as simply generic.

'So how must global brands cope? Some keep pushing their tried and tested ways of working. If it has worked for us in the last 100 years, then why change for some upstart? Some resort to buying out local brands in the hopes of capturing some of their authentic brand equity. Still others say that we must behave like start-ups and launch innovations into the market as fast as we can.

'While I do not claim to know the best answer to this challenge, what I do believe is that understanding and delivering value to LOCAL consumers is still the best way to win in a GLOBAL marketplace. If we don't win the local consumer, then there is no global marketplace. In a way, it is indeed behaving like a start-up, not so much by hyper-ventilating innovation launches, but more by applying the entrepreneurs' mindset of seeing a need in the market and doing all we can to be the first to fulfill this need better than anyone else.

'Beyond product innovations, I believe the same is true for brand building. I have become cynical of the myth of Global Big Ideas for global brands that force-fit one advertising campaign across multiple markets. Time and again, I have seen such global campaigns work in some markets but fail in many others. Or worse, global brand managers resort to settling for the least common denominator of 'what works in most markets' to come up with campaigns that are essentially generic. In both cases, local brands that have a better connection with the nuances of local consumers win in the market. While these local brands may not have a multi-country presence, the reality remains that they are winning the hearts, minds and wallets of consumers in the country where they do operate.

'The resurgence of local brands could be short-term. I tend to believe it is a deeper trend that global brand builders must come to terms with. Large-scale manufacturing is being challenged by micro-manufacturing. The rise of craft beers as well as craft coffee blends prove this point. Already 3D printing is being applied to food products such as customized chocolate shapes and flavours. So if global brands are to survive in this new era, we need to let go of old industrial 'economies of scale' mindsets and learn how to deliver value to local consumers, one person and one market at a time.'

EXTENDED CASE STUDY: PHILIPS, A STUDY IN HEALTHY INNOVATION

Philips is a Dutch-based brand, well-known for its many successful products all over the world, particularly in the healthcare category, so looking at its evolution – how it expanded and then focused – and its emphasis on innovation can help any global brand manager succeed and the brand to stay relevant.

Little did people think that Philips would be such an innovative brand when it was born in 1891, as it focused on manufacturing light bulbs in a modest factory that Frederik Philips had purchased.[32] His goal was done to bring cost-effective, reliable electric incandescent light bulbs to all who needed them. After all, although the light bulb was invented by Thomas Edison, the actual commercialization of it was split among many others. Frederik Philips aimed to be among them.

Then, between 1915 and 1925, Philips started its pioneering research into X-ray technology as well as producing medical X-ray tubes. They also became the world's largest manufacturer of radios and radio tubes, based on their research into that area.[33] Philips' range of products expanded; they showcased their first television at the 1938 Annual Fair in Utrecht[34] and launched their pioneering rotary electric shaver, the Philishave, one year later.[35] In fact, over the next 50-plus years, they continued with additonal technological breakthroughs, including advancements in transistors and integrated circuitry, enabling research into the treatment of malignant tumours[36] and launching the Compact Audio Cassette in 1963,[37] which became the standard for recording, and, one year later, optical telecommunication systems, the LaserVision optical disc, and the highly successful Compact Disc, which they developed with Sony.

Even during these early days, when 'branding' was not considered important, Philips focused on creating international markets for its products. In those days, personal connections and winning large orders were essential for advancing the success of any commercial manufacturing facility.[38] When the Russian Tsar ordered the installation of electric lights in his winter palace, Philips was the winner.[39]

Another smart decision by the company was to devote funds and energy to product innovation, which led to the inception of their 'NatLab,' a centre dedicated to studying physical and chemical phenomena as a way of stimulating product innovation.[40] This offered a unique positioning for them, helping them differentiate themselves from the other manufacturing-focused organizations of the time, who were just happy to book orders of existing products without thinking 'what's next?' While it's important to note that talking about innovation is not a differentiating point anymore, 'walking the talk', ie, being innovative, is what will make the cut and make people see you as an innovative company. After all, actions speak louder than words.

While a well-established global brand, they simplified their structure in the 1990s, reducing the number of operational areas.[41] In the healthcare sector, Philips also adopted a people-centric approach to product design, with the aim of making medical systems easier for clinicians to use and more comfortable for patients.[42] However, they still focused on product innovations in other areas, again partnering with Sony to introduce the DVD in 1997, which became the fastest-growing home electronics product in history.[43]

Philips today is involved in a range of product categories, including: Sound and Vision, Personal Care, Mother and Child Care, Household Products, Lighting, Health, Automotive and Accessories that work with or support the other categories. And, in the professional healthcare arena, their products range from their long-standing engagement in radiology and X-ray systems to respiratory care and emergency care and resuscitation systems. These business categories are universal and touch the lives of people wherever they live. It is hard to believe that any brand in such large influential categories would ever aspire to be only a national or regional brand. And they don't. One immediate indication that Philips truly stands out as a global organization is that their key people include nationals from the Netherlands, USA, India, Israel, Belgium, Germany, Brazil, France, China and Switzerland, reinforcing the concept that a truly global brand can be identified easily by looking at the make-up of its management team, the executive committees, board of directors, supervisors and others in its organization. Philips' impressive collection of brain power and cultural identities, market-specific knowledge and obviously deep understanding of consumer needs in various parts of the world is key to this brand's strength. Any brand that can demonstrate such commitment to understanding consumer behaviour is a truly global brand.[44]

Philips is not known for producing glitzy ad campaigns. In fact, its advertising and marketing activity is quite low-profile when compared to relative newcomers such as Samsung.[45] In 2017, Philips appointed Ogilvy to launch a global campaign under the title: 'Better me, better world.'[46] The initiative is part of Philips' stated goal of improving the lives of three billion people each year by 2025.[47] In 2018, the company claimed to have helped 2.1 billion through working on campaigns such as United Nation's Every Woman Every Child initiative, which aimed to improve the lives of women and children in Africa and South East Asia.[48,49]

Another part of their campaign was to personalize care by looking at specific sub-groups of patients, such as children. This led to the development of its Ambient Experience Computed Tomography (CT) suite.[50] As we all know, young people are anxious and reluctant to go through medical procedures, especially because hospitals and clinics look like, well, hospitals and clinics. Philips developed ways to make children feel less anxious during their CT scans through the use of calm lighting, entertaining projections and soothing music. The invention increased the quality of diagnostic images, lowered the potential for repeat scans and improved the morale of medical practitioners engaged in the process.[51] A complete win-win-win, building the brand as well.

Philips also noticed that innovation could drive the provision of efficient healthcare at scale through 'industrialization'. After all, there are aspects of healthcare that do indeed mimic industrial processes. While technology has overhauled traditional factory lines in the manufacturing industry, there is still plenty of room in the healthcare sector to automate certain tedious tasks, such as patient monitoring and diagnostic image processing. Philips has helped hospitals make headway in this area by tapping into digitization and the internet of things (IoT).[52] By collaborating and engaging third-party developers who helped accelerate the pace of innovation, they now have 9.7 million IoT devices connected to their HealthSuite

Cloud.[53] Not many brands show this amount of commitment to improving the entire process in which their products are used.

While Philips puts an emphasis on the technological and production innovation, it also pays a significant amount of attention to the people involved in the creation and ideation of new product concepts. A good brand must always pay attention to those who bring it to life every day. Philips is known for fostering a culture of co-creation and collaboration among various disciplines, so they can achieve maximum value for the end consumer and the client (a hospital, for example).[54] As Philips' Chief Design Officer once said, 'With this complex and changing world, it is impossible to innovate alone. Finding better solutions and creating value requires collaboration between different people and organizations.'[55]

While some think of Philips as primarily a healthcare brand, it is still bringing amazing products into our lives in other categories. For instance, prior to 2012, there was very little significant innovation in the light-bulb category product for many years. They had become a commodity and many people didn't care who manufactured their bulbs. But in 2012, they launched The Philips Hue LED Lighting System, which some magazines voted as best new product of the year.

It's important to note that prior to their latest ad campaign, Philips' advertising theme was: 'Sense and Simplicity', which was launched in 2005.[56] The advertisements were designed to give customers a distinctive image of a sharper, more focused enterprise, which – through its activities in healthcare, lifestyle and technology – was held together by a common drive to deliver simpler end-user experiences. Gabriele Wrede, global head of marketing and brand management, said at the time: 'Thanks to our consistent focus on building brand loyalty amongst all our customers – with the brand campaign as an important element – we've seen a 7 per cent increase in the value of the Philips brand to US $8.7bn, outpacing the average increase for 4 per cent shown by brands measured in the 2010 Interbrand ranking."[57]

As you can see, through their history of innovation, Philips has always worked to make life easier. Philips after all is never satisfied with its current level of success and is always looking beyond the horizon to find the next opportunity. For them, innovation is a way of life. For any global brand manager, no matter your title, that outlook should be adopted. It's the way to ensure that your brand thrives for 130 years or more.

KEY TERMS

- adoption
- brand touchpoints
- demographics
- maturity
- PEST
- SWOT

DISCUSSION QUESTIONS

1 What are some additional dos and don'ts when customizing a multinational brand to a local market?

2 What are the fundamental management decisions at the brand-life-cycle inflection points?

3 What are the key considerations that help determine whether a brand should expand into a new market?

4 When and how should a brand manager customize multinational brands to a local market?

5 Describe the basic conditions for success in vast and competitive marketing environments.

Notes

1 Zorfas, A and Leemon, D (2019) An emotional connection matters more than customer satisfaction, *Harvard Business Review*, https://hbr.org/2016/08/an-emotional-connection-matters-more-than-customer-satisfaction (archived at https://perma.cc/BV2E-PT7W)

2 Trott, D (2019) Copywriting Conference 2013: Dave Trott, Predatory thinking for copywriters, YouTube, https://www.youtube.com/watch?v=rl3SELihHqs (archived at https://perma.cc/9W9J-Z7AV)

3 Jarrett, C (2019) Psychology: How many senses do we have? BBC, http://www.bbc.com/future/story/20141118-how-many-senses-do-you-have (archived at https://perma.cc/27BW-5K8K)

4 Verywell Mind (2019) How heuristics help you make quick decisions, https://www.verywellmind.com/what-is-a-heuristic-2795235 (archived at https://perma.cc/CU8T-JMQA)

5 Woodruff, J and Thompson, J (2019) What is Premium Pricing Strategy? Smallbusiness.chron.com, https://smallbusiness.chron.com/premium-pricing-strategy-1107.html (archived at https://perma.cc/UDZ9-LMZX)

6 Rao, A, Bergen, M, and Davis, S (2019) How to fight a price war, *Harvard Business Review*, https://hbr.org/2000/03/how-to-fight-a-price-war (archived at https://perma.cc/DU84-L8A2)

7 Arrington, M (2019) Expanding Your Portfolio? Remember These 5 Things, *Entrepreneur*, https://www.entrepreneur.com/article/273556 (archived at https://perma.cc/3FZH-HHN7)

8 Murphy, G (2019) Leverage your partnerships to enhance your service offerings, Channel Futures, https://www.channelfutures.com/business-models/leverage-your-partnerships-to-enhance-your-service-offerings (archived at https://perma.cc/LK92-5G4E)

9 Nunes, P, Dull, S and Lynch, P (2019) When two brands are better than one, Mthink.com, http://mthink.com/legacy/www.crmproject.com/content/pdf/CRM4_wp_nunes.pdf (archived at https://perma.cc/B9KM-LRYX)

10 Feldman, A (2019) How to make a brand more attractive to licensees and retailers, lmca.net, http://lmca.net/wp-content/uploads/2016/01/How-to-Make-a-Brand-More-Attractive-to-Licensees-and-Retailers.pdf (archived at https://perma.cc/TTA3-877W)

11 Smedstad, S (2019) Why your employer brand needs to be magnetic, Social Recruiting Strategies, https://socialrecruitingstrategies.com/blog/why-your-employer-brand-needs-to-be-magnetic (archived at https://perma.cc/ERD3-7KNY)

12 Vizard, S, Hammett, E, Gloyne, R, Woollen, P, Fleming, M, Hemsley, S, Rogers, C and Joy, S (2019), How Heineken is evolving its employer branding strategy, *Marketing Week*, https://www.marketingweek.com/2019/01/29/heineken-new-employer-branding-strategy (archived at https://perma.cc/ZF2F-9GMK)

13 Cleverism (2019) Threat Of Substitutes, Porter's Five Forces Model, https://www.cleverism.com/threat-of-substitutes-porters-five-forces-model (archived at https://perma.cc/2CG2-C74C)

14 Cleverism (2019) Threat Of Substitutes, Porter's Five Forces Model, https://www.cleverism.com/threat-of-substitutes-porters-five-forces-model (archived at https://perma.cc/2CG2-C74C)

15 Creativepool.com (2019) Job Description: Brand Manager, https://creativepool.com/articles/jobdescriptions/brand-manager-job-description (archived at https://perma.cc/9PPP-N7PD)

16 The Economist (2019) Nothing special: MBAs are no longer prized by employers, https://www.economist.com/whichmba/nothing-special-mbas-are-no-longer-prized-employers (archived at https://perma.cc/6LLV-N9D9)

17 Aaker, D and Joachimsthaler, E (2019) *Brand Leadership*, Free Press (a division of Simon & Schuster), New York; Google Books, https://books.google.com/books?hl=en&lr=&id=Jha-ykJWgDUC&oi=fnd&pg=PT9&dq=brand+leadership+model&ots=yEQsL-c9S0&sig=eFLB54DoY86kri5jRo6lzyfqYzY#v=onepage&q=brand%20leadership%20model&f=false (archived at https://perma.cc/56FK-METC)

18 Emeraldinsight.com (2019) Brand image and customers' willingness to pay a price premium for food brands, *Journal of Product & Brand Management*, 23 (2), https://www.emeraldinsight.com/doi/abs/10.1108/JPBM-10-2013-0414 (archived at https://perma.cc/3GN7-GAX4)

19 Deloitte (Produced by the Deloitte Center for Health Solutions) Medical tourism consumers in search of value (2019), Globalwellnesssummit.com, https://www.globalwellnesssummit.com/wp-content/uploads/Industry-Research/Americas/2008-deloitte-medical-tourism-consumers.pdf (archived at https://perma.cc/6X7L-9CRB)

20 Hospitals.webometrics.info (2019) Ranking Web of Hospitals, http://hospitals.webometrics.info/en/world (archived at https://perma.cc/8GHF-76GZ)

21 Theananti.com (2019) Ananti Cove, https://theananti.com/eng/cove/drosclinic.asp (archived at https://perma.cc/A57V-V99N)

22 Twitter.com (2019) Twitter, https://twitter.com/gucci/status/1093345744080306176/photo/1?ref_src=twsrc%5Etfw%7Ctwcamp%5Etweetembed%7Ct, wterm%5E1093345744080306176&ref_url=https%3A%2F%2Fwww.washingtonpost.com%2Fnation%2F2019%2F02%2F07%2Fhaute-couture-blackface-gucci-apologizes-pulls-racist-sweater%2F (archived at https://perma.cc/L63H-JU3Z)

23 The Daily Beast (2019) Dolce & Gabbana never met a controversy they didn't like – until now, https://www.thedailybeast.com/dolce-and-gabbana-never-met-a-controversy-they-didnt-like-until-now?ref=home (archived at https://perma.cc/Q94D-UKDW)

24 Hbs.edu (2019) HBS Professor Frank Aguilar Dies at 80, News, *Harvard Business School*, https://www.hbs.edu/news/releases/Pages/aguilar-obituary.aspx (archived at https://perma.cc/T9LZ-3MC9)

25 Aguilar, F (1967) *Scanning the Business Environment*, Macmillan, New York

26 Friesner, V (2019) History of SWOT Analysis, Marketingteacher.com, https://www.marketingteacher.com/history-of-swot-analysis (archived at https://perma.cc/483W-S6FY)

27 Mindtools.com (2019) PEST analysis identifying big picture opportunities and threats, https://www.mindtools.com/pages/article/newTMC_09.htm (archived at https://perma.cc/585F-7YNN)

28 Morrison, M (2019) The complete history and guide to SWOT Analysis, *RapidBI*, https://rapidbi.com/swotanalysis (archived at https://perma.cc/Y5VM-Q523)

29 Friesner, V (2019) History of SWOT Analysis, Marketingteacher.com, https://www.marketingteacher.com/history-of-swot-analysis (archived at https://perma.cc/483W-S6FY)

30 Snopes.com (2019) FACT CHECK: Did the Chevrolet Nova fail to sell in Spanish-speaking countries? https://www.snopes.com/fact-check/chevrolet-nova-name-spanish (archived at https://perma.cc/5UCH-RMN4)

31 DuetsBlog (2019) That story about the Chevy Nova? It's a no go, https://www.duetsblog.com/2012/07/articles/branding/that-story-about-the-chevy-nova-its-a-no-go (archived at https://perma.cc/7EH9-9QEP)

32 Philips (2019) Our heritage – Company – About, https://www.philips.com/a-w/about/company/our-heritage.html (archived at https://perma.cc/N7MU-VJW9)

33 Philips (2019) Our heritage – Company – About, https://www.philips.com/a-w/about/company/our-heritage.html (archived at https://perma.cc/N7MU-VJW9)

34 Costello, O (2018) Philips one of the great 4K UHD bargains around this holiday period, *SmartHouse*, https://www.smarthouse.com.au/philips-one-great-4k-uhd-bargains-around-holiday-period (archived at https://perma.cc/S7J8-3AGG)

35 Anon (2019) https://www.philips.com/a-w/about/philips-design.htm (archived at https://perma.cc/655X-Z2VH)

36 Philips (2019) Our heritage – Company – About, https://www.philips.com/a-w/about/company/our-heritage.html (archived at https://perma.cc/N7MU-VJW9)

37 Dormonm, B (2013) Happy 50th birthday, Compact Cassette: How it struck a chord for millions, Theregister.co.uk, https://www.theregister.co.uk/2013/08/30/50_years_of_the_compact_cassette (archived at https://perma.cc/7SLK-82TL)

38 Philips (2019) Our heritage – Company – About, https://www.philips.com/a-w/about/company/our-heritage.html (archived at https://perma.cc/N7MU-VJW9)
39 Philips (2019) Our heritage – Company – About, https://www.philips.com/a-w/about/company/our-heritage.html (archived at https://perma.cc/N7MU-VJW9)
40 Philips (2019) Our heritage – Company – About, https://www.philips.com/a-w/about/company/our-heritage.html (archived at https://perma.cc/N7MU-VJW9)
41 Philips (2019) Our heritage – Company – About, https://www.philips.com/a-w/about/company/our-heritage.html (archived at https://perma.cc/N7MU-VJW9)
42 Philips (2019) Our heritage – Company – About, https://www.philips.com/a-w/about/company/our-heritage.html (archived at https://perma.cc/N7MU-VJW9)
43 Philips (2019) The history of the CD – The beginning – Research, https://www.philips.com/a-w/research/technologies/cd/beginning.html (archived at https://perma.cc/D8NA-KU9V)
44 Philips (2019) Supervisory Board – Our management – Company – About, https://www.philips.com/a-w/about/company/our-management/supervisory-board.html (archived at https://perma.cc/N4UN-5QNC)
45 Low, E, Farveen, F, Tam, I, Ramli, Y, Tay, V, Farveen, F, Tan, J, Boost, R, Ng, L, Manjur, R, Wee, L and Xuan, O (2019) Philips overhauls marketing approach, Marketing Interactive, https://www.marketing-interactive.com/philips-overhauls-marketing-approach (archived at https://perma.cc/MJ2X-6WDD)
46 Tan, E (2017) Philips launches global marketing initiative 'Better me, better world', Campaignlive.co.uk, https://www.campaignlive.co.uk/article/philips-launches-global-marketing-initiative-better-me-better-world/1445374 (archived at https://perma.cc/T224-65QK)
47 News-Medical.net (2019) Philips reinforces commitment to improve 3 billion lives each year by 2025, https://www.news-medical.net/news/20170922/Philips-reinforces-commitment-to-improve-3-billion-lives-each-year-by-2025.aspx (archived at https://perma.cc/35YT-SD4A)
48 Campaignlive.co.uk (2018) Philips launches global marketing initiative 'Better me, better world', https://www.campaignlive.co.uk/article/philips-launches-global-marketing-initiative-better-me-better-world/1445374 (archived at https://perma.cc/T224-65QK)
49 YouTube (2018) Better me better world, Philips, https://www.youtube.com/watch?time_continue=32&v=eXZuJ8n-KSA (archived at https://perma.cc/9LPJ-FW96)
50 Philips (2019) Ambient experience, Philips Healthcare Consulting, https://www.usa.philips.com/healthcare/consulting/experience-solutions/ambient-experience (archived at https://perma.cc/BL22-3SAS)
51 Philips (2019) Ambient experience, Philips Healthcare Consulting, https://www.usa.philips.com/healthcare/consulting/experience-solutions/ambient-experience (archived at https://perma.cc/BL22-3SAS)
52 Philips (2019) Ambient experience, Philips Healthcare Consulting, https://www.usa.philips.com/healthcare/consulting/experience-solutions/ambient-experience (archived at https://perma.cc/BL22-3SAS)
53 Pennic, J (2019) Philips and Samsung partner to connect Samsung's IoT platform to Philips HealthSuite digital platform, Hitconsultant.net, https://hitconsultant.

net/2018/03/08/philips-samsung-partnership/#.XH8JGM9KjMI (archived at https://perma.cc/Z4BP-8WTX)

54 Pennic, J (2019) Philips and Samsung partner to connect Samsung's IoT platform to Philips HealthSuite digital platform, Hitconsultant.net, https://hitconsultant.net/2018/03/08/philips-samsung-partnership/#.XH8JGM9KjMI (archived at https://perma.cc/Z4BP-8WTX)

55 Asian Scientist Magazine, Science, technology and medical news updates from Asia (2018) Co-creating the future of healthcare, https://www.asianscientist.com/2017/12/features/future-healthcare-ipi-singapore (archived at https://perma.cc/5C23-GMDC)

56 Businesswire.com (2019) Philips launches new wave of brand advertising campaign; innovative campaign continues to promote image of healthcare, lifestyle and technology company and 'Sense and Simplicity', https://www.businesswire.com/news/home/20050516005215/en/Philips-Launches-New-Wave-Brand-Advertising-Campaign (archived at https://perma.cc/3YJX-FZ5C)

57 WIRE, B (2018) Philips Launches New Wave of Brand Advertising Campaign; Innovative Campaign Continues to Promote Image of Healthcare, Lifestyle and Technology Company and 'Sense and Simplicity', Businesswire.com, https://www.businesswire.com/news/home/20050516005215/en/Philips-Launches-New-Wave-Brand-Advertising-Campaign (archived at https://perma.cc/3YJX-FZ5C)

10

Brand architecture

READING OUTCOMES

At the conclusion of this chapter, you should be able to:

- explain the difference between a house of brands, a branded house and a hybrid of the two;
- describe the differences between a sub-brand, an endorsed brand and a brand extension;
- define the process for achieving optimal corporate ROI by rationalizing a brand portfolio;
- articulate the value of having strategic, clear, logical, flexible, synergistic brand architecture.

Introduction

When two friends start a company in the house garage or business incubator, while filled with optimism, they never know where the initiative will go. They have no clue if the business they create is just a nice idea that has to be tested or if they will become a multinational conglomerate. They simply play with an idea and try to make money. In fact, we have encountered many students who approach us with questions about starting a business, with only one thing in mind: making money, fast. Branding is not a consideration.

One of the best examples of friends starting a company is the pairing of Steve Jobs and Steve Wozniak, who liked each other and bonded with an idea to find a cheap way to make long-distance calls, by inventing a technology that routed around the AT&T system. It was all a prank to start with, and only later did they think: 'wait a minute, maybe we can make money out of it.'[1] This was the beginning of Apple, one of the mightiest brands in the world.[2] When Apple grew into a larger organization, they needed to develop product lines or sub-brands and decide under which umbrella each individual stock-keeping unit (SKU) would live.

All successful companies reach a point where they start marketing more than just one product and, perhaps, more than one brand. For that, they need to understand 'brand architecture', or 'brand hierarchy', to help them organize these products or brands. What is the best way to organize all the various the products in your company? As a branded house, where all of the products and services carry the same name and logo, and each product perhaps carries an extension to the name to identify it? As a house of brands, where each brand has a different name? Or a hybrid of the two, where some of the product or service brands carry the name of the owner brand and some do not?

Larger companies pay close attention to their brand architecture as well. Fast-moving consumer goods (FMCG), such as soap, soft drinks, toothpaste and canned and frozen foods often belong to large organizations that operate as houses of brands. Procter & Gamble, SC Johnson, Coca-Cola, Unilever and others have a stronghold on consumers globally. Many other brands that affect our lives in different ways can be found in branded houses. Aeroplanes are mainly manufactured by two branded houses, Boeing and Airbus, for instance. Multinational banks offer financial services that range from current and savings accounts to life insurance and investment products, all identified under the same brand. And then there are all of the 'in between' situations. Which is best? It depends. This chapter will help you decide which is right for your organization.

Overview

In this relatively short but important chapter, we open by describing the various ways of organizing product or service brands in a business. One of the most important decisions the brand manager has to make is whether to create a house of brands, a branded house or a hybrid of the two. To help you answer the question for your organization, we explore each in detail, examining their advantages and disadvantages. We then explore brand portfolio rationalization, the process of auditing an organization's collection of brands or the product and services lines within a single brand to determine which to emphasize and which, if any, to sell or eliminate. We conclude the chapter with a 'guest perspective' from Professor Lubna Nafees, who looks at how brands can go global, using India as an example, and finally we have a case study exploring how GM reorganized its brand architecture.

Do you want to have a house of brands or a branded house?

Look at the structure in many large corporations and you'll find that each brand is managed separately from its other brands, has its own P&L, distinct marketing objectives and often separate ad agencies. In addition, the responsibilities and day-to-day tasks of someone who has the job title 'Brand Manager' can vary from brand to brand in multi-brand corporations. Furthermore, in multi-brand corporations the product categories and the consumer problems can be widely different from one brand group to another. But even with all of these differences, the brands have to work together – and make sense being together under the same corporate umbrella – in order to advance the ultimate growth and profit goals of the corporate owner.

How the various brands are structured in the corporate organization is called 'brand architecture'. As branding guru David Aaker and co-author Erich Joachimsthaler wrote in their classic, *Brand Leadership: Building Assets in an Information Economy*, 'Brand architecture organizes and structures the brand portfolio by specifying brand roles and the nature of relationships between brands.'[3] The generally accepted benefits of implementing an appropriate brand-architecture strategy include:

- positively contributing to brand equity and loyalty;[4]
- capturing and transferring positive brand equity among offerings;[5]
- increasing sales and revenues by helping the target segments understand and choose brands;[6]
- improving the efficiency of marketing efforts and PR decisions and executions;[7]
- facilitating product-development process;[8]
- simplifying future naming, branding, packaging and distribution decisions;[9]
- improving brand consistency across all brand touchpoints.[10]

In other words, employing the proper brand architecture or structure for the organization's brands can facilitate overall growth and build consumer loyalty, ensuring long-term corporate stability. But what is the proper structure? That is the golden question. Settle on the wrong structure and the organization might eventually need to undertake a painful reorganization, not to mention a costly rebranding process, taking your focus away from other needs. Worse for the company, the wrong structure might confuse employees and customers, not generate the sales needed for sustained growth, require that you burn through marketing dollars to maintain share, and have to forego other business and brand-building opportunities.[11]

The answer depends on the strategic goals of the organization. Is there cohesion across the product lines? Do you aim to buy and sell the product lines? Are there benefits for standardizing packaging? How do you see expanding your portfolio of products and services? Can the product line or service in one category shine a halo on the product lines in other categories? These are just some of the questions that you need to ask when exploring your strategic goals. How you answer then will help determine how you will structure (or restructure) your brand portfolio.

Finding a home in a house of brands

What is a house of brands? Walk into your bathroom and you may find that many of the personal-care brands that you know and have used for many years actually come from the same source. Just go down this list and see which ones you and your family uses: Ace, Align, Always, Ambipur, Ariel, Aussie, Bold, Bonux, Bounce, Bounty, Braun, Cascade, Cheer, Clerblue, Comet, Crest, Charmin, Dash, Dawn, Daz, Dodot, Downy, Dreft, Era, Febreze, Fairy, Fixodent, Gain, Gillette, Head & Shoulder, Herbal Essences, Ivroy, Joy, Lenor, Luvs, Meta, Naturella, Olay, Old Spice, Oral-B, Scope, Secret, Tide, Pantene, Pampers, Pepto Bismol, Prilosec Puffs, Rindex, Rejoice, Safeguard, Salvo, Sarasa, SK-II, Swiffer, Tampax, Venus, Viakal, Vicks and Whisper.[12] At the time of writing, they are all owned by one, very famous house of brands: Proctor & Gamble (P&G). In fact, they own more than 50 brands, divided into such diverse product categories as dishwashing, laundry detergents, feminine hygiene and skin care.[13] Another famous house of brands is Unilever. They own more than 200 brands throughout the globe, including Braun, Gillette, Crest, Ariel and Olay.[14]

With a house of brands, there is very little association between the parent name, such as Procter & Gamble or Unilever, and the brands they own. Each independent, unconnected customer-facing brand within a house of brands has its own, unique brand foundation. When a consumer uses a brand owned by a house of brands, we rarely think of the name of the holding company that owns it.

THE ADVANTAGES OF A HOUSE OF BRANDS SYSTEM

There are some clear advantages to the house of brands system, which we set out below.

Multiple target markets Having a house of brands gives you the ability to appeal to multiple target markets within a country and across borders. A selection of brands might contain similar ingredients and even be made in the same plant, but the brand name in one country or with a segment within a country may not have the same appeal in another. Sometimes names that are extremely popular in one part of the world sound offensive in another location. As a holding company, a house of brands can operate in many markets at the same time and even compete with themselves, without creating any visible conflicts.

Ease of testing the appeal of new products We know that it doesn't always pay to launch a new product on a massive scale, either nationally or globally. A house of brands offers the opportunity to launch new brands, some with multiple innovations, into markets that could be used as a test for further expansion. In cases where the test doesn't work, the test brand can be eliminated without causing significant damage to the owner or reflect poorly on other brands in the portfolio. If it looks like the brand won't be able to expand beyond the initial segment(s), but could still be profitably managed, it could become a niche market brand for the organization.

Damage-limitation to brands in the same stable A house of brands helps to prevent contamination across brands or to the holding company. Imagine that a house of brands, such as Unilever or Procter & Gamble, is launching an innovative new brand, one that takes shaving into a completely new place. Instead of having to actually shave, men will just take a pill the night before and their hair will stop growing for 24 hours. This concept product could be quite radical and even intimidating to many. An experienced house of brands company such as Unilever or Procter & Gamble would never embark on such an adventure knowing that it might be a significant risk for the entire holding company. All of the other brands in the men's health, wellness and personal hygiene category will continue their manufacturing and marketing efforts without any interference. The new revolutionary brand could be launched, tested, tweaked and criticized by the media without jeopardizing or even hurting the other more traditional brands in the stable, since they simply have no connection with each other. Their entire operation for the new brand, including its production, marketing, sales and research, can be kept separate. The personnel involved in the new product could also be completely different, and even the geographical location where the product is sold might have nothing to do with the distribution of their other brands. If things go wrong with the new brand, it can even close its doors, and with very little brand association, the closure will not cause damage to other brands in the house.

Ease of sale of brands A house of brands gives you the ability to easily sell a brand or even an entire category of brands. For example, take the niche product mentioned in the section above. If the company discovers that one of their new products can't generate the scale they want or need or that they cannot manage it profitably but other companies think they can, they can sell it, enabling them to recoup their product-development costs and focus on their core competencies. Finally, the company can sell a brand, a collection of brands or even an entire category of brands should their ownership of them cause confusion for their shareholders or other stakeholders. An athletic shoe company, for instance, might own a line of sports drinks or protein bars. Selling those consumer brands might underline to their investors that they are dedicated to their core competency, athletic shoes, helping improve their valuation and stock prices or address any concerns with their overall strategy.[15]

Ease of purchase of other brands Since one brand doesn't reflect on the others within a company, the organization can easily acquire growing brands started by entrepreneurs or even from other house-of brand-organizations. As a result, the organization doesn't have to take the risk of growing a small niche market or testing a new product, eliminating product-development costs and the initial marketing activities when returns are typically lower. Once they have acquired the brand, they can use their network to increase distribution to recuperate the purchase costs. They might also buy brands from other houses of brands that are exiting the category or simply can't grow sales for the brand. Of course, if the house of brand predicts that they have maximized the potential for a brand and others think that they can grow it, they can also easily sell the brand.

Brand licensing If a house of brands is not strong in a particular market and another one is, the first one can license the brand to the second one for a particular market. In these situations, the owner of the brand is licensing the brand's equity, which they'd need to protect in the agreement by demanding a strict adherence to using the same ingredients, manufacturing processes and brand platform as adjusted to the market. The owner might also demand a review of any marketing materials for the licensee's territories to ensure the brand equity is not damaged. Conversely, if the house of brands is stronger in the market and has excess capacity, including manufacturing and marketing, they could always sign a licence to distribute other brands in their markets.

Cross-promotion A house of brands gives you the chance to enter categories or launch innovative features without detracting from the equities of an existing brand; not every innovation needs to or should result in a brand extension. Say a house of brands owns a successful product in a category; they don't want to take away from it, but they have an opportunity in the same or related category. One strategy would be to launch the new invention as a new brand. To help launch the new brand, the company can run messaging about the new brand on the packaging of the existing one, building the equities of the new one without detracting from the equities of the established one. They could also offer a voucher for the new brand in or on the packaging or the established one. Another option: they could offer the new brand as a gift-with-purchase of the existing brand, driving trial of the new one. All of these tactics fall under the definition of cross-promotion, which can be executed with brands owned by other companies, but is much easier when they're both owned by the same company. After all, not every invention should result in a brand extension.

One example of entering a new category without violating the space of an existing one is the story of how Crest launched it battery-powered toothbrush. As an established house of brands, Procter & Gamble owns many brands around the globe, but few are as successful as Crest. Crest today has Crest Gum, Crest 3D White, Crest Pro Health, Crest Complete, Crest Sensitivity and many other kinds of toothpastes. However, in 1996, it experienced failure when it wasn't able to launch a major mouth-hygiene product. As a result, Crest brand share started declining, with competitor brands Colgate, Mentadent and Aquafresh working to gain share.

According to Information Resources Inc, a market research firm in Chicago, the brand declined to 26 per cent market share from about 35 per cent that year.[16]

Around that same period, an inventor named John Osher created a product that had nothing to do with dental-hygiene products or practices but would soon impact it. What was his invention? The Spin Pop, a lollipop that sits atop a battery-operated handle, so consumers could twirl the sweet treat in their mouths. At the candy's inception the Spin Pop created an entirely new product category, now known as 'interactive candy'.[17]

This simple idea led John Osher and his design team to believe that they could apply his invention to other product categories. The perfect match came while exploring supermarket aisles, namely the toothpaste aisle. The driving idea was to design a toothbrush that would cost less than US $1.40 to manufacture and would not retail for over US $5. It had to be better than a manual one and it had to last a minimum of six months. The batteries for the toothbrush also had to last for at least three months. Obviously, this product would be a 'category killer' of the electric toothbrush, which was selling at a much higher price.

P&G understood the opportunity that this product represented for their toothpaste brand, in terms of growing the loyal customer base and moving into a mouth-hygiene tool. John Osher sold the SpinBrush to Proctor & Gamble in 2001 for US $475 million dollars and turned it into a successful brand, but not successful enough for them. They sold it to Church & Dwight Co for US $75 million in cash and an additional performance-based payment of up to US $30 million, a small fraction of the original price that P&G paid for it.[18] As owners of brands and the distributors of others in the personal-care category, including Aim, Arm & Hammer, Close Up, Mentadent and Pepsodent (as well as brands in the fabric care, health and wellbeing and home care categories), Church & Dwight Co were better situated to grow the brand.

THE DISADVANTAGES OF A HOUSE OF BRANDS SYSTEM

The disadvantages of a house of brands system is that they aren't able to realize economies of scale for marketing or synergies between products. In addition, the company may not be able to support investments in smaller brands to make them bigger. These brands risk decline or elimination if they do not succeed. Of course, the smaller brand could always be sold, as the SpinBrush example shows.

Products, services and sub-brands that live within a branded house

When you know a brand that keeps using one brand name throughout all its products, chances are the organization is a branded house. For instance, all Boeing aeroplanes are named Boeing, distinguished from one another by a number: 707, 727, 737, 747, 757, 767, 777, 787 and on and on. BMW is no different: all models

FIGURE 10.1 Common types of brand architecture

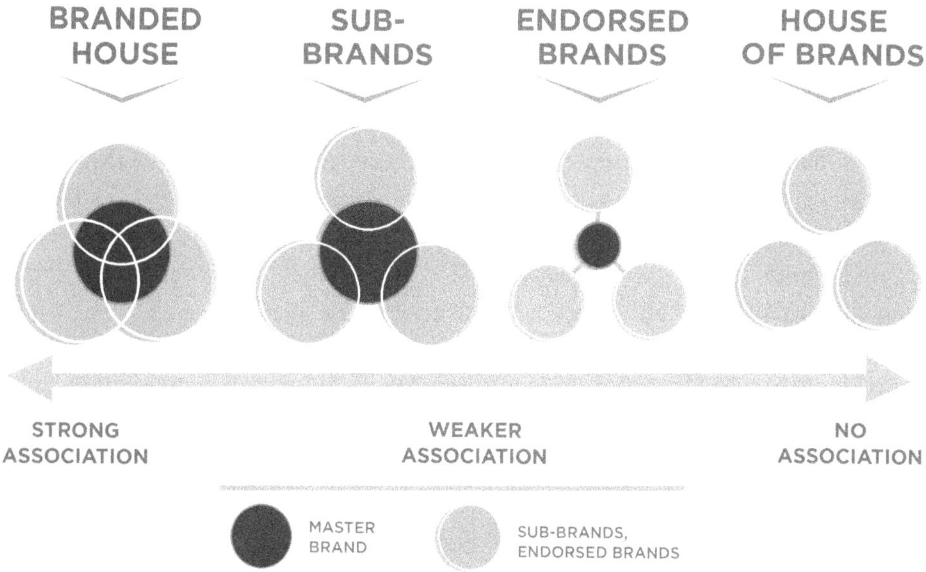

The 'right' brand architecture for each product or services lies somewhere on this spectrum, either on one of the sides or somewhere in between.

begin with an identifying number, which identifies the BMW Series they belong to 1, 2, 3, 4, 5, 6, 7, 8 and so on. Other examples of branded houses include General Electric, Sony and Philips.

The benefits of running a branded house include realizing an economy of scale for the company's marketing dollars, as equities translate from one product and category to another. When a branded house launches an innovative or breakthrough product, it can provide a 'halo effect' over the other products in their portfolio, making them seem better as well.[19] It also enables standardization of name, eliminating name ideation costs;[20] facilitates product introductions since many of the prospects are already familiar with the brand and what it represents;[21] and supports alignment of the priorities for their employees.[22]

The negatives, on the other hand, include a lowered ability to easily sell an underperforming product or product line, as the buyers either can't acquire or need to license the existing brand name, at least in the short term until they're able to rebrand, both of which can limit their ability to build the brand. A good example of the risks inherent in a branded house strategy were demonstrated in the fatal air crashes of Boeing's 737 MAX aircraft. All Boeing 737 MAX models were grounded worldwide. The brand reputation was in question, the share price plunged and there is still a cloud over the company which will be cleared only after a long investigation.[23] In other words, the benefits and negatives of a branded house are nearly a mirror image of the benefits and negatives of a house of brands.

There's one other caution with a branded house – acquiring new properties. Apple used to be a branded house – and many people still consider them to be one, with the Apple Mac, Apple iPad, Apple iPhone, Apple Watch, Apple Music, Apple TV and other sub-brands stemming from the master brand. But Apple bought Siri in 2019,[24] Beats Electronics (Beats by Dre in 2014)[25] and Shazam in 2018,[26] among other names that were not rebranded in the Apple naming conventions, so now they are actually a hybrid of the two main types of structures. This often happens when successful branded houses start buying up other brands. For example, Amazon bought IMDb (Internet Movie Database) in 1998, AbeBooks in 2008, Zappos in 2009 and Whole Foods Market in 2017, so they too are a hybrid organization. Another example is Facebook. You might think they are a branded house too. After all, they typically close the brands they purchase, since they tend to acquire companies for their platforms and technologies. But Facebook also owns Instagram and WhatsApp, which they operate as subsidiaries.[27] These hybrid combinations can cause confusion internally, as some may see the product brand with the same name as being the parent of higher priority.

Often in branded houses – and in houses of brands for brand extensions – they need to create sub-brands – products or services that are connected to a master brand and augment or modify the associations of the master brand.[28] While the master brand is primary, it is expanded by the sub-brands through added associations and/or personality traits. Sony PlayStation and Chevrolet Camaro are two examples. In both the B2C and B2B sectors, we do not need to think about the extension or sub-brand to understand many of its equities for established brands. Sony and Chevrolet, for example, convey clear attributes about the products and what they represent.

Within sub-brands, either the endorser or endorsed brand – ie, the brand or sub-brand – can drive the purchase decision. Have you stayed at a Marriott or Courtyard? Perhaps you selected a Chevrolet over a Camaro? Through the use of an endorser and endorsed brand, you can address conflicting strategic needs of the brand;[29] leverage existing brand equity, enabling you to conserve brand-building resources;[30] protect the endorser brand from being diluted by overstretsching it;[31] and signal that the endorsed brand is different from the parent.[32] Often endorsement by an established brand provides credibility and substance to the endorsed or sub-brand. Endorser brands typically represent the organization's equities, such as leadership, trust and innovation and these associations usually help the endorsed. Endorsers are somewhat insulated from the performance of the endorsed brand, but it could reflect badly back on the endorser if the endorsed brand doesn't perform.

The use of the endorser and endorsed brand formula can also help with rebranding, where you do not want to confuse existing customers. Say you want to move away from Brand A, perhaps because it was sold and the original owner was a branded house, and move to Brand B. Brand A would then become the endorser brand and Brand B would become an endorsed brand. As the endorsed brand becomes familiar with the target audience, the emphasis on the endorser can be lowered and the emphasis on the endorsed can become greater. Eventually, the original endorser name can go away, and the product can then be fully rebranded under the name of the endorsed brand.

Brand portfolio rationalization

Many organizations have too many active brands, which can be very costly to support. National and global companies have product and service brands, as well as additional business-unit brands that cause them to lose track of the variety, goals and costs as well as how consumers view them. In other cases, many companies become complacent about some of their dormant brands, which struggle to compete with newer, more relevant competitors' brands. These dormant brands could actually have a second wind, if sold to another company that may know how to market them better. At some point, the brand marketer might realize that its organization has too many brands and sub-brands to focus effectively on all of them. At that point, the company might decide it's time to sell or close a few of them. The process of figuring out what to keep and what to discard is called 'brand portfolio rationalization'.[33] Simply put, the process of strategic brand portfolio rationalization is a sophisticated way to cut costs, make sense of the multitude of brands, avoid duplication of marketing activities and expenses, and a chance for the business to rededicate itself to the products, services and brands that will position it for optimal future growth.

Experienced brand architects are professionals who plan the future of their brands without merely reacting to current market conditions. They research, study, deliberate and design a plan to manage and organize the consistent performance of their brands. As a result, they know where each brand fits into the picture, which brands need to be rationalized, which ones need to be combined and which types of brands need to be purchased to optimize their portfolio.

To start the process of brand portfolio rationalization, ask these five questions:

- Do our current brands cover every market and demographic we want to capture?
- Do we own brands that create duplication across markets and customers?
- Have we taken into consideration future market segments and unmet needs?
- Are we innovative enough to create new opportunities for new brands?
- Can we grow some of our existing brands to include new brand extensions?

When engaging in the brand rationalization process, organizations often incorrectly focus on how their internal marketing department is organized to guide the decision-making. This is never the answer to brand architecture. Instead, organizations should take a look at how their customers view their brands, which segments of the market they are targeting and which benefits they are emphasizing. They should consider how relevant their brands are, whether there are any scientific developments that might call for new products and whether there are any dynamics within the category that could position the brand or two or more for future growth or for a tougher time profitably generating sales.

When an organization is undergoing the brand rationalization process, it should not act until it fully reaches decisions about all of the brands in its portfolio. It should then establish a clear and fair process to guide management, brand managers and marketing associates such as ad agencies. After all, the brand rationalization process is not an exercise in merely shuffling marketing budgets and responsibilities within an organization. Rather, it can point out the winning brands and highlight ways to make them even more successful, as well as suggest ways to cut costs and losses on the lower-performing brands.

For our purposes, the Boston Consulting Group (BCG) approach with the classic SBU (Strategic Business Units) model works here as well. Bruce Henderson, founder of the BCG, wrote in 'The Product Portfolio' in 1970 that 'A company should have a portfolio of products with different growth rates and different market shares. The portfolio composition is a function of the balance between cash flows.... Margins and cash generated are a function of market share.'[34] In this model, companies define their products, services and brands as Stars, Cash Cows, Dogs and Question Marks:

- Stars are products with the best market share, generate the most cash and are in a fast-growing category. Stars are the products to invest in.
- Cash Cows are leaders in the marketplace, generate more cash than they consume, and are part of a slow-growing category. Companies could invest in Cash Cows to maintain their current level of productivity.
- Dogs are products with both a small market share and a low growth rate. These products are prime candidates for discontinuation, either through the sale of it (ideal) or closure.
- Question Marks are products with high growth prospects but low market share. They should be carefully analysed to determine if they're worth the investment required to grow the share.[35]

As a responsible organization, you should position each of the current brands in your portfolio on the current market map. This is a step that requires agreement and deliberation with internal teams to discover the conflicting opinions about the present position of each brand. When this is done, it will allow the team to move confidently to the next decision-making process. The market map should help any organization decide where they want their brand to be, and what kind of place it should take in the organization's portfolio of brands.

Taking all that into consideration, there are some very rational steps that must take place; emotional decisions will not be helpful here. The most important fact to consider in any brand portfolio alignment is the consumers' state of mind. Their needs, wants and behaviour in the product or service category provide the direction for any brand architecture.

At this point, key stakeholders in each brand should start making recommendations about investment levels in the brands, including the possibility of eliminating them all together, or selling them at the highest possible price. Once this is completed, the key stakeholders can start determining which model best suits their future brand portfolio. Once the decision about the brand hierarchy has been established, within each brand group the role of sub-brands, brand endorsers, driver role brands and more can be explored.

To see how the process should work, take a look at Pepsi. They realized that customers choose from a range of non-alcoholic beverages, and not just the carbonated ones, to satisfy their need for refreshment. In light of that, they made several acquisitions such as Gatorade, SoBe and Tropicana; developed new products, including Amp and Aquafina; and formed several joint ventures such as the one with Starbucks to distribute the bottled Frappuccino. A current trend among consumers is the awareness to environmental issues. The beverage industry is creating massive amounts of plastic by using bottled drinks. Soda Stream, the Israeli manufacturing company best known as the maker of a consumer home product that turns tap water into carbonated water, is a company that has eliminated the need for using plastic bottles. To compete in this area, Pepsi announced the acquisition of Soda Stream in August 2018, which could be a smart move based on the direction of consumer preferences.

The authors know of a company in the speciality beverage category that launched as a house of brands. However, through talks with their consumers and distributors, they realized that their parent brand was their most valuable asset and, as a result, decided that they needed to go through a reorganization and rebranding process to enable them to capitalize on their opportunity. While painful, the reorganization could better position them for faster growth. The authors anxiously await to see the results of this soon-to-be branded house.

BRANDS GOING GLOBAL – A GUEST PERSPECTIVE FROM LUBNA NAFEES, INDIA AND USA

Professor Lubna Nafees is best described in one word as enterprising. At the marketing department at the Walker College of Business, Appalachian State University, her teaching, research, training and consultancy interests include brand and marketing communications, digital strategy, visual imagery and semiotics and management education. Lubna has experience of teaching in business schools and conducts corporate training in multicultural classrooms in Asia, Europe, Australia and the United States. She has published papers and case studies in academic journals and popular media. She has co-authored a book, *Family-managed, Multinationals and Public Sector Enterprises: The strategic choices for global competitiveness* and has three edited books – *Brands Rising as Products Fall*, *Brand Research* and *Innovative Management Education Pedagogies*, aimed at preparing the next generation of leaders. Here is Professor Nafees on how several brands have successfully gone global.

> 'According to the American Marketing Association, a brand is a name, term, design, symbol or any other feature that identifies one seller's good or service as distinct from those of other sellers. Branding is endowing products and services with the power of a brand.[36] Branding is the process of giving a meaning to a specific company, product or service by creating and shaping a brand in consumers' minds. It is a strategy designed by companies to help people quickly identify their products and organization and give them a reason to choose their products over the competition's, by clarifying what this particular brand is and is not. The objective is to attract and retain loyal customers by delivering a product that is always aligned with what the brand promises.
>
> 'In the context of increasingly interchangeable product and service offerings, brands are crucial drivers for product purchasing and usage decisions. Thus, they constitute a substantial intangible asset for most companies. Brand experts like Kotler and Keller have for the most part emphasized consistency and the conveying of a single message. However, when markets expand across geographical boundaries, one is left wondering what this brand consistency is?
>
> 'Quick Service Restaurants (QSR) like McDonald's, Taco Bell and KFC have had to customize their menu and format as they enter markets outside the home country. Whereas they are mostly take-away in the United States (US) and popular for being quick and convenient, in countries like India and China, they are family hangouts, kids' party places and a go-to lunch/dinner place where people/families can sit down and have a meal. One can see this shift in brand positioning, yet at no loss to the company. In fact, these markets provide new avenues once the home market is saturated.
>
> 'Taco Bell opened its first quick-service restaurant in India in 2010. The Indian market with its increasing middle-class population was too lucrative a market to be ignored. Taco Bell in the US targeted the young at heart, particularly those between 18 to 24 years old, whose priorities were price and convenience. It was aimed at people who preferred their food served cheaply and quickly because they were busy and had less time to prepare meals. However, the Indian market was unique with its three Vs – value for money, variety and the vegetarian veto. The Indian audience wanted variety in the menu as well as value for money – two contradictory things. And if that were

not enough, the company had to deal with a vegetarian veto. That is, in a group of four, even if only one is vegetarian (many Indians are vegetarian for religious reasons), that person can veto and pull the other three into a restaurant offering more vegetarian options. Taco Bell's original menu was all about beef and pork, neither of which found any home in India.

'Taco Bell built a brand by successfully selling Mexican-inspired food in the US. An initial taste test with an Indian audience, however, came back with alarming results – people categorized the food as 'bland Indian food'. The challenge for Taco Bell was to keep the food Mexican-inspired and yet appeal to the Indian consumer. The menu was reworked and tailored to fit the preferences of the Indian audience.

'Another case in point is IKEA. IKEA opened its operations in India in 2018, targeting the young, middle class and upwardly mobile. These consumers prefer fashionable and stylish furniture and domestic products at low prices. They are brand-aware and fashion-oriented, and prefer well-designed, low-priced products. The IKEA group's unconventional approach to the furniture business has enabled it to rack up impressive growth worldwide. Throughout Europe, the IKEA group benefits from the perception that Sweden is the source of high-quality products and efficient service. The IKEA Group uses the cost-focus strategy. In the cost-focus strategy, a firm's lower-cost position enables it to focus on a narrow target market and offer lower prices than the competition.

'IKEA India plans to start retail operations in several Indian cities, namely Hyderabad, Bangalore, Delhi, Chennai, Kolkata, Pune and Mumbai, at an investment of over US $1.5 billion (£1.19 billion) by the end of 2025.[37] India is a country with a population of more than 1.21 billion population (according to a 2011 census)[38] with different cultural and ethnic backgrounds. People's tastes and preferences vary from one place to another. In Europe, IKEA is positioned as good-quality, stylish furniture at prices so low that everybody can afford it. Whereas, in China, for example, IKEA is a good-quality, Western-styled aspirational brand for the middle-class population.[39] Now IKEA has the challenge of conquering a completely contrasting Indian market.

'To penetrate the Indian market, the company has had to come to grips with some key differences, one of which is that 'unorganized' players dominate the Indian furniture market. The Indian consumer traditionally thinks of furniture as a onetime investment, something lasting over multiple generations. Availability of cheap labour in India beats the whole Do It Yourself (DIY) concept for which IKEA is known globally, and furniture on rent is easily available in India.

'IKEA has customized its product mix to fit into the Indian household and has tried to address the problems of product availability, timely delivery, display of all types of furniture in IKEA stores and customer service. IKEA follows a polycentric approach to pricing. This enables it to price differently in different parts of the globe. In India, since people do not like DIY, IKEA offers preassembled furniture delivered to the consumer's doorstep at a premium. DIY is the one of the core values of the brand and yet to establish itself in the Indian market, IKEA has had to adapt is offering.

'An example of a company that failed to customize to a new local market is that of Netflix. Video on demand (VOD) was a revolutionary idea, first offered by Netflix, Inc. (Netflix), a US-based company, in order to avoid the decline in its business of DVD rental service.[40] Netflix made its entry in the Indian market in the year 2016. At the time, Hotstar (owned by Novi Digital Entertainment Private Limited, a wholly owned subsidiary of Star India Private Limited) was the dominant player. The Indian market is in the growth phase and several international and local players are eyeing a share of the pie. Amazon Prime Video (owned and operated by Amazon.com, Inc.), too, made its way into the Indian market in 2017 and went on to beat Netflix in the number of subscribers. Netflix is a global leader in VOD and India is one of the only three markets in the world where Netflix has lost out to Amazon Prime, despite its first-mover advantage.[41]

'The major reason attributed to Netflix's slow growth in the Indian market was lack of understanding of the market itself. The Indian market is a price-sensitive market and people cannot imagine paying US $8 (£6) per month for a service such as VOD. Netflix originally wanted to target the upper middle class and higher-income groups in India and continue selling their regular content, which is popular in the US. It wanted to keep the core value of its brand consistent. However, with a competitive market scenario and multiple players, they were pushed into customizing content, collaborating with local partners and media houses.

'That leaves us with one significant question – what is the core of a brand? When one business model is not sufficient to work in different markets, it is not uncommon for companies to tweak the business model for doing business in a particular country. In an ideal world, that would be devastating for the brand, but in the real world it is a question of survival. The brand does have different meanings in different places. Many brands cash in on their aspirational image and others just blend into the society as if they belonged there like no place else.

'Brands need to develop the ability to engage customers in a way that feels local to them. Failure to 'glocalize' can lead to the demise of brands in certain countries. It is evident that brands that retain their core values and simultaneously tailor messages to suit individual markets reap a multitude of benefits, though it's not always easy for brands to know where to draw the line.'

EXTENDED CASE STUDY: THE REORGANIZATION OF GENERAL MOTORS' BRAND ARCHITECTURE

The General Motors brand is an old one, and relatively easy to understand from an architecture perspective. After all, most people drive cars and we all have a fairly good understanding of how we as consumers place them in our minds.[42] Of course, when it comes to brand architecture, sometimes the captains of industry are not in the same place as their consumers. Looking at their more recent marketing decisions, one might wonder if the entire area of brand hierarchy and brand architecture was misunderstood by GM's previous CEOs, Marketing Chiefs and Brand Managers.[43]

General Motors was incorporated on September 16 1908 in Flint, Michigan, USA. The industrialist William Crapo 'Billy' Durant was a pioneer of the automobile industry, who partnered with Josiah Dallas Dort to start the Durant-Dort Carriage Company, becoming a top manufacturer of horse-drawn vehicles.

Durant was initially sceptical of automobiles. But when the public demand for government-regulated petrol-powered horseless carriages grew,[44] Durant saw an opportunity to improve safety in those horseless machines. To enter the automobile industry, Durant purchased Buick, a local car company with few sales and large debts.[45]

With Buick as a base, he envisioned creating a large automobile company that would design, build and market several different makes and control the subsidiary component-making companies, much as he had done with Durant-Dort in the carriage-making world.[46] Durant's GM bought Cadillac, Oldsmobile, the Oakland Motor Company, later rebranded Pontiac, and a variety of different parts-manufacturing companies, paint-and-varnish companies, axle-and-wheel companies and others, merging them into GM around 1909.[47] With no contemporary discipline of 'Brand Architecture', the motivation for creating so many different brands was to simply reach more audiences across the country while controlling costs.[48]

Fast forward to the middle of the 20th century and the US automobile market was dominated by three major brands: GM, Ford and Chrysler. American-made cars were considered to be technical marvels, with every imaginable amenity and luxury item available, from air conditioning to automatic gear boxes, as well as the promise of unrivalled comfort, size and reliability.[49] Among the American car brands, GM's Chevrolet was so dominant, it controlled over a third of the entire car market by 1962.[50]

The car divisions of GM were known to be independent in those days,[51] and the emerging control of one brand became worrisome to the top management of GM and its lawyers.[52] But then GM started integrating Chevrolet into the rest of the corporation, resulting in a long period of diminishing the dominance of Chevrolet by giving more power to other GM brands. As part of their moves, they combined Chevy's manufacturing operations with those of Buick, Oldsmobile, GMC and Pontiac to form the General Motors Assembly Division.[53]

While this might have saved money for the company, consumers saw something different: that the cars started to look nearly identical. Outside of some slight differences in the outer shell, the different cars felt like they were exactly the same, no matter which brand badge was on the hood.[54] Gone were the days when the different GM brands had distinct designs of their own, such as the classic Corvettes designed by Harley Earl[55] and others, who strived to achieve some kind of uniqueness.[56] In 1984, following the advice of consulting firm McKinsey and Co, GM split into two groups – the Buick-Oldsmobile-Cadillac Group for big cars and the Chevrolet-Pontiac-Canada Group for small ones.[57]

GM's brand architecture was also influenced by rising oil prices, which pushed consumers and thus manufacturers to consider smaller cars.[58] GM was already distributing the Opel in Germany and Vauxhall in the UK, but these brands were never sold in the US.[59] They added to the stable by purchasing SAAB and sold its original cars, but the SAAB brand hurt when they dressed other GM brands in a SAAB costume, without changing the car.[60] GM also collaborated with Subaru of Japan, and dressed some of those cars with a SAAB badge.[61]

The only attempt GM made to launch a stand-alone brand was with Saturn.[62] In what could be considered a real attempt to consider brand hierarchy and brand architecture, GM launched the Saturn brand to offer a different and distinct small-car experience.[63] Since the 'Big Three' American car companies were known for producing large passenger cars, consumers were flocking to the Japanese and European brands. VW, Toyota, Honda and Nissan were taking market share from US cars.[64] Saturn was an attempt by GM to try new car technologies and new management methods.

To underscore its independence, Saturn was not even launched as a 'GM' brand. Rather, it was positioned as a 'different kind of car company', operated independently from its parent (for a time) with its own assembly plant in Spring Hill, Tennessee; unique car models; and a separate retailer network. Even the ad agency produced advertising that was not typical of American cars.[65] Around the time of its launch, Saturn grew quickly while the other GM brands were continuing to lose market share.[66]

During that time, the total number of car brands under GM's umbrella was growing while offering similar products at similar price points, all sold from the same car dealerships.[67] The GM brands during that period included Buick, Cadillac, Chevrolet, GMC, HUMMER, Oldsmobile, Opel, Pontiac, SAAB, Saturn and Vauxhall.[68]

Following the financial crisis of 2008, the US government bailed out GM, which was on the verge of bankruptcy,[69] and the company had to size down and eliminate many operations. That led to the 'rebirth' of GM as a slimmed-down corporation. Gone were Oldsmobile, Pontiac, Hummer, Saab, Opel and Vauxhall. In fact, the US corporation operates as of writing only four key brands: Buick, Cadillac, Chevrolet and GMC. To 'rationalize' their offerings, Chevrolet was positioned as the brand for every man. They have vast product lines, ranging from large pickup trucks and SUVs to small compact cars. GMC sells trucks and 'upgraded' SUVs with more options than Chevrolet, while actually being an identical line, except they do not offer passenger cars. Buick is now a 'semi-luxury' car, offering many upgrades and using some European car designs. It doesn't look or feel like any other GM brand and is considered to be a luxury car in markets such as China.[70] Finally, Cadillac, which was the luxury line of GM, moved its headquarters to New York, to create an image that it was 'cool and cosmopolitan'.[71] Despite improvements in its design and quality, Cadillac continues to struggle against other luxury car brands.[72]

KEY TERMS

- brand portfolio rationalization
- branded house
- house of brands
- hybrid brands
- strategic business units

DISCUSSION QUESTIONS

- What is the difference between a house of brands and a branded house? Give examples of each.
- What is a sub-brand, an endorsed brand and a brand extension and what are the differences between them?
- What is the process of rationalizing a brand portfolio to achieve optimal return on investment?
- What is the value of having a brand architecture that is strategic, clear, logical and synergistic?

Notes

1 Isaacson, W (2011) *Steve Jobs*, Simon & Schuster, New York, p 28

2 Zillman, C (2017) This is the world's best brand – for the 5th year in a row, *Fortune*, http://fortune.com (archived at https://perma.cc/4S5Z-RA6D), http://fortune.com/2017/09/25/apple-worlds-best-brand (archived at https://perma.cc/4S5Z-RA6D)

3 Aaker, D and Joachimsthaler, E (2014) *Brand Leadership*, Free Press, New York

4 Aaker, D and Joachimsthaler, E (2014) *Brand Leadership*, Free Press, New York

5 Aaker, D and Joachimsthaler, E (2014) *Brand Leadership*, Free Press, New York

6 Aaker, D and Joachimsthaler, E (2014) *Brand Leadership*, Free Press, New York

7 Aaker, D and Joachimsthaler, E (2014) *Brand Leadership*, Free Press, New York

8 Aaker, D and Joachimsthaler, E (2014) *Brand Leadership*, Free Press, New York

9 Aaker, D and Joachimsthaler, E (2014) *Brand Leadership*, Free Press, New York

10 Aaker, D and Joachimsthaler, E (2014) *Brand Leadership*, Free Press, New York

11 Element Three (2019) Why brand architecture matters, and what you can do about it, https://elementthree.com/blog/why-brand-architecture-matters-and-what-you-can-do-about-it (archived at https://perma.cc/BGQ4-UHCW)

12 P&G (2019) P&G brands and products, Us.pg.com, https://us.pg.com/brands (archived at https://perma.cc/7YK6-8AU8)

13 Morgan, P (2019)An overview of Procter & Gamble's 5 segments, Product Categories, *Market Realist*, https://articles.marketrealist.com/2015/07/overview-procter-gambles-5-segments-product-categories (archived at https://perma.cc/K4FE-C4KF)

14 P&G (2019) Procter & Gamble brands and products, Pg.co.uk, https://www.pg.co.uk/brands (archived at https://perma.cc/ZW3E-KF2K)

15 *Cincinnati Business Courier* (2008) Procter & Gamble selling Folgers brand to Smucker, Bizjournals.com, https://www.bizjournals.com/cincinnati/stories/2008/06/02/daily26.html (archived at https://perma.cc/CV7K-29LA)

16 Canedy, D (2019) Decline of Crest shows how a brand can fade, Nytimes.com, https://www.nytimes.com/1997/06/20/business/decline-of-crest-shows-how-a-brand-can-fade.html (archived at https://perma.cc/H866-DC3M)

17 Key, S (2019) The Man – The Legend – John Osher, Inventor of the Spin Brush Part I, AllBusiness.com, https://www.allbusiness.com/the-man-the-legend-john-osher-inventor-of-the-spin-brush-part-i-2-7665547-1.html (archived at https://perma.cc/FD72-96US)

18 Neff, J (2005) Church & Dwight buys Spinbrush from P&G, Adage.com, https://adage.com/article/news/church-dwight-buys-spinbrush-p-g/46789 (archived at https://perma.cc/2W25-GJ88)

19 Broc Consulting (2019) Branded house architecture – benefit from the established reputation, BROC consulting. http://broc.com.sg/insights-ideas/brand-strategy/branded-house-architecture-benefit-from-the-established-reputation (archived at https://perma.cc/W4EL-2QC9)

20 Lucas, L (2015) Coca-Cola and the shift to the 'branded house': should other marketers consider a similar move? Forbes.com, https://www.forbes.com/sites/onmarketing/2015/06/01/coca-cola-and-the-shift-to-the-branded-house-should-other-marketers-consider-a-similar-move/#62ba4b1f4217 (archived at https://perma.cc/PLB6-M4SY)

21 Lucas, L (2015) Coca-Cola and the shift to the 'branded house': should other marketers consider a similar move? Forbes.com, https://www.forbes.com/sites/onmarketing/2015/06/01/coca-cola-and-the-shift-to-the-branded-house-should-other-marketers-consider-a-similar-move/#62ba4b1f4217 (archived at https://perma.cc/PLB6-M4SY)

22 Gram, C (2017) In-house vs agency branding: 5 benefits of each approach, *Medium*, https://medium.com/new-kind/in-house-vs-agency-branding-5-benefits-of-each-approach-19869069d3f4 (archived at https://perma.cc/G998-D2E2)

23 Freedman, A (2019) What we've learned from the Boeing 737 MAX crashes, *Axios*, https://www.axios.com/boeing-737-max-crash-investigations-c4a9170e-4742-481f-9304-8931ca394538.html (archived at https://perma.cc/6ZYC-2J9Z)

24 Statt, N (2019) Apple buys AI voice startup that helps companies build Alexa and Google Assistant apps, *The Verge*, https://www.theverge.com/2019/2/15/18226836/apple-pullstring-ai-voice-chat-app-amazon-alexa-google-assistant (archived at https://perma.cc/EWS7-NTBX)

25 Soloman, B (2014) It's Official: Apple Adds Dr Dre with $3 billion beats deal, Forbes.com, https://www.forbes.com/sites/briansolomon/2014/05/28/apple-brings-dr-dre-on-board-with-official-3-billion-beats-deal (archived at https://perma.cc/9574-GHFF)

26 Welch C (2018) Apple completes Shazam acquisition, will make app ad-free for everyone, *The Verge*, https://www.theverge.com/2018/9/24/17896350/apple-shazam-app-acquisition-complete-free (archived at https://perma.cc/XH3K-JPF7)
27 Reiff, N (2019) Top Companies Owned By Facebook, *Investopedia*, https://www.investopedia.com/articles/personal-finance/051815/top-11-companies-owned-facebook.asp (archived at https://perma.cc/7MSA-JWFC)
28 UKEssays.com (2017) The role of brand extension, https://www.ukessays.com/essays/marketing/the-role-of-brand-extension-marketing-essay.php (archived at https://perma.cc/6Q92-VPQZ)
29 Aaker, D and Joachimsthaler, E (2014) *Brand Leadership*, Free Press, New York
30 Kajabi Blog (2019) What is brand equity, why it's important, how to build & examples, https://blog.kajabi.com/what-is-brand-equity-why-it-s-important-how-to-build-examples (archived at https://perma.cc/P27E-UUMV)
31 Aaker, D and Joachimsthaler, E (2014) *Brand Leadership*, Free Press, New York
32 Carter, L (2019) Brand hierarchy fundamentals for multiple brands to avoid confused customers or stagnant sales, *Persona Design*, https://www.personadesign.ie/brand-hierarchy-fundamentals-for-multiple-brands-to-avoid-confused-customers-or-stagnant-sales (archived at https://perma.cc/GL6M-XTE6)
33 Citeman.com (2019) Brand portfolio rationalization, https://www.citeman.com/1247-brand-portfolio-rationalization.html (archived at https://perma.cc/Q9CS-GH8B)
34 Henderson, B (1970) The product portfolio, bcg.com, https://www.bcg.com/en-us/publications/1970/strategy-the-product-portfolio.aspx (archived at https://perma.cc/JB64-C7K8)
35 Reeves, M (2014) BCG classics revisited: the growth share matrix, bcg.com, https://www.bcg.com/en-us/publications/2014/growth-share-matrix-bcg-classics-revisited.aspx (archived at https://perma.cc/9BEC-7WNG)
36 Kotler, P T and Keller, K L (2016) *Marketing Management*, 15th Ed, Pearson, London
37 'IKEA paves way for first Indian store,' (August 12 2016), BBC.com, http://www.bbc.com/news/business-37057254 (archived at https://perma.cc/S7PP-MWBS)
38 'Population Census 2011', Census 2011, https://www.census2011.co.in (archived at https://perma.cc/X5NP-KQSN)
39 Chu, V, Girdhar, A, and Sood, R (July 21 2013) Crouching tiger tames the dragon, *Business Today*, https://www.businesstoday.in/magazine/lbs-case-study/how-ikea-adapted-its-strategies-to-expand-in-china/story/196322.html (archived at https://perma.cc/C7MP-RPBN)
40 BBC.com (2018) Netflix's history: from DVD rentals to streaming success, http://www.bbc.co.uk/newsbeat/article/42787047/netflixs-history-from-dvd-rentals-to-streaming-success (archived at https://perma.cc/Q7JY-647F)
41 Bhattacharya, A (2018) How Amazon has flicked Netflix in India, *Quartz India*, https://qz.com/india/1205896/how-amazon-edged-past-netflix-in-india (archived at https://perma.cc/D9N3-4PUQ)
42 Lisa Merriam (2018) General Motors: a reorganized brand architecture for a reorganized company, http://lisamerriam.com/general-motors-a-reorganized-brand-architecture-for-a-reorganized-company (archived at https://perma.cc/57M2-QRE8)

43 Pfanner, E (2019) G M's global strategy: a brand for every place, Nytimes.com, https://www.nytimes.com/2008/02/04/business/worldbusiness/04gm.html (archived at https://perma.cc/H3Y6-K87M)

44 Durant, W C (2019) Myautoworld.com, https://myautoworld.com/gm/history/history/durant/durant.html (archived at https://perma.cc/Y239-A292)

45 Dr Folsom, B W (1998) Durant and the founding of General Motors, Mackinac Center for Public Policy, https://www.mackinac.org/article.aspx?ID=651 (archived at https://perma.cc/M8BW-HQJR)

46 media.gm.com (2019) GM opens historic Durant-Dort Factory One, https://media.gm.com/media/us/en/gm/home.detail.html/content/Pages/news/us/en/2017/may/0501-factory-1.html (archived at https://perma.cc/GD36-WEYK)

47 media.gm.com (2019) GM opens historic Durant-Dort Factory One, https://media.gm.com/media/us/en/gm/home.detail.html/content/Pages/news/us/en/2017/may/0501-factory-1.html (archived at https://perma.cc/GD36-WEYK)

48 Bellperformance.com (2019) How Alfred Sloan and GM changed American history, https://www.bellperformance.com/blog/general-motors-interesting-history-vision (archived at https://perma.cc/HQ92-RLHG)

49 nwitimes.com (2019) A history of GM's rise to power – and decline (1991), https://www.nwitimes.com/uncategorized/a-history-of-gm-s-rise-to-power--/article_fc381f19-f86a-5683-9355-9b02da5aafed.html (archived at https://perma.cc/897K-7QT2)

50 HISTORY (2018) The cars that made America, https://www.history.com/news/the-cars-that-made-america (archived at https://perma.cc/4W72-LNSD)

51 u-s-history.com (2019) General Motors Corporation, https://www.u-s-history.com/pages/h1809.html (archived at https://perma.cc/UL3L-WGC7)

52 Encyclopedia.com (2019) General Motors Corp, https://www.encyclopedia.com/social-sciences-and-law/economics-business-and-labor/businesses-and-occupations/general-motors-corp (archived at https://perma.cc/VSD4-XTMY)

53 Encyclopedia Britannica (2019) automotive industry, History, Developments, & Facts, https://www.britannica.com/technology/automotive-industry (archived at https://perma.cc/58KB-FHQJ)

54 Appel, T (2019) Fit and trim: the General Motors B-Body Coupes of 1977, The Daily Drive, Consumer Guide®, http://blog.consumerguide.com/fit-and-trim-the-general-motors-b-body-coupes-of-1977 (archived at https://perma.cc/4SA2-HNWE)

55 HARLEY EARL (2019) Corvette History, http://www.harleyjearl.com/corvette-history-101 (archived at https://perma.cc/Q2JL-6EDA)

56 *Automobile Magazine* (2019) The 25 greatest designers of all time, https://www.automobilemag.com/news/the-25-greatest-designers-of-all-time (archived at https://perma.cc/G72J-ZQTS)

57 *Automotive News* (2019) Roger Smith's grand plan: unravel division system, create a unified GM, https://www.autonews.com/article/20080914/ANA03/809150416/roger-smith-s-grand-plan-unravel-division-system-create-a-unified-gm (archived at https://perma.cc/Z4EL-XP5N)

58 Pophistorydig.com (2019), General Motors small cars, https://www.pophistorydig.com/topics/tag/general-motors-small-cars (archived at https://perma.cc/BT6P-367G)

59 *Automobile Magazine* (2019) Peugeot, Citroen, Opel, and Vauxhall in the US, https://www.automobilemag.com/news/peugeot-citroen-opel-and-vauxhall-in-the-u-s (archived at https://perma.cc/2LTT-LB5J)

60 Chicagotribune.com (2019) We are currently unavailable in your region, https://www.chicagotribune.com/news/ct-xpm-2003-04-17-0304170105-story.html (archived at https://perma.cc/K9KS-7MBM)

61 *Automotive News* (2018) Why did GM water down its strongest, most successful brand? http://www.autonews.com/article/20111031/CHEVY100/310319917/why-did-gm-water-down-its-strongest-most-successful-brand%3F (archived at https://perma.cc/NQC8-UESA)

62 Saturn Corporation History (2019) History of Saturn Corporation, *FundingUniverse*, http://www.fundinguniverse.com/company-histories/saturn-corporation-history (archived at https://perma.cc/GR29-S49Z)

63 Saturn Corporation History (2019) History of Saturn Corporation, *FundingUniverse*, http://www.fundinguniverse.com/company-histories/saturn-corporation-history (archived at https://perma.cc/GR29-S49Z)

64 Cheney, P (2015) The rise of Japan: how the car industry was won, *The Globe and Mail*, https://www.theglobeandmail.com/globe-drive/adventure/red-line/the-rise-of-japan-how-the-car-industry-was-won/article27100187 (archived at https://perma.cc/9RUB-XDB9)

65 Saturn Corporation History (2018) History of Saturn Corporation, *FundingUniverse*, http://www.fundinguniverse.com/company-histories/saturn-corporation-history (archived at https://perma.cc/GR29-S49Z)

66 Jones, R (2007) Saturn bluntly challenges Japanese rivals, msnbc.com, http://www.nbcnews.com/id/19413775/ns/business-the_driver_seat/t/saturn-bluntly-challenges-japanese-rivals (archived at https://perma.cc/8RC6-ZN3V)

67 Jones, R (2007) Saturn bluntly challenges Japanese rivals, msnbc.com, http://www.nbcnews.com/id/19413775/ns/business-the_driver_seat/t/saturn-bluntly-challenges-japanese-rivals (archived at https://perma.cc/8RC6-ZN3V)

68 u-s-history.com (2019) General Motors Corporation, https://www.u-s-history.com/pages/h1809.html (archived at https://perma.cc/UL3L-WGC7)

69 Crawley, J and Drawbaugh (2019) US auto execs plead for Congress to fund bailout, *Reuters*, https://www.reuters.com/article/us-autos-bailout/u-s-auto-execs-plead-for-congress-to-fund-bailout-idUSTRE4AD08120081118 (archived at https://perma.cc/K5BC-TVYG)

70 Baruth, J (2019) The last soldier prepares to cross the block, *The Truth About Cars*, https://www.thetruthaboutcars.com/2013/06/the-last-soldier-prepares-to-cross-the-block (archived at https://perma.cc/PP5T-7ADN)

71 Forbes.com (2019) Cadillac moves headquarters from Manhattan back to Detroit, retreating from brand emphasis, https://www.forbes.com/sites/dalebuss/2018/09/26/cadillac-retreats-from-brand-emphasis-by-moving-headquarters-from-big-apple-back-to-detroit/#398f10350348 (archived at https://perma.cc/3AC9-YD46)

72 Forbes.com (2019) Cadillac moves headquarters from Manhattan back to Detroit, retreating from brand emphasis, https://www.forbes.com/sites/dalebuss/2018/09/26/cadillac-retreats-from-brand-emphasis-by-moving-headquarters-from-big-apple-back-to-detroit/#398f10350348 (archived at https://perma.cc/3AC9-YD46)

11

Speciality application areas

READING OUTCOMES

At the conclusion of this chapter, you should be able to:

- identify and describe the wide variety of types of brands, including their key functional differences;
- make a clear distinction between the terminology and functions within the various types of brands;
- communicate all of the components within a personal branding and begin to describe yours;
- describe the benefits and attributes of a private-label brand as well as the best practices for it.

Introduction

While the majority of brand interactions and transactions fall within the Business-to-Consumer (B2C) arena, the transactions of larger monetary value lie within the Business-to-Business sphere (B2B). Therefore, corporate branding has more value in the B2B environment, while retail branding remains almost entirely in the B2C domain. Many companies see their brand as being essential to the prosperity of an organization, while others, including not-for-profits, do not see it as an asset. Meanwhile, many of us are beginning to pay attention to our own individual branding, since we are all competing for something, such as a job or social status, and see that adopting branding principles could be an advantage.

Why are there so many different versions of branding across such a wide variety of categories? The answer is simple: we're becoming sophisticated consumers and global citizens. Brand theory is evolving to address the specifics of each category. What works in one might not work in another.

As current and future brand managers, we need to fully understand the differences between all the application areas or categories for branding and approach each appropriately. Could it be that those who are in charge of a company that is building a service brand never have to deal with building the brand of a packaged good? Or will the stakeholders of product branding get involved with not-for-profits branding? Probably. What is needed in one category might not work in another, and most professionals build their careers in one or, at the most, two categories. There are occasions when a company evolves and brand managers find themselves having to adapt to working in a different category from the one they started in. Look at IBM; it was once known for its products, primarily mainframe computers, supported by services. Now the company is known purely for its services and has sold off most of its products.[1]

As a result, brand managers should know the theories, best practices and approaches for each category, because it might inspire them as they approach theirs, as well as stop them from exploring tactics and approaches that definitely won't work in theirs. This chapter looks at the major branding categories in greater depth, in order to make sure that brand managers are fully prepared for the new global marketplace. Let's get started.

Overview

In Chapter 1, we encountered a catalogue of brand types, everything from corporations, products and services to non-profits, celebrities and places. In this chapter, we'll examine more closely some of these types of brands, particularly those that tend to span multiple countries. We start with global corporate brands and then the kind of brand that most people are familiar with – fast-moving consumer goods or products. We also investigate the global implications of service brands and not-for-profit brands, as well as the role of luxury and celebrity brands and influencers in the world of global brand management. Finally, we switch our attention to destination branding. Our 'guest perspective' is from Dr Karen Sutherland, a professor at the University of the Sunshine Coast, Australia; she gives some expert advice on using social media in marketing global brands. The closing case study shines a spotlight on the success of an upstart, Xiaomi.

Why experience determines the types of brands you'll manage

Today will help determine tomorrow. As a brand manager, you'll generally just work on one or two types of brands during your career. In the first chapter, we listed many of them: product, service, corporate, place, nation, non-profit, celebrity, personal, ingredient, private-label, luxury, premium and activist. The brand will either be the leader of the category, a challenger (it's best to be the second in the category if your brand is a challenger) or a niche brand. Each of these types and positions requires different skills sets and marketing activities to be optimally successful. For instance, a leading brand often focuses on growing the category. After all, the more users of the category, the more they'll get. They try not to point out the competition – ie the challengers – because they don't want to give them exposure. If you're managing a challenger brand, however, you might seek to gain share from the leader rather than growing the category, since this could benefit the leader more than it would benefit you. It is generally harder for leaders to take share from challengers (the second level is usually thriving because a portion of people are rejecting the leader), just as it is for challengers to work to grow the category. Meanwhile, niche brands can be very successful working to grow their niche, taking share from the leader and the challengers. Finally, the brand could be marketing to consumers or shoppers (B2C) or to businesses (B2B), which generally have different timelines, sales funnels and processes.

As a result, your perspective as a brand manager will depend on where you work and the types of activities in which you engage. Many companies, especially at the beginning of their life, focus on a single product that helps them launch into the market. For instance, a corporate giant like Kraft Foods grew out of a simple wholesale cheese delivery business, which specialized in processing cheese products.[2] Nestlé, the world's largest food company, started its business as a condensed-milk manufacturer focusing on infant foods.[3] Finally, as you saw in Chapter 9, Philips started its journey by manufacturing incandescent lamps when the product was considered innovative. All three multinational brands are now well-known houses of brands, and almost all those brands are products grouped under consumer goods categories. Among typical houses of brands, one might find numerous individual product brands, many of which have succeeded beyond expectations and turned into master brands. As mentioned earlier, Dove, a multi-product global brand, started its life as a bar of soap.

During the start-up phase, a lot of companies do not see the long-term horizon, focusing on making the single-product brand a commercial success. Eventually, after the brand has proved a success, brand extensions are a natural development. Without branding the product properly, however, the chances of developing brand extensions and product extensions are limited. Apple started with a single-minded focus on one product: the personal computer. It evolved into other product categories related to 'things we can do with a computer', such as the iPod, and later extended beyond music into telecommunications. The idea of iPhones was a long way off when Steve Jobs and Steve Wozniak teamed up in that garage in Palo Alto.[4]

Focusing on product branding helps when companies aim to target a variety of audiences, at different income and education levels, or those who live in different cultures. As we saw in the previous chapter, Procter & Gamble, a large house of brands, sells a variety of washing powders across the world. They market many different brands, which are basically the same product, to appeal to different audiences. Brand managers at P&G might be overseeing a leading or a challenger brand, so within the same company the considerations and activities are different. Each brand manager is fighting to grow his or her share and might even be at odds with the other.

Likewise, the P&G corporate brand is not typically part of the consideration set when the consumer is debating whether to purchase Tide or one of its other product brands, so the brand managers do not include it as a part of their efforts. However, the P&G corporate brand should be at the top of mind for the chief executive officer (CEO), the chief marketing officer (CMO) and human resources, because of the role it plays in the functions beyond consumer-purchase decisions. These range from recruitment and setting the expectations for employee behaviour and performance to maintaining or growing the brand's stock-market valuation for investor relations and how employees interact with trade partners and distribution-channel suppliers. Depending on the organization's structure, the corporate brand could play a role in setting expectations for franchisees and licensers. Overall, however, the main goal behind building a corporate brand is to support corporate entity, not necessarily the products that it makes or the services it offers.

Managing a global corporate brand is a very complicated and often behind-the-scenes activity. The experience at every touchpoint for every stakeholder, from clients to employees to shareholders, needs to align. Obviously, that branding activity is very different from the one that consumers experience online, in stores and elsewhere along the points of contact. Depending on the brand architecture, some organizations may find themselves protecting a single brand, should it face trouble, and others may have to defend the entire organization. In Chapter 2, we saw a clear case of needing to defend a brand when VW was caught cheating on measuring emissions from their diesel cars in 2015[5] and the organization couldn't prove that their top management was not aware of it.[6]

Attention should be paid to not confusing the corporate brand with a product's brand. In some cases, the organization's overall image may hinder the success of the actual product brand, such as with VW or Sears; the latter is an example of a brand that is spiralling towards death at the time of writing.[7] But Kenmore, Craftsman and Die Hard are successful brands that have stood their ground under the failing Sears corporate brand. Some brand assets have been sold and some will be – in order to contribute to the coffers of the failing corporate brand.

Corporate brands, or organizational brands, as they are also called, result from all the activity at the organization's brand touchpoints and often have nothing to do with the quality of their products and services. Under corporate branding, customer service, treatment of employees, interviews with the CEO and other corporate leaders, stock performance and news reports, among other things, deliver the key brand impressions that result in the brand associations. Conversely, the brand can affect the employee's delivery of their company's customer service, its stock performance and other areas that help inform the brand. Corporate or parent brands, as well as the behaviors that contribute to the reputation, grow in importance as product life cycles became increasingly shorter, particularly in the technology fields.[8]

One of the most important elements of corporate branding is its Corporate Social Responsibility (CSR) and in many cases it follows the demands of customers and civic organizations calling for improvements in environmental performance and other ethical behaviours. Brands that do not participate in activities seen as gracious or benefiting the customer audiences stand to lose.

A corporate brand thrives if there is strong alignment between its culture and its business strategy for addressing each of its stakeholders and between its vision, corporate culture and image (VCI).[9] Mergers and acquisitions, however, make it harder to maintain consistent corporate branding. There are plenty of cases where this has happened, among them the merger of United Airlines with Continental, two of America's legacy airlines, which caused many problems and confusions about the final corporate brand. For a long time after the merger, some aircrew members took pride in their previous culture, and even presented themselves to the flying public as being part of their 'old company'.[10] Therefore, when a merger or acquisition is being discussed, the brand manager should develop a plan for transitioning the respective visions, corporate cultures and imagery into alignment.

Tangible comments about non-tangible service brands

Many of the brands we use today are not tangible. In other words, they are not something we can own, take home, physically hold and use whenever we please. As we've mentioned earlier, services are brands. Every bank, credit card, airline and hotel is a brand. The same goes for ride-sharing services and other app-based services. We select, use, prefer and repeat-purchase them because of the experience the brand delivers and the memory we have formed of them as a brand.

The challenges of service branding are far greater than those of product branding. Today's consumers are demanding when it comes to the level of satisfaction they expect from an experience, owing in part to the large number of competing and related services from which they can select. In addition to the traditional 4Ps, a number of other 'P' elements, such as people, process and physical evidence (cues), have to be factored in when dealing with services. The brand manager must fully understand consumers' and employees' needs and wants, the process by which the service brand can be delivered most effectively, and the surrounding environment where the service takes place. There should also be cues such as signs or employee actions in that environment reminding consumers that they are experiencing the service. A simple example is folding the edge of the toilet paper in a hotel room to indicate that it had been cleaned. In reality, the hotel staff might have just straightened up the room and not changed the bedding, but guests assume the room is clean when those little signs are present.

Human resources are key for enhancing service brands. Finding and retaining the right people for conveying the brand personality, brand promise and brand experience are crucial. Service branding does not work if those delivering the brand experience do not understand their role as brand ambassadors and are not properly trained to make the brand experience top of mind. Human resources should be working to ensure that it becomes a key responsibility of the brand manager.

One type of service is non-profits or not-for-profits (NFP). The term can be misleading. Some may think that because there is 'no profit' there is no business, and therefore does not need a brand. The truth is, every NFP is a business and may need a strong brand even more than a for-profit organization. The very first thing to consider is that any NFP organization has competition. That fact alone calls for a strong brand to differentiate it. The other important thing to remember is that for every dollar contributed or donated, a significant amount of money has been invested in making the NFP meaningful to the contributors.

A mutual element in NFP organizations is worthy intentions. They all have a defined objective and are purpose-driven organizations with a clear mission. The total number of NFP organizations in the US alone is estimated at around 1.5 million.[11] Some examples of well-known NFPs from across the political spectrum are Amnesty International, an organization which works to end human rights abuses; the International Committee of the Red Cross (and Red Crescent), a global organization that helps victims of wars, armed conflicts and natural disasters, among other lifesaving initiatives;[12] and The United Nations Educational, Scientific and Cultural Organization (UNESCO), which helps promote global collaboration in the areas of its name.[13] The reason almost all of us have opinions – positive and negative – about these organizations is because they're brands. We can't ignore them, and many smaller, poorer NFP organizations wish that they could have the budgets and exposure that these brands enjoy. Had these organizations neglected their public branded activities, chances are we might not have heard of them either. The truth is that any NFP can increase their branding activities by being disciplined and organized about it. Most NFPs operate with a volunteer team that also includes the board of directors, who ultimately make the decisions about branding and marketing. But some have leaders focused on building their brands. The NFPs that focus solely on convincing wealthy contributors to join the board of directors, however, may neglect the need to build a brand, which can lead to less recognition compared to competing NFPs.

Public thoughts on private-label brands

A private-label product is usually produced by a contracted outside manufacturer and sold under a store brand name or related name, mostly in the consumer goods and consumer product categories. Some of the more common product groups offering private labels are: personal care; beverages; cosmetics; paper products; household cleaners; condiments and salad dressings; dairy items; and frozen foods. An example of a private label is 'Kirkland Signature', Costco's private label. Sold exclusively through Costco's website and warehouses, Kirkland Signature is trademarked by the company. The name is derived from the original location of Costco's corporate headquarters, Kirkland, Washington.[14] Under this private label, one can find bottled water, clothing, luggage, food products, batteries, beer, coffee, gasoline, golf products, among other items.

Kirkland Signature brand offers big savings on high-quality products. Costco has focused a lot of its efforts on making sure that the company's store brand can compete with name-brand products. These private-label products offer high quality compared to the brand-name competitors, but at a much lower price. A large retailer, such as Costco, can specify everything about the product attributes: packaging, ingredients, quality level and label design. They also sell the original brands side-by-side with their own store brand to show that theirs cost less but, through design cues, they imply that they have the same quality. Target likewise sells a variety of their own food products under the Archer Farms brand, their private label, alongside comparable branded snacks from companies like General Mills and Frito-Lay. We can also find many private-label products in hair salons that create their own branded line of shampoos, conditioners and styling products. For retailers, the advantages of offering private-label products include:

- managing and controlling production: third-party manufacturers work for the retailer, under their direction, offering the retailer complete control over product ingredients and quality;
- controlling profitability: because the retailer controls the product, they can ensure a higher margin than the branded products they sell;
- adaptability to market conditions: retailers are closer to the customer and can often spot emerging product demands faster than manufacturers of branded products;
- controlling brand imagery: the retailer determines the brand name and packaging design of their private-label products, so they can use them to convey key attributes of their overall brand;
- enabling exclusivity: retailers can develop products that can't be purchased elsewhere, so fans of those items need to visit their stores or online channel, which can drive purchases of other items. In addition, some of the exclusive private-label brands are being positioned as premium products, a smart strategy because it allows the retailer to demand a higher price tag.

Most of all, the private-label products can serve as cues as to the quality of the retailer, reinforcing their brand equities, important since retailers are essentially services. Without the tangible benefits of the private-label products, they can only build their brand on the intangible experiences within their environments online and off. On the other hand, some of the pitfalls and dangers in adapting private-label strategy include:

- dependency on third-party partners: since production is in the hands of an outside manufacturer, it's important to partner with reputable companies. Switching manufacturers can result in changes in flavour, packaging and other attributes that can produce a break in delivery of the brand promise.
- roadblocks to building loyalty: established and well-known brands have the advantage and a clear advantage in the distribution channel. A private-label brand will only be sold in specific stores and only on the label's website, limiting customer access to it. In some cases, limited availability could also create an advantage, giving customers a reason to believe in the exclusivity of the brand, leading to repeat purchase.

What to put into an ingredient brand?

Every brand we consume has ingredients that make it better, faster, healthier or offer some other benefit and these ingredients or parts can themselves be brands. A brand of brakes or tyres can promise to make a car safer. Shimano's name appears on many different brands of bicycles, because they make their gears. The Gore-Tex label appears on a wide range of apparel and footwear items. In addition, 'some large manufacturers own product brands which they use to enhance their final product offerings, like Trinitron from Sony, Quattro from Audi, Northstar from Cadillac and many more. Here we talk about Ingredient Branding through self-brands.'[15]

Intel is another example. The Intel chip can make the computer more desirable to many people, serving as a 'proof point' for the machine's quality. In fact, according to the *Harvard Business Review*: 'Intel is the ultimate ingredient brand. Zero sales to end consumers yet Intel built a consumer demand pull for its chips that required every PC manufacturer to incorporate them and to advertise Intel Inside on their products and in their ads.'[16]

Ingredient brands add to the brand association for the products that house them. Using a well-known ingredient brand whose attributes are relevant to the target audience reinforces the strengths of the master brand and positions the quality of the master brand. It can enable a product to command a premium price and differentiate itself from competing, similar brands that do not contain the ingredient brand. Finally, it can also secure exclusivity in a specific product category, giving the master brand an aura of differentiation and uniqueness.

The downside of using an ingredient brand is that it can prohibit you from employing competing ingredient brands. For example, manufacturers of computers may not be able to involve other chipmakers if they engage with Intel. Exclusivity agreements with ingredient brands could limit how the brand advertises and promotes itself, affecting the impressions they can create. Master brands also run the risk of negative publicity if the ingredient-brand company gets into financial trouble or generates negative publicity. Another potential hazard is when the ingredient brand becomes more dominant than the master brand. In such cases, it can detract from the public opinion about the master brand.

Celebrities and influencers and their place in global brand management

We all know and pay attention to celebrities. Many of us can't take our eyes off them, can't stop listening to them, want to be like them, eat like them and dress like them. The first question: is being a celebrity enough to become 'a brand'? Probably not. The reason is quite simple: it is easy to become one and it can be fleeting. Social media has turned us all into potential celebrities, and the question is which one of us will become huge and develop a loyal following. Anyone can post a video that ends up being watched by millions of people and, as a result, the poster becomes a minor celebrity. But viewership alone doesn't guarantee long-term commercial or emotional value for the consumer, and initial celebrity status does not mean that they have a robust, differentiated brand promise that will drive long-term consumer affinity. Strong brands, however, not only focus on being profitable, but also focus on delivering their higher purpose or brand promise.

But most celebrities who last do become brands and can find themselves in a position to endorse other brands, lending their brand equity and credibility to the product or service. The product or service, conversely, will reflect on the celebrity endorser, so the respective mission, vision and values need to align. For consumers, it could be enough that the celebrity simply holds the product, demonstrates its use, or is seen with it in public to be viewed as endorsing it and validating that the product or service brand is indeed a good one. Celebrities, of course, also endorse worthy causes, raising awareness of social issues and, of course, politicians and political initiatives. Again, these endorsements reflect on the celebrity's brand as they promote the other brand.

Celebrity endorsements can become a powerful branding tool. During the 1970s, Japanese consumers saw American celebrities as appealing. As a result, Japanese brands hired American movie and sports stars, as well as other American celebrities, to endorse their products in Japan – everything from coffee and Coc-Cola to wristwatches. Japanese advertisers maintained that, properly used, foreigners can attract the interest of the average Japanese. Brooke Shields, Farrah Fawcett, Diana Ross, Paul Newman and other internationally known figures were used. 'Foreigners look different,' said Kazuo Yamamoto, international relations manager for Tokyo's Matsuya Department Stores at the time. In addition, the Japanese ad agency Hakuhodo reported that, 'A foreigner can break the tranquility of the ad and make the audience wake up.'[17] While this exact branding strategy won't work in Japan today, it can inform today's brand building.

One form of celebrity today are 'influencers', a term slowly replacing the term 'opinion leaders' – people who inform and advise, leading to the acceptance by others of their position.[18] Not like the celebrities historically used for endorsing a brand or product, they're simply other 'consumers' voicing joy, excitement, thrill and gratitude for the experience they have just had with a brand. It is immediate and relevant. Some of these influencers make it a business to be online virtually 24/7 and report their experiences to others. Other consumers take great joy in being among the first experiencers of a brand, as well as having the bragging right of spreading the news. Others are paid either through cash, gift cards or free products.[19] Legally, they need to identify any financial considerations, but many do not disclose them.[20] The common thread is that influencers are in fact businesses owners (their platforms), become keynote speakers at conferences, and even publish books and other offline materials. And of course, they spend a lot of time on social media. It takes dedication and commitment to become an influencer, but almost anyone can do it. The majority of the influencers, however, are younger and have a background in technology and entrepreneurship.[21]

Brand marketers can find social-media influencers in virtually every category, including business-to-business, to help broadcast their news. During some product launches, tweets and posts from influencers are anticipated with great anxiety. Anytime a new iPhone model is being launched, for instance, people look to influencers who follow the technology world, such as Guy Kawasaki (@GuyKawasaki) who used to work at Apple as the Chief Evangelist. Guy has an incredible list of followers in almost all social-media outlets.

GUY KAWASAKI'S FOLLOWERS

LinkedIn followers: 2.6 M, Twitter followers: 1.51 M, Instagram followers: 65.6 K, Facebook followers: 450 K, YouTube subscribers: 5.7 K. Guy also serves as a brand ambassador for Mercedes Benz and a keynote speaker for Apple, Nike, Audi and Microsoft among many others. He's written 13 books, many of them *New York Times* and *Wall Street Journal* bestsellers.[22]

Since we're on the topic of people as brands, we are all in a way branded from birth. The first mark of the brand is the name. There comes a point when it's hard to separate the name from the person and the personality that comes with it. When that happens, we have a personal brand. As we grow, we either like our names and keep them, or we feel that for some reason the name does not reflect who we really are and 'rebrand' by changing our names to something that fits the feeling that we'd do better in life under a different name. Real products and brand in the real world are no different.

We self-brand ourselves for many purposes, but mostly to advance in our jobs and careers. Your employees, teammates, co-workers, supervisors, clients, prospects, potential employers and others all hold impressions about your on-the-job competencies, which can affect the influence you have over them. If you want them to correspond to how you want to be perceived, you need to develop your personal brand. Any person who wishes to develop one must start from a list of fundamental components that make a brand, including the following:

- Our body is the first to be considered in the concept of Personal Branding. It is our 'packaging', the first tangible entity we present to the world. Just like any other brand, the way we see our bodies is completely different from one to another. It is up to us to develop the appreciation that we wish for our 'body brand' and to express it through the clothes we wear, as well as how we talk, which form the first tangible hints at our unique brand promise, our level of success and our world beliefs.
- The next component is the values and character we hold dear. Honesty, punctuality, loyalty and authenticity are just a few of the values that people hold as their guiding character. Of course, our actions need to be consistent with our core values and character to be believed. After all, claiming to be honest does not make one so. Just like product and service branding, it's what others perceive that is important.
- People also judge our personal brand by looking at our competence and success. At any stage of life, we can measure our accomplishments. Success can be monetary, of course, but can also be measured by the degree of mastery and relationships in our given field.
- Social roles fill a significant space in the total creation of our self-brand. The higher a position we have in society (work, politics, family, organizations), the higher our perceived status.
- Finally, our personality informs our personal brands too. We might be calm, explosive or moderate. Our traits can include patience, wisdom, tenderness, open-mindedness or indifference. The list can go on and the specifics inform the opinions others have about us, which is the definition of a brand.

The success and longevity of luxury brands

It is astonishing to see that many of the most expensive products and services survive tough economies, which is one of the most convincing arguments for the power of branding. But success in hard times makes sense, because the target audience for luxury brands is much smaller than the mass market. It is very clear that not everybody can buy a Bugatti Chiron or, for a slightly lower price, a Rolls Royce, but that is not the only reason why luxury brands have a strong sustainability power. Successful luxury brands work hard at managing and protecting their equities to ensure they're enduring.

The Bugatti brand is a good example. Like many luxury brands, Bugatti carries the name of its founder. Carlo Bugatti started a jewellery and furniture-design business and was followed by his sons Ettore and Rembrandt. The Bugatti car business began in 1909 after Ettore Bugatti found that his talents were less in expressive arts, like his father and brother. Yet, he managed to build cars that were themselves considered works of art.[23]

Despite some tragedies the family had experienced, both Rembrandt's sculptures and the early cars of the Bugatti shop are today selling for millions.[24] There are less than 8,000 original Bugatti automobiles manufactured by the family.[25] The brand was bought by Volkswagen in 1998. While Bugatti doesn't belong in the brand portfolio of a mass production company, VW is handling it wisely, and very few people make any connection between the brands. The name Bugatti has such allure that they launched a Bugatti named Veyron in 2005. The car exhibited the guiding principles of the design established by Ettore but combined with modern engineering and technologies. The result was a car with a unique appearance and performance. VW understands the power of the Bugatti brand. They never manufacture Bugatti cars in large quantities. Rather, they're limited editions, topping at around 500. The average price is US $3 million (£2.4 million).[26]

As a prudent measure in brand architecture, the VW group rarely mentions the Bugatti name. Within VW's luxury group, one can find VW/Skoda, mid-range in price and perceived quality; Audi/Porsche, more luxurious cars, with Porsche being at the sport luxury end; Ducati, an Italian sporty and fast motorcycle brand; Bentley, a British brand that was once owned by Rolls Royce; and Bugatti, the top of the line. As mentioned earlier, there is clear differentiation between each brand, and although the term 'luxury' could apply to most of them (Audi, Porsche, Bentley), the Bugatti brand stands alone. Because of its positioning and separation from the rest of the group, the VW scandal we explored in Chapter 2 hasn't affected it.[27]

Coco Chanel is another established luxury brand that started from absolutely nothing. Gabrielle Bonheur Chanel was raised in an orphanage, where she learned to sew, and started her career as a singer but was unsuccessful. She started designing hats, and a male friend, who trusted her enough helped her launch a shop in Deauville, France, where she sold simple sportswear. In the true spirit of a professional brander, she sensed that differentiation would set her apart from the stifling fashion rules of society at the time. The jersey fabric she used gave her the opportunity to create a different look that resonated with women at a time when fashion dictated corseted styles. She created the look of a 'poor girl' and attracted the richest and most influential women in Paris. Chanel believed in the simple positioning that 'luxury must be comfortable, otherwise it is not luxury;'[28] she stressed simplicity and comfort and turned the fashion industry on its head.

By the late 1920s, the Chanel brand was successful and expanded into areas related to fashion, such as a couture house, jewellery, textile mills and perfume laboratories. She knew how to promote her products by promoting her uncompromising personality, something that many fashion designers have since copied to also became successful. Rhonda Garelick, a professor of English at the University of Nebraska at Lincoln, who wrote a Chanel biography, *Antigone in Vogue*, said: 'She is a successful poseur who came from nothing and blasted her way into society and celebrity.' Chanel improvised as she went, 'tapping into desires that are far more than sartorial.'[29]

Chanel understood that after assessing her competition, there was no one who was innovating and creating fashion for the rich who wanted to dress as the 'everyday girl'.[30] She built an everlasting brand out of being a 'peasant girl' who barged into the circle of the elite Parisian world. Her key was persistence, consistency and an unwillingness to compromise.

As we can see from the Bugatti and Channel examples, luxury brands present and offer an entry to a lifestyle. Luxury brands never focus on their functionality. They never offer coupons or discounts. Instead, a person who purchases luxury goods uses them to announce his or her standing in society. Luxury products imply that their owner is powerful, wealthy, sophisticated and a member of an elite group. The brand becomes an ambassador for their personality and desire to belong in that elite group.

Luxury brands always offer uncompromising quality and simple, superior design. To serve a lifestyle that manifests superiority, the products of any luxury brand must also be superior to others in the same category. If nothing else, it enables people to justify its high cost. When brands are manufactured in large numbers, quality control often goes down. Meanwhile, as distribution increases, large brands lose the element of exclusivity, which is essential for luxury brands.

The act of buying a luxury brand becomes part of the luxury experience. Personal attention to individual consumers is customary. To purchase a Bugatti, for instance, one must make an appointment. After all, acquiring a luxury good isn't merely a financial deal. It's an entry point into the lifestyle promised by the brand, and customers of luxury brands know each other; they belong to a 'club'. Luxury brands create bonds among people of the same social standing. The brand represents their standing in the world. Notice that most advertising for a luxury brand is typically highly visual, featuring sensual imagery of the product or products. It is designed to connect with consumers on an emotional level and fuel the desire for the lifestyle it presents.

Luxury brands should use scarcity to make them feel exclusive and create demand. Scarcity fosters a sense of urgency among the target audience, a tactic that other brands can use as well. Through scarcity a particular model or fashion item can become the ultimate status symbol, making some consumers feel that they simply can't go on with their lives if they do not own it.

How to build a brand for a country's tourism and commerce sectors through place branding

One of the most memorable symbols of all time is the 'I♥NY' logo created by Milton Glaser in 1976.[31] I LOVE NY was an idea for a tourism campaign conceived by the ad agency Wells Rich Green, following a request from the New York State Department of Economic Development (DED).[32] Legend has it that Milton Glaser created the image on a piece of paper in the back of a New York taxi. The original is now part of the MOMA collection. This particular logo became a symbol that caught the attention of many people because of its uniqueness, simplicity and direct communication using a human emblem, a heart. While it was popular in NY to begin with, the imitations never stopped appearing all over the world. The simple notion of being able to use a graphic symbol, which is not a registered trademark, ♥©, and add to it any additional letters, turned this into a global message. But the logo was not the only brand element that the ad agency created for the New York State Department of Economic Development. They collaborated with all the stakeholders in the city, from cab drivers to celebrities, to Broadway and beyond, to carry the message. A famous song 'I LOVE NY' was created, and it is the state's song till this day.

Given that New York City is one of the world's most famous destinations, a unique destination brand without a doubt, did they really need the 'I♥NY' logo to help sell it? There are many arguments for and against building a destination brand.

A leading policy advisor and author of the *Good Country Index*, Simon Anholt, argued in the late 1990s that a powerful and positive national image was valuable for stimulating trade, tourism and foreign investment. But the phrase he coined in 1998, 'nation brand', soon became problematic. He said:

> 'I first began to write about an idea I called "nation brand" in 1996. My original observation was a simple one: the reputations of countries (and, by extension, of cities and regions too) behave rather like the brand images of companies and products, and they are equally critical to the progress, prosperity and good management of those places. Unfortunately, the phrase "nation brand" soon became distorted, mainly by naïve governments in willing collusion with ambitious consulting firms, into "nation branding", a dangerously misleading phrase which seems to contain a promise that the images of countries can be directly manipulated using the techniques of commercial marketing communications. Yet despite repeatedly calling for it over the last fifteen years, I have never seen a shred of evidence to suggest that this is possible: no case studies, no research, and not even any very persuasive arguments. I conclude that countries are judged by what they do, not by what they say, as they have always been; yet the notion

that a country can simply advertise its way into a better reputation has proved to be a pernicious and surprisingly resilient one.

'I also have to admit that despite studying the topic for many years, I'm not at all sure I even know what "branding" is. "Brand" can mean at least three different things in the world of commerce: first, it can refer to the designed identity of a product (the look of the product itself, its packaging, its logo, its livery, its communications and so forth); second, it is sometimes used more ambitiously to refer to the culture of the organization behind the product; and third, it can refer to the product's or corporation's reputation in the minds of its target audience (this is the sense in which I used the word in my first essay on the subject in 1998, *Nation Brands of the Twenty-First Century*, although the term "brand image" is a more precise one in this context).

'Hence, one might suppose, "branding" must be related to one or another of these meanings: it is either the business of designing the livery of products (which is indeed what branding agencies do); or else it has something to do with building or creating an enhanced sense of corporate culture or mission within the organization (in fact the word is not often used in this context); or it is the means by which the product acquires its reputation, and this is where the trouble starts.

'Used in its first sense, branding actually does have some relevance to countries and the ways they present themselves to the rest of the world, but it is a humdrum business, which doesn't begin to justify the excitement about "nation branding". Countries, through their many state agencies, have numerous dealings with various professional audiences around the world, and one can certainly argue that it gives a better impression of the country if all those agencies use consistent, well-designed materials when they carry out their transactions. A single logo, a professional 'look and feel' on their stationery, business cards, corporate videos, information leaflets, communiqués, press releases, websites and so forth, undoubtedly reinforces the impression of a well-organized, modern, self-respecting state with effective and efficient structures, processes and mechanisms.'[33]

The stakeholders in destination branding are many: directors of city and municipality marketing organizations; marketing leaders from tourism boards; marketing staff working with inwards investment, economic and residential growth; property and real-estate companies working with place-making and development projects; and advisors, agencies and consultancies working with city and governmental clients. Of course, there is one other key stakeholder: people who live and work in the destination and benefit from increased traffic to their location.

EXAMPLE REQUEST FOR PROPOSAL

As in many cases, governments, municipalities and other organizations call on ad agencies to create a logo and promotional campaign for their beloved country, city, village or region. Often, there is also a public tender, calling on anybody to submit proposals for the project. Here are the typical parameters that an agency will receive with sample content to help familiarize yourself with the language:

Request for Proposals
Tourism and Business Attraction Branding Campaign

BIDS DUE: (It could be weeks, months and even a year)

Our (type of destination) is now engaged in a major effort to reimagine and rebrand itself for the purpose of projecting a more favourable image to the world. Under the leadership of a jobs-focused Governor and General Assembly, the state has dedicated substantial political and financial resources to bringing together its people around a new vision for the state – one that brands us as the best place in the country to live, grow a business and visit as a tourist or business traveller.

To that end, the (governmental body) is requesting proposals from firms and groups of firms for compelling outreach, design, branding, marketing and advertising campaigns that rebrand our (type of location) and promote it effectively and memorably as a place to visit, live, work or start a business.

We are seeking responses that offer a fresh look at the state and flexible solutions in areas that include, but are not limited to: public outreach, design, strategy, brand development, public relations, advertising and market research.

The selected bidder(s) shall:

- engage stakeholders throughout our state to harness the many different state's experiences;
- leverage this engagement to drive public buy-in and generate regional and national attention;
- develop an authentic, captivating brand that advances civic engagement, tourism and business attraction;
- engage public and private partners to deploy this brand;
- provide public relations, marketing and advertising services to promote the State as a place to live, work, visit, or start a business.

In response, the branding firm or an ad agency will present a response that includes such items as:

- executive summary
- technical approach
  - services required;
  - milestones and timetables;
  - reporting, status and monitoring specifications;

    - staffing specifications;
    - where services are to be performed.
- technical experience
    - number of years of experience;
    - level of technical expertise;
    - services and other relevant experience.
- personnel
    - CVs or bios
- financial capacity
    - financial statements
- changes to the RFP
- required forms
    - qualification form;
    - business and directory information;
    - references;
    - public contract number;
    - minority, female, person with disability status and subcontracting;
    - conflicts of interest disclosures;
    - taxpayer identification number;
    - information regarding terminations, litigation and debarment.
- other attachments (depending on the governing body managing this RFP)

As in many cases, a committee originates the process of engaging members of the public, including professionals and sometimes amateurs. Many of them are publicly elected officials, who may or may not be there by the time the project is being developed or nearing completion.

KEY CONSIDERATIONS WHEN USING SOCIAL MEDIA IN THE MARKETING MIX OF A GLOBAL BRAND – A GUEST PERSPECTIVE FROM DR KAREN SUTHERLAND, AUSTRALIA

Dr Sutherland is an award-winning lecturer and the Discipline Lead of Public Relations, coordinator and creator of the Social Media minor and a social media researcher at the University of the Sunshine Coast in Queensland, Australia. Her passion is finding simple social-media solutions for business and non-profit organizations that build positive and ongoing relationships with their customers and stakeholders. Dr Sutherland has been employed in a range of marketing, communication and public relations roles at organizations such as Australian Broadcasting Corporation (ABCTV), Grundy Television, Fremantle Media International, the Australian Red Cross Blood Service and Monash University. Having published widely about social media, Dr Sutherland is often invited to speak on the topic and provide expert commentary to the media. Here is DR Sutherland's advice on how to use social media in marketing a global brand

'Effectively managing a brand in a global market has always been a challenge, and the rapid adoption of social media has not simplified this task. While social media has assisted marketers in overcoming geographical barriers, including it in the marketing mix of a global brand adds yet another layer of complexity to marketing communications if not approached with caution.

'By 2019, it is estimated that more than 2.77 billion people globally will use social media.[34] As such, social-media technology has become a necessity for businesses and non-profit organizations to reach and engage with consumers around the world. However, marketers are advised not to panic. While the tools may be relatively new and constantly changing, the fundamental principles of marketing communication still apply even in the ever-changing social media landscape.

The balance between global and local

Managers of global brands often have to strike a delicate balance between maintaining a recognizable presence while customizing their marketing efforts to maintain relevance for local markets. This mix of a global and local or 'Glocal' approach to brand management also applies to social media. However, there are some key areas that should remain standardized throughout the world to avoid diluting the brand and confusing consumers, whereas others can be customized in order to provide consumers with a more meaningful and relevant product or service.[35]

Areas to standardize

- Branding
  - Ensuring consistent branding across countries results in a higher degree of brand recognition in multiple markets. The key with global branding is to be identifiable to current and prospective customers in any location. Having clear branding guidelines and communicating the importance of upholding them to local marketers is paramount.
- Positioning
  - The overall brand position must remain the same. Similar to branding, an organization's unique offering and image should remain consistent across its global markets. This helps to build and maintain trust with consumers.

Doing so will result in positive brand associations in the way of consistency and dependability in terms of offerings in any country. Consumers will know that what your brand offers is the same wherever in the world they choose to engage with it.

- Social customer care
  - Consistent processes must be in place throughout every market to ensure that the customer experience is of a high standard in any location where a consumer interacts with your brand. Social media has enabled customers to air their grievances on a global stage with negative brand experiences, reaching larger networks of people further and faster than ever before. Therefore, it is essential for global brand managers to ensure that customer care is a number one priority in every market and on its social-media channels.
- Benchmarking practices
  - Measurement is an essential part of brand management and this also applies to social media. Having consistent benchmarking practices across global markets facilitates like-for-like comparisons at a macro level and allows for the identification of issues (and successes) in specific countries. Marketing decisions need to be informed by data, and social media generates meaningful data to facilitate this process.
- Research
  - Research is the most important part of strategy development and implementation. A strong commitment to continuous research and improvement must be possessed by all marketers managing global and local markets. The only constant is change, and research is the only way that brand managers will be able to maintain flexibility to thrive in a constantly evolving social-media landscape.

Areas to customize for the local market

- Positioning vis-à-vis local competition
  - A strong commitment to research should also include a constant analysis of local competitors in order to retain a competitive edge. While it is important to maintain a consistent brand position overall, it is also vital to be able to tweak communication and delivery in order to keep up with trends and remain relevant and unique when competing in local markets.
- Language
  - It is essential to be able to communicate clearly and effectively with consumers in every local market and the only way to do this is to accurately translate content into the native language of each country and to have native speakers interact

with consumers on social media at a local level. This is an area where investment is necessary, because inaccurate translation can negatively impact brand reputation and can also cause offence. For example, a brand came under fire when someone in the Australian Head Office cropped an image with Mandarin written on a wall in the background. The remaining Mandarin was perceived as an insult to native speakers who read it. This could have been avoided with local native speakers checking social-media content before it was posted.

- Cultural preferences
  - Again, having local marketers on the ground in each location is essential to ensure that the cultural nuances of the region are understood, addressed and encapsulated within social-media content. What works in Western markets may be misunderstood in Asian markets and vice-versa. This may result in offence, as already mentioned, or it may just cause confusion within the local market. Either way, consumers will become disengaged owing to the brand's irrelevance at a local level.
- Posting time and frequency
  - It is risky to assume a social-media strategy that works effectively in a brand's home country will also succeed in other global markets. Again, this is where research and the gathering and analysis of social-media performance data should inform all decisions in relation to the best days and times to post and how often to post in local markets. Guessing (or assuming) that all countries are the same is one of the fastest ways to waste time, money and other resources, particularly when social-media advertising is involved.

'Overall, while branding, positioning, benchmarking, the customer experience and researching must remain consistent, global brand managers are strongly advised to do their homework in each local market. With knowledge of the local market, experienced marketers and customer-care staff can be employed on the ground and global brand managers can make informed choices as to how to customize their global social-media strategy to ensure that it is relevant and appropriate to positively resonate with local consumers.'

EXTENDED CASE STUDY: A BRIEF LOOK AT THE QUICK GLOBAL GROWTH OF THE XIAOMI BRAND

Xiaomi ('Little Rice' in Chinese) positions itself as 'a Chinese electronics company headquartered in Beijing. Xiaomi makes and invests in smartphones, mobile apps, laptops and related consumer electronics.'[36] But in reality, this brand is known for its smartphones and very little else. When passing the windows of their retail outlets, your first thought might be that it's an Apple Store, but it's not. Indeed, the similarities are many: wide-open space, tables featuring the latest smartphone models and other technology gadgets, the walls filled with tech accessories and the extra-large video screens featuring slick shots of the latest phone models. Was it intentionally designed to appear as if it's imitating another brand? Is it a compliment? Should brands engage in looking, feeling and sounding like another brand? Or is Xiaomi actually a stand-alone brand, with its own distinct personality, character and appeal?

Let's examine the brief history of Xiaomi and the reasons it became such a success story. Xiaomi is a new brand. It started in 2010 with the active involvement of several technology veterans: Lin Bin, VP at the Google China Institute of Engineering; Dr Zhou Guangping, senior director at Motorola's Beijing R&D centre; Liu De, department head of industrial design at the University of Science and Technology, Beijing; Li Wanqiang, general manager of Kingsoft Dictionary; Wong Kong-Kat, principal development manager at Microsoft China; and Hong Feng, senior product manager at Google China.[37]

While their accumulated experience is impressive, timing was also an important factor. From the start, the executives admired Steve Jobs and his work at Apple. In an interview with *The New York Times*, conducted in 2012, the head of Xiaomi said: 'When Steve was alive, he was the best, nobody could surpass him. Nothing could surpass the iPhone.'[38]

As we all know, the smartphone market was already red-hot in 2010, and the competition between the leading brands was fierce. The main war on market share was between Apple and Samsung. Nokia had already been pushed out of the picture and was falling fast.[39] As a result, there were two systems in play: Apple and Android. While Apple controlled its OS software, Android was open to allowing many brands to use it.[40]

Xiaomi is using Android, but they tweaked it and made it more user-friendly. One difference is that Xiaomi enables consumers to design their operating system.[41] It frequently releases software updates for users in China and other countries.[42] This is an unusual way of engaging consumers, enabling the brand to be at the front of technology updates, consumer trends and opinions. As a result, they were able to be seen as being more people-oriented and approachable than Apple, creating a favourable image for their brand.

In China, the Apple product, specifically the iPhone, had a cult like following. Xiaomi paid attention to every detail of the meteoric rise of the iPhone brand and many other 'brand behaviours' that Apple presented to its followers. Xiaomi in fact adopted a marketing strategy of carefully following Apple's brand mannerisms. Even its product-introduction events included bits of Apple's famous product unveilings. For example, at a Xiaomi event in 2012 in a trendy art district in Beijing to show off the new Xiaomi smartphone to a roomful of cheering fans, Mr Lei strode onto a stage dressed in a black polo shirt, jeans and black Converse shoes, mimicking Steve Jobs.[43]

For many years, Western products were copied and sold in China and other markets. As a result, some luxury brands whose products suffered from cheap imitations opened their own stores in China, to guarantee that original products could be obtained in that market. Apple had also opened a few stores in China, but the iPhone was beyond the means of the average Chinese consumer. When Xiaomi first came out, it was hard to distinguish between the look of its products and those made by Apple. A great compliment to Xiaomi came from a consumer who said: 'Xiaomi is the real fake'.[44]

It appears now, however, that the brand image is becoming less of a factor, and price is becoming more important. While smartphone sales are still growing globally, the 'demand for premium and high-end smartphones continued to suffer due to marginal incremental benefits during upgrade. Demand for entry-level smartphones (sub- US $100) and low mid-tier smartphones (sub- US $150) improved due to better-quality models,' Anshul Gupta, research director at Gartner, said.[45]

As of 2018, Xiaomi is considered to be one of the world's leading phone brands. It stands only behind Apple and Samsung and is tied with another Chinese brand, Huawei. It is important to notice that when considering the popularity of a Chinese brand, it operates in a market with 1.5 billion consumers. Many of the consumers in China would like to own a Western brand for prestige and status, but they simply cannot afford it. The region surrounding China constitutes 50 per cent of earth's humanity. No wonder the sales figures are impressive. While Xiaomi, Huawei and Oppo are successful in Asian markets, they are largely unknown in other markets. Xiaomi is almost absent from Europe, Africa and Australia, and sold only via Amazon in the US. So, what can we learn from Xiaomi's example regarding global brand management? Several things:

- A group of experts can always start a company, once they have the money.
- The strategy of creating a brand out of admiration for another leading brand is not always easy.
- The same strategy can work on a limited audience, but not always globally.
- Not everybody appreciates a 'me too' brand, since it's already been done.
- Not having enough originality in a brand can be a problem.
- In the end, copycat brands are driven by price, not by innovation, and that could be an issue.
- To survive, Xiaomi has to have become known for products, services and user experience that is unique to this brand.
- Competition might vary from market to market owing to local copycat brands.

KEY TERMS

- challenger brand
- glocal
- ingredient brand
- leading brand
- luxury brand
- master brand
- niche brand

DISCUSSION QUESTIONS

- What are some of types of brands and what are their key functional differences?
- What are the components a personal brand and how do you describe yours?
- What are the benefits, attributes and drawbacks of a private-label brand for retails?
- What are the best practices for developing and managing a private-label brand?

Notes

1 Leathers, H (2017) IBM: the next generation wants a solution, not a product, *Seeking Alpha*, https://seekingalpha.com/article/4107584-ibm-next-generation-wants-solution-product (archived at https://perma.cc/7C62-94J4)

2 Reuters (2019) Factbox: Kraft Foods vital statistics and history, https://www.reuters.com/article/us-cadbury-kraft-factbox/factbox-kraft-foods-vital-statistics-and-history-idUSTRE60I1JI20100119 (archived at https://perma.cc/KA9M-Q5P9)

3 http://www.nestle-ea.com (archived at https://perma.cc/7RKE-E353) (2019) History, https://www.nestle-ea.com/en/aboutus/history/history_detailed (archived at https://perma.cc/4WUP-GC7F)

4 http://www.nestle-ea.com (archived at https://perma.cc/7RKE-E353) (2019) History, https://www.nestle-ea.com/en/aboutus/history/history_detailed (archived at https://perma.cc/4WUP-GC7F)

5 BBC News (2019) Volkswagen: The scandal explained, https://www.bbc.com/news/business-34324772 (archived at https://perma.cc/SH2V-66WA)

6 BBC News (2019) Volkswagen: The scandal explained, https://www.bbc.com/news/business-34324772 (archived at https://perma.cc/SH2V-66WA)

7 *Forbes* (2019) Dead brand walking: Sears is going out with a bang, https://www.forbes.com/sites/stevendennis/2018/12/17/dead-brand-walking-sears-is-going-out-with-a-bang/#44765a34477a (archived at https://perma.cc/DP6T-WBEB)

8 Schultz, M & Hatch, M J (2009) Of bricks and brands: from corporate to enterprise branding, *Organizational Dynamics*, **38** (2), pp 117–130, http://majkenschultz.com/wp-content/uploads/sites/10485/2016/03/Org-dynamics-Schultz-Hatch.-2009..pdf (archived at https://perma.cc/G8MY-CWF7)

9 Schultz, M & Hatch, M J (2009) Of bricks and brands: from corporate to enterprise branding, *Organizational Dynamics*, **38** (2), pp 117–130, http://majkenschultz.com/wp-content/uploads/sites/10485/2016/03/Org-dynamics-Schultz-Hatch.-2009..pdf (archived at https://perma.cc/G8MY-CWF7)

10 Glassdoor.com (2019) https://www.glassdoor.com/Reviews/United-Airlines-merger-with-continental-Reviews-EI_IE683.0,15_KH16,39.htm (archived at https://perma.cc/B7X2-TGUV)

11 GrantSpace (2019) How many nonprofit organizations are there in the U.S.? http://grantspace.org/tools/knowledge-base/funding-research/statistics/number-of-nonprofits-in-the-u.s (archived at https://perma.cc/B9YK-VKRH)

12 Amnesty.org. (2019) Amnesty International Home, https://www.amnesty.org/en (archived at https://perma.cc/7NAR-GLX2)

13 Mastersinnonprofitmanagement.com (2019) Top 6 most famous non-profit organizations in the world, http://www.mastersinnonprofitmanagement.com/top-6-most-famous-non-profit-organizations-in-the-world.html (archived at https://perma.cc/DG7N-BHJ8)

14 Freedman, L (2018) This is the meaning behind the Kirkland Signature brand name at Costco, @kitchn, https://www.thekitchn.com/costco-kirkland-signature-brand-name-meaning-263610 (archived at https://perma.cc/NQ65-AUZR)

15 Havenstein, M (2003) Ingredient branding, *WiSt – Wirtschaftswissenschaftliches Studium*, **32** (4), pp 231–234

16 *Harvard Business Review* (2019) How to Build a B2B Brand, https://hbr.org/2007/11/how-to-build-a-b2b-brand-1 (archived at https://perma.cc/3753-AHYR)

17 Trucco, T (1982) Why Paul Newman is on all those Tokyo billboards, *The Christian Science Monitor*, https://www.csmonitor.com/1982/0723/072339.html (archived at https://perma.cc/8PLY-PUZQ)

18 Mittal, B (2017) *Consumer Behaviour*, 4th ed, Open Mentis, Cincinnati

19 Johnson, T (2019) How much do influencers charge? Paying Influencers 2019 Guide, Retail Performance Marketing Blog – *CPC Strategy*, https://www.cpcstrategy.com/blog/2018/06/how-much-do-influencers-charge-paying-influencers-2018-guide (archived at https://perma.cc/2G58-P5LT)

20 Johnson, T (2019) How much do influencers charge? Paying Influencers 2019 Guide, Retail Performance Marketing Blog – *CPC Strategy*, https://www.cpcstrategy.com/blog/2018/06/how-much-do-influencers-charge-paying-influencers-2018-guide (archived at https://perma.cc/2G58-P5LT)

21 Cbsnews.com (2019) Top social media influencers of 2018, https://www.cbsnews.com/pictures/social-media-influencers-influential-2018 (archived at https://perma.cc/HW4M-6VTH)

22 Guy Kawasaki (2019) Guy Kawasaki – About, https://guykawasaki.com/guy-kawasaki (archived at https://perma.cc/6UKY-QFB7)

23 Anon (2019) Bugatti – History, https://www.bugatti.com/tradition/history (archived at https://perma.cc/VCV5-A526)

24 Elsom, D (2019) The classic 1930s Bugatti that's worth DOUBLE the price of a brand new Chiron. *The Sun*, https://www.thesun.co.uk/motors/5129202/the-classic-1930s-bugatti-thats-worth-double-the-price-of-a-brand-new-chiron (archived at https://perma.cc/63WM-UWY2)

25 Braithwaite-Smith, G (2019) Extreme machines: the story of Bugatti, Motoring Research, https://www.motoringresearch.com/car-news/features/the-story-of-bugatti-cars (archived at https://perma.cc/CNY3-58P4)

26 Constantine, C (2019) Bugatti sold 70 Chirons this year, *The Drive*, https://www.thedrive.com/sheetmetal/17179/bugatti-sold-70-chirons-this-year (archived at https://perma.cc/CKH5-BTVM)

27 Anon (2019) Bugatti – Home, https://www.bugatti.com/Home (archived at https://perma.cc/9V73-XC2U)

28 Bartleby.com (2019) What is luxury? – 3096 Words, https://www.bartleby.com/essay/What-Is-Luxury-P3KNKCS57KGEZ (archived at https://perma.cc/77N5-X36X)

29 Ferla, R (2019) Chanel's life and works continue to inspire others, Nytimes.com. https://www.nytimes.com/2009/09/24/fashion/24chanel.html (archived at https://perma.cc/4PUX-CB57)

30 Bartleby.com (2019) What is luxury? – 3096 Words, https://www.bartleby.com/essay/What-Is-Luxury-P3KNKCS57KGEZ (archived at https://perma.cc/77N5-X36X)

31 Kara, R. (2017) How the 'I Heart NY' logo transcended marketing and endures 4 decades after its debut, *Adweek*, https://www.adweek.com/brand-marketing/how-the-i-heart-ny-logo-twice-transcended-marketing-and-endures-4-decades-after-its-debut (archived at https://perma.cc/27ZM-2X2J)

32 Kara, R. (2017) How the 'I Heart NY' logo transcended marketing and endures 4 decades after its debut, *Adweek*, https://www.adweek.com/brand-marketing/how-the-i-heart-ny-logo-twice-transcended-marketing-and-endures-4-decades-after-its-debut (archived at https://perma.cc/27ZM-2X2J)

33 Anholt, S (2019) Beyond the nation brand: the role of image and identity in international relations, SURFACE, https://surface.syr.edu/exchange/vol2/iss1/1 (archived at https://perma.cc/7AHC-JXLC), Used with permission of the author.

34 Statista 2018, Number of social media users worldwide from 2010 to 2021 (in billions), https://www.statista.com/statistics/278414/number-of-worldwide-social-network-users (archived at https://perma.cc/2RJB-9JTT)

35 Social Bakers (2018) Setting up a Strong Local-Global Social Media Strategy, https://www.socialbakers.com/social-media-content/studies/setting-up-a-strong-local-global-social-media-strategy (archived at https://perma.cc/H2XJ-JAQ3)

36 Thenewsminute.com (2019), https://www.thenewsminute.com/article/how-xiaomi-positioning-itself-more-smartphone-brand-india-89252 (archived at https://perma.cc/LC3D-VUYM)

37 XiaomiToday (2019) The Xiaomi's history until now – XiaomiToday, https://www.xiaomitoday.com/xiaomis-history (archived at https://perma.cc/5J8L-PWU7)

38 Wong, S (2019) Challenging Apple by imitation, Nytimes.com, https://www.nytimes.com/2012/10/29/technology/challenging-apple-by-imitation.html (archived at https://perma.cc/4T2W-GC28)

39 Medium (2019) Why did Nokia fail and what can you learn from it? https://medium.com/multiplier-magazine/why-did-nokia-fail-81110d981787 (archived at https://perma.cc/64YZ-8S6W)

40 Diffen.com (2019) Android vs iOS – difference and comparison, *Diffen*, https://www.diffen.com/difference/Android_vs_iOS (archived at https://perma.cc/LLS9-96M4)

41 Blog.mi.com (2019) [News] Xiaomi pioneers technology innovations with groundbreaking Mi 8 series – Mi Blog, http://blog.mi.com/en/2018/05/31/news-xiaomi-pioneers-technology-innovations-with-groundbreaking-mi-8-series (archived at https://perma.cc/45V3-834H)

42 Notebookcheck (2019) Xiaomi OS update roadmap revealed – Redmi Note 4 to remain on Nougat, https://www.notebookcheck.net/Xiaomi-OS-update-roadmap-revealed-Redmi-Note-4-to-remain-on-Nougat.309146.0.html (archived at https://perma.cc/38D7-PUWY)

43 Heath, A (2019) Chinese entrepreneur impersonates Steve Jobs and sells iPhone knockoffs, *Cult of Mac*, https://www.cultofmac.com/230180/chinese-entrepreneur-impersonates-steve-jobs-and-sells-iphone-knockoffs (archived at https://perma.cc/JSB4-YZPC)

44 Wong, S (2019) Challenging Apple by Imitation, Nytimes.com, https://www.nytimes.com/2012/10/29/technology/challenging-apple-by-imitation.html (archived at https://perma.cc/4T2W-GC28)

45 Gartner (2019) Gartner says global smartphone sales stalled in the fourth quarter of 2018, https://www.gartner.com/en/newsroom/press-releases/2019-02-21-gartner-says-global-smartphone-sales-stalled-in-the-fourth-quart (archived at https://perma.cc/62L4-X265)

12

Digital asset management and other strategies for managing brands

READING OUTCOMES

At the conclusion of this chapter, you should be able to:

- communicate the theory behind developing an effective marketing communication approval process;
- articulate the strategies for effectively managing global branding elements to ensure consistent execution;
- explain the ideal contents of an effective brand-guidelines manual, as well as the process for creating one;
- describe the key role that online project-management systems can play in effectively managing global brands.

Introduction

Theory is good only in so far as it can be drawn on to create effective brand-building programmes in the real, habitually messy, quickly changing world. For instance, it's easy to control logo, colour and font usage and make sure that the accurate brand elements are being employed when there is only one art director or designer creating all of the messaging. Consistent usage is much harder to ensure when there are hundreds of art directors and designers designing messaging for a brand across the globe.

The same holds true for the development of verbal brand messaging, particularly for capturing the appropriate tone and manner, let alone the messages. The hardest task is ensuring the alignment of on-brand atmospherics, which we discussed in

Chapter 6, as well as consumer-facing employee behaviour across offices for professional services and outlets for brick-and-mortar retailers.

What's more, many companies with global products and services have hundreds of people working on brand-building initiatives for each of its markets. With it, each professional can bring his or her interpretation of the brand, and some interpretations might run counter to others. (There's an old joke about marketing experts: put two in a room and you'll get three opinions.) As a result, there can be an additional break in ensuring brand consistency.

Finally, there's the mammoth job of physically managing the brand assets, so that every one of the hundreds of the professionals working on the brand are employing the appropriate versions. Logos get updated; fonts get tweaked; colours, images and brands sounds might be slightly revised; and, for place-based brands, olfactory scents get changed. Imperceptibly modernizing their brand elements is one way in which many brands stay current.

Fortunately, the theory set out in this book can be implemented on a global scale. The first hurdle is ensuring that the brand can be consistently represented by more than one person or by even a small group. To overcome it, there are guides to explain the brand and online asset-management systems, often tied to product-management tools. Let's start exploring this final chapter, which, though short, will be useful to you throughout your career.

Overview

We open by looking at a traditional brand-guidelines manual and, as a lucky-strike extra, we've included samples of the kind of language you might expect to find in one. We then run through online digital-asset- and project-management systems and the theory and practice of reviews and approvals. We'll conclude the main section with some failed attempts at creating a universal message for a brand – a powerful warning for any brand manager ready to embark on managing a globally distributed product or service. John Morrow, the leader of successful global business-process improvements for Colgate-Palmolive, Procter & Gamble, PepsiCo and Bristol-Myers Squibb, explores how technology enables global brand management. We close the chapter (and the book) with a look at Richard Branson and the Virgin brand.

Tools for managing a global brand

Managing a global brand is exponentially more complicated than managing one that is only available in a region, which in turn is exponentially more complicated than managing one that is only available in a single market. The easiest to manage are personal brands and those that are only available in a single location. But there are strategies and tools to help manage multi-market and global brand situations, with more tools becoming available every day, thanks in part to ever more sophisticated marketing technologies.

The first place to start is with the brand-guidelines manual, which can live online in a central portal or offline in a printed booklet. The main purpose of the manual is to ensure that the brand assets are applied in a uniform way. Knowledge is not enough when it comes to the dos and don'ts of how the brand should be delivered to the world. Employees must buy into the branding system and learn to protect it, and this starts with the branding guide. These guides should first present the corporate, product or service identity, demonstrate the correct use of the logotype and graphic elements, and explain the principles upon which the logotype and graphic elements have been designed. The typical table of contents for a brand-guidelines manual looks like this:

- General introduction
- Message from the CEO
- History
- Values
- Vision
- Mission
- Logotype
- How to use the logotype
- Logotype dos and don'ts
- Brand signature/tagline
- How to use colour
- Colour specifications
- Typography
- Vocabulary and word mark Requirements
- Trademark
- Materials guidelines, business cards, letterhead, envelopes, mailing label
- PowerPoint presentation
- Website
- Marketing communication expressions

Branding manuals are extremely important to anyone involved in the reproduction of the company's visual assets. Most people are not graphic designers or marketing professionals. However, in today's digital environment, many people have access to the graphic elements of many brands, and they use them at liberty. Trying to prevent individual interpretations of a logo application can only be done by issuing exact instructions in plain language. Here is an example of a comprehensive Branding Manual, also known as a 'Graphics Standards Manual'. Obviously, the tone and manner of the guide will be different for each brand and should be written in a way that reflects the personality of the brand. Pre-internet days, these manuals were printed and distributed among active members of the brand-identity keepers, stakeholders, ad agencies, printers and others in the supply chain. Today, these manuals generally live in the digital domain and are only accessible to authorized individuals.

In developing a brand manual, the instructions must be clear and direct. Senior executives must also stress the importance of flawless execution and execute flawlessly as well. The text below provides samples of the words, instructions and inspirations for a successful corporate identity programme. An introduction might include:

> The purpose of this manual is to provide information and direction by [The Company or Brand] for using and protecting our [corporate/product/service] brand identity. It is important that this information be consistently and conscientiously applied. Doing so strengthens the brand identity's reputation, credentials and value with our prospects, customers, investors, employees and others.
>
> Please read this thoroughly and keep for future reference. Maintaining brand consistency is important to us and all who do business with us, because it ensures that the [corporate/product/service] brand is applied in a standard manner.
>
> The pages that follow present our corporate identity. We've tried to make this manual as concise, convenient and as easy to use as possible. It provides the tools and instructions in the creation of new materials, from our sales presentations and internal documents to packaging and in-store communications. The instructions should make it easier to make the right decisions, according to the proper positioning of our brand.
>
> No deviation from these guidelines is permissible without prior consultation with [name person or department]. Where deviations exist or occur, please consult with [name person or department] so course corrections can be made.

It might also include a message from the CEO, something like:

> Every employee of [The Company] has an important stake in the consistent presentation of our brand and use of our logotype and graphic elements. You may also have a role in helping ensure that the brand is being used correctly by our customers and other external stakeholders. For that reason, we are sharing this Brand Identity Manual with all of you.
>
> [The Company] brand has evolved and grown over the years. Our business continues to grow by providing value to our customers not only through the product itself, but through the impact our brand has on consumers as well. We have invested in advertising, marketing support and consumer research to strengthen our brand in the minds of our target consumer, and we will continue to do so in the future. We believe these efforts will allow us to serve a greater number and variety of customers – [name job titles] by increasingly distinguishing our brand from competitors, who try to take advantage and capitalize on our success by using elements of our name and brand identity.

Customers see our brand on a variety of marketing materials, presentations and company communications, as well as on our website and social media. Customers often use our brand identity on their own websites and see our brand on packaging, in-store environments and in advertising and other communication channels. Most of this activity is created, coordinated or supervised by the Marketing Department. During your work at [The Company], you may have a need to order printed materials, or use our logotype and other brand elements on social media or in some other manner or medium. Whenever you do so, you will be communicating the brand to [audience]. To ensure that our brand continues to create the maximum possible value for our customers, it is vital that we use it consistently. Please read through this Manual carefully and consult it whenever you intend to employ the brand in communication, regardless of form.

I hope you share my enthusiasm for the brand identity, and that you will feel as strongly as I do about the importance of protecting its value by speaking and referring to the brand accurately, using the logotype, identity elements and guidelines contained in this Manual in a consistent manner.

Thanks for your cooperation and continuing contribution to our success. [Signature of CEO]

Next, a history of the organization should be included, starting from its earliest days. It might be similar to the legendary collaboration of Steve Jobs and Steve Wozniak (if you are lucky) and should include the driving inspiration behind the company. It should mention every key step that led to your company's most current success story.

Other contents should include your corporate values, social and environmental initiatives. Sample phrases might include:

- As a company dedicated to social and environmental responsibility, we're proud of our initiatives in these areas. We feel that our commitment is reflected in everything we do.
- Each year, we make a contribution to [charity]; and an international non-profit organization founded to [name mission and focus areas].
- We're certified by [name], in accordance with [name] standards.

For your environmental programme, you might want to go into more depth, including the ways your organization is working to reduce the amount of waste it produces as well as how it is recycling items and encouraging the reuse of other items, which are key concerns of many employees. For example:

Company-wide recycling

Our environmental programme is defined by [drop in how the company is contributing to the protection of the environment], including re-bagging most of our outgoing products into the original packaging, reducing our need to use additional packaging. In instances where the original bags are not suitable for reuse, we recycle them to be manufactured into other packaging. In addition, all employees are actively involved in our company-wide recycling programme, which encompasses paper, plastics, cardboard, metals and glass. In addition, all dust or chaff that is removed from raw materials as a result of our pre- and post-cleaning process is directed to a local compost facility. Finally, where possible, our printed materials and brochures make use of the most environmentally friendly stock available. We often use 100% recyclable, chlorine-free paper that is partly composed of post-consumer waste.

As you can see, it's important to be explicit in the expectations and standards. Of course, every company or brand is different, and the initiatives and expectations need to align with the brand. Next, the manual should talk about the name, logotype and brand colours. For example:

Our Logotype

The Company logotype involves three major elements:

- The Symbol: identify in words
- The Type: identify in words
- The Colours: identify in words

Each of these elements has been carefully crafted so that it contributes to the overall impact of our brand in all its environments. Therefore, none of these elements should be removed, changed or altered in any way. Remember, consistency is important.

[The Company] logotype will be reproduced on printed materials and in online and in-store environments, so all stakeholders who will use this logotype no matter what the environment or surface must adhere to the following basic rules. First, it is important to use [The Company] logotype in its entirety for several reasons:

- The use of the logotype is not an exercise in aesthetics, but rather an execution of business strategy.

- A logotype is only as strong as the perception associated with it, and that perception needs to be continually reinforced as demonstrated by consistent usage.
- Consistent display of [The Company] logotype builds the brand, while minimizing confusion.

How to use the logotype

- Position: being a circle, [The Company] logotype is a perfect, well balanced and anchored shape, and should never be tilted or turned upside down.
- Clear space: whenever the logotype is used, no matter how large or small, maintain enough clear space around the logotype for maximum impact and clarity. The clear space should be of the same height as the 'X' in our logo and there should be the same space all around the logo, in all directions. See the diagram indicating how to determine the amount of space to leave around the logotype.
- Logotype art files: when reproducing the logotype, use the appropriate master art files, which are available from [The Company Marketing Department or name the individual responsible]. These master art files should never be altered or manipulated in any way or be recreated from scratch. The master art files should be used as a basis for all applications of the logotype.[1]
- Sizing: depending on where it is used, the logotype may be reproduced in different sizes. However, it should never be reproduced in a size smaller than X/X" (X.X cm) in diameter.

Following these general rules will ensure legibility and the importance or effect of the logotype in all printed materials and communications.

The Company logo is available on the [name the location].

- Logotype dos:[2]
  - Always use [The Company] logotype as a circular unit [for example] without adding any space, in white or colour, around the black or white border lines. Notice that the only place to use the blue colour [for example] is in the inside circle, and never on the mark, the ® or the outer black circle.
  - The logotype can be produced entirely in black when needed.
  - Remove the black border line when the entire background is dark in tones, or the logotype is placed on photography, as demonstrated here.
  - Keep the black border line when the entire background is light in tone.
- Logotype don'ts:
  - Do not change the proportions of the logotype. Keep the entire circular unit intact under all circumstances.

- Do not use the black border line when the entire background is a dark tone, or the logotype is placed on photography, as demonstrated here. Do not reverse the background of the logotype out of dark or photographic backgrounds, as demonstrated here.

Brand signature/tagline

- Brand signature – a defining characteristic of the brand used in conjunction with the brand logotype.
- Tagline – a brand positioning line or promise used in advertising and marketing materials.
  - As market conditions evolve, [The Company] tagline may change. This is why we have kept any taglines or brand signatures outside the border of the circular shape of the logotype.
  - Currently, we are using the line: [drop in line] and that line should always be used as shown. However, for the purposes of packaging design, in-store communications and other promotional activities, that tagline could be dropped with the circular logotype used as a free-standing design element.

Colour

The use of colour in The Company corporate identity requires a very simple colour palette. First, be aware of the materials that the logotype will be printed on. The Company logotype requires a white background. If the graphic execution requires a colour stock, please make sure to add the white colour under The Company circular logotype. When using PMS coded colours, be sure to distinguish between Coated, Uncoated and Matte stocks. The letters C, U and M next to the colour number identifies these alternatives.

When [The Company] logotype is used in a four-colour printing process, make sure that the blue portion of the logotype is made of 68% Cyan and 34% Magenta. In spot colour applications, use PMS 279 as the blue colour. Online, use the following RGB values for the blue colour: 102.102.255 [sample only].

Always use 100% solid black for the colour of the other elements of the logotype [sample only].

It is preferable to use the CMYK breakdowns by converting PMS colours to CMYK within any software such as Adobe Illustrator®, Adobe InDesign®, or QuarkXPress™ [sample only]

Colour specifications

The colours shown are The Company colours. You may use the PANTONE colours indicated to the right instead of the SWISS WATER® Process colours. The standards for the PANTONE Colors are shown in the current edition of the PANTONE Colour Formula Guide. The PANTONE MATCHING SYSTEM® is a worldwide printing, publishing and packaging colour language for the selection, marketing and control of colour.[3]

- Specifications: for all key print and on-screen requirements, it is preferable to use the CMYK breakdowns by converting PANTONE® colours to CMYK within any software such as Adobe Illustrator® or QuarkXPress™.
- Marketing, Advertising and Printed Promotional Materials: for commercial printing and duplication of marketing, advertising and promotional materials, a PMS or CMYK colour is required. Chart should be provided for specifications.
- Web: each colour in the primary and highlight colour palettes is assigned a web-safe colour. These equivalents are the only colours that are appropriate for use. No substitutions are to be considered. Chart should be provided for specifications.
- PowerPoint: a template has been created with a colour palette to accommodate the unique requirements of Microsoft PowerPoint®. These specific colours are embedded within the template. These equivalents are the only colours that are appropriate for use.

Typography

The primary font for The Company brand communications and materials is Trade Gothic, from the Trade Gothic family, a Linotype AG typeface distributed by Adobe Systems Inc.[4] The font embedded in the logotype should never be altered under any circumstances. Always use Trade Gothic for graphic design in print and online applications. However, employees who prepare sales presentations, whether printed or projected, can use non-serif fonts such as Arial and Verdana as replacements for Trade Gothic, when necessary.

Text should be presented simply and directly. It should not be rendered three-dimensionally, in outline or with drop shadows.

All specifications of type, point size, alignment and leading have been embedded into the featured samples of Microsoft Word® and PowerPoint® templates.[5] The use of these templates not only ensures consistent style, but also avoids the need to adjust settings for each letter or presentation.

Vocabulary and word mark requirements

- Brand name
  - As previously noted, the brand name is [The Company]®. Abbreviations such as TC® or The C are to be avoided, as we need to set the standard for our customers and suppliers to follow with respect to proper treatment and protection of our brand as a registered trademark. In printed material, the brand name should always be used as an adjective, in capital letters with the trademark notice. The Company® word mark must always appear as two words, 'The' and 'Company', in lower-case letters of equal height. Spacing between characters should not be altered. The two words 'The' and 'Company' must appear on the same line of text unless restricted by space limitations. In headlines, subheads and body copy of promotional material, 'The Company®' must be set in Trade Gothic font.

- Company name
  - The official name of our company is [The Company Inc]. When using the company name in documents or printed materials, write it with capital and lower-case letters for the words 'The' and 'Company' and leave off the trademark notice ®, which should not be included in the company name at any time. Please use 'The Company' in the first instance without the abbreviation after it. When speaking about the company or referring to it, use the full name, not a shortened form of it. For example, do not say: 'I work for T Company,' or 'Good morning, The C.'
  - Please reference the company name, The Company, and the brand name, The Company®, in their entirety when communicating with suppliers and customers, particularly over the phone or via email. Do not reproduce any art from printed pages of this document by scanning or copying. Always use the correct downloaded file for your project.

Trademark

The required trademark footnote text must accompany the logotype on printed materials. It should appear in black only at the bottom of the panel in which the logotype appears. The text should be set in 5pt Trade Gothic Medium. When setting the type, do not use the keyboard ™ symbol, spell it out as 'TM' so that it is the same height as the other capital letters. ®/TM are trademarks of The Company.

For more information

- Content or technical support
  - For content issues, technical support related to the Brand Identity Manual, electronic templates and artwork and technical support on how to use them, please contact The Company Marketing Department, or submit your questions via email: [The Company], Marketing Department, 800.XXX.XXXX or 1.800.XXX.XXXX ext. XXX, info@thecompany.com.
- Templates and art files
  - Templates can be obtained by contacting the Marketing Department. The Company® logo is available on the company drive, in the folder '/marketing/graphics/logo'.

Business card

The following guidelines and example will help you develop, create and reproduce the business card. The business card should be created in 2" X 3.5" only. It should be printed using two colours: blue PMS 279 [for example] and black. Do not try to print these business cards using CMYK process and colour separation. The recommended paper for business cards is: Crane's Choice Fluorescent White Wove Cover, 110lb. An alternative could be: International Paper Strathmore®, ultimate white, 97% brightness, wove, 110lb.[6] Templates can be obtained by contacting the Marketing Department.

Letterhead

The following guidelines and examples will help to develop, create and produce our official letterhead. Do not try to print any official letterhead using CMYK process and colour separation. Our official letterhead is printed on 8.5" x 11" paper. It should be printed using two colours: blue PMS 279 and black. Recommended paper specifications are: International Paper Strathmore® Writing, Ultimate White, 77% brightness, 25%, cotton, wove, laser-compatible, 24lb. Templates can be obtained by contacting the Marketing Department.

Envelopes

The following guidelines and examples will help to develop, create and produce #10 envelopes and 10" x 12" envelopes. Do not try to print any official letterhead using CMYK process and colour separation. Use #10 and 10" x 12" standard envelopes. Recommended paper specifications are as follows: International Paper Strathmore® Writing, ultimate white, 77% brightness, 25% cotton, wove, laser-compatible, commercial flap. Templates can be obtained by contacting the Marketing Department.

PowerPoint presentation

The following guidelines and examples will help you develop PowerPoint® presentations. For electronic presentations, you will require Microsoft® PowerPoint 20XX, or a later edition. PowerPoint templates allow for creativity, while also maintaining consistency by providing predetermined fonts and colour palette, which are embedded within the templates.

Remember that less is more in presentations. Keep the amount of information on each slide to a reasonable length. Instead of trying to include everything on a particular subject in one slide, divide the information into several slides. Generally speaking, use one key point or topic per slide. Use 'headlines' at the top of each slide, with more detailed, supporting information in the body. The best presentations have a flow from slide to slide. Use animation sparingly, for emphasis of key points. Be selective when importing photography and try to keep it consistent in style. Templates can be obtained by contacting the Marketing Department.

Managing a global brand beyond the brand-guidelines manual

The brand-guidelines manual and other formalized guidelines are your first step to managing a brand. Global brands need a centralized location to keep all of the materials, ensuring up-to-date key messaging direction and brand elements. Many different systems have already been developed to ensure compliance with brand standards and guarantee consistency in brand manifestation in all global markets. There are many providers who offer cloud-based portal services for brand assets platforms. These platforms offer essential services for as little as US $150 (£120) a month, usually for small brands. Those services may include content management, a portal for up to 100 monthly visitors and storage of up to 250GB. They will allow for custom branding, unlimited sharing, email and chat support, InDesign plug-in and help from the hosting company.

These services, limited as they may seem, can help ensure the integrity of a brand. Brand managers can rely on them as an important safety mechanism for future growth into regional, national and even international territories. For larger brands, the monthly fee will increase, but so will the level of service, storage (it can go up to 2TB) and number of unique monthly visitors. Larger organizations, perhaps with a global brand presence, can hire monthly services of brand platform compliance for about $1,000 (£800) a month, including unlimited storage as well as all of the other services we've already mentioned.

Because data is overwhelming almost any brand today, there are other ways to protect a brand through monitoring the content published about it. Certain services monitor web pages, influencer content and opinions, affiliate links related to the brand, relevant content, social posts and blog feeds related to the brand and more. Furthermore, they can examine and analyze content for compliance with the brand by comparing content against the brand policy rules.

It's important to note that the word 'content' can mean different things in different locations as well as within different locations, especially for global products or services, creating an extra challenge for those working to maintain the integrity of their brand. Maintaining a consistent image for a global brand, however, is a very powerful message to all, one that requires full compliance and very strong strategic corporate communication ability. Brands must develop very clearly defined brand compliance standards, to allow the brand compliance technology to perform its job.

One point of view on how things should be done was presented by Angie Geffen, vice president of marketing for Perion Networks, in an interview with Matt Robins for his blog: 'Many brands already market to different countries, but they tend to focus on individual countries rather than a global strategy. Therefore, they have multiple campaigns running, and each is operating independently. Each campaign is tailored to the specific country in question. However, those campaigns are not operating in conjunction with one another. They might as well be for different brands – they are so different and have absolutely nothing to do with one another.'[7]

Centralized brand-compliance resources

One strategy utilized to keep brand strategy and implementation on-point in multinational markets is to leverage brand-management software to pull in resources into one cohesive system worldwide. Many are already using a global marketing portal as an online, on-demand repository that assists marketing departments and sales teams with approved brand assets. This tool is being used as the undisputed authorized authority on how to access, customize and distribute all marketing content in all global environments, including social selling situations. Organizations can even organize their materials by the different cultures, languages, consumer behaviours and economic and ethnic demographics that they serve.

These tools allow a centralized brand team to control the brand while giving employees content when and how they need it. Without such a brand compliance portal in place, employees tend to argue, invent new ways, or even independently create such content as proposals, presentations, brochures, reports, micro-sites, invitations, blog posts and sales emails. Of course, such activity is counter-productive and even harmful in the long run.

As mentioned earlier, a centralized brand-assets-management system offers a corporate-controlled collection of the approved digital assets and multi-channel templates for every brand touchpoint. Local operators can use them with corporate HQ's pre-permission and authorization. These operators can also customize and create relevant brand assets or campaigns that meet the specific needs of local demographics and target audiences, allowing local marketers to apply customization while maintaining brand consistency at every global brand touchpoint.

When all company branches, as well as ad agencies, have access, localization and ways to distribute the latest marketing materials, they are able to secure a more consistent customer experience with a brand, as every brand touchpoint is on-brand strategy, updated constantly and relevant. Such marketing asset portals allow companies to enable all employees and trade partners to have equal access to materials that can be customized within pre-approved brand guidelines.

Tim Calkins, Clinical Professor of Marketing at the Kellogg School of Management at Northwestern University, sums it up consistency as 'getting an entire organization to embrace the brand and live up to the brand promise over time. Brands are created through a wide range of touchpoints; every time customers interact with a brand, they form associations. Consistency matters, and it matters at every turn.'[8] Large multinational brands are capable of doing all of this work on their own, and many do. The task of overseeing these activities is not always an exclusive activity of the marketing department but can be assigned to special units with different names within an organization.

What's more, 'technology can move brand management's perspective from the past to the present and the future. Because real-time tools are now available, the point of reference has changed from what was done three months ago to what is being proposed for the next three months,' reported Danielle Sauvé, Vice President of Marketing at Esko, in a recent email to the authors. In addition, technology can increase the efficiency of the brand's management activities.

One way in which these new technological platforms can increase efficiency is by reducing the number of points needed for human creative reviews and approvals. In an ideal world with perfect knowledge and execution, no reviews and sign-offs, in theory, would be needed. The marketers would simply create the on-brand messages, the art directors and designers would bring the ideas to life with all of the branding elements being applied correctly (and with the most recent elements), and coders and printers would produce on-brand executions. Unfortunately, it's not a perfect world and the traditional strategic and creative presentations and executional reviews are helpful at the primary points where something can go wrong through off-brand messaging and improper interpretation or execution of the brand standards. In many ways, it's a 'fix-on-fail' system. However, artificial-intelligence-based marketing technology can now be used to review the executions, with often better results than a review by professional marketers, greatly reducing the number of needed reviews and sign-offs.[9]

The promise for future enhancements is even greater. In the same email, Danielle also wrote, 'Advances like virtual and augmented reality, artificial intelligence, connectivity and automation are not solely reserved for consumer experiences. All of these tools can be powerfully applied to the way in which companies create products and packaging. This digital transformation of how work is done promises to deliver more speed to market, higher quality and lower costs.'[10] Of course, most of all, it can help ensure greater consistency for global brands.

Some failed attempts at creating a consistent and appropriate brand message

When it comes to global brand building efforts, we're programmed to think globally, every corporation aspires to be a global one and sell products and services in multiple markets – and business schools educate today's MBA students to think globally. However, not everybody agrees that developing one global campaign for a brand is indeed the best solution. It's important to listen to these reservations when it comes to determining the global brand approach. For example, Jeremy Swartz, Vice President of customer engagement firm Thunderhead in Australia and New Zealand, said in an interview with B&T: 'It all starts with listening. Rather than projecting what you think a customer should be doing, rather than guessing the journey you think your customer is taking to buy your products, investigate to see what is actually going on. Once marketers start listening it will soon become clear what the next best channel is. But it all starts with the passive listening.'[11]

Technology allows all of us to listen, and there is no doubt that many brands do just that. There is also no doubt that what they hear is different from one side of the globe to the other. Cultural habits alone would be a reason not to create 'one size fits all' brand campaigns and brand behaviour all over the globe. And yet, sometimes large, famous and respected brands do not pay enough attention.

Pepsi, for instance, attempted to address racial issues by positioning the brand as one with unifying and good intentions. The PepsiCo Global Beverage Group President, Brad Jakeman, teamed with Pepsi's Content Creators League, an in-house agency, to create a spot featuring Kendall Jenner, who was shown at a protest march handing out cans of Pepsi to the riot police.[12] Not only was the spot rejected by many on social media, it was also ridiculed on late-night shows in the US market.[13] Eventually, it was pulled, and Brad Jakeman had to resign his post.[14] It is hard to believe that this ad was planned for global distribution via TV and on social media.[15]

Another example of an inappropriate ad was one that Audi aired in China, in which a groom's mother pops up in the middle of the wedding ceremony to 'examine the merchandise', checking to see if the bride is worthy of marrying her son.[16] The ad was considered distinctly insulting to women. While the ad did not support the global brand positioning of Audi, the brand stewards in China felt that for local consumption, this kind of humour would be appropriate.[17] Even if the message was felt to be appropriate in the Chinese market and consistent with the Audi brand, we must not forget that TV commercials are used in more media than just broadcast. They're featured on YouTube and other places. The Audi ad was rightfully shared on social media by many who wanted to shame the company for the offending commercial.

An ad that was racist, pure and simple,[18] was put out by well-known and well-liked global brand, Unilever's Dove Soap. In it, the visual changed from one model to another, sending out a simple message: Dove is good for any skin. Despite the fact that the brand stayed on message and strategy, it was found to be offensive because the model's ethnicity changed from African-American to white.[19] It didn't take long for this ad to create a global social-media firestorm,[20] which put Unilever in the position of having to implement damage-control measures over enabling brand growth.

Onwards

We hope and believe that this book has given you the strategies, tools and perspectives not only to avoid these failed attempts, but to build programmes that succeed in growing and managing a global brand. There's one more thing to remember: as Calvin Coolidge, President of the United States 1923–9, reportedly said, 'Press on!' Persistence is indeed the key trait for building a successful career as a global brand manager. And now you have the tools to get started.

HOW TECHNOLOGY ENABLES GLOBAL BRAND MANAGEMENT – A GUEST PERSPECTIVE FROM JOHN MORROW, USA

While managing brand assets on a global scale can sound theoretical, it's done every day. To get the inside scoop on how to do it, we asked someone with extensive experience – John Morrow. He has led successful global business process improvements at Colgate-Palmolive, Procter & Gamble, PepsiCo and Bristol-Myers Squibb. His work has covered Packaging Artwork Systems, Omni-Channel Marketing Systems, R&D/Product Development Systems and Quality Assurance Systems. Most recently, John was Worldwide Director of Global Artwork Operations at Colgate-Palmolive where he led the successful implementation of Colgate's Global Artwork Management System. This included the global rollout of the Esko Webcenter software and resulted in a two-thirds reduction in global artwork cycle-times.

John earned a Bachelor of Science degree in Chemical Engineering from the University of Notre Dame and an MBA in Marketing from Xavier University. He retired from Colgate in early 2018 and now runs his own consulting practice for business process improvements. Here's what John has to say:

> 'Marketplace disruptions caused by the rapid growth in e-commerce and social media are posing major threats and opportunities for CPG companies. Designing innovative products and packages that delight consumers has always been important, but innovation today needs to be faster, more effective and less expensive than ever before. Strong marketing implementation has also always been important, but the complex environment today requires a highly efficient integrated omni-channel approach. Technology can help enable these transformations.
>
> Design innovation will continue to play an increasingly important role for CPG companies. Many articles have been written about why design-led companies are more successful than other companies. Companies that follow 'design thinking' principles are simply more successful at understanding true consumer needs, and at brainstorming, prototyping and testing new ideas that better meet consumer needs.
>
> 'The first three steps of the 'design thinking process' are highly people-centric activities where cross-functional teams 'empathize' with consumers to understand their needs, 'define' a problem statement, and 'ideate' potential solutions. When they move to the prototyping and testing phases, there is a major need for rapid prototyping capability to quickly and cost-effectively iterate through multiple different scenarios. This is an area where technology can play a major role.
>
> '3D design technologies and virtual reality technologies provided by companies like Esko and Dassault can allow global cross-functional teams to quickly and inexpensively create multiple realistic prototype ideas and then test them in simulated store-shelf and/or home-use environments. Learnings from one iteration can then be quickly incorporated into the next iteration of prototyping and testing until the successful idea is developed and validated.
>
> 'In addition to aiding marketing designs, technology can also be used to facilitate better functional package design. For example, companies at the leading edge of e-commerce implementation are realizing that they often need different types of packaging uniquely designed for the e-commerce channel. Again, 3D design technology and simulated testing technology can help make this process faster, more

effective and less expensive. These technologies can also help in the design and implementation of more sustainable packaging, a critically important idea for many consumers and for society in general.

'Strong marketing implementation today requires an integrated omni-channel approach. Companies must communicate a consistent and compelling message across all channels. This includes e-ommerce, social media and direct-to-consumer channels without forgetting about more traditional brick-and-mortar, point-of-sale and print channels. This poses a major data complexity challenge which is a major opportunity for new technology.

'Package label design is often at the centre of this complexity and opportunity. This is often the one place where key brand information such as logos, graphics, colours and marketing claims come together with key product information such as ingredient statements, warning statements, usage instructions and product endorsements. It is an important brand-management requirement, and often a legal requirement, that all of these individual elements be correct and consistent across all products and all distribution channels.

'Since many of these individual elements are developed and approved by different groups, this creates a major logistics and data-management challenge. This is where technology, process and organization improvements are often needed.

'To manage this situation, many companies start with sophisticated artwork management software such as Esko Webcenter or Blue Software. These provide the platform for global cross-functional teams to collaborate on the development and approval of all artwork elements, which is a great start. But it is only a start.

'Since many of the individual elements of the artwork are often developed and approved in different places, this can lead to delays, inefficiencies and errors. That is why it is also important for companies to use internally developed or externally purchased content-management systems to integrate all of the individual systems into one efficient and accurate process.

'Once the package is developed and approved, it is also important that it be consistently and appropriately presented across all distribution channels. The image and required information will look different on a smartphone, a tablet, on a store shelf or in a promotional pack. But they all need to be accurate and they all need to convey a consistent brand message. In order to manage this complexity, many companies are integrating their artwork management software with digital asset management software.

'Technology by itself is not enough to address these challenges and opportunities. It is also critical to optimize the process workflows themselves, and to optimize organization structure and roles and responsibilities. For example, instead of developing individual package elements separately and sequentially, it could be more efficient and effective to have processes and org structures that coordinate the design and development of on-shelf packs, promotion packs and images for e-commerce and social media at the same time.

'The implementation of a new technology can often be used as the justification for also optimizing the process workflow and organization roles and responsibilities. And of course, it is absolutely critical to have strong senior management support, or the entire effort could be a waste of time.

'All of this is complicated enough if you are operating in one geography. It becomes even more complicated for large global companies who need to balance the needs of global-brand consistency with the needs of local-market implementation. But the solution is the same. You need well-defined processes, with clear roles and responsibilities, and the help of robust technologies.

'E-commerce and social media are causing major market disruptions that are creating major challenges and opportunities for CPG companies. Companies that embrace and lead transformations in process, organization and technology will likely be successful in the future. Companies that fall behind in these transformations will likely lose market share, and many may eventually go out of business.'

EXTENDED CASE STUDY: VIRGIN, A DIFFERENT KIND OF GLOBAL BRAND

Virgin is a truly all-encompassing global brand, which includes products, services and everything in between, in all five continents. Virgin-branded companies include Virgin Atlantic, Virgin Mobile, Virgin Media, Virgin Life Care, Virgin Digital, Virgin Poker, Virgin Credit Card, Virgin Trains, Virgin Radio, Virgin Games, Virgin Coffee and Virgin Green Fund.

No other brand to our knowledge has ventured into such rich and different categories of consumer goods and services. There must be something special and magical about the brand and its founder, something that separates it from other corporations and gives this cheeky brand a chance as it competes with some of the world's biggest conglomerates. It all started with music.

Every piece of research about Richard Branson points to the significance of his early days and the student magazine he published, where young unknown musicians such as Mick Jagger were interviewed.[21] Legend has it that the name 'Virgin' came about when one of the employees at Branson's music company observed that they were all new to the world of business, virgins without much experience.[22]

Looking back, the name is appropriate because Virgin ventures into many business categories without having much experience in that particular category. After all, Virgin Atlantic, the airline, was born out of a complete accidental turn of events.[23] It was the first line of business that Branson chose to try his hands at outside the music business, where he was already considered a veteran. The way Virgin conducts business is not for the sake of 'invading' business categories they don't know, but because they find a way to improve something for the consumer. They add value and customer experience to any brand that they create or purchase.

Since the early days, when Virgin was in the music business, they found that their music stores could compete head-on with the large music retail outlets and offer better price and service. Eventually, the Virgin record shop opened on London's Oxford Street and ventured further into the music recording business under the brand Virgin Records. Here the brand had the good fortune to lease recording time to artists such as Mike Oldfield, The Sex Pistols, Rolling Stones, UB40, Steve Winwood and other rock stars. The close association of these big stars with the recording label generated a great brand image for Virgin. No other record label of those days could feature executives and managers that looked and sounded like Mick Jagger.[24] Virgin was a current and relevant brand with which fans could identify and feel an affiliation for. Virgin was a fun brand!

Branson instinctively knew how to do things differently. The cultural scene in London of the late 1960s was awash with a new, radical movement. These were the years when The Beatles, Rolling Stones, Mary Quant, Carnaby Street, Twiggy and mod subculture were dominant. The scene was about fun and hedonism.[25] Richard Branson understood the mood and the behaviour models of the consumers during that time. His Virgin brand was a perfect match for the needs and wants of those customers.

Branson was once quoted as saying: 'There is no point in starting your own business unless you do it out of a sense of frustration.[26] Indeed, he was always frustrated with big, boring, slow-moving, boardroom-driven corporations that didn't deliver enough good service, and whose products were not innovative or consumer-value-driven. He always positioned his brands as the underdog, fighting the established bureaucratic firm with new creative offerings. He cultivated a brand personality that:

- flaunts the rules;
- has a sense of humour, which is occasionally outrageous;
- positions itself as an underdog willing to take on the establishment;
- executes flawlessly with high standards.

In addition, the brand has a wealth of symbols:

- Richard Branson the person and his perceived lifestyle;
- Virgin blimp, a great promotional tool used only by a few, most notably Good Year;
- Virgin script logo, unique and different – it's almost a personal signature.

Its core identity elements include:

- service: consistent best-of quality delivered with humour and flair;
- innovation: first with value-added features and services;

- entertainment: Virgin is a fun company;
- value: present in all its offerings, not just the high-priced option.

In essence, the Virgin brand is about iconoclasm and breaking with tradition. Based on our outsider analysis, the Virgin brand identity and value proposition elements could be broken down thus:

- functional benefits: a value offering with quality, plus innovative extras delivered with flair and humour;
- emotional benefits: pride in being associated with the underdog with an attitude; fun, good times;
- self-expressive benefits: willingness to go against the establishment, to be a bit outrageous.

Based on the Virgin case study, as well as insights from the rest of the book, here are some key takeaways. Every brand should own at least one superior position on a key feature or product attribute. Functional benefits are not to be underestimated simply because most product features can be imitated. For example, Volvo has claimed safety safety as its 'superior product attribute' since its introduction to America. Brand symbols, including logos, can be good metaphors for a product's functional benefit. The Pillsbury Doughboy, for example, is a metaphor for fresh and light foods, and the classic Prudential Rock indicates financial strength. Symbols are a great way to communicate factual information.

Emotional benefits are easier to maintain and keep distinct from competitors'. They give the customer a positive feeling. Volvo's safety feature is doubly strong because it makes the customer feel safe as well. A person can feel warm and caring when buying a Hallmark card or rugged owning Caterpillar boots. A study by the marketing and communications company Young and Rubicam showed that, on their own, functional benefits are more effective than emotional benefits, but that the two working together are stronger than either individually.

KEY TERMS

- brand compliance standards
- brand guidelines-manual/brand manual
- corporate identity
- global marketing portal

DISCUSSION QUESTIONS

- What is the theory behind developing an effective marketing communication approval process?
- What are some key strategies for effectively managing global branding elements to ensure consistent execution?
- What are the contents of an effective brand-guidelines manual? What is the process for creating one?
- How do online project-management systems help brand managers effectively manage global brands?

Notes

1 Note: with online digital-asset-management systems, the logotype should always be taken from it for every project to ensure that it's the latest version.

2 Note: As far as possible, describe the visual elements in detail.

3 All registered trademarks are property of their respective owners.

4 All registered trademarks are property of their respective owners.

5 All registered trademarks are property of their respective owners.

6 All registered trademarks are property of their respective owners.

7 Roberts, M (2019) 3 Strategies used by global companies to ensure brand compliance, *MarcomCentral*, https://marcom.com/blog/three-strategies-used-by-global-companies-to-ensure-brand-compliance (archived at https://perma.cc/3KB9-3P7J)

8 Tybout, A and Calkins, T, Eds (2018) P Kotler, Foreword, *Kellogg on Branding, The marketing faculty of the Kellogg School of Management*, John Wiley & Sons, Inc, Hoboken

9 Sellers, A (2019) The Intersection of technology, design and packaging: what we can learn from a Rochester Institute of Technology Professor, https://www.simplifymypackaging.com/home/2018/2/15/the-intersection-of-technology-design-and-packaging-what-we-can-learn-from-a-rochester-institute-of-technology-professor (archived at https://perma.cc/GLZ3-YSUE)

10 Sauvé, D (2018) VP, Marketing, Esko, in an email to the authors

11 Bastick, J (2018) Why global campaigns often don't work globally, *B&T*, bandt.com.au, http://www.bandt.com.au/marketing/why-global-campaigns-often-dont-work-globally (archived at https://perma.cc/EM43-54VC)

12 YouTube (2017) Full Pepsi commercial starring Kendall Jenner, https://www.youtube.com/watch?v=uwvAgDCOdU4 (archived at https://perma.cc/ADP9-MAZX)

13 Whitehead, M (2019) Kendall Jenner's Pepsi ad is being absolutely ridiculed online, *HuffPost* (Australia), https://www.huffingtonpost.com.au/2017/04/04/kendall-jenners-pepsi-ad-is-being-absolutely-ridiculed-online_a_22026158 (archived at https://perma.cc/C8VK-C2XX)

14 Schultz, E J (2017) Brad Jakeman is leaving PepsiCo to start a consultancy, Adage.com, https://adage.com/article/cmo-strategy/brad-jakeman-leaving-pepsico-start-a-consultancy/310943 (archived at https://perma.cc/P7VF-9LAY)

15 YouTube (2017) Full Pepsi commercial starring Kendall Jenner, https://www.youtube.com/watch?v=uwvAgDCOdU4 (archived at https://perma.cc/ADP9-MAZX)

16 YouTube (2017) This Audi commercial in China compares women to used cars, https://www.youtube.com/watch?v=UEKgxwBfw_c (archived at https://perma.cc/U95A-4KL6)

17 YouTube (2017) When Chinese Audi's advertising creates a bad buzz, https://www.youtube.com/watch?v=VCEkkcGKrB8 (archived at https://perma.cc/3UQX-ELLC)

18 YouTube (2017) Dove apologizes for what some called a racially insensitive ad, https://www.youtube.com/watch?v=JdmUu0txO3I (archived at https://perma.cc/2HWV-GQCE)

19 YouTube (2017) People are accusing this Dove ad of being racist, https://www.youtube.com/watch?v=zkIrbVycAeM (archived at https://perma.cc/2GLA-A6DA)

20 YouTube (2017) #DoneWithDove: racist soap ad creates social media furor, https://www.youtube.com/watch?v=-KHMs_iBATY&t=4s (archived at https://perma.cc/5TW2-266W)

21 *India Today* (2019) Richard Branson reveals his relationship with The Rolling Stones in his autobiography, https://www.indiatoday.in/lifestyle/culture/story/richard-branson-the-rolling-stones-mick-jagger-finding-my-virginity-book-lifest-1075264-2017-11-05 (archived at https://perma.cc/C7NM-SLXL)

22 Virgin. (2019) What's in a name? https://www.virgin.com/richard-branson/whats-name (archived at https://perma.cc/5EZJ-57NB)

23 Virgin. (2019) Why did Richard Branson start an airline? https://www.virgin.com/travel/why-did-richard-branson-start-airline (archived at https://perma.cc/5RH6-DR4E)

24 Ressner, J (1992) Stones sign deal with Virgin, *Rolling Stone*, https://www.rollingstone.com/music/music-news/stones-sign-deal-with-virgin-183866 (archived at https://perma.cc/X5UT-RBMJ)

25 Amazon.com (2019) https://www.amazon.com/Swinging-London-Inside-Story-Capital/dp/1783130091 (archived at https://perma.cc/LJQ4-GVQL)

26 Armstrong, M, Miller, W, Menders, D, Johnson, Z, Jones, K, Thomas, A, Fang, M, Escalona, A, Merilee Kern, M, Braun, A, Gosnell, K, Beckley, B, Nicole, E, Giguère, J (2016) 10 Success Rules From Richard Branson's Playbook, *YFS Magazine*, https://yfsmagazine.com/2016/03/11/10-success-rules-from-richard-bransons-playbook (archived at https://perma.cc/T4NF-EE5F)

INDEX